Stress Testing for Risk Control under Basel II

Stress Testing for Risk Control under Basel II

Dimitris N. Chorafas

AMSTERDAM • BOSTON • HEIDELBERG • LONDON • NEW YORK • OXFORD
PARIS • SAN DIEGO • SAN FRANCISCO • SINGAPORE • SYDNEY • TOKYO
Butterworth-Heinemann is an imprint of Elsevier

Butterworth-Heinemann is an imprint of Elsevier
Linacre House, Jordan Hill, Oxford OX2 8D
30 Corporate Drive, Suite 400, Burlington, MA 01803, USA

First edition 2007

British Library Cataloguing in Publication Data
A catalogue record for this book is available from the British Library

Library of Congress Cataloguing in Publication Data
A catalogue record for this book is available from the Library of Congress

ISBN-13: 978-0-7506-8305-0
ISBN-10: 0-7506-8305-8

For information on all Butterworth-Heinemann publications visit our website at http://books.elsevier.com

Printed and bound in Great Britain

07 08 09 10 11 10 9 8 7 6 5 4 3 2 1

Contents

Preface

Starting with the 1996 Market Risk Amendment to Basel I, and following up with the 2006 Basel II's New Capital Adequacy Framework, the Basel Committee on Banking Supervision institutionalized the control of risk through models and testing methodologies. For the financial industry, however, risk management – and, most specifically, advanced testing – is not just a regulatory requirement; it is also a major:

- Operational,
- Cultural, and
- Technological challenge.

To help the reader face the risk management challenge, this book addresses the cultural and technological issues connected to an advanced methodology, and most particularly *stress testing*, which is a fairly recent development. A crucial question with new methods and tools is how they should be learned and applied in an environment of complex exposures, as in that of banks, which can suffer simultaneously through:

- Corporate bankruptcies,
- Derivatives exposure, and
- A shrinking value of investments.

More precisely, which factors should be taken into account in computing exposure, how the different types of risk should be combined into an aggregate picture, which critical limits could or should be applied and where, how one institution can be compared against another in terms of risk being assumed, and how stress testing can make these risks reveal their secrets.

This text is written for banking and, more generally, financial industry professionals and managers, who are not mathematicians, but need to deal with new regulations, models and advanced tests, for compliance with regulatory authorities and to keep ahead of the competition. Sixteen chapters provide the necessary background to understand:

- What is involved in using financial simulation and experimentation, and
- What kind of contribution technology can make to risk control, by means of stress testing.

Part 1 explains why an advanced testing methodology protects the bank from the unknowns that always exist in risks being assumed. Chapter 1 brings to the reader's attention the high impact of extreme events that are not being always accounted for, pays attention to the contribution of confidence intervals (a new theme in banking), and explains what is meant by an advanced testing methodology for risk management.

It has been a deliberate choice to leave the definition of risk and of risk appetite until Chapter 2, to allow a broader look at testing methodology and the way in which it should be implemented to gain competitive advantages. For the same reason, the task of explaining the dynamics of stress testing within the framework of enterprise risk management has been assigned to Chapter 3.

The tools of stress analysis are the theme of Chapter 4. These range from scenarios to sensitivities, and the use of statistical inference, including the methodology that should characterize the use of advanced tools. Chapter 5 presents case studies on worst case analysis, including drills for a meltdown and the concept of a 'bad bank'.

Because an advanced testing methodology cannot be effectively implemented without the appropriate technological infrastructure, Chapter 6 has been added to Part 1 to outline and document what is involved in a successful technology effort. This text also includes the technical requirements for projecting and implementing an enterprise architecture, a 'must' for enterprise-wide risk management.

Part 2 addresses the stress testing of expected losses. This includes the stress probability of default (SPD), stress loss given default (SLGD), stress exposure at default (SEAD), and the prerequisites to be fulfilled to proceed successfully with SPD, SLGD and SEAD studies. Chapter 7 explains the need for including and studying the contribution of volatility patterns in connection with stress testing, and what kind of improvements need to be made to volatility models to improve their deliverables.

The focal point of Chapter 8 is stress testing the counterparty's creditworthiness. The text includes the contribution of power curves, as well as problems posed by unwillingness to perform. The text is enriched with case studies. Stress probability of default and the way it is estimated is the subject of Chapter 9, including probability of default buckets, errors in stress probability of default estimates and the contribution of benchmarking.

Chapter 10 concentrates on the challenge of computing stress loss given default, and stress exposure at default (SEAD). It also presents the way in which legal risk and other operational risks impact negatively on SEAD losses. Part 2 concludes with the themes covered in Chapter 11: counterparty credit risk (as distinct from straight credit risk), ways and means for credit risk mitigation, and wrong-way risk in case of double default.

Part 3 presents the most important background factors behind expected and unexpected losses, as well as their after effects and algorithms associated with their computation. Chapter 12 concentrates on stress testing expected losses, and how the results of tests for tier-one, hybrid tier-one, tier-two and tier-three capital impact on regulatory requirements. Strengths and weaknesses of credit risk models are examined, and their implementation is evaluated from a holistic risk control perspective.

Because the analysis of reasons for unexpected losses should definitely involve the impact of macroeconomic developments, significant attention is paid to this in Chapter 13. The text includes stress testing macroeconomic risks, stress testing interest rates and stress testing losses from business risk. Economic capital allocation and algorithms for stress testing unexpected losses are the subjects of Chapter 14. They have been included to provide the reader with a comprehensive approach to the management of unexpected losses.

Closely associated with the subject of unexpected losses, and their impact on the banking industry, is the exposure taken with leveraged and volatile financial assets.

Chapter 15 starts with a brief overview of hedge funds, which manage such assets, then explains the need for stress testing the worth of highly leveraged institutions. Chapter 16 concludes this book by explaining through practical examples why stress testing is a means for better governance. The text also emphasizes the contribution of Pillar 2 and Pillar 3 of Basel II in better governance.

Because, to a large extent, the assets of a bank are liabilities of other entities, stress tests should consider not only counterparty risk, but also the fair value of these assets. A comprehensive approach to exposure contributes greatly to better governance and, along timely management control, can be instrumental in improving the bank's staying power and, therefore, market edge. Advanced testing is broadening both management's mind and the range of options in pursuing business opportunities.

My debts go to a long list of knowledgeable people and their organizations, who contributed to the research that led to this text. Without their contributions this book would not have been possible. I am also indebted to several senior executives for constructive criticism and valuable suggestions during the preparation of the manuscript.

Let me take this opportunity to thank Karen Maloney for suggesting this project, Charlotte Pover for the editing work and Melissa Read for the production effort. To Eva-Maria Binder goes the credit for compiling the research results, typing the text and preparing the camera-ready artwork.

Valmer and Vitznau Dr Dimitris N. Chorafas
November, 2006

Warning

The Merger of EL and UL and the Weakening of Basel II

A first draft of *Basel II*, by the Basel Committee on Banking Supervision, was released in June 1999. This was a consultative paper (CP) containing general outlines of proposed regulation in connection to *credit risk* and *operational risk*. CP1 also included some very clear thinking about how to handle these two important exposures.

This new capital adequacy framework made several major contributions to risk measurement and risk control. One of them has been, for the first time ever, the institution of capital requirement for operational risk. Another crucial concept, which helped to restructure the thinking of bankers in respect to exposure, was the distinction between *expected losses* (EL) and *unexpected losses* (UL).

- Capital for expected losses, which is *regulatory capital*, buys the bank a license to operate.
- Capital for unexpected losses, a new concept, addresses the long leg of the loss distribution as well as its spikes.

Until quite recently, provisioning for financial resources connected to unexpected losses has been made through *economic capital*, a non-regulatory funding. In its background is *Pillar 3* of Basel II. This active and transparent use of *market discipline* encourages monetary financial institutions (MFIs) to:

- Hold more capital than strictly required by regulators, and
- Allocate that capital to their business units, enabling them to face losses due to outliers and extreme events.[1]

Many market participants looked at UL provisions as *signalling capital*, telling the market that the bank has the resources to face exceptional shocks. This has been a neat approach with clear organizational guidelines, made by geniuses who also introduced *stress testing* concepts associated to UL:

- Stress probability of default (SPD)
- Stress loss given default (SLGD)
- Stress exposure at default (SEAD)

Over the last six years, *stress testing* proved to be one of the top contributions of Basel II, surpassing the two aforementioned original goals in terms of its potential to improve risk management policies and practices. Moreover, stress testing is a necessary complement to the discipline of modelling. Ingeniously used, it can serve in exercising some control over *model risk*, which is always present.

Regulatory authorities look very favourably at commercial banks' expertise in stress testing. The Basel Committee on Banking Supervision is underlining that:

- Banks *must* do stress tests under *Pillar 2*, and
- Therefore, stress testing is now in the domain of national supervisors.

Pillar 2 is the steady review of capital adequacy, along with other criteria of prudential bank supervision exercised by national regulatory authorities. This mission for greater attention placed by national supervisors on stress testing, comes over and above other already existing duties.

The concept of placing stress testing under Pillar 2 is good. But there are two challenges which need to be addressed. One lies in the fact that not all national regulatory authorities employ *rocket scientists*, or have the skills necessary for controlling stress testing models and procedures of commercial banks. A basic management principle is that:

- *If* there is no control
- *Then* there is no way to assure compliance. Therefore, prudential supervision means nothing.

This leads to the second challenge: The need for global homogeneity in prudential regulation, which has been the Basel Committee's goal in the first place. Assigning stress testing responsibility to national supervisors will eventually see to it that there is a bifurcation in the sophistication of stress tests.

- The few national supervisors employing rocket scientists will be the *leading edge*, moving well ahead of the lot.
- But the majority of national supervisors lacking such skills, will fall behind and become Basel II's *bleeding edge*.

It is nobody's secret that many supervisory authorities are behind the commercial banks in their jurisdiction, in regard to technology and analytical skills. This is bad not only for supervisors but also for commercial banks, as it increases by an order of magnitude:

- The risk of conflicts of interest in modelling,
- The attention they should pay to model risk, and
- The expertise they should acquire in stress testing.

This book has been deliberately organized in a way to assist in the effort of stress testing for risk control – both for commercial banks and supervisory authorities.

It needs no explaining that *if* Basel II is to become effective, *then* supervisors should establish a most rigorous plan on how to move ahead of the curve in:

- Stress testing, and
- Model risk control.

* * *

The state of business described in preceding paragraphs regarding gaps in high technology and analytical skills, is not extraordinary. Classically, national supervisors have been tooled for control of regulatory capital requirements which were linear, and much simpler than those now under *Pillar 1* and *Pillar 2* of Basel II. Pillar 1 specifies two methods for regulatory capital calculation regarding credit risk:

- The standardized approach, an upgraded version of Basel I, and
- Internal ratings-based (IRB) method, with two alternatives: F-IRB and A-IRB.

Originally, under Basel II, the computation of expected losses under either IRB approach was provided in an elegant, comprehensive manner, expressed through the algorithm:

$$EL = PD \cdot LGD \cdot EAD \tag{1}$$

On 10/11 October, 2003, this neat concept ceased being the model for expected losses. At that time, the Basel Committee met in Madrid to decide on over 200 responses and comments received on the third consultative paper (CP3), plus results from *quantitative impact studies*. (QIS 1 of 1999, QIS 2 and QIS 2.5 of 2001, and QIS 3 which was taking place that very month of 2003.)

In the course of that fatal Madrid meeting, the EL equation was dropped because responses to CP3 by commercial banks pressed the point they were already making reserves for expected losses, and formula (1) was a duplication. The Basel Committee accepted this thesis which, in my opinion, was not the right decision – and it has been, in a way, reversed (more on this later).

Sometime after October 2003, two events worth recording took place: one was QIS 4, and the other was the advancement of an UL formula based on stress testing. (Prior to this there were a couple of UL equations, an excellent one advanced by the Deutsche Bundesbank.) The stress testing formula is:

$$UL = SPD \cdot SLGD \cdot SEAD \tag{2}$$

QIS 4 has been the last quantitative impact study in which American regulators participated: Federal Reserve, Office of the Controller of the Currency (OCC) and Federal Deposit Insurance Corporation (FDIC). From what is known from US Congress hearings:

- OCC and FDIC do not subscribe to precommitment on regulatory capital made by commercial banks by means of models.
- Sometimes marking to model is like marking to myth, says Warren Buffett, the well-known investor.

FDIC and OCC would like to see *as a minimum* 8 per cent regulatory capital for credit risk, as prescribed by Basel I – no matter what the models say. To be at the side of prudence, since regulatory capital is a proxy for avoidance of systemic risk, American regulators:

- Will follow their way, and
- Conduct their own quantitative impact studies.

By contrast, other central banks in the Basel Committee proceeded with QIS 5, as explained in the main text of this book. American regulators contributed to this QIS 5 study QIS 4 results. QIS 4 was conducted only one year earlier than QIS 5, but among G10 countries it was restricted to the US and Germany. Therefore:

- The Basel Committee considered the results of QIS 4 and QIS 5 comparable, and
- Selected data from QIS 4 was included in the QIS 5 analysis.[2]

With QIS 5, EL has also come back to life. According to the Basel Committee's *International Convergence of Capital Measurement and Capital Standards*, of June 2006, a potential difference between total EL and total eligible provisions – known as *regulatory calculation* difference – will be deducted from regulatory capital.[3]

Now comes the surprise. QIS 5 targeted UL, though unexpected losses are covered by economic capital. UL has never been a regulatory capital requirement under the original A-IRB and F-IRB of Basel II. By contrast, with QIS 5 the IRB approaches are calibrated on *UL only* (emphasis added). I don't think this is the right decision because it destroys the very neat concept of a line dividing:

- *Expected losses*, which every well-managed bank knows how to handle.
- From *unexpected losses* which, as their name implies, hold many unknowns and surprises – for commercial bankers and regulators alike.

Anything that unsettles the clarity of an important issue is the enemy of good governance. Moreover, technically speaking, the characteristics of EL and UL are totally different. Precisely this fact made the person who invented this distinction between EL and UL a genius:

- *Expected losses have a fairly common pattern*,
- To the contrary, every financial institution has *its own risk appetite* – and, therefore, *its own pattern of unexpected losses*.

The fact that EL and UL have totally different risk distributions – the first characterized by high frequency low impact (HF/LI) events, the second by low frequency high impact (LF/HI) events – should have been enough to keep them separate. Every junior high school student knows that they should not add together apples and grapefruits, even if both are round.

Mixing up EL and UL by basing regulatory capital on UL (God forbid) has self-evident contradictions. Unexpected losses are, by definition, outliers. If not, they would have been expected losses. Beyond the minimal doubt, every credit institution's *own pattern* of extreme events must be studied at much higher level of sophistication than expected losses.

- Minimum capital requirements computed by summing up EL and UL – without stress factors – *mean nothing*.

Both the weeding out of the aftermath of extreme events in UL and the inclusion of UL into regulatory capital, make me feel very uncomfortable – which explains the reason for this *Warning*. Its aim is to bring to the reader's attention these worries. Also, to comment on what seems a low level of capital requirements for credit institutions revealed by QIS 5. Gaming the regulatory system is done through:

- Correlation coefficients, and
- Risk weighted assets (RWAs).

QIS 5 has demonstrated that a fairly significant reduction in regulatory capital requirements takes place in spite of a shrinkage of equity capital (Tier 1), already made because of Hybrid T-1, Hybrid T-2, deferred tax assets (DTAs), and other fuzzy reasons. Also, in spite of the inclusion into QIS 5 capital requirements for credit risk, of:

- Operational risk, and
- *Market risk* (curiously enough).

* * *

Allow me to open a parenthesis which helps to better appreciate the comments which follow. The Basel Committee's *Results of the Fifth Quantitative Impact Study (QIS 5)*, of June 16, 2006, states that this test took place in 31 countries among 51 Group 1[4] G-10 banks, 146 Group 2 G-10 banks, and 155 banks from other countries.

The sample is unquestionably statistically significant. This makes the results so much more worrying regarding *the huge shrinkage in regulatory capital requirements*; and hence, in relation to the stability of the global financial system. According to QIS 5, with A-IRB:

- Group 1 G-10 banks *will reduce* their capital requirements by 7.1 per cent (!)
- Group 2 G-10 banks *will reduce* their capital requirements by 26.7 per cent (!!)
- Other non-G-10 Group 1 banks *will reduce* their capital requirements by 29.0 per cent (!!!)

That's free lunch, and everybody is invited to the party. It is not funny, but it is still a laughing matter if for no other reason than because these hefty regulatory capital reductions are made courtesy of *unstable models*. To make matters much worse:

- This shrinking regulatory capital base *is supposed to cover credit risk, market risk, and operational risk.*
- Notice that operational risk was originally supposed to represent an additional 20 per cent, then 12.5 per cent, over and above credit risk.
- Moreover, market risk has been a subject of the 1996 Market Risk Amendment – not of Basel II (more on this later).

What the above mentioned capital reductions document is that Basel II has become *ultra light*. Given these horrendous figures, it would have been advisable to put Basel II, its procedures, and its models under a 5-year test in parallel to Basel I – until its many bugs and loopholes are weeded out.

* * *

The careful reader will notice that, officially, these (–7.1 per cent, –26.7 per cent, –29.0 per cent) very superficial figures represent *the change in total minimum required capital – that is, including credit, market and operational risk.*

- Officially, it is said that this is the difference in regulatory capital between Basel II and Basel I.
- But such comparison is lopsided because the 1988 Basel I regarded only credit risk.

Such super reduction of regulatory capital happens at a time when it has been officially announced that derivative exposures currently stand at about $330 *trillion*, in notional principal amount. Just three big institutions: JP Morgan Chase, Bank of America, and Citigroup, share among themselves $110 trillion in derivatives exposure.

As explained in the body of this book, in terms of credit equivalence under stress conditions, the $110 trillion in notional principal morph into $22 trillion in *real money*. This corresponds to almost 2 years of the US gross national product (GDP) – a level of exposure which:

- Gives vertigo to bankers and regulators, and
- Increases most significantly the likelihood of systemic risk.

It is therefore a great disservice to the commercial banks themselves, at least to those who put survival ahead of yearly profits, to lump together all sorts of heterogeneous types of losses. And, having done so, to also decrease the level of regulatory capital. John Law, of Mississippi Bubble and Royal Bank fame, would have loved this kind of 'solution'.

The question these references pose to the Basel Committee and all national regulators is whether there is a plan to review and rethink UL, because of risks presented by the aforementioned capital reduction. Will commercial banks also keep their classical credit risk reserves beyond UL? The answer I got is that banks will keep their credit risk reserves which are subject to national accounting rules, rather than the Basel II Framework. Is Basel II going to be further degraded?

Another question in connection to the theme under discussion, concerns the very foggy and utterly unsettled issue of *correlations* in finance and banking. While chairman of the Fed, Dr Alan Greenspan had said that the study of covariance in finance is still in its infancy. Moreover, a 2001 document by the Joint Forum of the Bank for International Settlements (BIS) states that:

> The correlation between different risk types may be very difficult to measure.[5]

That's absolutely correct. With IRB, the correlation coefficient is set by the Basel Committee. Two big issues come up: the first is what sort of control, for instance through sampling, there exists to assure this is exactly the correlation coefficient the banks are using with IRB.

The official answer seems to be that in QIS 5, banks provided input data for the Basel II risk-weighted functions which indeed include correlations set by the Committee. The results of QIS 5 therefore reflect the regulatory minimum capital requirements. This does not respond to the query about post-mortem control by Basel and/or national regulators.

- *If* the correlation coefficients given for A-IRB and F-IRB are sort of averages.
- *Then* the results being obtained are unreliable; correlations are the Achilles heel of Basel II.[6]

There is no evidence that during QIS 5 the Committee asked commercial banks to provide *their* internal correlation estimates, or economic capital figures. Officially it has been said that bank and market data had been taken into account in the original calibration of correlation coefficients. *Calibration?*

The question mark on calibration is in the background of yet another issue. Even if one accepts that RWAs and correlations based on averages are admissible with expected losses, which tend to be normally distributed, this can *never* be the case with unexpected losses, their outliers and their spikes.

As an American saying goes, thinking through averages is a state of mind which says that if you have your head in an oven and your feet in a freezer, on average you will feel alright. Averages will not do, even if they are properly computed, and steadily updated. Confidence *intervals* play both the freezer and oven roles.

- Rating agencies look at a 99.97 per cent level of significance when they give AA credit rating.
- It is an illusion to think that averages, the 50 per cent level, can satisfy regulatory capital requirements, in any serious approach to the control of systemic risk.

Taking everything into account, for the time being, a reliable computation of correlations remains the weakest link of every modelling approach to regulatory capital requirements. No two banks have the same type, magnitude and impact of exposures:

- Therefore, their correlations should enter into regulatory capital, *after* rigorous supervisory control.
- 'Standard correlations' for banks with hugely varied risk appetites and amounts of exposure, don't really make sense.

Yet another weakness of current calculations made for regulatory capital reasons – whether EL, UL, both of them or something else – is the very short time frame of one year. With few exceptions, banks don't fail in one year. The drift to default takes several years of mismanagement. Therefore, an extension to a 10-year time frame would have been a valuable improvement.

* * *

In conclusion, the reader should retain the following points:

1. *Stress testing remains very important*, even if UL is no more the product of stress tests of EL factors.

Stress testing now comes under Pillar 2. Evaluation of stress test results is at the discretion of national supervisors.

2. Capital for unexpected losses has become a sort of regulatory requirement.

In fact, QIS 5 primarily addressed UL, not EL. By all evidence, IRB methods of Basel II are now targeting UL only; a questionable practice.

3. Correlation coefficients have been given, and will continue being given, by the Basel Committee.

In the preceding pages (and in the body of this book) I have expressed my reservations about using one-size correlations for institutions with most diverse exposure. It is time to scotch the myth that average correlations are serious business.

Last but not least, credit-risk-only reserves will be subject to national supervisory rules, rather than Basel II. This is a significant weakening of Basel II – but at the same time it increases the importance of stress tests, and of the stress testing methodology discussed in the text the reader has on hand.

Notes

1. D.N. Chorafas, *Economic Capital Allocation with Basel II. Cost and Benefit Analysis*, Butterworth-Heinemann, London, 2004.
2. QIS 2 and 3 were conducted before the final Basel II Framework was published, and therefore the rules on which they were based were different. Additionally, macroeconomic conditions prevailing at their time were not the same as those of QIS 5.

3. See paragraphs 43, 380, 383, 386 and 563 of Basel Committee for Banking Supervision *International Convergence of Capital Measurement and Capital Standards*, BIS, Basel, June 2006.
4. These are diversified, internationally active institutions, with capital in excess of Euro 3 billion ($3.8 billion (£2 billion).
5. The Joint Forum *Risk Management Practices and Regulatory Capital*, BIS, Basel, November 2001.
6. D.N. Chorafas *After Basel II. Assuring Compliance and Smoothing the Rough Edges*, Lafferty/VRL Publishing, London, 2005.

PART 1

Stress testing defined

1 The need for advanced testing methodology

1.1 Introduction

The objective of this chapter is to explain the reason why an advanced testing technology has become absolutely necessary to risk management in banking, and in the financial industry at large. It has been a deliberate decision to delay the definition of risk until Chapter 2, and of *stress testing* until Chapter 3.

1.2 Risk distributions and extreme events

The genius of great investors is based on their capacity to take pains, not only risks. This capacity, however, is not unlimited. Experience shows that it can last for as long as their resources see them through. The way to bet is that beyond that point may lie a torrent of red ink. Hence, two basic investment characteristics are:

- The ability to live with uncertainty, and
- The availability of a system that permits to exercise timely and effective damage control.

Uncertainty is not limited to investments. It is an integral element of many economic and financial decisions, especially those regarding trades, as well as loans, extending into the future. Testing can be instrumental in gaining insight in situations involving uncertainty; classical tests, however, provide a very limited perspective because of the increased *complexity* of transactions.

The new landscape of capitalism, known as the *market economy*, is far more sophisticated and complicated than previous versions have been. In fact, compared with banking in the post-World War II years, market economy sophistication has increased by more than a factor of ten.

Dr Willis Ware, my professor at the University of California, Los Angeles (UCLA), in the early 1950s, taught his students that when something changes by an order of magnitude our:

- Concepts,
- Methods, and
- Tools

must also change. This change affects the way we look at the world, at our business and at the information we receive, and also at the use we make of such information. Data analysis pertaining to economic conditions and financial transactions has been always based on *statistics* (noun, singular), making use of *probabilities* and studying what might lie behind a distribution. But our notions of what that distribution may be have changed.

In classical testing procedures the prevailing concept is that of the *normal distribution* characterized by a mean (x), the so-called true value; standard deviation (s), the measure of dispersion; and *skewness*, the third momentum of a distribution. In the 1980s *kyrtosis*, the fourth momentum, became popular. The twenty-first century brought along the need for *stress tests*, which is a quantum jump in data analysis. (More on this later.)

That market values, or any other type of measurement, will fit a normal distribution has always been a hypothesis very rarely documented by the facts. Therefore, the references made to the bell-shaped normal distribution are an approximation that are made largely because of:

- Tradition in analysis,
- Easiness in conceiving the bell-shape of values, and
- The existence of rich statistical tables, developed over the twentieth century, that allow statistical tests to be performed.

In addition, not only in an investigation do we assume that events are normally distributed, as shown in Figure 1.1, but we also tend to concentrate on those of higher frequency. Increasingly, this proves to be a misleading approach because such events may have low impact, while events mapped at the tails have high impact.

Experienced analysts know that the normal distribution hypothesis is a near-sighted approach that can lead to significant errors. They know this for the simple reason that they appreciate many financial transactions and economic phenomena are complex

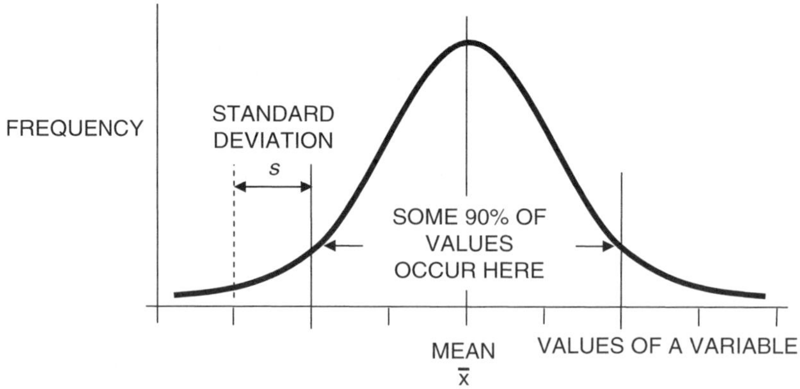

Figure 1.1 Not only do we assume that events are normally distributed, we also concentrate on those of higher frequency

and do not follow the rules characterizing normally distributed events. Hence, we are caught between two contradictory goals:

- The wish to conduct a realistic and accurate analysis, and
- The fact that in order to analyse risk events we generally need to simplify complex realities.

Many real-world situations are simplifications made through mathematical formulae, known as *models*. Bankers, traders and analysts need models to gain an idea of future movements in prices or other variables, to prognosticate the impact of market changes on their investment and to exercise control over exposure. A model, however, must adequately represent the relevant structural relationships between the variables that it addresses. This is not always achievable because of:

- Model uncertainty, and
- Data uncertainty.

This is a simple but powerful way of bifurcating *model risk* into its two main components. It has been presented in a seminal paper published in the Monthly Report of the Deutsche Bundesbank in June 2004, in connection with macroeconomic modelling. The bifurcation of uncertainty is generally applicable to all artefacts representing real-world situations, which generally include uncertainties on:

- The analyst side, and
- The user's side.

Model uncertainty refers to a lack of knowledge about the most crucial variables that should be chosen. It also reflects limited knowledge about the exact transmission mechanism that characterizes the economic, financial or technical environment under study.

Many models are theoretical and, therefore, not very precise in how they define the key variables and (most particularly) their behaviour. There often exist competing theoretical models, which explain the same phenomenon in very different terms. Moreover, different models may contradict one another in the:

- Selection of explicitly included variables,
- Type of interrelations between them, or
- Data required for simulation and experimentation.

Data uncertainty denotes incomplete and unreliable information about developments affecting the chosen variables up to the current observation period. In addition, the data being collected may not be accurate, or fail to include extreme values, yet advanced type analysis target these outliers in particular.

The lack of extreme values that have low frequency, but high impact, is one of the most significant factors in creating the false belief that a distribution of events is

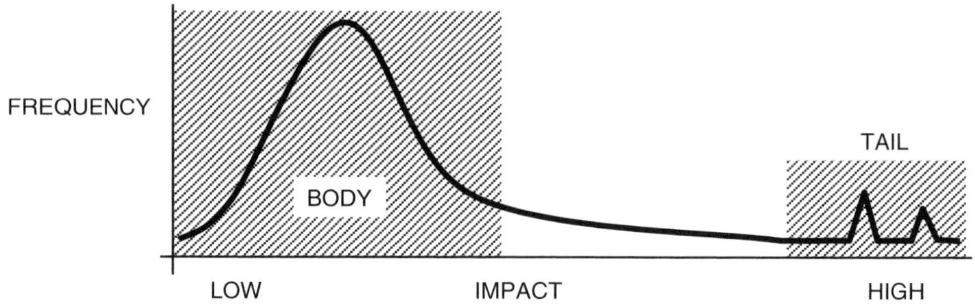

Figure 1.2 A distribution of credit risk can be divided into a body, which is almost normally distributed, and a tail with own characteristics

normal, whereas in reality it is not. Figure 1.2 provides an example from credit risk. This distribution of credit exposure could be divided into two main parts:

- A *body* whose values are *almost* normally distributed, and could be studied through classical testing, and
- A *long tail* consisting of low-frequency events with spikes, characterized by high impact in terms of end results.

For starters, *spike* is an extremely short-lived price movement in the spot market. Spikes can also be created by a market disturbance, when the worst feared by economists, investors and analysts continues to worsen.

This long-tail distribution must be studied through *stress testing*, which is the theme of this book. Part 1 defines stress testing methods, procedures and tools. Part 2 provides the reader with practical examples on stress testing using, as practical example, the Basel II *credit risk* criteria. The theme of Part 3 is *expected* and *unexpected losses*. Expected losses tend to fall towards the body of the distribution, while unexpected losses concentrate themselves in the tail.

1.3 Model uncertainty in simulation and testing

Stress testing has both proponents and critics. The latter say that while, as a discipline, it permits risk analysis of the long leg of a distribution, it also involves a great deal of model uncertainty. The best way to answer this argument is through Francis Bacon's dictum: 'If a man will begin with certainties, he shall end in doubts. But if he will be content to begin in doubts, he will end in certainties'. In a nutshell, this describes what stress testing aims to achieve.

As for model uncertainty, section 1.2 has given the message that this characterizes all simulations and all types of tests. (A simulation is a working analogy constructed either through algorithms and heuristics or by means of analogue models.) In practice, along with the problem of model uncertainty, there is also the problem of data uncertainty arising because relevant statistics provide obsolete, incomplete or unreliable information about:

- The value of 'this' or 'that' variable, and
- The interconnection, or correlation, that prevails between variables included in the model.

An additional type of data uncertainty occurs because several variables that play a decisive role in theoretical models cannot be observed directly in the real world. Therefore, they have to be estimated, and the precision of estimation(s) is strongly dependent on the underlying model.

Irrespective of whether management's objective is to maximize returns, subject to security and liquidity requirements, or to exercise risk control, along lines that derive from a portfolio's purpose, there will be both model and data uncertainty. Senior management may elaborate guidelines and benchmarks, but it is the duty of the testing methodology, and its deliverables, to come up with prognostications of exposure that impact on projected profits and losses (P&L). It is the thesis of this book that:

- Being constrained through normal distribution concepts, traditional testing approaches provide results of relatively low dependability.
- By contrast, by moving from the *body* to the *tail* of the distribution, as shown in Figure 1.2, one escapes the confines of 3 standard deviations. By using 5, 10 and 15 standard deviation events, stress testing increases the dependability of deliverables.

Figure 1.3 provides a bird's-eye view of the bandwidth of deliverables with normal tests and stress tests. The example is a comparison between underlying risk in a portfolio based on an $x \pm 3s$ test, and the likely output of an $x \pm 10s$ stress test. The boxes display envelopes of the perception of embedded risk. The horizontal lines represent the estimated risk levels that are:

- Poor without appropriate test conditions
- Better with traditional type tests, and
- Best under stress testing, as the bandwidth of perceived risks significantly increases.

Apart from the fact that level(s) of perceived risk are presented at a higher level of confidence (see section 1.5), an increased band of perception provides a way of compensation for part of the prevailing uncertainty in the time-span between, say, an investment decision and the occurrence of events that impact on the P&L of that decision.

For instance, an interest rate cut may be designed to jump-start a flagging economy, by increasing the velocity of circulation of money (and therefore the money supply). At the same time, however, it may unravel positions taken on the hypotheses of tight liquidity conditions maintained through higher interest rates and greater reserve requirements.

The references being made, and examples being given, address some of the issues to be found in model uncertainty's downside. Other measures may be taken with the aim

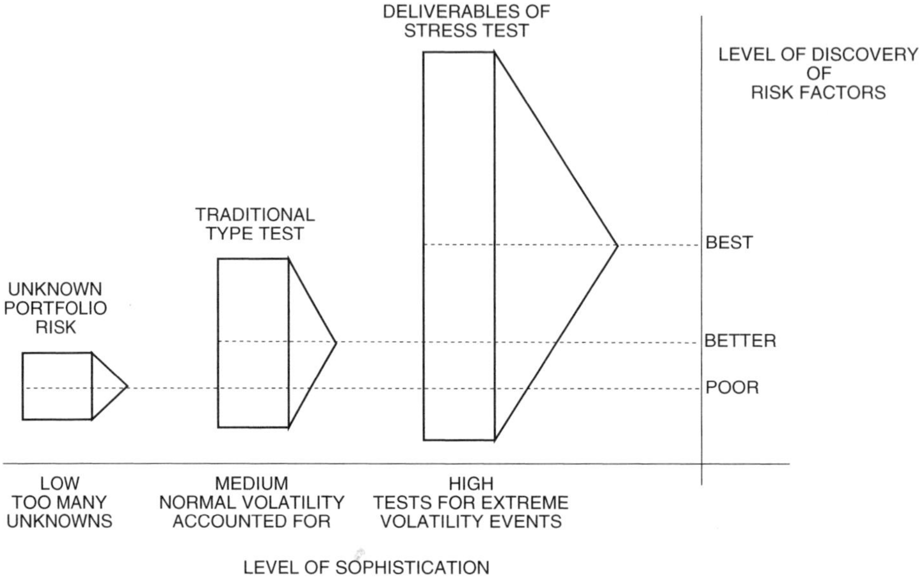

Figure 1.3 Likely structure of the bandwidth of deliverables between traditional and stress tests

to improve upon data uncertainty. For instance, in connection with monetary policy decisions, when assessing risks to price stability, central bankers increasingly chose:

- Not to concentrate on only one indicator variable, such as inflation,
- But instead, to analyse a wider range of critical factor and information elements associated with them.

The underlying thought in the foregoing discussion is that the possible shortcomings on each individual data set, in a wide range of decisions, may be compensated for by errors in other data sets, as not all uncertainties necessarily fall on the same side. This is known as the *Fermi principle*, and it can be applied in physics as well as in trading, loans, investments and monetary policy. Accuracy can be improved because some of the errors tend to cancel themselves out.

While this opinion is well founded, whether or not such cancelling out will materialize depends on how serious measurement errors have been in one variable compared with other relevant variables, and on whether systemic bias exists. At the same time, whether in traditional tests or in stress tests, data quality alone cannot serve as the sole criterion for choosing which variables to use in modelling.

1.4 Stress testing and the need for transparency

Section 1.2 has explained that traditional tests can only capture basic features and behaviour patterns that fall within the realm of a normal distribution (plus or minus 3 standard deviations from the mean). Another shortcoming of such tests is that time series rarely extend beyond five or ten years, yet longer observation periods can, under several circumstances, have a considerable impact on the results.

Short time series do not respect a basic principle in analytics, that both the range of values taken by variables, and *correlation(s)* between variables, may change fundamentally at some point in time. Moreover, an often encountered practice with traditional testing is that not all data that are relevant to the analysis of a situation are statistically valid samples, representative of the underlying population.

Another reason for lack of accuracy is that some data (noun, singular) that is collected is subject to *measurement problems*. Some of these problems may be the result of a lack of transparency in records that reflect transactions and commitments, whether these are due to trading, loans, investment or other types. Therefore, in its Core Principles of Methodology, the Basel Committee outlines the following essential criteria for banking supervision,[1] edited to fit an individual institution's requirements:

- Operational independence, accountability and governance structures of each supervisory authority should be prescribed by law and publicly disclosed.

While this criterion is written for supervisory authorities, banks and other financial institutions would be well advised to make it a pillar of their own by-laws. There should be no interference that compromises the operational independence of each business unit, and each control function, including the ability of risk controllers to obtain all information needed to carry out their mandate.

- Senior management must publish test objectives (including stress testing), and it remains accountable, through a transparent framework, for exercising its duties in relation to those objectives.

Whether in central banks, commercial banks or investment banks, senior management must understand stress testing to be able to establish objectives for, and control the results of, stress tests. Paraphrasing the Basel Committee's directive, the stress testing unit must be financed in a manner that does not undermine its independence. Appropriate budgeting should permit it to conduct effective risk analysis studies. The budget should:

- Provide staff in sufficient numbers, and
- Pay for skills commensurate with the size and complexity of the institution.

In addition, senior management should appreciate that stress testing is not just a mathematical exercise. There is a whole philosophy of management that goes along with it. The stress testing unit, which is typically part of the larger risk management organization, must also have powers to address compliance with supervisory requirements, in terms of:

- Sharing information with supervisors,
- But also protecting the confidentiality of such information.

The stress testing unit should present and document the results of its studies in a way that permits senior management to set prudent and appropriate limits to exposure, as well as minimum capital adequacy requirements for each business unit and for the institution as a whole. Under Basel II, capital adequacy must:

- Reflect the risks that the bank undertakes, and
- Define the components of capital, bearing in mind its ability to absorb losses.

The Basel Committee suggests, in the aforementioned document, that: 'Supervisors must be satisfied that banks and banking groups have in place a comprehensive risk management process (including Board and senior management oversight) to identify, evaluate, monitor, control, or mitigate all material risks; and to assess their overall capital adequacy in relation to their risk profile. These processes should be commensurate with the size and complexity of the institution'. In the case of credit risk (which is the theme of Part 2), supervisors must be satisfied that banks:

- Have a credit risk management process that takes into account the risk profile of the institution, and
- Follow prudent policies, with processes able to identify, measure, monitor and control credit risk, including granting loans and making investments.

In its guidelines on core principles, the Basel Committee also pays particular attention to large exposure limits: supervisors must be satisfied that banks have policies and processes that enable management to identify and manage concentrations within the portfolio. In the author's experience, such concentrations, as well as exposures to related parties, are best studied through stress tests.

There are also other domains where stress tests can be instrumental. For example, they can be used in prognosticating liquidity risks, thereby contributing to a sound liquidity management strategy that takes into account:

- The risk profile of the institution, and
- Its policies and processes to identify, measure, monitor and control liquidity risk on a day-to-day basis.

Still another domain where stress tests can provide assistance is the making of contingency plans for liquidity problems. They may also help in evaluating, by means of limits testing, whether the institution's internal controls are adequate for the size and complexity of their business.

A novel, still in development, use of stress testing principles is that of processes relating to *know your customer* rules, which promote ethical and professional standards in the financial industry. This requires the institution to develop and maintain a thorough understanding of operations, and of policies to prevent it from being used, intentionally or unintentionally, for criminal activities.

Further uses of a stress testing methodology include: customer acceptance policies that identify business relationships that the bank will not accept, as well as their past aftermath and possible future flaws; customer identification, verification and due diligence programmes; and policies and procedures to monitor and recognize unusual or potentially suspicious transactions, particularly in high-risk accounts. This type of stress test follows the *accountability* principle.

1.5 Stress testing and confidence intervals

The late 1970s and early 1980s saw a wave of deregulation in the financial industry. In the aftermath, two things have changed: there is a wider spread of banking activities in different sectors of the economy, through the repeal of the Glass-Steagall Act of the 1930s; and a redefinition of supervisory activities, including compliance. The latter has been effected through the Capital Adequacy Accord of 1988 (Basel I), and enhanced by the New Capital Adequacy Framework (Basel II).[2]

In essence, Basel II has been a redefinition of banking supervision, with capital adequacy for credit risk at its kernel. Some years earlier, the 1996 Market Risk Amendment, also by the Basel Committee, had added requirements for market exposure to credit risk capital adequacy. This reinforced compliance requirements to which the board of directors, chief executive officer (CEO) and senior management should address themselves. National supervisors now require that directors and managers:

- Understand the underlying risks in their business, and
- Are committed to a strong risk-control environment.

Stress testing helps senior executives in performing this mission which, with Basel II, has taken on the characteristic of risk-based capital accuracy. Moreover, among well-managed banks economic capital allocation has become an integral part of their mission. Another important novelty has been the fulfilment of qualitative requirements. The supervisors:

- Determine whether there is an appropriate balance in the skills and resources in control functions, and
- Have the power to require changes in the composition of the board and senior management, to address any prudential concerns related to the satisfaction of risk-control criteria.

Precisely because they provide the ability to prognosticate critical future developments in terms of exposure, stress tests have become an important part of a bank's risk management responsibilities. Their pragmatic results not only help the interests of the individual bank, but also make a valuable contribution towards overall financial stability, a reason why they are appreciated by supervisors.

Some bankers say that value at risk (VAR), the market risk model introduced with the 1996 Market Risk Amendment,[3] is plenty in terms of exposure metrics (see Chapter 7 for a brief history of VAR); particularly because, by now, it has become generally applicable. Part of this argument is that VAR can perform the functions assigned to stress tests. This is, however, an inaccurate statement and a dangerous assumption, for several reasons.

- As an artefact, VAR has all of the characteristics of model uncertainty and nothing to compensate for them.
- The assessment of risk on the basis of VAR is bound to historical data, which means that it is not possible to extend stress scenarios to future hypothetical events.
- Commonly used VAR approaches are unsuited to assessing tail events, representing losses in extreme market situations, and

- VAR is a very simplistic, approximate approach to market risk, at the 99 per cent level of significance, omitting those extreme events that typically fall in the other 1 per cent.

There are reasons for these shortcomings. In regard to the fourth bullet point, in 1991/92, when VAR was developed as the '4.15 pm market risk report' to the top management of J.P. Morgan, the concept of *confidence intervals* was well known to statisticians, physicists and engineers, but it was not yet a conscience in banking. Today it is.

Tier-one financial institutions now appreciate that the *level of confidence* applied to risk measurement is a most crucial part of a test methodology. To appreciate why, look briefly at the *operating characteristics* curves in Figure 1.4. Any sampling plan, and every test being applied, has the risk of:

- Rejecting a lot of good quality, and
- Accepting a lot of bad quality.

This is as true of loans as it is of manufactured goods. The first risk is known as α, type I error or producer's risk. It defines the kernel of *significance* in test results, by presenting the likelihood of an unwanted but often unavoidable happening, and, therefore, the confidence which is attached to test results.

The challenge presented by the second bullet is known as β, type II error or consumer's risk. (The β in Figure 1.4 should not be confused with β indicating

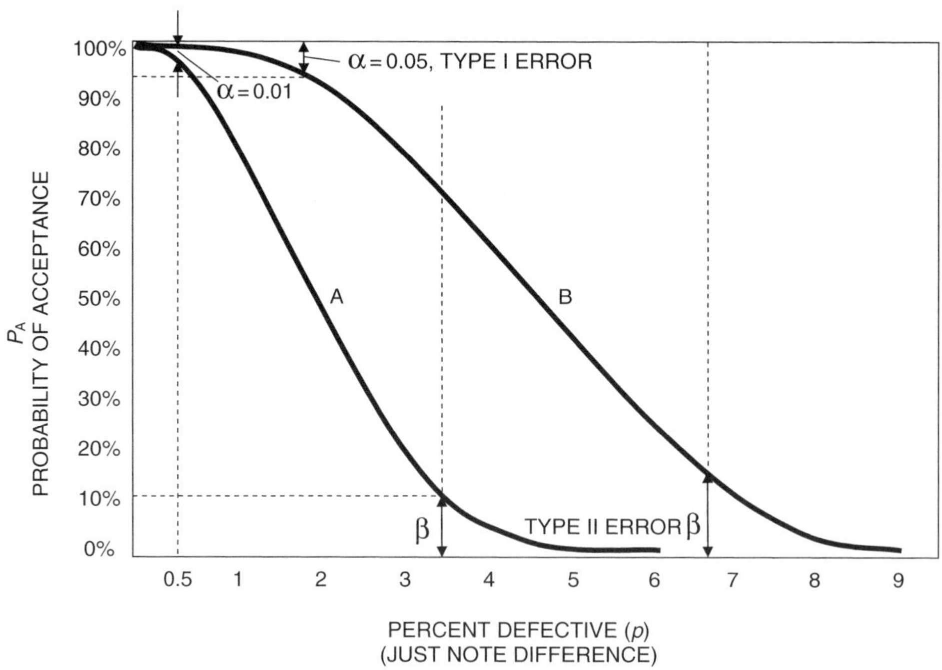

Figure 1.4 Operating characteristics curves for sampling plans

volatility.) One way of improving the operating characteristics of a test is to decrease the standard deviation of the statistic being tested. Because the variance around the mean represents variability in the measurements that are made, high quality has a small standard deviation:

- High quality usually results in fairly uniform items, but not in clones.
- Low quality is characterized by significant differences among crucial dimensions of items, and their measurements.

This principle of α and β risks associated with a sampling plan and its testing is valid throughout science, even if traditional type tests fail to account for it. The same principle prevails with *correlation coefficients* and their impact on testing results.

An example is given in Figure 1.5. The scatter of points indicates that the correlation is too low. Therefore, the regression line is meaningless. The example is taken from the financial industry and it concerns client concentration, a key issue in compliance. Low correlation coefficients, and negative aftermath of risk concentration, may happen for several reasons. Taking credit risks as an example:

- The covariance of chosen variables is in doubt.
- The sample is too small. A large sample might have given better results.
- The portfolio is concentrated in one industry. Therefore, it is highly dependent on that industry.
- There have been other types of concentration beyond credit risk.
- The portfolio gave equal weights to all borrowers, yet the amount of money involved differed by order of magnitude.

Advanced testing would ensure that the regression line, which emulates an expected value line, is only indicative, and its pattern is enriched with confidence intervals as shown in Figure 1.6. As can be seen from the figure, the central line (a proxy of the regression line) gives only 50 per cent assurance; therefore, it is meaningless.

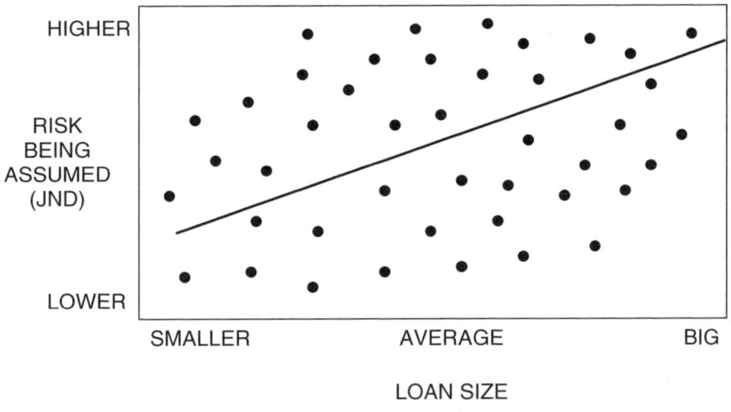

Figure 1.5 Risk associated with client concentration

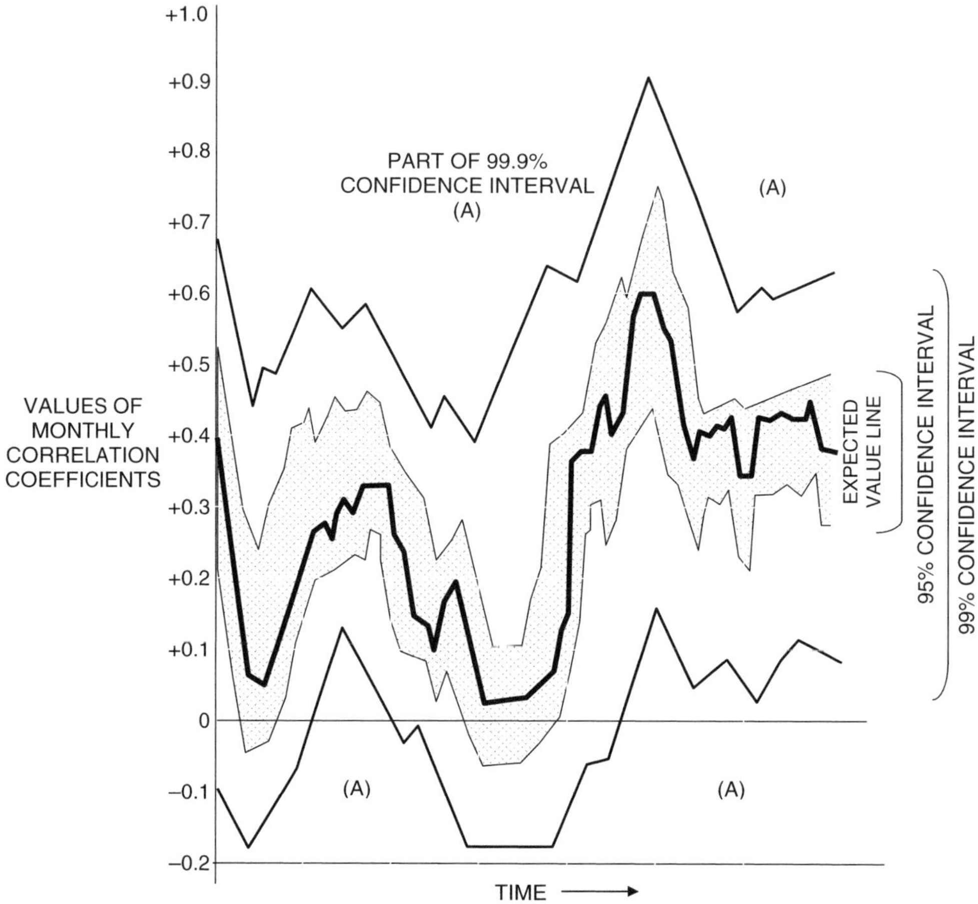

Figure 1.6 Confidence intervals of correlation coefficients of two principal variables of a financial risk model

The 95 per cent level of confidence also provides a very poor assurance, leaving 5 per cent of all risks outside its area. The 99 per cent level of confidence is better, but not much better. As for the 99.9 per cent level of confidence, a good chunk of it does not fit in the graph. For AA rating banks need a 99.97 per cent level of confidence in capital adequacy.

The reader should remember this example the next time he or she talks about risk measurement and diversification. It should also be remembered that client diversification often follows a similar pattern, which is subject to both:

- Model uncertainty, and
- Data uncertainty.

With supervisors becoming increasingly orientated towards analytical solutions, confidence intervals are destined to play a significant role in regulatory reporting. For board members, chief executives and senior managers who think that the expected value line of a correlation coefficient, which represents 50 per cent of cases, is plenty, the best treatment is Warren Buffett's query: 'Would you jump out of an airplane with a parachute that has 50 per cent chance of opening?'

1.6 Advanced testing methodology for better governance

The thesis presented in section 1.4 is that stress testing not only consists of examining the tail of a risk distribution for spikes and other high-impact events, but also is subject to a level of confidence that can speak volumes about the examples being obtained. Part 2 will return to this issue in connection with stress probability of default, stress loss given default and stress exposure at default.

- A higher confidence interval is also a stress test, and
- It provides management with assurance on the population of risk events covered by the results.

In Figure 1.6, the expected value of the correlation coefficient is never negative. But at the 95 per cent level of confidence ($\alpha = 0.05$) the two key variables of the model also correlate negatively. This happens practically all the time at the 99.9 level of confidence. When senior management decisions on risk control account for negative correlation, the quality of governance is significantly improved. (More on better governance in Chapter 16.) Notice that:

- Such negative correlations may be low frequency,
- But when they happen, they have significant impact. Management may find that its bets have been on the wrong side of the balance sheet.

During World War II, which saw the first major spike in rigorous analytics related to weapons systems, quality inspection took as the expected value of a process the average percentage defective, or average number of defects per hundred units of product submitted by the supplier for inspection. Today, it is known that while this is necessary, by itself it is not enough:

- The mean is an interesting statistic, but it gives only half a message.
- The other half is the level of confidence associated with reported statistics, which helps to relieve a good deal of uncertainty regarding the likelihood of results.

Supervisors are increasingly using confidence intervals to determine whether a bank has a well-tuned compliance function, which assists the board and senior executives in effectively managing risks. The level of significance of tests being made helps the compliance function to be fully independent of the business activities of the entity.

- Ensuring that policies and processes are compliant with supervisory guidelines well beyond averages, and
- Reviewing, through stress tests, the risk position resulting from the bank's business, at a high level of confidence.

Advanced analytical tools help to identify material risks run by the entity, and to classify these risks according to their current severity and future impact. To promote a practice of better governance, the Basel Committee's Core Principles Methodology[4] advances an assessment process based on a four-grade scale:

- Compliant,
- Largely compliant,
- Materially non-compliant, and
- Non-compliant.

While this has been written by the Basel Committee in connection with the classification of countries as a function of their quality of bank supervision, the concept has much broader applicability. Boards of directors and CEOs would be well advised to use these four categories in connection with the quality of the bank's internal control.

According to the aforementioned Basel classification, a country is *compliant* when all essential criteria applicable for this country are met without any significant deficiencies. A *largely compliant* country presents only minor shortcomings in supervision, which do not raise any concerns about the authority's intent and ability to achieve its stated objectives.

People with experience in senior management will appreciate that these definitions are applicable to auditing, internal control and risk management. The same is true of the following definitions. A *materially non-compliant* country has severe supervisory shortcomings, despite the existence of formal rules and procedures; also, when there is evidence that:

- Supervision has not been effective,
- Its practical implementation is weak, and
- Shortcomings are raising doubts about the authority's ability to achieve its goals.

By contrast, a country will be considered *non-compliant*, under core supervision principles, whenever there has been no substantive implementation of these principles, several essential criteria are not complied with, and bank supervision is manifestly ineffective. An entity can establish similar criteria for its headquarters, business units and subsidiaries in connection with:

- Auditing performance,
- Effectiveness of risk management, and
- The way in which the feedback channels work in satisfying internal control requirements.

The four-way classification of compliance is a very useful methodology for all activities outlined in these three bullets. An alternative is the *normal, tightened* and *reduced* inspection implemented for the Manhattan Project in World War II (see MIL-STD 105A).[5] This standard establishes sampling plans that have helped the US government to determine the type of inspection needed with respect to product quality submitted by a particular supplier.

MIL-STD 105A specifies that the government shall, in its sole discretion, determine whether to use normal, tightened or reduced inspection at the start of a contract. During the life of the contract, the government's quality inspectors shall determine which type of supervision should be used, according to the following criteria:

- *Normal inspection* must be used when the estimated process average is inside the applicable upper and lower limits shown in the quality standards table.
- *Tightened inspection* shall be instituted when the estimated process average exceeds the applicable upper limit in the quality standards table in question.
- *Reduced inspection* may be instituted *if* a high quality level is maintained, and the government inspectors so desire, provided that all conditions outlined in terms of quality control are fully satisfied.

In addition, normal inspection shall be reinstated if the estimated process average is equal to or better than the specified quality level, while tightened inspection is in effect. Similarly, if a reduced inspection is in effect and the average quality deteriorates, the quality control plan requires a return to normal inspection, and from there, perhaps, to tightened inspection.

Quality control charts by variables plot sample means $\bar{x}$ against an $\bar{\bar{x}}$, the mean of means averaged over time. They also have associated with them range charts (R). In World War II, the government estimated the process average by an arithmetic mean computed from the results of its sampling inspection, reserving the right to exclude from the estimated process average the results of inspection considered to be abnormal. Today, advanced testing techniques use confidence intervals to quantify and qualify the level of risk, well beyond average values.

1.7 An introduction to the role of information technology in gaining competitiveness

An advanced testing methodology, and its tools, cannot be implemented by keeping notes on the back of an envelope, or through the medieval technology that is still in use by many entities. Advanced applications require sophisticated technological solutions, which are part of a state-of-the-art way of conducting business.

Networked resources, any-to-any linkages real-time systems, cross-functional workgroups working in global and geographically dispersed organizations, on-line data-mining and the mapping of functional operations into models, are part of this state-of-the-art solution. The transition from medieval to advanced approaches takes a large amount of re-engineering effort. Information must be seamless:

- At any time,
- On any issue,
- With any counterparty,
- Anywhere in the world.

The accuracy of stress testing, risk management and damage control is enhanced with real-time collaborative applications. The identification of exposure taken with any instrument and counterparty is facilitated through networks, simulators and rich databases even if, as stated in section 1.2, there is model uncertainty and data uncertainty.

The success of computer-aided design (CAD) in the 1980s[6] ensured that since the early 1990s distributed vaults of information elements have become common in engineering applications. By the middle of the 1990s, banks who capitalized on advanced software for CAD extended its usage into process and workflow management in the financial industry.

Among well-managed institutions, the use of CAD software became popular not only in network design and maintenance, but also in trading applications and risk control. In the early to mid-1990s, the Union Bank of Switzerland, where the author was consultant to the Board, was using thirty-six CAD stations, half of them in non-engineering projects in the financial industry.

This cross-fertilization in the implementation of information technology benefited from the fact that functional software in one discipline provides capabilities for effective usage in other disciplines. It also permits organization-specific attributes for *objects*, such as client accounts or exposure limits, to be identified and used.[7]

- Through object-oriented applications, each client, and client advisor, was given the opportunity to customize banking services.
- The next step was to extend the advisory relationship on-line, and empower the client to make more informed and confident decisions regarding his or her wealth.

Sophisticated commodity software originally projected for engineering design offered the capability to define and manage instantaneous classification structures in banking operations and, then, to attach specific objects to appropriate classes. A number of conditions had to be fulfilled, however, before implementing this solution. The following questions are appropriate in defining the characteristics of the real-time system.

1. *Architecture*. Is the system design easy to extend? Is it open? Can it evolve over time and accommodate developing user needs? (See Chapter 6.)
2. *Functionality*. How well, and in what manner, does the system support the functions important to the bank and its clients, both now and in the foreseeable future?
3. *Fully distributed environment*. How does the system support highly distributed peer-to-peer implementation? Can it be extended over time as the applications grow?
4. *Heterogeneous platforms*. How effective is the support provided for platforms that are heterogeneous, but important to the bank, including the remaining legacy subsystems?
5. *Application interfaces*. Are the interfaces already provided user friendly? Are they robust? What sort of improvements are necessary as new, more sophisticated applications are tuned in?

Among top-tier organizations, in the background of these technological issues has been a new business strategy for the institution, based on fundamental business propositions. Since the year 2000, as an industry, banking has come to a strategic crossroad. Although one bank's strategic direction differed from another's, all well-managed institutions looked for an opportunity to:

- Shape their future, and
- Define their services in terms that add value to their functions, and to their customers.

Basically, apart from the control of risk, this is a major goal for implementing high technology and for adopting advanced testing methods. Any managers worth their salt will ask themselves: Will we rise to the occasion or just stand by and watch our primary income sources continue to shrink? Are we to keep being idle until our current customers become tomorrow's competitors?

Clear-eyed managers know that there is no time to lose in moving the organization forward. And they appreciate that if they fail to take control while there is still time for strategic alternatives, their customers, competitors and shrinking profit margins will make the decision for them. Two themes are present on every board, at nearly every meeting:

- Strategic choices, and
- Advanced technology to see them through.

These themes are not specific to banking. They are present throughout business and industry and they constitute a great challenge in themselves. Mature professionals see technology as a very important tool in the management of risk, and as the key ingredient in developing new value-added services for customers. Over the past few decades, says Kenneth A. Hines Jr, of Citigroup, technology has benefited the banking industry in three ways:

- *Capacity*, by allowing us to handle higher volumes of transactions,
- *Quality*, by making it possible for us to perform our jobs better through error reduction,
- *Creativity*, by making feasible activities never previously considered, which now are within the reach of well-governed firms.

In the last analysis, models, networks, databases, knowledge artefacts and increasingly sophisticated tests like those presented in this book, are themselves technology. For instance, agents enriched with case-based reasoning are carrying out ad hoc filtering and exception reporting. Other artefacts are used for zooming, to magnify knowledge-chosen findings, lifting them well above a base level. Still others are executing:

- Financial analysis,
- Predictive chores,
- Logistics planning, and
- Next-generation user interfaces.

In terms of credit risk, market risk, country risk, interest rate risk and currency risk, in spite of the uncertainty embedded in them, models act as a magnifying glass in risk assessment. A networked approach ensures that the bank's far-flung branches and operations work as *one team*, eliminating time-consuming delays caused by manual document elaboration and searches. At the same time, the implementation of advanced technology has prerequisites, as explained in Chapter 6.

Notes

1. Basel Committee, *Core Principles for Effective Banking Supervision*, BIS, Basel, April 2006. These core principles are conceived as a voluntary framework of minimum standards for sound supervisory practices.
2. D.N. Chorafas, *Economic Capital Allocation with Basel II. Cost and Benefit Analysis*, Butterworth-Heinemann, London, 2004.
3. D.N. Chorafas, *The 1996 Market Risk Amendment. Understanding the Marking-to-Model and Value-at-Risk*, McGraw-Hill, Burr Ridge, IL, 1998.
4. Basel Committee, *Core Principles Methodology*, BIS, Basel, April 2006.
5. Obtainable from US Government Printing Office, Washington, DC.
6. D.N. Chorafas, *Engineering Productivity Through CAD/CAM*, Butterworth, London, 1987.
7. D.N. Chorafas and Heinrich Steinmann, *Object-Oriented Databases*, Prentice-Hall, Englewood Cliffs, NJ, 1993.

2 Risk and its management

2.1 Introduction

This chapter addresses the notions of risk and its management. It introduces the reader to ways and means for risk control, presents examples on credit and market exposures, and elaborates on the notions of risk appetite and risk aversion by market players.

2.2 Risk defined

Dictionaries define *risk* as the chance of injury, damage or loss; a hazard. In insurance and banking, risk is expressed quantitatively as the degree, or probability, of an adverse effect and its financial aftermath. The computation of this probability of loss is not a matter of pure mathematics, although statistics and analytics are necessary to measure it. Rather, risk, its likelihood and its magnitude are a function of:

- The type of loss that is covered,
- Prevailing market conditions, and
- The amount of leverage behind the transaction, or inventoried position.

Exposure in volatile markets comes from changing exchange rates, interest rates, equity indices, equity prices and the price of other commodities; also from exposure to default concerning the counterparty with which we are dealing, and from this party's willingness to perform. No wonder regulators aim to make bankers, traders, treasurers and investors more sensitive to the inequalities of borrowers, and other parties, with whom contracts are drawn up.[1]

The realization that a great deal of the banking business should focus on managing risk is the inevitable result of assuming an increasing amount of exposure. *Risk management* is really a process of management of change, by means of systems and procedures sounding a warning about limits being approached or broken. At the same time, as Chapter 1 has shown, while the management of risk is our business, it is an impossible task without the appropriate conceptual tools, analytical methods and technological infrastructure.

- The act of determining functions or actions of risk may seem a relatively straightforward exercise,
- But it is most difficult quantitatively and qualitatively to measure, let alone forecast, risk without a properly focused and concentrated effort.

Notwithstanding the myriad of regulations, financial and social responsibilities to which companies are subject, industrial and business enterprises are, after all, entities with profit objectives. To reach these objectives they are assuming risks. With time, *risk taking came to a strategic crossroad*, requiring the board, chief executive officer and senior management to

- Establish a strategy regarding exposure, and
- Define, in no ambiguous terms, how they can be in charge of risks assumed by the enterprise.

Every entity is exposed to the *credit risk* of financial loss, arising from a counterparty's failure to service its debt in a timely manner and other reasons (see section 2.3). A different type of exposure is *market risk* associated with a decline in the total value of the entity's assets, or increase in its liabilities. This happens because of adverse changes in market variables such as interest rates, exchange rates and other commodities (see section 2.4).

Another type of risk that came in the spotlight with the new capital adequacy framework (Basel II), by the Basel Committee of Banking Supervision, is *operational risk*. This includes exposure to fraud, errors made in transaction, substandard technology leading to financial losses, damage to the entity's reputation, or other reasons caused by people, failed or inadequate processes and systems, or external events.[2] A company also faces *liquidity risk*, of being unable to meet its financial obligations as they become due, without incurring unacceptable losses because of twelfth hour salvage operations. Part of operational risk is also legal risk, which has always been present, but has become particularly pronounced during the past two decades.

Chapter 1 explained, in no ambiguous terms, that *stress testing* is one of the fundamental tools in risk control, because it helps in analysing extreme events, and in prognosticating conditions that find themselves beyond the beaten path of daily business. As long as we steadily maintain our knowledge on how to deal with uncertainty and adversity, and the instruments for doing so:

- We can take risks to gain competitive advantages,
- By contrast, failing to control exposure can result in chaos.

In mathematical terms, risk is the measure of variance around an expected value. Algorithmic formulae try to pinpoint the target (expected) value and to calculate the probability of reaching this goal. As explained in Chapter 1, however, contrary to popular thinking, risks are not normally distributed.

- They may be approximated through a normal distribution in the left part (body).
- But they have a totally different pattern at the tail, characterized by generally low likelihood, spikes and high impact.

Figure 1.1 has been redrawn in this chapter to help the reader to differentiate between *expected risks* (at the body), and *unexpected risks* (at the tail). The concept

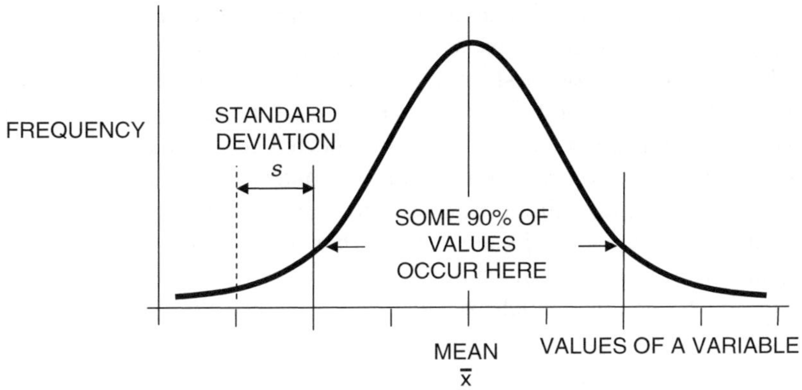

Figure 1.1 Not only do we assume that events are normally distributed, we also concentrate on those of higher frequency

is illustrated in Figure 2.1, where the frequency of losses represents loans. The loss distribution is divided into:

- *Expected losses*, typically covered by profits resulting from current operations, and reflected as profit and loss (P&L) in end-of-year financial reporting, and
- *Unexpected losses*, which are lower in frequency than those expected, but represent a significantly higher level of impact per event and must be faced through reserves and equity.

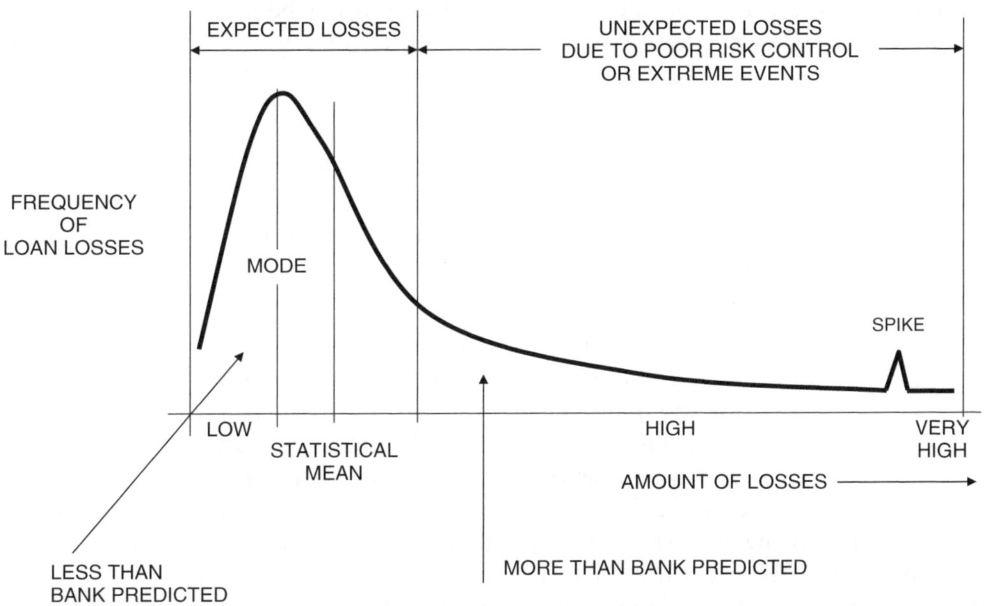

Figure 2.1 The statistical distribution of loan losses classified into expected and unexpected

The emphasis on unexpected losses and their treatment is relatively new (see Part 3). Their origin may be *extreme events* with catastrophic impact, but unexpected losses may also be due to very poor risk management or changes in economic conditions that have not been appropriately projected and accounted for. A great deal also depends on the extent to which the law of unexpected consequences comes into play.

In addition, rare or extreme events come in spikes. Few people truly appreciate that these spikes multiply with leverage, and their amplitude increases. Finally, when assessing risk factors, we should keep in mind that transactions that we carry out and positions that we take reflect the type of entity, or person, we are. They also map the economic factors under which we operate, as well as the type and amplitude of exposure that we assume.

2.3 Risk associated with the counterparty

The term *counterparty* denotes an entity or person to whom a bank has an on-balance sheet and/or off-balance sheet credit or market exposure, or a potential exposure of some other type. That exposure may, for example, take the form of a bridging loan, a foreign exchange deal or a derivatives transaction, or another commitment that has not yet been settled.

Money lost with the Bankhaus Herstatt, and Franklin National Bank of New York, is an example of counterparty risk associated with not yet settled transactions relating to forex operations. The bankruptcies of Barings and Drexel Burnham Lambert are other cases where counterparties have been licking their wounds.

Both expected losses and unexpected losses may result because of failure on the part of any customer, correspondent bank or other third party to fulfil its obligations towards our entity or towards ourselves. Sometimes, a single event such as the invasion of Kuwait by Iraq in 1990 results in several counterparties being faced with significant losses (see section 2.6 on event risk).

These examples point towards a definition of counterparty risk that is broader than that of credit risk taken alone. Counterparty risk is not only associated with *default risk*, as is the case with credit risk. The definition of counterparty exposure includes more than one risk factor:

- *Default risk* means that a counterparty will not be able to fulfil its obligations in accordance with the agreed terms of a transaction, because of financial distress.
- There is also the case of *unwillingness to perform*, particularly when the counterparty is faced with huge losses or is protected by politicians. This is different from bankruptcy, because the counterparty has the necessary assets.
- *Transfer risk* can ensure that a counterparty is unable to meet its foreign currency obligations owing to restricted access to foreign currency or other reasons not involving bad faith, but usually being associated with country risk.
- *Settlement risk* is due to failure of settlement or clearing entities of financial transactions, where the exchange of cash, securities or other assets is not simultaneous, as it is with delivery versus payment systems.

Credit risk should be assessed at several levels within this landscape of counterparty exposure. The first bullet addresses counterparty rating; the second, its moral standard. (More on this later.) *What if* this specific counterparty's rating changed from AA to A status? To BBB? To B? *What if* a future rating downgrades? For instance, what if a significant number of *our* institution's correspondent banks are known to increase their derivatives exposure by 30 per cent per year?

- Where will this leave *our* banking book? Our trading book?
- What emergency measures will be necessary? Which of these measures are practical? Feasible?

Similar queries should characterize the analysis that it conducted in regard to transfer risk, country risk and settlement risk. There is always a counterparty behind credit risk exposure that might be harmful to our institution.

Sometimes, counterparties receive warning from changes in the credit rating of entities with which they are dealing, even if this comes as a surprise. For instance, in the 1990s J.P. Morgan lost its triple A rating by Moody's, and this was a blow to the pride of one of the world's biggest and most powerful banks. (Morgan was the last American bank to enjoy a top rating from both Moody's and Standard & Poor's.)

Moody's said that the shift towards investment banking was responsible for the downgrade of its two US bank subsidiaries, Morgan Guaranty Trust Company and J.P. Morgan Delaware, to AA1 from the top AAA grade. Morgan was one of a select band of blue-chip institutions to enjoy a triple A rating from all three major independent rating firms (the other being Fitch), alongside Deutsche Bank, Union Bank of Switzerland and Rabobank Nederland. (The only non-government supported bank that finally retained the AAA rating was Rabobank, although eventually Union Bank of Switzerland regained the highest rating.)

- Morgan's businesses had become increasingly sensitive to the behaviour of global financial markets, and
- Earnings from capital activities such as equities and derivatives dealing have been much more volatile than those from corporate and personal banking, on which Morgan has previously relied.

Essentially, Morgan had been following banking industry trends. After the two major oil shocks of the 1970s competitive pressures forced most money centre banks in the same direction. The change in business orientation left only a handful with triple A ratings from Moody's, Standard & Poor's or Fitch (then London-based IBCA).

It is the duty of independent rating agencies to be extremely sensitive to the creditworthiness of banks and other entities that they rate. When, in late 1997, the bottom fell out of the South Korean banking and financial system, rating agencies were severely criticized for not having been alert to the need for a massive downgrade.

In Europe, too, during the great bull market of the late 1990s, some analysts interpreted as worrisome the fact that since 1989 the average rating of the top fifty

European banks has dropped from AA+ to AA–. The trend was for credit risk averages of banking institutions to continue falling. The cost is that:

- Whether in banking or in other industry sectors, entities with lower ratings generally find it more expensive to obtain credit lines or to issue bonds, and
- Bigger companies can sometimes be more reluctant to do business with counterparties of lower rating, because strong ratings are frequently used as evidence of corporate security and dependability.

This trend evidently poses the question: why is credit risk deteriorating? There are plenty of reasons behind the loss of creditworthiness. At the top of the list is poor management, followed by high leverage. These two reasons correlate, and the result is strengthened by other weaknesses.

Beyond poor management and leverage, another crucial factor is the growing complexity of credit risk assessments, particularly in connection with new financial instruments. This leads to misconceptions about different types of exposure, amplified by wanting information technology, substandard modelling solutions and fairly poor databases (see Chapter 1).

Still another crucial role in the increase of counterparty risk is played by concentration of exposure, rather than the often touted diversification. Many people, including experts, confuse concentration with diversification.

- Consolidation in the banking industry generally leads to concentration of risk.
- At the same time, the contents of the trading portfolios and loan books of many institutions are fairly similar, increasing the resulting exposure.

Based on statistics by the European Central Bank (ECB), the histogram in Figure 2.2 shows the consolidation of credit institutions in Euroland, over two decades. This is expressed through the number of remaining independent entities. (ECB brings to attention the fact that statistics for 1985 and 1990 are only indicative.)

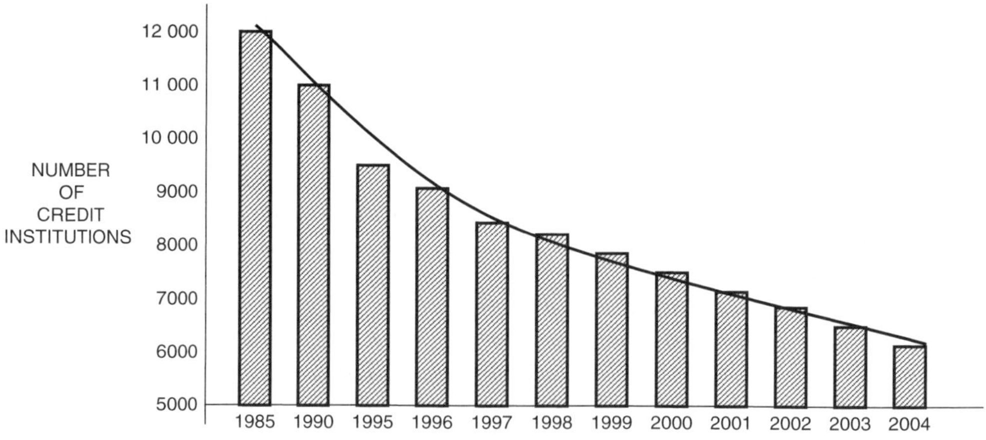

Figure 2.2 Trendline characterizing twenty years of consolidation among credit institutions in Euroland (statistics by European Central Bank)

The ECB notes that despite a notable decline in the number of banks, in most Euroland countries the number of branches has remained fairly stable, or even risen.[3] In the aftermath, the pattern being observed so far supports the hypothesis that, in terms of cost-effectiveness, the benefits of restructuring have not yet shown up. By contrast, the consolidation of portfolios of derivative financial instruments, and look-alike loans, has increased, with an evident impact on the banks' exposure.

- Classical testing will not reveal the extend of assumed risk, as it fails to account for extreme events and spikes.
- Therefore, it is necessary to stress test creditworthiness, taking full account of the fact that commercial and investment institutions depend to a very substantial degree on correspondent banks.

The principle is that correspondent banks might have been weakened, not strengthened, through mergers and acquisitions (M&As) because most frequently the consolidation of portfolios reduces the diversification prevailing before an M&A. Other important reasons for loss of creditworthiness are wanting principles of and solutions to risk management because of the confusion (and musical chairs) following a merger. These are often aggravated by:

- Avoidance of personal accountability, and
- General laxity in moral responsibility, which leads to taking fully unwarranted risks.

Few people truly appreciate that *credit* is a financial term with a moral lineage, which goes beyond its meaning of debt. Credit is *trust* given or received, typically in expectation of future payment for property transferred, fulfilment of promises given or other reasons such as performance. Therefore, stress tests for creditworthiness must pay due attention to moral responsibility, and to the lack of it. Short of this, the results will be half-baked at best.

2.4 Market risk and its variants

Market risk is the all-inclusive term connected to a portfolio's exposure to the volatility of market prices. This volatility may regard interest rates, exchange rates, equity values or other variables exposed to changes in the market. A practical classification of market risk is into *general* and *specific*.

- *General market risk* is connected to the whole market activity. For instance, it can be expressed as risk associated with the volatility of an equity index such as Dow Jones.
- Specific market risk reflects the price behaviour of one company. It may work in synergy with general market risk or it may exhibit a countertrend.

The *general market risk* is relatively easy to understand. In the case of interest rates, for example, the general risk results from the change in the yield curve featuring

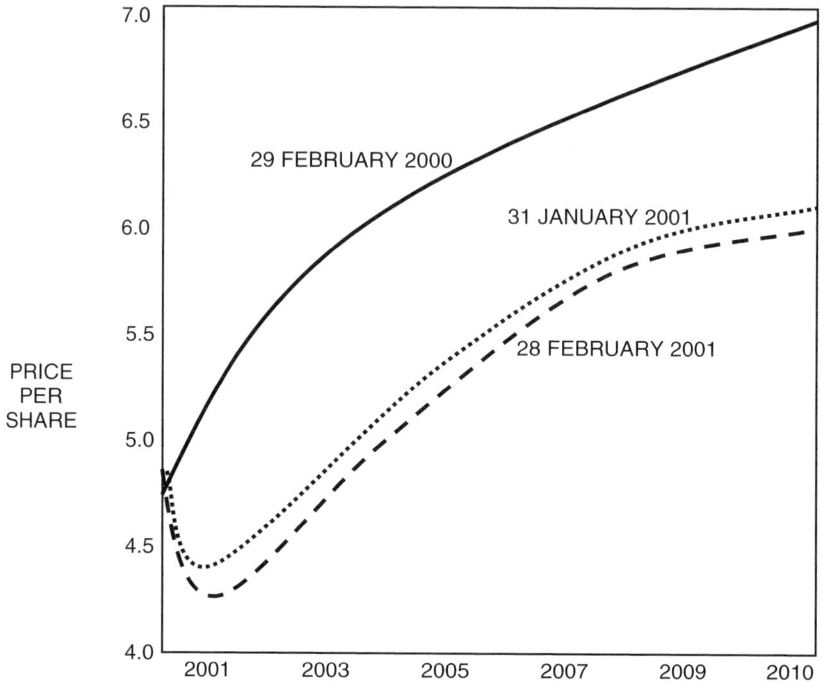

Figure 2.3 Ten-year curves of implied forward overnight interest rates in Euroland (in 2000 and 2001, percentages per year, daily data) (*source*: ECB Monthly Bulletin, March 2001, with permission)

different interest rates from those contracted. As an example, Figure 2.3 shows three ten-year curves of implied forward overnight interest rates in Euroland, in the 2000 and 2001 time-frame.

General market risk may also have other origins. For instance, it may come from changes characterizing the stock market index or exposure connected to currency exchange. In principle, changes in prices of key commodities with wide consumption have direct, indirect and second level effects.

Specific market risk is one of the issues that is not so clearly defined by the 1996 Market Risk Amendment.[4] In a way (which follows financial reporting practices in America), the Amendment says that there is a link between specific risk and the standardized method of reporting exposure to regulators. But specific market risk is not explained in unambiguous terms. Rather, it is lumped together into a *value at risk* (VAR) measure.

The most likely accepted definition of *specific market risk* is the one connected to the instrument and/or the issuer of the instrument. In the case of interest rates, different issuers and different instruments have different spread. This spread is defined by the market on the basis of:

- The rating of the issuer, or
- The information that it possesses on that particular instrument.

Both general and specific market risk should be subjected to stress testing. Since the 1996 Market Risk Amendment the model advanced by regulators for market risk reporting has been VAR. A stress test of VAR is done by increasing the level of confidence from 99 per cent to 99.9 per cent and 99.97 per cent. The latter corresponds to an AA rating by independent agencies at the long leg of the risk distribution.

The importance of *confidence intervals* was explained in Chapter 1. Increasing the confidence interval from 99 per cent to 99.9 per cent is an order of magnitude improvement, and at the same time a stress test. Indeed, nothing less than 99.9 per cent is acceptable in risk reporting.

- 99 per cent means that 1 per cent of all risk cases are not accounted for.
- Through this 1 per cent may pass a swarm of exposures, including unexpected risks, tail events and spikes, which bring the firm to its knees.

However, uplifting a weak model such as VAR is not the best possible strategy. What is needed is a rigorous approach to market risk evaluation. For face-lifting purposes, some banks use variants by combining VAR with delta- and gamma-neutral positions. Others combine VAR with the general autoregression conditional heteroschedasticity (GARCH) method. Still others:

- Evaluate different stress testing levels;
- They do so through comparison with the price of options augmented as a function of an increase in market risk.

Different financial institutions, and different analysts within the same bank, use their own criteria in analysing general and specific market risk. No two methods are exactly the same, and none of these available is definitely better than its alternatives. A similar statement is valid about ways and means followed for the control of market risk, coming, in the general case, under *hedging*.

It is only normal that an investor or a company, exposed to interest rate risk, foreign currency risk, equity price risk or other risk relating to the volatility of market prices, would like to protect itself. In many cases, although not always, a portion of these risks is hedged, but market volatility can still have an impact on the results of operations and financial position commodities.

Entities usually hedge the price exposure of raw materials and other commodities, as well as a portion of anticipated revenue to foreign currency fluctuations. They do so primarily with option contracts. Treasurers monitor the foreign currency exposures daily, or even better several times daily, to ensure the overall effectiveness of their hedge positions.

Considerable attention must also be paid to exposure associated with fixed income securities, which are subject to interest rate risk. This is true even if the portfolio is diversified, and it consists primarily of investment grade securities to minimize credit risk. Companies hedge their exposure to the interest rate risk with options. Securities held in the equity portfolio, too, are subject to equity price risk. Volatile equity securities are also hedged with options.

Even 'perfect hedges', however (in case these exist), do not provide complete cover from market risk. Worse still, sometimes hedges may turn against the hedger, who has not been able to prognosticate market uncertainties. Summing up the message conveyed through the preceding paragraphs, *market risk* is mainly due to unexpected price changes in stocks, bonds, interest rates, currencies and other commodities. As such, market risk causes:

- Capital losses, or
- Lower income in the future.

There are two preconditions to the able management of market risk. One is the proverbial deep knowledge of the instruments in which one is investing, and their volatility. With simple financial instruments, rich databases and analytics, market risks are relatively well understood. But constraints remain because of:

- Macroeconomic impact
- Non-linearity between risk and return
- Instability in correlations between market variables
- Aftermath of defaults and credit cycles (more on this later), and
- Other factors, such as yield curve changes and spreads.

In addition, under certain conditions, market risk and credit risk correlate, with market risk morphing into credit risk and, sometimes, vice versa. This is particularly true with modern, complex financial instruments, because:

- Their market behaviour is not transparent, and
- Traditional know-how, tools and methods have not been made for them.

Complexity ensures that, in a growing number of cases, this is true of both general and specific market risk, the latter relating to the instrument (or issuer) and the former to the structural evolution of the global financial system, from one dominated by banks, to one with deep and liquid capital markets.

Because of this major structural change, credit risk becomes market tied, with prevailing unknowns turning some time-honoured notions of the economy, and of finance, on their head. The ongoing structural changes due to globalization increase price volatility, promote transborder financial flows, and create an urgent need to rethink and re-establish capital adequacy terms. For instance, loan loss provisioning may become unstable because of market risk morphing into credit risk.

2.5 Risk appetite and risk aversion

The notion of *risk appetite* relates to the willingness of investors, bankers, speculators and other market participants to take risks. Risk appetite is a measure of assumed exposure by people and companies; as such, it invariably relates to leverage, type of risk assumed, and condition of the financial markets, as well as of its performance.

Risk appetite changes over time, because of its being subject to cyclical fluctuations. By contrast, economists look at risk *aversion* as a relatively time-invariable degree of defensive positioning in terms of investment. In the background of risk aversion is uncertainty regarding future consumption market behaviour.

Risk appetite and risk aversion relate in a possibilistic way.[5] Their sum is not equal to 1. The reason for this lack of complementarity lies in the fact that rather than describing risk reception within a specific financial market environment,

- Risk aversion reflects the underlying attitude to all types of financial risk;
- This contrasts with the notion of risk appetite, which can be subject to sharp short-term volatility.

These are the definitions prevailing today in the financial industry. To illustrate their meaning, a risk curve is shown in Figure 2.4, which holds true in every field of activity from engineering to finance. *If* prevailing market conditions were invariant, *then* in this U curve:

- High risk can be found in the early years of a product, as well as in its old age when it becomes overexploited by speculators.
- Relatively low risk lies in the useful years of the product, past teething troubles, when it becomes settled and before its massive exploitation by smart operators.

In terms of assumed risk, this risk curve evidently moves north when the economic environment is confronted with financial crises. Riskier market conditions increase the exposure assumed at every point of the U curve, but the teething troubles and worn-out peaks remain.

This pattern towards a generalized higher exposure accounts for the fact that, in general, financial crises cannot be explained solely by fundamental economic factors.

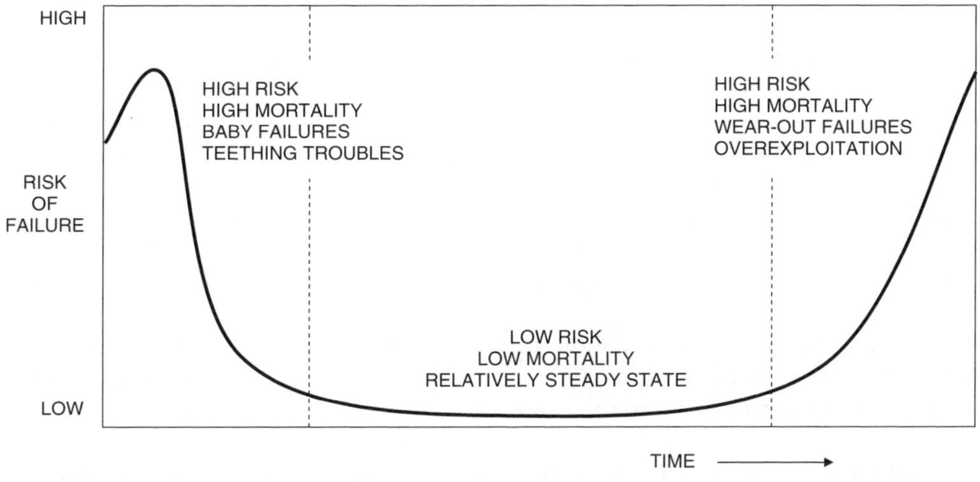

Figure 2.4 All systems, all products and all entities go through a U-curve transition in mortality

The unexplained part is thought to be due to the risk appetite of market participants, which is subject to volatility. The willingness of investors to bear risks is not steady, and modern economists believe that any serious analysis should pay attention to both:

- Risk aversion, and
- Risk appetite.

From the viewpoint of regulators, risk appetite poses a threat to financial stability, particularly because mismatches between risks being assumed and returns being received cannot be systematically identified *ex ante*. This makes it virtually impossible to specify a fair valuation level for pricing of risk(s).

However, there are some exceptions to this statement. For instance, a change in risk appetite is reflected in the risk premiums of those assets more exposed to the market's whims. Evidence is provided by yield spread of relatively low rated corporate bonds over Group of Ten government bonds. Such spread is not steady over time:

- It diminishes with investors' higher risk appetite, and
- It increases with lower risk appetite, sometimes to hundreds of basis points.

Contrarians to this statement say that volatility in yield spread cannot be simply seen as pointing to an equivalent variance in risk appetite. The reason for wider spread could also lie in liquidity risk, not only in credit risk, and liquidity changes as the market evolves.

There is no doubt that a model based on both credit risk and volatility risk will be more sophisticated than one based on market risk alone. This being said, however, a *drop* in risk appetite generally leads to higher financing costs, as:

- Yield expectations of investors increase even if the overall risk remains unchanged;
- Hence, it becomes more difficult to raise capital in the equity and debt capital markets.

Usually, a change in general risk appetite of market participants contributes to the volatility of risk premium. At the same time, a high risk appetite can result in unprofitable projects because investments are poorly scrutinized before being made. An example is the sharp reduction in risk premiums in 2004/05.

According to financial analysts there are various reasons behind sharp and protracted deviations in risk appetite, but there is no general agreement on these reasons. In general, empirical analyses show that there is a positive correlation between economic performance and the willingness to assure risks, which essentially means that:

- In bull markets, investors are more prepared to bear additional exposure, and
- Bear markets typically lead to a decline in risk appetite, with a different correlation characterizing these two variables in every time.

Based on such empirical findings, economists suggest that, in the general case, the risk premium is negatively correlated with risk appetite, but it also has a positive correlation with actual risk. All told, although experts speak of a relationship between risk appetite and fundamental market factors, their analysis has not progressed in a way that permits documented conclusions.

One of the hypotheses is that risk appetite and risk aversion are more fundamental behavioural factors characterizing the actions of market players than is generally thought to be the case. According to some experts, the risk-related behaviour by market participants has associated with it limitations of cognitive abilities, because people have only a limited ability to:

- Absorb information,
- Process it quickly,
- Reach decisions, and
- Store the reasons behind them over long periods.

Cognitive restrictions lead to simplified rules of conduct; and such simplified rules do not correspond with the customary notion of 'rational markets'. Research in this frame of reference is handicapped by the lack of reliable indicators for measuring risk appetite. In the late 1990s, in the middle of stockmarket boom, Dr Alan Greenspan spoke of investors' 'irrational exuberance', but:

- Evidence was hypothetical, and
- No measures were taken to correct the balances.

Financial institutions have recently started to develop metrics addressing investors' risk appetite. In 2001, an indicator was developed by Crédit Suisse First Boston (CSFB), which drew on the correlation between risk appetite and the relative performance of two quarter spaces:

- The top riskier assets, and
- The bottom, less risky, assets.

The CSFB model is based on the assumption that an increasing risk preference shifts the demand from less risky investments to assets associated with higher risks. In the aftermath, it pushes their prices up relative to low-risk assets. However,

- *If* the prevailing market condition is that of lower risk appetite,
- *Then* there is a preference for risk-free assets whose prices increase as a result of higher investor demand.

Other indices of risk appetite have been developed by Goldman Sachs and J.P. Morgan. The Goldman Sachs model draws on a consumption hypothesis, based on the capital asset pricing model (CAPM) for assessing risk appetite of investors. The liquidity, credit and volatility index (LCV) of J.P. Morgan comprises seven subindices capturing credit risk, liquidity risk and volatility in different financial markets.

Based on indicators of risk appetite, another mathematical model calculates the *expected shortfall*, along the pattern shown in Figure 2.5. The unit in the abscissa is pure capital at risk. The model address both expected and unexpected losses.

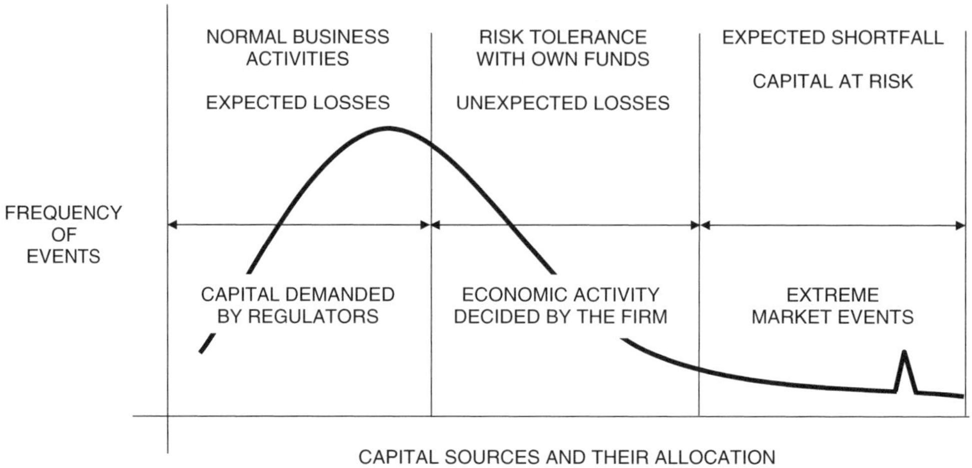

Figure 2.5 The view of capital adequacy in connection with risk appetite and expected shortfall (this gives a percentage of financial staying power from the outside)

The developers of this concept present it as a better alternative to VAR. (Expected losses and unexpected losses are covered in Part 3.)

2.6 Systemic risk and event risk

Section 2.3 introduced the notion of counterparty risk. The definition of counterparty risk is much broader than that of credit risk alone, because it involves not only default risk but also settlement risk, transfer risk and other aspects of exposure.

Section 2.4 brought to the reader's attention the fact that up to a point market risk and credit risk correlate, and may morph into one another. This is particularly true with the ongoing expansion of credit due to globalization, where the lender (or investor) is remote from the entity being trusted with wealth in terms of loans.

At the positive end, the expansion of credit greases the wheels of a market economy. At the same time, however, it is an important factor in the build-up of imbalances in the financial system, which may lead to *systemic risk*. The term systemic risk denotes an economic and financial crisis that severely impairs the work of the financial system, and may eventually cause its complete breakdown.

- Uncertainty in terms of the ability to avoid systemic risk becomes greater as the number of market unknowns increases.
- Managing systemic risk in a proactive manner is a new task, made more urgent as the exposure of the banking system stands at trillions of dollars and continues mounting (see the drill for a meltdown in Chapter 5).

Deregulation, innovation in financial instruments and globalization ensure that regulators must run quickly to stay in the same place. In monetary regimes where paper money and electronic funds transfers dominate, the main exogenous constraints on the creation of credit in monetary terms are interest rates and reserve requirements. Nowadays, monetary authorities use interest rates to:

- Regulate the velocity of circulation of money, and
- By controlling the monetary base, impact on money supply.

Systemic risk can also originate through major credit events such as the collapse or near collapse of significant market players; for example, Drexel Burnham Lambert, Continental Illinois, the Bank of New England, LTCM and the savings and loans industry. Although these events occurred in the late 1980s and the 1990s, many supervisors believe that the availability of liquidity under stress conditions has not been fully tested. Therefore, it remains uncertain:

- How the use of an even greater amount of leverage can affect the markets under stress, and
- What the aftermath of a simultaneous failure of two, three or more big financial institutions would be.

Supervisory authorities monitor closely the condition of credit institutions and other regulated entities, by means of qualitative and quantitative disclosures that provide an overview of the company's business objectives, its risk appetite, diversification of exposure and how its different business activities fit into its stated objectives.

An integral part of required disclosure is the types of internal control procedures that are in place for managing what is often a diverse business environment served by a wide-spanning range of instruments. To a significant extent the compliance notions, as discussed in Chapter 1, fit within this perspective.

At the heart of compliance is how well the entity's ongoing activities conform to rules and regulations. Investors, speculators, lenders and other market players, however, can be overtaken by events that either are poorly detected in advance, or hit at the most inappropriate moment, with more or less devastating effects. This is the sense of *event risk*.

While the discussion in the preceding paragraph has focused on market risk from volatility in equity prices, the impact of volatility is omnipresent and its prognostication is still an arcane art. For instance, in terms of volatility specific market risk can be significantly greater than general market risk, because it is influenced by many factors involving unknowns.

- *Event risk* can happen at any moment.
- Therefore, tier-one banks have developed expertise on how to simulate event risk and study its impact.

Event risk can ensure that even good knowledge of the instrument, and its exposure, can turn a forecast on its head. For instance, it can turn credit into ashes almost overnight. Moody's Investors Service had given Orange County a debt rating of Aa1. That was the highest for any county in California; but after the December 1994 meltdown of Orange County's treasury, Moody's declared its bonds to be junk.

Another example of the after effect of event risk has been the rapid meltdown of the formerly prosperous 'Asian tiger' economics in mid-1997. This was followed by the near bankruptcy of the go-go economy of South Korea, at the end of the same year. Both equity and bond investors were deeply hurt. Practically all major independent rating agencies failed to anticipate a latent bankruptcy because the highly geared Asian entities had miraculously escaped scrutiny. Still other examples are:

- LTCM's bankruptcy in September 1998,
- Enron's bankruptcy in December 2001, and
- Parmalat's bankruptcy in December 2003, which was the greatest corporate default ever.

Experience teaches that it is unlikely that the real reasons underpinning financial catastrophes, such as the Great Depression, or the underlying laws of such major events, will be discovered in straightforward manner. Nor is it likely that a dramatic breakthrough will wrap things up neatly, as often happens in fictional stories. For modelling purposes (see Chapter 1), a web of circumstantial evidence needs to be constructed, which is so strong that the conclusion is inescapable.

- The strands of this web should be as independently anchored as possible.
- Independence ensures that, in case one strand breaks the whole web will not unravel.

Rocket scientists and financial analysts are faced with an analogous situation as they struggle to weave a web of evidence for future risk events. They need all the independent strands of evidence they can master to be able to see certain patterns, and to develop plausible hypotheses of future events. In this connection, stress tests provide an invaluable contribution.

'We welcome the growing emphasis in stress testing, to make people aware of outliers and extreme events', said Barbara Ridpath of Standard & Poor's. 'The challenge is to get consistent stress tests across all risk types', added Tim Thompson of Barclays Bank. Consistency in stress testing is still an issue in its infancy.

2.7 Developing a system for risk management

The general experience has been that very few people realize there is a great deal of similitude between the way tycoons work and make a business fortune, and the manner in which engineers and scientists conduct their endeavours. Science begins with an empirical observation and proceeds by recognizing its possible implications. Subsequently, the scientific method:

- Confirms the importance of observations by experiment, and
- Battles against every sort of difficulty to gain acceptance of experimentally confirmed results, until such results unravel because of an unexpected new piece of evidence.

Whether in business or in science, the key ingredients of a great professional are imagination and breadth of vision, as well as the drive to push forward the current limits, whether these are physical constraints or frontiers in knowledge. People make the difference. The range of personal skills and drive is so great that leading experts hypothesize that results obtained by the best person and by an average person can vary by a factor of fifty to one (as suggested in a study from the Massachusetts Institute of Technology).

Personal leverage works to amplify what is obtained in terms of deliverables, and to compress the timescales from start to finish. In addition, in science and in business, discovery is exciting. Working out the implications of a discovery needs knowledge, patience and determination. These characteristics are most fundamental in achieving results, whether in:

- Scientific discoveries,
- Exploiting new business opportunities, or
- Establishing an effective risk management system.

The most famous scientists and best known businessmen do not go by the book. They observe, analyse, make up their minds and take action. Able managers know this. 'We don't care what you do as long as you make a mess in this laboratory. It has been too clean for a number of years', said the rector of the University of Sheffield to Dr Howard Florey, who developed a way of mass producing penicillin, when he hired him.

This should be the mission given to every newly hired chief risk management officer. 'Making a mess of exposure profiles' can be done through stress tests, for rigorous risk management reasons. Indeed, a good domain for stress tests is the asymmetries that exist in most financial transactions, and in the global financial system at large; for instance, between:

- Coexisting sound and unsound economic policies by sovereigns,
- Rational and irrational allocation of capital at risk in credit institutions,
- The disparity in the treatment of lenders and borrowers by legislators, and
- Systemic crisis prevention and systemic crisis intervention by supervisors.

Scientific research presents many parallels to this requirement of analysing asymmetries, and of examining what encountered anomalies may mean. Like a juggler who can keep a dozen balls in the air, a good scientist must keep five or six lines of research endeavour in motion, without losing track of his or her objectives. A great businessman is doing exactly the same, because he knows that few of his projects have a real chance of success.

The paradigm of similitudes extends to many aspects of exposure. The businessman, the scientist and the risk manager produce results when they are endowed with a great sense of independence. Independence of mind is like opening mental windows, letting the fresh air of realism clear away the stuffy air of conventional thinking which is, at best, sterile.

This process of independence of mind should in effect be used in developing a novel but also rigorous risk management system. The best solutions are made for the

Table 2.1 Development process of a risk management system

Original concept	First prototype	Second prototype	Implementation and upkeep
Concept selection Credit risk data Market risk data Operational risk data Coarse design Structural paths Interdependencies Impedences Target definition	Concept refining Measurement of simulated results Comparison to real-life target Evaluation of structural paths Redefinition of interdependencies Control of impedences Simulation and experimentation	Real life implementation in 2 selected divisions Performance evaluation Cost evaluation Cost improvements Performance improvement Acceptance by end-users Acceptance by senior management	Corporate-wide implementation Test of the total system Test of reporting structure Test of quantitative results Test of qualitative results Walkthroughs for accuracy control Backtesting and update

entity in which they will be implemented. Table 2.1 divides this process into four steps, each with its own specific performance characteristics:

- Original concept,
- First prototype,
- Second prototype, and
- Implementation and upkeep.

The original concept sets the direction. This is important because a vital factor in the success of a scientist's efforts is his or her sense of direction in the research. This principle fits well the type of work the risk manager is required to do, particularly in connection with advanced testing.

An important common characteristic of high-grade professionals is the attention that they pay to the cause and effect of interlinked variables. This is most important to nearly all risk management projects. Some of the firms blasted out of existence in the 2000/01 severe market downturn:

- Were parties in long chains of interlinked contracts, and
- While these contracts needed to be unwound, some of the counterparties involved in the deals had gone bust.

Risk managers who are worth their salt are always dubious about statements that 'things will take care of themselves' or 'they will turn around some time down the line'. Quite often, to see what is in other people's minds, risk controllers look at faces. They sit up, watch directly the play in the eye of the person whom they are interviewing and record reactions. In so doing,

- They use soft language, but are absolutely clear about what they are after, and
- They are mindful that the number of past successes is, in no way, proof that these will be repeated in the future.

Moreover, both businessmen and scientists know all too well that having a carefully worked out, internally consistent analysis is no guarantee of being precisely right. It is entirely possible things would turn out otherwise. However, not having such analysis increases significantly the probability of being wrong.

Time and again, rocket scientists and risk controllers appreciate the wisdom of what Harry Truman once said: 'You can always amend a big plan, but you can never expand a little one'. Therefore, they shape their plans and systems in a way that makes it feasible:

- To cover a larger domain,
- While at the same time, remaining flexible and adaptable to changing market factors.

Last but not least, the results obtained must be presented in such a way that assumed exposure is properly understood by all parties (see also the discussion on user interfaces in Chapter 6). The problem is that traditional financial reporting tools rarely, if ever, provide the type of detail needed to make critical decisions in a timely manner. What every party in position of responsibility needs is:

- A fully comprehensive presentation,
- Quick, interactive access to very current information, and
- Powerful means permitting experimentation with this information in a meaningful sense.

The result of risk management must be a consistent view of exposure across instruments, transactions, entities, product lines, individual counterparties, customer groups, market sectors, countries or any other defined criterion. Timeliness, accuracy and consistency are at a premium, so that decisions can be based on a clear perspective about where and when to invest resources, establish limits and capitalize on new opportunities, or close down non-performing projects.

Notes

1. D.N. Chorafas, *Economic Capital Allocation with Basel II. Cost and Benefit Analysis*, Butterworth-Heinemann, London, 2004.
2. D.N. Chorafas, *Operational Risk Control with Basel II. Basic Principles and Capital Requirements*, Butterworth-Heinemann, London, 2004.
3. European Central Bank, *Monthly Bulletin*, May 2005.
4. D.N. Chorafas, *The 1996 Market Risk Amendment. Understanding the Marking-to-Model and Value-at-Risk*, McGraw-Hill, Burr Ridge, IL, 1998.
5. D.N. Chorafas, *The New Information Technologies – A Practitioner's Guide*, Van Nostrand Reinhold, New York, 1992.

3 The dynamics of stress testing

3.1 Introduction

The theme of this chapter is an introduction to stress testing, its mechanics and its dynamics. The reader will find two definitions of stress testing: a broader one and a narrower one. The broader definition, together with its methodology and investigative tools, will be the basis for all subsequent discussion on the implementation of an advanced testing technology, no matter which issue is being brought under the microscope of analytics.

3.2 Stress testing defined

Stress testing is a generic term, which does not necessarily mean the same thing to different companies or to different people. In the general case, the term describes various methods, techniques and conditions used to gauge the potential vulnerability of a given entity, portfolio, condition, position or group of investments (including loans, securities, derivatives and other items). The stress test aims to unearth, ahead of time, vulnerability to exceptional, or unexpected but plausible, events. A stress test can be conducted through:

- Scenario writing,
- Sensitivity analysis,
- Statistical inference under extreme conditions,
- Drills for a meltdown.

This is a broad palette of ways and means available for implementing stress testing, necessary for the broad definition of stress tests. A much narrower definition considers stress testing as a subsection of model validation. The added flavour is that exact details and requirements are seen as a matter between the entity conducting the stress test, for instance a bank, and its regulator.

Because stress tests are not the past but the future, narrow definitions are counterproductive and, therefore, they should be avoided. For this reason, this text will follow the broader definition, looking at stress testing as an investigative tool:

- Akin to applied research,
- But with the characteristic that it is specifically aiming at *risk analysis*.

Such risk analysis will be conducted around the outline for families of tools. The tests to be performed will be based on historical evidence and/or on hypotheses. They will also have a goal. For instance, one may aim at stress-testing exposure embedded in a portfolio by simulating the ramifications of large market swings, reflecting:

- A repetition of past evidence, or
- Tentative statements on market volatility and possible, but unlikely, extreme conditions.

The careful study of historical evidence can be most rewarding. In the mid- to late 1990s, Dr Brandon Davies, the treasurer of Barclays Bank, had his people studying outliers over 200 years of the British economy. There is nearly always historical evidence of transient phenomena, and their study may reveal some predictors. Figure 3.1 presents a twenty-first century example: the January 2001 spike in power costs in mid-Columbia (north-western USA).

- The plausibility of such an occurrence is small, and this may be a first time event, not detectable in past time series,
- But the impact is great, overrunning the after effect of better known and more frequent, and therefore expected, events.

In the background of stress testing financial occurrences, along the frame of reference described by these bullets, lies the fact that markets are always in motion. There are very interesting exceptional events that should be studied, but when using traditional tools (see Chapter 1) the ability to do so in regard to market movements is limited. Slowly, we have come to appreciate that we need a microscope.

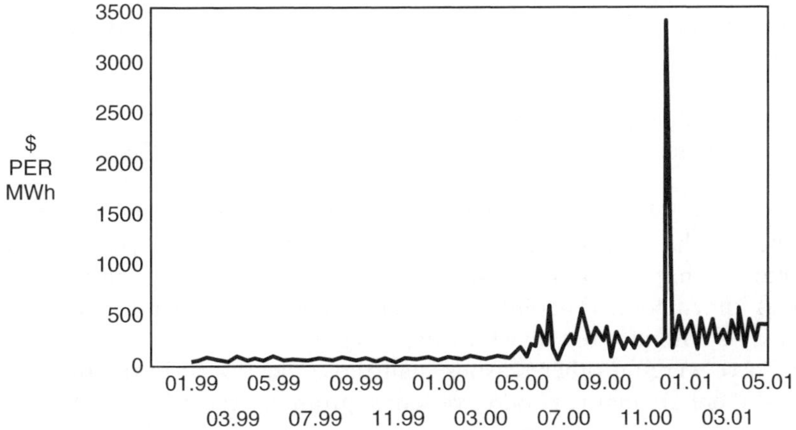

Figure 3.1 The 2001 spike in US mid-Columbia power costs.
MWh: megawatt-hour

While using the microscope of analytics provided by stress testing, it should be appreciated that movements taking place in markets can be good predictors in interpreting the state of the economy. To do so, however, one must be able:

- To study asymmetries characterizing markets and instruments, and
- To take account of the fact that the message they convey is written in their language; hence, it must be interpreted.

The misalignment between currencies and interest rates is an example of such asymmetries. Some of the benefits derived from stress tests come from the fact that crises cannot be made to run to a timetable, but panics can be emulated by means of test conditions on an experimental timetable. Subsequently, the aftermath is studied. This prognostication is made possible by means of experimentation, which:

- Goes beyond *normal risks* attached to traditional widely held forms of investment in a market with rather low volatility, and
- Focuses on background reasons of *extreme risks*, which characterize new and highly leveraged instruments; also, more classical ones under conditions of high volatility.

The reasons behind this hunting for outliers in a risk distribution are both theoretical and practical. An example of the practical side is the assurance that risk stays within limits (see section 3.4). Such limits are established by the board of the institution and their intend is not simply to reduce risk. The real goal is reliable:

- Measurement,
- Pricing of risk, and
- Timely reporting of assumed exposure.

In a similar manner, the real objective of risk management standards by regulators is not to eliminate failures of individual banks, or to abolish the process of creative destruction that provides the market with its dynamism. Neither is risk measurement and risk pricing intended to replace the individual responsibility of board members, the chief executive officer and risk managers. The goal is to:

- Enhance individual accountability, and
- Promote a greater and more objective market discipline (see Chapter 16).

Another reason why standards are in place and analytics are necessary is appreciation of the fact that institutions cannot function satisfactorily unless they operate in an environment characterized by transparency, personal accountability and reliability of financial information. Therefore, financial standards are vital, and tests in their regard must be administered in a fully dependable manner.

Even if there were no other reasons than those mentioned in the preceding paragraphs, and there are many, good governance promotes the practice of stress testing. Cooked up books, dubious formulae, muddy accounts, unreliable financial statements, inflated earnings and hidden losses are examples of research areas where available information has to be tortured to reveal its secrets.

3.3 Advanced testing and new financial instruments

One of the fundamental forces propelling stress testing is that the traditional testing tools and control methods are subject to *standards fatigue*. Classical tests for exposure have been left behind by innovation in financial instruments, and market dynamics propelled by deregulation, globalization, technology and a growing risk appetite (see Chapter 2). Legacy types of risk analysis are at a disadvantage because of:

- The current higher degree of complexity, relative to the old business model of operations,
- New requirements posed by financial and commercial relationships between providers of services and their clients,
- The failure of old tests to analyse the underlying reason(s) or motivation, connected to greater sophistication of instruments, and
- The location of significant operations in multiple jurisdictions, with differences in legal matters and regulatory regimes.

Many of these issues relate to corporate governance; others are specific to products and services, but all have a major impact on exposure. Well-managed institutions appreciate that the control of risk is a steady intraday affair, which must be focused and precise. This contrasts with the way in which poorly managed organizations run their business, where nobody is really in charge of exposure.

In addition, guidelines related to financial reporting and risk management, as well as to capital adequacy, do not mean much in the absence of sound accounting conventions. That is what the International Financial Reporting Standards (IFRS) are all about.[1] Regulatory accounting standards must be supplemented by dependable valuation of assets, robust auditing practices and timely internal controls. Under this perspective,

- Stress testing is an integral part of the system of management control action, and
- The need for increasingly more powerful, and more scientific, tests is further promoted by the frequency and severity of risks being taken.

Efforts aimed at improving financial stability are more likely to be effective if they work in unison with market forces, harnessing the prudential instincts of serious market players, and promoting codes of market behaviour, by providing measurements and benchmarks on which practitioners can depend. Classical tests, and old reporting standards, do not have the polyvalence required by a globalized market environment. Another defect is their inability to differentiate between:

- Normal events, and
- Low-frequency events of high impact.

Rephrasing the concept introduced in Chapter 1, in connection with the normal distribution, what are usually considered normal events are high-frequency events occurring within 2–3 standard deviations of the mean, and their impact is more or less average. By contrast, low-frequency events occur in the long tail of the distribution, and there may be spikes.

As far as analytics are concerned, timing considerations are also important and these, too, are not covered by traditional tests. For instance, in connection with operational risk,[2] *high-frequency* (spot) events are recognized within one to five days. Such high-frequency operational risks can be empirically observed, with the result that it is often possible to track them and to price their impact.

In contrast, *low-frequency* operational risk events usually represent a forward sort of exposure that may pass undetected. That kind of risk may not even be already known, or it shouts over the head of managers, and therefore it is not appropriately observed. Many high-impact operational risk events consist of background or residual happenings that:

- Went undetected by management, and
- Were allowed to grow over time, because nobody was in charge.

In lending, an example is provided by failure to re-evaluate steadily the creditworthiness of borrowers, calculating and stress testing probability of default (see Chapter 9), stress testing loss given default and stress testing exposure at default (see Chapter 10). Default stress testing must be done steadily for all major accounts in the loans portfolio, with particular emphasis on lower rated and big borrowers.

Many high-impact events in areas other than lending are directly connected to new financial products, such as derivative instruments. Derivatives are increasingly used by banks and other entities for reasons ranging from hedging to profit making. Although hedging derivatives risk is supposed to limit the impact, often the opposite result is reached, with hedging leading to higher exposure.[3]

Indeed, one of the major problems with new financial instruments is that they have not been fully tested in adverse circumstances. Many derivatives, the majority contracted over the counter, have questionable liquidity, under virtually all circumstances, something that classical tests of exposure do not appropriately detect.

- Estimates of value at risk (see Chapter 7), based on historical price volatility, are not a good guide to potential losses under dynamic market conditions, and
- Liquidity in the underlying market(s) can dry up unexpectedly, leaving economic agents more exposed than they expected to be, on the basis of classical model estimates (see Chapter 9).

It is not surprising, therefore, that well-managed institutions look at stress testing as a way to overcome these limitations. Both the concepts underpinning stress tests and the tools being used play an important role in identifying potential vulnerabilities. By so doing, they support senior management's efforts to deal with them by spotting weaknesses, or gaps, in the institution's financial armoury.

The message the reader should retain from this section is that attaining the objective of sound governance is a moving target, which requires steady evolution of methods, tools and standards. Innovation in management control practices ensures that such practices are no longer as simple as they used to be. Indeed, the complexity of the financial system makes a simplified approach ineffective.

3.4 What is the benefit of stress testing?

Invariably, the failure properly to manage and control the risks incurred in daily business results in damage to the staying power and, eventually, to the reputation of an entity. This leads to its downfall. To keep exposure in check, management sets operating limits, which are allocated among business units. Section 3.2 stated that limits help in measurement, pricing of risk and timely reporting of exposure. Moreover,

- Limits are the means for controlling the risk appetite of different units and of the company as a whole.
- To be effective, however, they have to be planned and gauged against expected risk and return.

In the past, setting limits to exposure has been pure guesswork. As this has proved to be inadequate, well-managed companies developed methods for limits planning through advanced testing. This has become an *ex ante* use of stress tests.

Another use is *ex post*, because, although necessary, planning the limits structure is not enough. Experimentation helps internal control to keep a close watch on the observance of limits, with the aim of protecting the company from unacceptable damage to its annual earnings capacity, its dividend paying ability, its reputation and, ultimately, its ongoing viability.

Intelligently used, stress testing provides a valuable input to internal control which is management's feedback. As Figure 3.2 shows, internal control shares common interests with accounting, auditing and risk management. In the intersection of these vital functional areas lies the domain of financial measurements, where again advanced testing plays a crucial role.

In measuring, monitoring and reporting, stress testing can provide an analytical picture of operations, highlighting less likely, but plausible, deviations from lines of conduct. This overcomes the limitation of *ex post* evaluations through classical means, which lies on two grounds:

- Such events have already passed, and
- Operational data tend to hold many secrets, until they are stress tested.

The fact that observed crude data do not reveal, to the naked eye, all the information they contain, finds its counterpart in nature and in the physical sciences. Astrophysicists and cosmologists believe that over 90 per cent of matter in the universe is hidden, and it may be of a different nature from the matter that we are made of.

Most particularly, physicists say, lots of the nanoworld around us remains a mystery; and, in its miniature form, matter pays little heed to the familiar world of Newtonian physics. The laws of gravity, optics and acceleration represent averages, not the quirky behaviour of each single nanoparticle. To discover these principles researchers must

- Venture into quantum physics, and
- Use more advanced tools of investigation than those traditionally available.

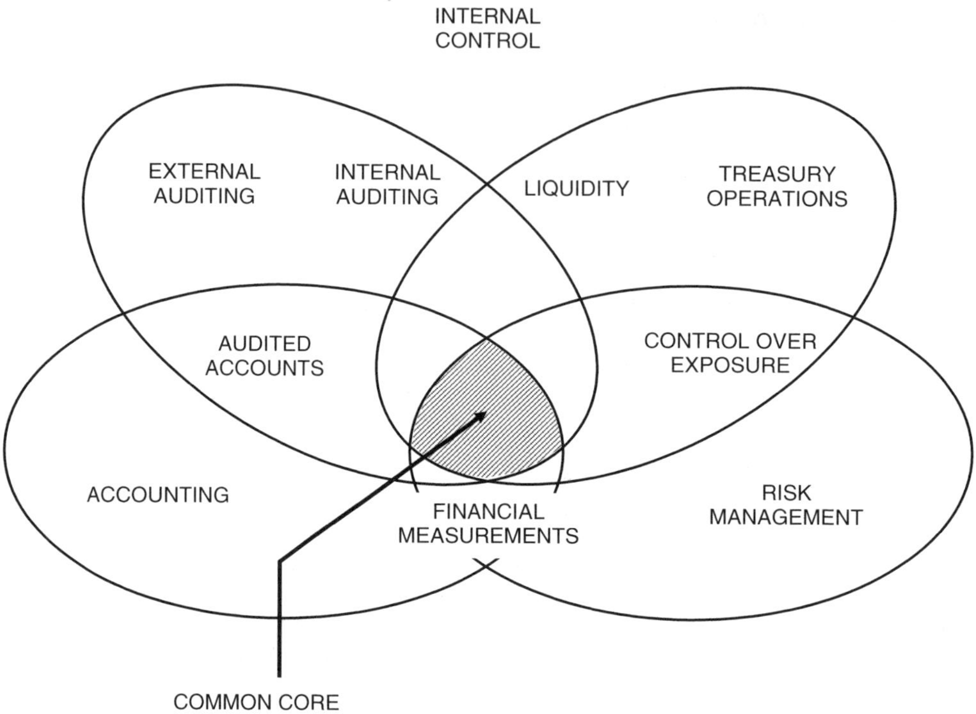

Figure 3.2 Stress testing performs well at the common core of internal control, auditing, accounting, treasury and risk management

This reference to the physical sciences finds its counterpart, in terms of advanced testing, in finance. To come to grips with the realm of hidden causes and effects, and to harness the power of operational data, available information elements must be placed under stress. While the exact nature of stress tests varies from one case to the next, the concepts discussed in this chapter are, to a substantial extent, invariant.

Take as an example the new Capital Adequacy Framework (Basel II) by the Basel Committee on Banking Supervision.[4] The Basel Committee believes that credit institutions adopting the internal ratings-based (IRB) method should hold adequate capital to protect against adverse or uncertain conditions. Therefore, the new regulations require the performance of meaningful stress tests discussed in Chapters 7–11.

In a way, the interests that regulators and commercial bankers have in an advanced testing methodology coincide. For both, the goal is to ascertain the extent to which financial losses may increase under adverse conditions. A stress scenario includes:

- Economic downturns,
- Depressing industry conditions,
- Severe market risk events,
- Different types of liquidity squeezes,
- Solvency problems, and so on.

Stress tests, the methodology and models on which they rest, must be meaningful and reasonably conservative. Worst case scenarios (see Chapter 5) bring out evidence of financial weaknesses that often remain hidden. They also alert us to possible collateral damage, which is often an unknown quantity under classical testing.

Under traditional approaches, entities consider their exposure class by class: credit risk, market risk, legal risk, and so on. But in a complex financial environment risks are polyvalent, making advanced testing so much more important. Today's instruments are exposed to more than one class of risks, as shown in Figure 3.3. Therefore, stress testing must take full account of possible collateral damage.

In addition, a preoccupation at the board of directors' level should be steady upkeep of the entity's own risk control strategy. Both executive management and board members must appreciate that while simpler models help in *risk identification*, stress tests provide more rigorous responses, particularly in connection with new instruments and complex or unusual transactions, and in response to external events concerning the global market.

In conclusion, every entity should have in place a methodology and tools for stress tests covering all risk categories. In a credit institution, for example, putting the existing exposure in the trading book and banking book under stress conditions provides a glimpse of tail events that are never revealed through legacy-type risk measurement.

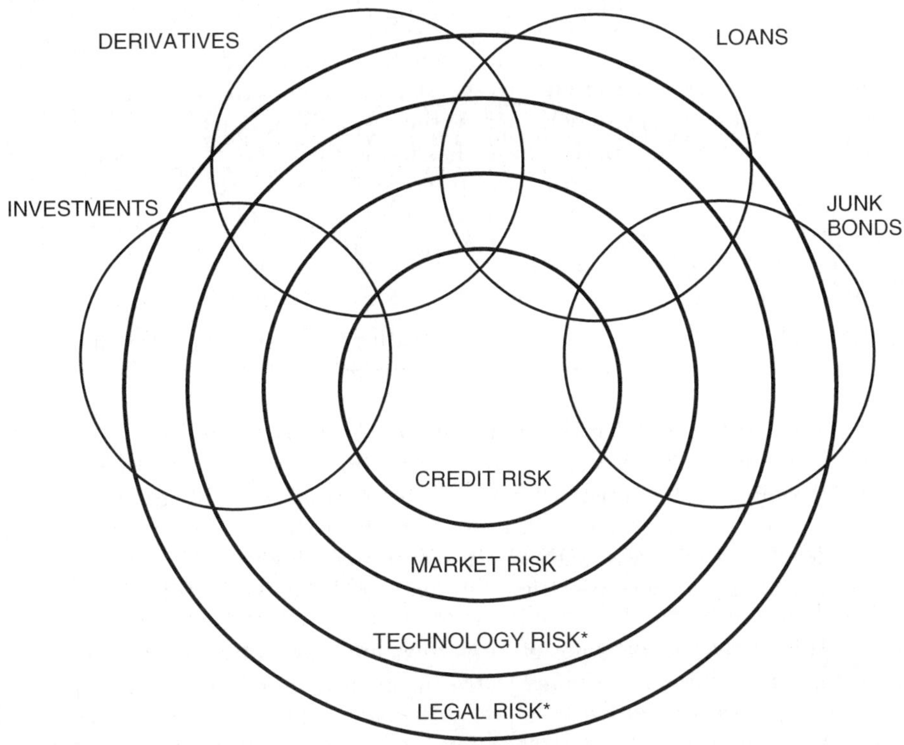

Figure 3.3 Overlapping types of exposure that make stress tests more complex.
*Both operational risks

A stress loss framework must keep on being enhanced and progressively extended, not only to all classes of risk, but also down to single risk level. The identification and quantification of assumed exposure under stress conditions is an integral part of a properly tuned internal control, and it is an evidence of good governance.

3.5 Scenarios, sensitivity analysis and statistical inference

Section 3.2 briefly outlined four methods for stress testing. The first three, scenarios, sensitivity analysis and statistical inference, are introduced in this section. A more detailed discussion, including the scientific method underpinning them as well as practical application examples, is given in Chapter 4. Drills for a meltdown are discussed in Chapter 5.

Previously, among banks and regulators, stress tests were not the subject of a taxonomic effort. The first meaningful classification of stress tests was the object of a 2001 study by the Committee on the Global Financial System, of the Bank for International Settlements (BIS).[5] The forty-three banks that participated in this study were asked to report on the work that they were doing in connection with stress scenarios and sensitivity stress tests. In response, they submitted 424 examples of stress tests, or roughly ten stress tests per institution, many of them being run at a bank-wide level.

The participating credit institutions were also asked to classify each stress test they reported as either a stress scenario or a sensitivity stress test. Having categorized the examples, the Committee concluded that they comprised 239 stress scenarios, while the remainder were sensitivity stress tests. The Committee also noted that there appeared to be some inconsistencies across the responding banks.

From his own research, too, the author has found that there is a persistent problem with definitions of stress test terms, and of stress test processes. Therefore, some of the notions that exist in the trade have been rewritten. As defined in the present book, *scenario writing* is a narrative of generally qualitative aspects. The scenario maps a situation consisting of:

- Players, who may be people, companies, products or something else, and
- Risks involved with players, markets and instruments.

Such mapping is done through numerous nodes and links which, among themselves, make up the scenario. Most often, a stress test scenario reflects one or more events that, in the opinion of a financial institution, its analysts and its experimenters, may occur in the foreseeable future, even if the probability of occurrence is small. Scenarios developed by stress analysis are essentially a high-level 'what if' type, and more sophisticated than scenarios made for expected events. The objective is:

- To compute the extent of exposure under *extreme assumptions*, or
- To evaluate the aftermath of *unexpected* but plausible events of high impact.

Each of those goals is quite different from *the likely loss* that may be faced because of expected risks. (See also in Part 3 the difference between expected losses and unexpected losses.) With stress scenarios, correlations between markets, instruments and counterparties are chosen for maximum effect. As explained in section 3.2, these may be hypothetical or historical, by unearthing outliers that have appeared in the past.

In a way, scenario writing is like constructing a spider's web, while keeping in mind that nodes and links will be subjected to testing. Because complexity presents a serious challenge to analysis, it is preferable to change one factor at a time. A maximum of two factors may be changed, provided they are independent of one another. As Dr Alan Greenspan once said, covariance is still in its infancy in financial analysis (see Chapter 14).

In scenario writing, it is essential to have a method of combining analytical results into a coherent and comprehensive pattern. The Delphi method (discussed in Chapter 4) offers one of the best examples of scenarios developed by means of combining expert opinions on the timing (or impact).

Sensitivity analysis contrasts with scenario writing, because it isolates the after effect on a chosen variable, for instance, a portfolio's value. A sensitivity analysis may also address one or more predefined moves in a particular risk factor. If a number of closely linked risk factors are involved, then the study puts the method of sensitivity analysis itself under stress.

Banks usually perform sensitivity stress testing in relation to market exposure, but the method is equally valid with counterparty risk, as well as with selected operational risks; for instance, legal risk (see Chapter 10). The study of exposure embedded in the banking book provides a good example of sensitivity analysis applications.

The fact that in most countries the majority of loans are granted with floating interest rates means that the credit institution has both credit risk and market risk in its banking book. Market risk associated with interest rate volatility can be studied through sensitivities by analysing the effects of a change in interest rates. Since the meltdown of savings and loans (S&Ls, thrifts) in the late 1980s, the Office of Thrift Supervision (OTS, their regulator) requires that every night the 1100 or so S&Ls submit an estimate of their exposure at ± 100, ± 200, ± 300 and ± 400 basis points change in interest rates (details in Chapter 13).

Credit risk effects on a portfolio should also be analysed by means of credit downgrades of counterparties, using a transition matrix of credit ratings (see Part 2). A mistake frequently made by implementers of sensitivities is the assumption that sensitivity analysis is the same sort of test as statistical inference. This is not true. Unlike rigorous statistical inference, sensitivity analysis typically uses simple business statistics. It:

- Does not handle non-linearities,
- Does not involve possibility theory, and
- Does not use experimental design.

In contrast, in the realm of stress testing, *statistical inference* involves tests under extreme conditions which go well beyond sensitivities. It also uses available methods for design of experiments with controlled variables; in short, statistical inference comes at a higher level of sophistication, but it may also be relatively simple in its details.

A simple approach may use 'what if' hypotheses to evaluate the effect of a given event today, by analysing time series and spikes in these time series. A more complex approach will use estimates of outliers, stress conditions and unexpected events. The best way of looking at statistical inference is as part of a broader process of studying plausible but unlikely results ahead of time, through inference. For instance, a risk manager may:

- Select a set of likely but extreme moves for key market parameters, and
- Subject these key variables to a test of 5, 10 or 15 standard deviations, or ± 400 basis points, as briefly mentioned in the OTS example.

In so doing, the experimenter is using historical evidence or hypotheses to measure a simulated change in portfolio value. At the same time, for inference purposes he or she mines databases for effects of similar market moves, comparing real-life results with those obtained through analysis or simulation.

As mentioned in Chapter 1, however, everything the experimenter does is subject to *data uncertainty* and *model uncertainty*. This is true for all types of test, including stress tests. The two Heisenberg principles, which were written for studies in physics but also apply in finance (Dr Werner Heisenberg, who stated that these principles apply in the physical world, was also a number scientist), explain the sense of this reference:

1. You can predict nothing with zero tolerance.

Nothing walks on a straight line. Tolerances and control levels are all over the place, and they affect every variable. Therefore, there should always be *confidence limits* (see Chapter 1). A narrower tolerance, and its steady observance, lead to a higher quality of results.

2. If something is closely observed, the chances are it is going to be altered in the process.

For instance, *if* an equity is in tight consolidation, and then breaks out on the day financial analysts upgrade the stock to 'strong buy', *then* the odds of a price move upwards are high, but the likelihood that this breakout would be sustained is small. Every study affects the data, just as every traveller has some impact on the country he or she visits. This is a background principle that characterizes the behaviour of data and variables in all sciences, from engineering and physics to financial analysis.

3.6 Capital at risk under extreme conditions: an example

As described in section 3.5, a stress scenario may involve (and often does) simultaneous moves in different *risk factors*, such as equity prices, interest rates, currency exchange rates and other commodity prices; or market events of a political or social nature. And, as mentioned in section 3.1, while the timing may be hypothetical,

- The nature of the test may well be based on a significant occurrence experienced in the past, leading to a *historical stress test*, or

- It may concern a plausible market event that has not yet taken place, but is likely to happen, which is the case of a *hypothetical stress test*.

Historical type scenarios are the most common. Hypothetical stress tests, however, are crucial to the future of the economy (and of a firm), because of the sword of Damocles hanging over the head of the global financial landscape owing to trillions of dollars of exposure, in notional principal amounts, at each of the major banks. Derivative instruments have changed not only the financial landscape, but also the unit of risk measurement. (See the case study on the measures taken by the Bank of England to assume its preparedness, in Chapter 16.)

Over and above market risk there is, on and off, a mounting level of credit risk. A good example is when independent rating agencies downgraded General Motors and GMAC debt to junk status. Normally, GMAC is a mom and pop lender, keeping the auto as collateral. The huge losses have come from GM, the parent company's side. The crucial question was then: 'What would happen if one of these mammoth financial organizations blew up?'

To appreciate the complexity of a hypothetical test, induced by its nature, the reader should keep in mind that credit risk and market risk correlate. In the case of a credit institution, for example, capital adequacy rules by the Basel Committee focus on credit risk. At the same time, however, the banks' core capital is so small compared with their derivatives exposure that it would last for a very short time in a blow-up.

The precedence is the bankruptcy of Long Term Capital Management (LTCM) in September 1998,[6] an event to which several references are made in different parts of this book. What is more, this core capital is tied up as a buffer to expected losses from credit risk, and it grows very slowly, while the derivatives exposure at major banks increases by 20–30 per cent per year or even more, depending on:

- The institution, and
- Its risk appetite (see Chapter 2).

A hypothetical stress test under extreme conditions will not necessarily take the whole notional principal amount of the derivatives portfolio at 100 per cent as being imminently at risk. How much of it is at risk depends on the type of inventoried positions, general economic climate and other factors, which together help in computing the *toxic waste*, a term coined to mean the irreducible amount of capital at risk because of derivatives exposure.

Well-managed entities try to squeeze this toxic waste out of their system. In an article that he published on derivatives risk, Warren Buffett stated that the purchase of American Re by Berkshire revealed a loaded derivatives portfolio, on the side of the acquired company. Buffett added that he spent a couple of years trying to dispose of it, but still something was left. This is the toxic waste.

A good way to compute exposure in a derivatives portfolio is to estimate the real money that is on the table by stress testing the notional principal amount. This is the *capital at risk*. Under normal market conditions, in the absence of exotic derivative products and, particularly, of a nervous market, capital at risk tends to be about 5 per cent of the notional principal amount. Therefore, a divisor (*demodulator*) of

20 will do. In a time of crisis, however, the aforementioned demodulator shrinks, and it can decrease all the way to 6 or 5, as demonstrated by:

- The bankruptcy of the Bank of New England in 1990, and
- The meltdown of the banking industry in East Asia in 1997.

The division of a notional principal amount in a derivatives portfolio by 5 or 6 essentially means that between 17 and 20 per cent of its value becomes capital at risk, and eventually toxic waste. In other terms, should a global economic crisis hit, the exposure in real money due to derivatives may, overnight, become:

- 7000 per cent or so of the bank's core capital, and
- A very high percentage of its assets, which essentially belong to clients.[7]

Demodulation of inventoried derivatives positions through the hypothetical scenario of extreme events, presented in the preceding paragraphs, is better known as *credit equivalence*, which practically means their market value in a panic, in case the counterparty in a transaction goes bust.

This example with derivative instruments and capital at risk has been a stress test, partly based on historical evidence, which can be applied at different levels of severity by varying the demodulator's size. A similar stress test should be applied to the banking book, but with a fair value of inventoried loans assets.

- The value of a credit institution's loans portfolio fluctuates because of credit risk and market risk, and
- The change in the value of proprietary securities and other assets belonging to the bank, such as real estate, should also be the object of stress tests.

Under normal conditions, there is no great difficulty in distinguishing risks connected to loans. However, *megaloans* can turn expected losses estimates on their head. For instance, during the first six months of 2001, after the bursting of the stockmarket bubble, telecoms debt defaults went to the stars. A total of 100 rated, or formerly rated, companies defaulted on US $57.9 billion worth of debt in North America and Europe.

Banks and institutional investors paid the price of gambling on loans to start-ups, and for massively buying junk bonds from these companies. Table 3.1 shows the

Table 3.1 The top eight telecoms debt defaults in the first half of 2001

	Country	First rating	Debt (US $ m)
PSINet Inc.	USA	B–	2733.9
Winstar Communications Inc.	USA	B–	2091.4
Viatel Inc.	USA	B–	1833.2
Call-Net Enterprises Inc.	Canada	B+	1781.6
360networks Inc.	Canada	B+	1675.0
Globalstar, LP	USA	B+	1450.0
RSL Communications Ltd	USA	B–	1415.6
360USA	Canada	B+	1200.0

losses of over $1 billion, all of them in the USA and Canada. The plight of these companies was exacerbated by a deterioration in general economic conditions, which cut off traditional funding sources for telecoms, and was sealed by the loss of their market. This being the case, the banking sector found itself in the frontline of red ink, along with institutional investors.

Two other examples of melting assets are the *junk bond* hecatomb and defaults on Latin American debt. January to August 2001 was an accelerated disintegration of the junk bonds market beyond the confines of the telecoms industry. Invented as a mass instrument in the 1980s, below investment-grade bonds went out of favour in the early 1990s, but they returned in force after 1995. With the euphoria of a booming stockmarket, over the 1996 to 2000 time-frame, junk bonds were issued in large numbers to finance all sorts of expansion plans, as well as takeovers.

- According to Moody's Investors Service, during the first quarter of 2001, ninety-three American companies defaulted on $35 billion of junk bonds, a record volume.
- On 23 July 2001, the *Wall Street Journal* reported that the recovery rate for junk bonds was 12 cents in the dollar, less than half the 25 cents in the dollar in 1999–2000.

These were ominous statistics because, at the time, the US market for junk bonds was valued at $690 billion, a colossal amount, although it represented 'only' 7 per cent of the $10 trillion market of all US corporate and treasury bonds.

One of the outstanding risks of a massive junk bond failure, which should be studied in advance through stress testing, is that it can bring down with it the larger bond market. This is particularly true if it is coupled with failures in bonds issued, and loans contracted, by defaulting Latin American and other emerging countries.

At the time of the junk bond meltdown, the foreign debt of Argentina, Brazil and Mexico added up to more than $900 billion. This did not include the huge domestic debt of these three countries, whose interest rates were spiralling upwards. Argentina defaulted on $100 billion of its bonds, and what bondholders recovered was between 25 cents and 30 cents to the dollar, a historical precedent to be kept in mind in stress tests.

3.7 Stress testing and the devil's advocate

Risk management systems are usually established by knowledgeable people, but this does not mean that there will be no omissions, gaps or bias. Therefore, for every risk management system, including stress-testing methods, tools and procedures, somebody with a very open mind at senior position, or an outside expert, or both, should be given the role of *devil's advocate*. The crucial question is what can go wrong with the chosen solution.

A very frequent error is that the stress tests are too mild to reveal hidden risks. When in the late 1990s stress tests started becoming popular, many companies limited them to 5 standard deviations from expected value. As documented by years of practice, this is absolutely inadequate. Extreme events, particularly those of high impact, may lie 15 standard deviations from the mean, not just 5.

- Only those stress conditions that test the limits can serve as tools and reference platforms to the devil's advocate.
- In October 1987 the stockmarket crash in New York was a 14.5 standard deviation event; this legitimizes the 15 standard deviation stress test.

In addition, while a stress-testing procedure should use what is currently available in mathematical tools and methods, experimenters should also explore analytical opportunities farther out than those already in use (see the reference to algorithmic insufficiency in Chapter 14). Speaking from experience, plenty of opportunities are presented by methods and tools established in engineering and in the physical sciences that should be used in finance.

An example is *experimental design*, which makes feasible a systematic search for underlying reasons of variations and provides documented evidence connected with them. Extensively used in applied experimental psychology, experimental design is a mathematically based approach to the role of the devil's advocate, taking fully into consideration a system's crucial variables. Analytical solutions worth their salt must help in the search for weaknesses in risk management:

- From hypotheses being made,
- To methods of measurement, test mechanisms and benchmarks.

To improve a risk management plan's performance, feedback from operations should be steadily used to update the method in use, and its procedures. Equally important is satisfaction of the need for broadening and deepening the investigation of failures, which are unavoidably being made.

For instance, a big problem in any project, particularly one addressing the management of exposure, is a poor quality of knowledge embedded into it. Complex projects evolve over a period of time, and often coinvolve different experts at different stages or sectors of the plan. Audits by the devil's advocate should address:

- What has been designed as a system,
- Its individual component parts, and
- The risk management expertise embedded in its nodes.

An approach used by this author for several decades in auditing the risk management system is based on a framework of dynamic constraints satisfaction, as applied with engineering tolerances. Combined with control limits, the use of tolerances makes possible explicit control of:

- Assumptions,
- Design choices, and
- Performance after implementation.

Moreover, assumptions, choices and obtained results can be used *ex post* to set parameters for adaptation, where only dimensional references are changed; and for functional adaptation, where the arrangement, as well as number and type of component parts, may also need to be modified.

For any practical purpose, the system solution outlined in the preceding paragraphs is the alter ego of General Electric's Six Sigma,[8] which has been used successfully both in manufacturing and in the financial industry, for instance, by GE Capital and J.P. MorganChase. Six Sigma is not a stress test per se; it is a methodology that can contribute a great deal to:

- The process of stress testing, and
- The function that the devil's advocate should perform.

The reason for emphasizing these approaches is that a stress testing system is dynamic and, therefore, requires a methodology able to handle dynamic processes. A difficulty with all types of adaptations to changing market conditions and/or the changing nature of risk is that the design has to satisfy criteria originating in many different places and involving a number of variables. The dynamic upkeep of a complex system is often like changing the tyres of a car running at 100 miles per hour. For the enterprise risk management system to remain functional and effective, it must be possible to make design conflicts resolvable:

- Without limiting the investigation of exposure, and
- Without requiring a totally new design, because this would mean interruptions in deliverables.

Furthermore, an integral part of the role to be performed by the devil's advocate is the search for inconsistencies among component elements of the risk management system. This includes auditing methods and tools, as well as the ability to review and revise choices that have been made among different major options.

One of the most frequent failures seen in regard to auditing risk management systems is that their output was not sufficiently crisp and comprehensive to all of their users. This leads to misinterpretation of information on exposure, or plain negligence in looking at it. Experience teaches that this happens for several reasons.

- Limited imagination of system designers.

This is, more or less, a universal characteristic. When people encounter a new phenomenon they try to fit it into an existing framework. Until enough experiments have been conducted, they do not know whether there is really a difference between *this* problem and 'other' problems; neither are they clear in regard to the best way to report it.

- It may be the *same thing* over and over again.

This is the opposite of the previous bullet point. Sometimes the markets have more than one way of doing things, but while they repeat their story over time we think something has changed. As a result, information concerning exposure leads to false alarms. It is also possible that.

- Data look different, while describing aspects of the same thing.

A frequently encountered problem with what has largely become 'normal tests' is that there is a larger picture underneath, from which things can be broken into parts that look different, like fingers on the same hand. Only advanced testing can reveal which figure is of real concern, and the size of the deviation.

- Non-financial reports, and footnotes, are not being paid enough attention.

Non-financial reports are a good area to exercise the devil advocate's type of vigilance. While financial reports observing accounting standards lead to misinterpretations, the risk is even more pronounced with non-financial reports. With them, firms volunteer an overview of what they describe as their business, including its environmental and social impact during the previous year. Today, however, there are no appropriate non-financial reporting standards provided by regulators. Therefore, storytelling seems to win the day.

3.8 Advice on implementing the stress test

The examples given in the preceding sections are a reminder that stress testing must be focused, and it should be characterized by clear objectives. To fulfil these requirements, the risk manager must clearly establish what is to be tested. Then, he or she should outline likely but rather extreme moves of chosen variables and associated market parameters. This done, the experimenter:

- Subjects the chosen variable(s) to value changes, and
- Measures the outcome of simulated changes in market parameters.

Most of the notions briefly outlined in the preceding paragraphs are not alien to risk managers; they are part of their daily job. What is new is the interest in looking for outliers and extreme moves, rather than setting one's search within the 99 per cent confidence intervals of the normal distribution which, as explained, is an inadequate practice.

While looking for extreme events, the experimenter should appreciate that despite focusing on the long leg of the distribution, stress testing is not necessarily a worst case analysis. Moreover, even a worst case may include scenarios at different levels of likelihood and of variance. Along with the decision of the specific level of confidence (see Chapter 1) at which the stress test should be conducted, special consideration must be given to instruments or positions that may be difficult:

- To liquidate, or
- To offset in a crisis.

Depending on risk factor(s) under investigation, the focus of a stress test may be a shift in the distribution of values, rather than the examination of outliers. Based on statistics by the BIS, Figure 3.4 provides an example with a shift to the left of the probability distribution of exchange rates.

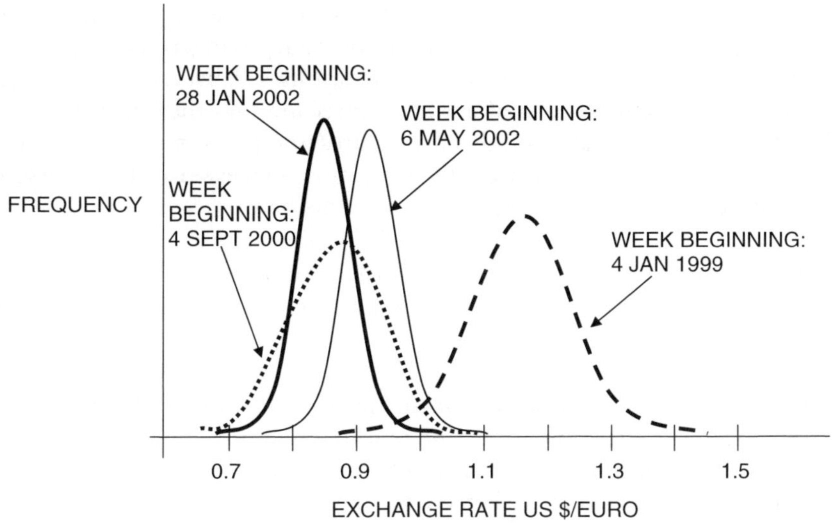

Figure 3.4 Shift to the left of the probability distribution of exchange rates: US dollars versus euros, over forty months (*source*: BIS, 72nd Annual Report, Basel, 2002)

Among the experimenter's list of worries are correlations, which may exist between currency exchange rates, interest rates, increases and decreases in equity index values, and other variables. Some of the often recurring facts and factors connected with a stress test on interest rates, are the correlations that may exist with changes in credit risk and probability of default (see Chapter 14). Other examples are correlations with:

- Steepening or flattening of yield curve,
- Changes in interest rate spread,
- Changes in swaps spreads,
- Increase and decrease in one-, two- and three-month volatilities by x per cent of prevailing levels.

These 'worries', which are characteristic of stress tests, are worth facing. Traditional tests have a limited ability of penetrating the important domain of synergy of increase and decrease in currency exchange and equity index volatilities, as well as the synergy of liquidity and volatility changes.[9] By contrast, stress testing can provide the basis for consistent methods of experimentation, including non-linearities that may be present in:

- Corporate bankruptcies,
- Derivatives exposure, and
- Value of equity investments in widely ranging markets.

Fuzzy engineering, used in connection with risk control, provides an effective basis for combining different types of exposure into an aggregate picture.[10] For risk management purposes, an aggregate picture helps in establishing a plan of action to be put into effect if the stress test points to a potentially dangerous situation.

Although not every company looks at stress testing's deliverables as a trigger for damage control, the better managed entities appreciate that they must have in place not only stress-testing policies, but also procedures and processes assisting in control action. As a senior executive of a credit institution suggested in the course of this research, as part of its stress-testing programme, his bank:

- Measures its solvency target, over the life of all contracts in each netting set, and
- Compares results against the measure of expected positive exposure, and associated capital adequacy requirements.

Stress tests should also provide an assessment of the entity's ability to withstand a severe economic or industry downturn, and market illiquidity conditions. With respect to customer relationships, stress testing should target the adequacy of collateral under stressed market risk and credit risk factors, as well as the protection provided by covenants.

Account should be also taken of the fact that as the complexity of financial instruments increases and users of test results become more demanding, the stress tests themselves must be more and more sophisticated. For instance, banks using the double-default framework (see Chapter 11), involving the likelihood of simultaneous failure of obligor and guarantor, consider as part of their stress-testing framework the impact of a deterioration in the credit quality of protection providers.

A practical example is the impact of guarantors falling outside the eligibility criteria relating to A-rating, and consequent increase in risk at time of default. Well-managed banks also conduct stress tests which account for credit risk concentrations, which usually have an adverse effect on the creditworthiness of each individual counterparty making up the concentration. Concentration risk arises through:

- Direct exposures to obligors, and
- Exposures to protection providers.

Stress testing is particularly important in this connection because the aforementioned concentrations are not addressed in the Pillar 1 capital charge for credit risk. While credit risk concentrations may be reduced by the purchase of credit protection, *wrong-way risk* might be greater than that reflected in the calibration of a double default treatment.

Notes

1. D.N. Chorafas, *IFRS, Fair Value and Corporate Governance. Its Impact on Budgets, Balance Sheets and Management Accounts*, Butterworth-Heinemann, London, 2005.
2. D.N. Chorafas, *Operational Risk Control with Basel II. Basic Principles and Capital Requirements*, Butterworth-Heinemann, London, 2004.

3. D.N. Chorafas, *Managing Risk in the New Economy*, New York Institute of Finance, New York, 2001.
4. D.N. Chorafas, *Economic Capital Allocation with Basel II. Cost and Benefit Analysis*, Butterworth-Heinemann, London, 2004.
5. Committee on the Global Financial System, *A Survey of Stress Tests and Current Practice at Major Financial Institutions*, BIS, Basel, February 2001.
6. D.N. Chorafas, *Managing Risk in the New Economy*, New York Institute of Finance, New York, 2001.
7. D.N. Chorafas, *Wealth Management: Private Banking, Investment Decisions and Structured Financial Products*, Butterworth-Heinemann, London, 2005.
8. D.N. Chorafas, *Integrating ERP, CRM, Supply Chain Management and Smart Materials*, Auerbach, New York, 2001.
9. D.N. Chorafas, *Understanding Volatility and Liquidity in Financial Markets*, Euromoney Books, London, 1998.
10. D.N. Chorafas, *Chaos Theory in the Financial Markets*, Probus, Chicago, 1994.

4 Stress analysis and its tools

4.1 Introduction

To be considered *advanced*, any analysis that includes sensitivities, scenarios and statistical inference for risk testing, must be based on scientific methodology. Therefore, the method of scientific research is the focal point of this chapter. It also examines relatively novel approaches to surveys targeting a qualitative evaluation by experts, such as the Delphi method.

4.2 The need for a scientific approach

In all fields of enquiry, whether in physics, engineering, finance or any other, there is a danger of not seeing the wood for the trees. Nowhere is this danger greater than in the analysis of assets, liabilities and embedded risks in a leveraged financial environment. Derivative financial instruments that can change at any time from assets to liabilities, and vice versa, depending on their market value, augment the need for advanced approaches to analytical investigation.

The thesis developed in Chapter 3 was that there is *no single risk* factor making up, by itself, the assumed amount of exposure. Instead, there are diverse, separate but also interrelated aspects of different risk factors, which contribute to the end result. Therefore, to obtain commendable results, the scientific method of the investigation is the only basis for conducting tests and experiments. Its basis consists of:

- Careful preparation of the process of analysis, and of test premises,
- Choice, and clear statement, of the hypothesis to be tested,
- Assurance that the procedure to be followed can be repeated as it is and, if repeated with the same data, it would lead to comparable results,
- Performance of the experiment, conclusion and documented decision based on that conclusion.

Among themselves, these four bullet points bring the message that scientific performance of analyses, tests and experiments does not resemble grains of sand put together to make a hill. There are prerequisites to be fulfilled and many aspects to be examined a priori. In addition, several of these aspects acquire their full significance when considered in relation to the chosen variables; but:

- Interrelations are not necessarily apparent at first sight, and
- They can be revealed only by means of rigorous tests, which have been properly organized and conducted.

In the majority of cases, stress testing of financial variables requires pooling of experience. Today, research is by and large a team project, rather than that of a single individual. The acquisition, organization and use of knowledge, which are essential factors in analysis, also require team effort. Indeed, it is this process of acquisition, organization and use of knowledge that is often called the *scientific method* (see section 4.3).

In principle, a person uses the scientific method, and associated scientific tools for investigative reasons, is free of prejudices, because prejudices introduce bias. This person is ready to test facts against experience, as well as to challenge established theories through observation and experiment. A good researcher:

- Operates on the principle of increasing certitude in conjunction with confidence intervals (see Chapter 1), and
- Is able, in large measure, to document the results obtained through enquiry by means of factual conclusions reached during the test.

These points describe the principles underpinning the work of *rocket scientists*: mathematicians, physicists and engineers who previously worked in aerospace, nuclear science, weapons systems and other advanced industrial sectors. By migrating into financial analysis, rocket scientists bring with them not only plenty of experience, but also their expertise in using the scientific method.

Since the mid-1980s the financial world has appreciated the role of rocket scientists because it understands that *analytical thinking*, modelling tools and a sound methodology are pillars of every process aiming at leadership in the market. This has meant that rocket scientists became the *technologists of finance*, enriching with their skills processes that are as old as humanity.

Figure 4.1 suggests that the scientific method can be instrumental in analysing complexity, which is typically found at the junction of different risks. Confronted with complexity, trial-and-error approaches cannot deliver. In many cases different aspects of the omnipresent counterparty risk and market risk:

- Correlate among themselves, and
- Interlink with management risk, because of near-sighted decisions and faulty oversights.

Along with the scientific method, another major contributor to analytical investigation is technology (see Chapter 6). *Science* and *technology*, however, should not be confused with one another.

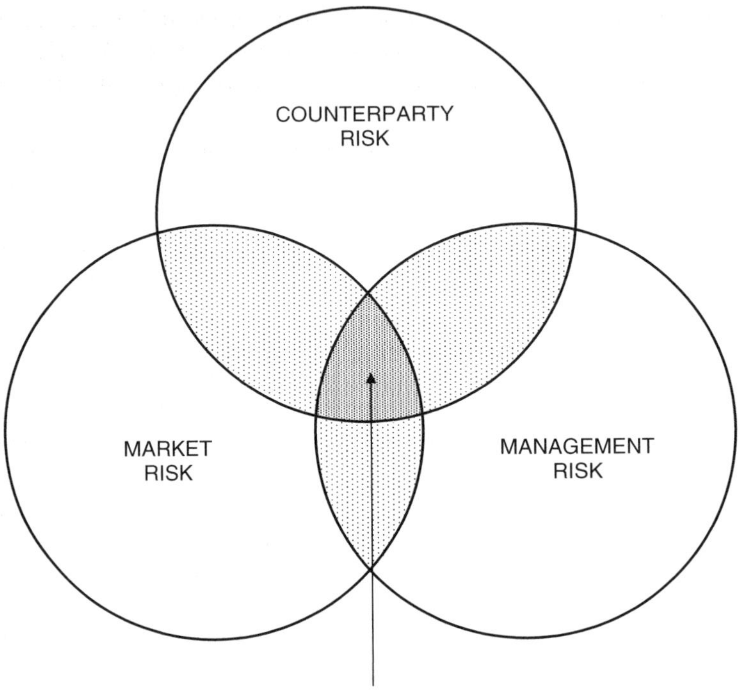

Figure 4.1 Well-managed institutions use the scientific method at the junction of risks they face, where complexity is high

- The scientist investigates the laws underpinning physical processes, and the changes taking place in nature,
- The *technologist* studies structures, develops systems, right-sizes organizations and aims to produce deliverables characterized by value differentiation over their predecessors.

Rocket scientists are primarily technologists. Therefore, their role is crucial in the management of change. In a business environment, *change* is the expression of hidden, bottled-up forces. The process of analysis tries to understand these forces, predict their trend and judge their aftermath. This must be done in a way that is transparent, documented and factual:

- Science is allowed to be esoteric.
- Technology must always be extrovert and useful.

The role played by rocket scientists in financial analysis can only have a purpose, and justify its costs, when it is truly of service to the institution employing these people. This should be to a substantial extent an adaptable role, because business needs and driving concepts vary from time to time, from place to place, and from culture to culture.

Within this context, this chapter examines the contributions of the scientific method and of financial technology to analytical thinking and testing, whether this is done under normal conditions or under stress. As the preceding chapters brought to the reader's attention, in the background of stress testing lies the fact that markets are good at reading the writing on the wall, especially when the message is written in their language.

- Stress tests go beyond classical analytics by capitalizing on the fact that crises cannot be made to run to a timetable,
- By applying stress conditions in study and experimentation, timetables are accelerated and the aftermath of events is analysed.

This is the best type of prognostication made possible through experimentation, and the results can be both quantitative and qualitative. *Qualification* is more important. Some people are so taken in by the beauty and precision of numbers that they frequently:

- Lose track of non-quantifiable characteristics,
- Neglect the qualitative factors that are often determinant,
- Overlook the simplification made to achieve some sort of quantitative precision, and
- Overemphasize their calculations which, after all, are merely cold numbers.

In conclusion, as a general principle, whether made under normal or stress conditions, the results of tests must be focused, accurate and honest. Even the worst aspects of a given situation must be reflected in them. Qualitative scenarios and quantitative computations, such as those involved in sensitivity analysis and in statistical inference, complement one another. This thesis will be followed throughout the present chapter.

4.3 Science and the scientific method

One of the virtues of scientific studies is that the framework they provide makes it easier to channel the judgement and intuition of experts in diverse fields towards the same goal. A sound methodology allows different types of results to be combined, systematically and efficiently. This helps not only in investigation and analysis, but also in *challenging the obvious*.

Science can challenge established theories and principles because it is based on analytical thinking and on experiments. Freedom of discussion is the necessary lubricant for the process of thinking. Where there is no freedom to elaborate, express, defend and change one's opinions, there is no freedom of thought and therefore no creative thinking.

- Whether in science or in business, the very absence of argument, criticism and dissent tends to corrode decisions.
- Where there is no freedom of thought, there can be no freedom of enquiry. By consequence, there is no scientific progress.

For these reasons, the first principle of a scientific methodology is the vigilant, focused criticism and constant questioning of all tentative statements, of all basic assumptions; of all theories and all their postulates. There is nothing more sacred in science than this principal method of *construction* and eventual *destruction*.

- We regard as scientific a method based on deep analysis of facts.
- Theories and scientific views are presupposed to be unprejudiced, unafraid of open discussion.
- Theories are made to be criticized, dismantled, revamped or sent to oblivion.

In science, conclusions are reached after debate, by overcoming dissent. This contrasts with authoritarian centralism and the spirit of the Middle Ages. Under still prevailing medieval concepts, as few people as possible have the authority (but not necessarily the knowledge) to decide as secretly as possible about facts, theories, policies and beliefs.

- Stress testing is, by and large, a destructive force, and
- For this reason, it is one of the basic pillars of the scientific method.

Both the philosopher and the scientist embrace the scientific method, because they proceed by hypotheses that they try to verify. Thereby, they are enriching their body of knowledge. The scientist does so by means of experiments; the philosopher through his or her penetrating thoughts. In ancient Greece two schools confronted one another in terms of what philosophy is, or should be:

- The *sophists*, led by Protagoras, regarded philosophy as education and training on how to perceive and do things
- *Socrates*, and his disciples, looked at philosophy as a process of acquiring knowledge of the nature of things, largely through a network of focused questions.

Long thought of as contradicting one another, these two schools constitute, between themselves, the underpinning of the scientific method. To Socrates, the successful pursuit of any occupation demanded the mastery of a particular field, skill or technique. Politicians, generals, other philosophers, scientists, poets and craftsmen came under the scrutiny of his method. To his dismay, Socrates said, he discovered that, except for craftsmen, none of them knew the meaning of the words he used (which is also true today).

The craftsmen have *how-to-do* knowledge. Whether in the arts, in science or in any other walk of life, hands-on, direct *experience* is a great guide. However, it also has its limitations. Albert Einstein wrote that 'Experience may suggest the appropriate mathematical concepts, but they most certainly cannot be deducted from it. [Yet] experience remains the sole criterion of the utility of a mathematical construction.'[1]

Along with experience, *thinking* underpins the history of progress in philosophy, science and the arts. Thinking ensures that a constructive, if tentative, theory can be found that covers the product or process under investigation. Yet, to some people it seems to be safer not to think at all, let alone develop theories. Others are afraid of what people may think. Things are different with creative people because they understand that:

- A thought is like a child inside a woman's womb. It has to be born.
- If it dies inside us, then, intellectually speaking, we die too.

Because they promoted the concept of the intellect and the deliverables that human thought can produce, philosophers and scientists played a very important role in antiquity, where a philosopher and a scientist were the same person. Socrates went further than this when he said that tragedy and comedy are the same thing; and it should be written by the same person.

From this duality developed the principles of the scientific method, as they are known today. In the foundations of the scientific method lies the fact that, as a process, science is seeking specific facts and the laws that underpin them. We think that a truth has been discovered when a thought is found that satisfies our:

- Intellectual need,
- Investigative spirit, or
- Method of testing our findings, or a new theory.

If one does not feel the necessity for discovering new truths or revamping old ones, the pursuit of scientific truth will not be appealing. In 1926, Edwin Hubble, the astronomer, made the observation that, wherever we look, distant galaxies are moving rapidly away from us. In other words, the universe is expanding. He also suggested that there was a time, the big bang, when the universe was infinitely dense and infinitesimally small. Under the then prevailing conditions, all the laws of science, as we know them today, would break down.

Other scientists have challenged Hubble's hypotheses, which rest on tentative statements that cannot be proven. For instance, Fritz Zwicky, Hubble's Caltech colleague, disagreed with the master's statement that all galaxies have roughly the same number of stars and the same brightness. Zwicky gave two arguments as to why dwarf galaxies should exist:

- The principle of *inexhaustibility of nature* is unlikely to allow for only two types of galaxy, and
- If Hubble said that dwarf galaxies did not exist, then almost certainly they do exist.[2]

A myriad of examples in scientific work demonstrates that the freedom to express disagreement and challenge other researchers' findings, or hypotheses, is at the root of the scientific method. This is the principle of *negation and subsequent reconstruction.*

- Negation and reconstruction is a powerful method, which can be very useful.
- The most basic art is to look for hypotheses, statements, theories or systems of thought that pretend to absolute truth, and to deny them.

The concept behind Zwicky's approach is that the intellect *creates*, but only scientific verification can *confirm*. This is one of the basic principle on which rests the scientific method. Confirmation is likely to be tentative, because the available tools are usually primitive compared with the magnitude of the task on hand. Or, as Protagoras (480–410 BC) put it, '. . . many things hinder knowledge: the obscurity of the matter, and the shortness of human life.'[3]

4.4 Fundamentals of stress analysis

Methods and procedures for *stress analysis* conform to the principles of scientific discipline discussed in section 4.3. The aim of an orderly approach is to provide a higher level of reference than could be assured by traditional ways to risk control. *Stress tests* look at the effects of extreme movements in the market (or important changes in creditworthiness) and, through their findings, affect risk drivers embedded in the trading book and banking book. The aim is to:

- Observe and describe,
- Classify and analyse,
- Relate and generalize,
- Formulate a comprehensive hypothesis,
- Test for weaknesses and hidden exposures,
- Predict, and verify the accuracy of the prediction.

With stress analysis, the portfolio is revalued (usually downwards) according to chosen parameters and projected values. In all likelihood, the outcome will not be in line with statistics derived from operational data, unless the experimenter uses historical extreme events. However, the most fundamental differences between stress analysis and a traditional procedural solution to testing, such as value at risk (VAR), lie in the methodology used in research:

- Stress tests explicitly focus on confidence intervals well beyond 99 per cent; for instance 99.9 per cent and 99.97 per cent.
- By contrast, VAR and other by now classical approaches concentrate at or below the 99 per cent level of confidence (see Chapter 1), where events are relatively low impact.

People who are inclined to stonewall, basing their decisions on obsolete information, do not appreciate this most important difference in testing and in the confidence which can be placed on test results. By doing so, they are living in a world detached from reality, because they fail to account for prevailing volatility (see Chapter 7) and growing exposure.

As an example, Figure 4.2 shows the time series of a volatile equity. The careful reader will observe that what constitutes an outlier is conditioned by the level of confidence that is chosen. An outlier of a 95 per cent level of confidence may be a normal distribution event at 99 per cent. (Levels of confidence and their role in stress testing were explained in Chapter 1.)

A higher level of confidence, such as 99.9 per cent in Figure 4.2, is an envelope that includes a larger number of real-life values of the variable under study; in this

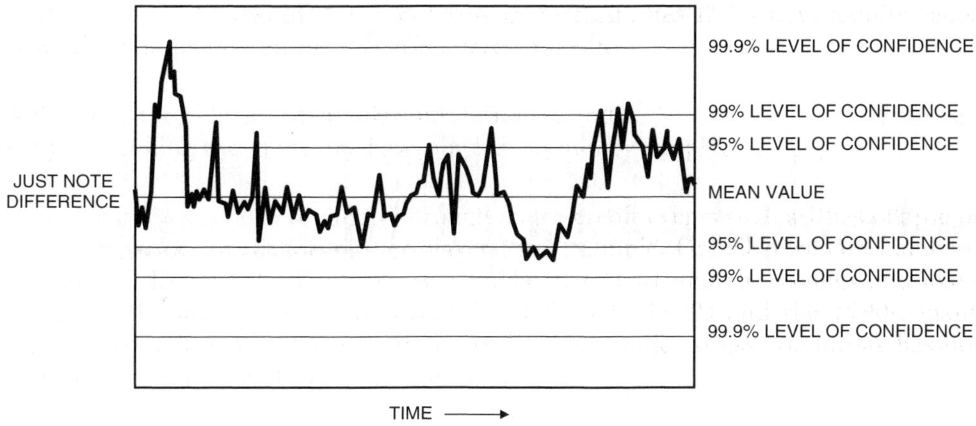

Figure 4.2 Outliers connected to a time series at different levels of confidence

case an equity. The points beyond the 99 per cent interval, in this graph, are those of interest to the stress test. They have been encountered already as tail events.

In this particular example, the tail events are historical. In other cases of stress analysis, they are hypothetical; the subject of a 'what if' investigation of plausible extreme values of a given equity. An interesting pattern of advanced analysis could also result by placing normally distributed values of an equity under stress conditions.

- Several scenarios may be developed to map the effect of stress on what seems to be normal events.
- The most interesting values for further analysis are usually those showing, somewhere down the line, a step function or spikes.

From an analytical viewpoint, the pulse of the market shown in Figure 4.2 presents many similitudes with the pattern of the electrocardiogram in Figure 4.3. Terry, our dog, died of a heart attack; the electrocardiogram foretold this event. Notice how the frequency and amplitude of Terry's pulse changed to a chaotic output.

Although, as shown in subsequent sections, the art of scenario building for stress analysis differs from one company to another, it has some common characteristics. One very important characteristic is that they target *accuracy*, rather than precision. Another common characteristic is that no stress analysis can remain valid forever. This is as true of financial studies as it is of studies in physics and engineering. Scenarios for stress analysis should therefore be updated with every change in the market, or in the instrument whose risk they target. Yet another common characteristic of scenarios developed for stress analysis by different firms is that they are essentially of the 'what if' type. The difference lies in the fact that:

- Tier-one banks test the limits,
- While less sophisticated institutions use conservative tests.

Moreover, a well-performed stress analysis calls for combining numerical results with qualitative outcomes, properly identifying the assumptions underpinning

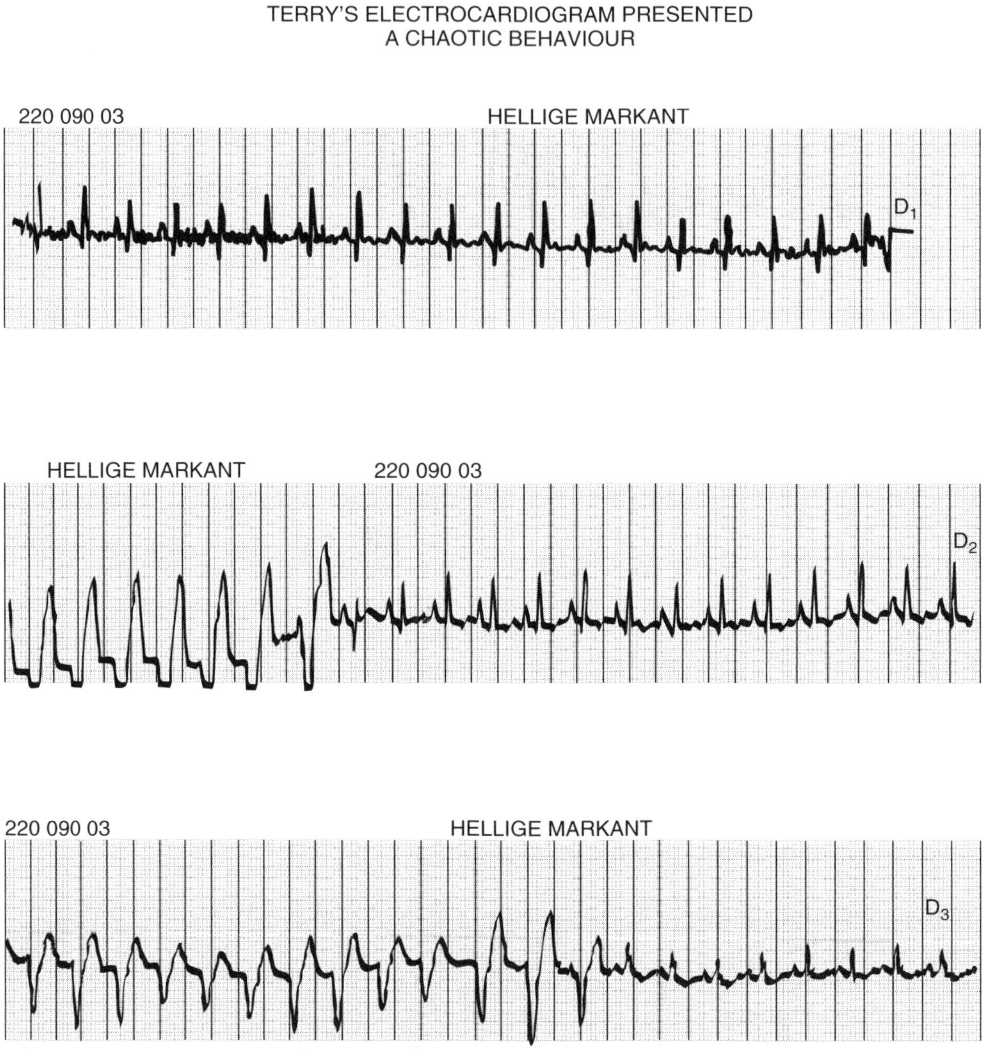

Figure 4.3 The electrocardiogram showed chaotic behaviour

experimentation; for instance, short rates moving more than long rates, or shifts in bonds yield curve combined with rise (or fall) in equity markets.

Clear and detailed identification of all factors entering into experimentation is vital to every analytical effort, not only because this is demanded by a scientific methodology, but also for the reason that the success of stress testing depends a great deal on assumptions being made and on the way in which the tests are executed. Last but not least, the usefulness of results to be expected is a direct function of the skill of experimenter(s) in:

- Coming forward with the right hypotheses,
- Evaluating the underlying model of the real world,

- Examining the quality and consistency of data,
- Proceeding with the examination of different changes, and of their aftermath,
- Analysing the effect of switches in crucial values, and
- Skewing the model towards whichever side needs to be magnified, to reveal its secrets.

The message carried by these bullet points can serve all processes of analysis. Regarding a holistic approach to a test, much can be gained by integrating expert opinions, contrasting one against the other all the way to its logic and its reasoning. In principle, the opinion of experts is most useful in defining the nature of extreme events that could occur in the future, and their possible impact, but it is not likely to find experts who are in accord with one another, as shown in section 4.6.

4.5 Case studies with scenario analysis

Scenario analyses can be of two types: one is based on *expert opinions*, tied together through a plot or play. This plot indicates events, reflects on their magnitude, guesses their timing and may also inject new scenes of behaviour. An example is a cast of characters, or sequel of events, that were not part of the original scenario. (More on expert opinions in section 4.6.)

The second type is based on *simulation*, through analogous thinking. For instance, a scenario analysis uses credit simulation to examine the path of stochastic variables such as default probabilities or recovery rates. Mote Carlo simulation, for example, makes it possible to experiment on:

- The concentration of credit risk exposure in the loans books, or
- The likely decay of a securitized loans pool, through repayment of individual mortgages.

Both types of scenario analysis, simulation and expert opinion, are valuable in active risk management. Experimentation on potential exposures, because of credit quality, helps in anticipating adverse movements. This leads to proactive decision making on:

- Restructuring exposures in a portfolio, or
- Implementation of credit risk-mitigating techniques.

Scenario analysis at the level of an investment portfolio must be performed in a way that reflects the characteristic of positions and trades. Exposures due to outliers are produced by identifying low-probability events connected with abnormal market conditions, such as exceptional price movements or a dramatic deterioration in liquidity.

Scenarios are also based on macroeconomic events precipitating radical change in parities, emerging political difficulties and other cases that assist in estimating the maximum potential downside. Examples of macroeconomic events with a global impact are:

- The multiple tightening of interest rates and bond market crash of 1994,
- The exchange rate mechanism crisis in September 1992 and its effect on the British pound, and
- The two major oil shocks of the 1970s.

Many experts consider scenario analysis to be an essential component of the market risk measurement framework. Properly done, it makes it possible to measure exposures by dynamically revaluing positions, by projecting incoming changes to market parameters. Because unearthing hidden market signals requires more powerful tools than ever before, stress testing of portfolios has become an integral component of active risk management procedures.

- Stress tests are particularly useful in calculating more accurately the impact of large market moves, and
- Projected sectorial exposure can be combined with portfolio aggregation techniques to provide a holistic risk forecast.

Sophisticated scenarios offer to management the ability to model exposures dynamically by assuming combinations of extreme market and default events. To offer realistic results, however, these scenarios must:

- Remain relevant to the business being conducted,
- Capture all significant risks, by avoiding oversimplifications,
- Be comprehensive and consistent across risk types, and
- Meet or exceed regulatory and industry standards in regard to risk control.

At no time should model uncertainties and data uncertainties (see Chapter 1) be forgotten. For this reason, apart from the accuracy of the model, attention must be paid to the data being used. Although, in many cases, two years of underlying information is used to derive market movements for VAR calculations, this is absolutely inadequate for stress testing. Leading institutions use at least ten-year time series, or even better twenty-year events.

The way in which information elements are organized and exploited also has an impact on research results. Depending on the objective of the stress test, positions may be aggregated by type of risk, by product, by counterparty or according to some other criterion. For instance, interest rate exposure includes risk arising from:

- Bonds,
- Money market,
- Swap transactions,
- Interest rate options,
- Foreign exchange,
- Equity investments, and
- Commodity options, among other instruments.

Quality-control charts can help to plot risks as a function of time.[4] Whereas VAR calculates potential loss arising from a given portfolio for a predetermined probability and holding period, using market movements determined from historical data, scenario analysis is used to estimate the *potential loss* after market parameters come under stress. Projected movements in market can be derived from:

- Past events, and
- Assumed changes based on expert opinion.

As the foregoing examples document, for more than one reason scenario analysis is an essential component of an institution's evaluation assumed exposure. Properly done, it allows market risk and credit risk embedded in portfolio positions to be measured by stressing market parameters. Historical information is changed according to different stress strategies, to permit the viewing of cases where investors are nervous, bank credit dries up or market conditions are totally disrupted.

4.6 Using the Delphi method

One of the best ways for performing scenario analysis is the Delphi method. It permits a systematic and direct use of expert judgement, taken from a statistically significant sample. Named after the ancient temple of Apollo, Delphi provides a framework that makes it feasible effectively to use informed intuitive judgement involving a given parameter, such as credit estimates. Delphi derives its importance from the realization that:

- Projections into the future, on which decisions must rely, are based largely on personal expectations, rather than on predictions sustained by theory or statistics.
- Even when a formal mathematical model is available, the hypotheses, input assumptions, range of variation of parameter(s), method and interpretation of output are all subject to intuitive intervention by individuals.

The best way to look at Delphi is as a method of qualitative analysis used to prognosticate the likelihood (or occurrence) of important events, to suggest better focused measures than currently available, to develop and compare alternatives to a course of action, to select a preferred allocation of capital resources, and for other purposes. Knowledgeable opinions are collected if the panel of experts is familiar with the problem under investigation.

Delphi prognostications use interviews and/or questionnaires to extract estimates, or forecasts, on a specific event (or issue) from a valid sample of experts. Typically, this event is subject to a conditional probability, also known as *abduction*:

- Something happens,
- If something else takes place.

The experts' prognostication is subjected to iterations. The responses obtained are presented to the same experts to confront them with *dissension*. This process of iteration and dissension helps them to focus their judgement. Dissension is a sort of criticism, but Delphi avoids face-to-face confrontation. It also provides anonymity of opinions, and of arguments advanced in defence of these opinions. There are different ways of implementing Delphi. In one version,

- The participating experts are asked to give not only their opinions, but also the reasons for these opinions, and
- Direct debate is replaced by an interchange of information and opinions, through a carefully designed sequence of questionnaires.

Successive iterations are stepping stones towards the definition of a likely outcome, or the selection of the most crucial factor among several top-level variables. Once a high-ranking small group of critical factors has been identified, the experts will be informed of their peers' choices and given a chance to change their opinion, and the procedure will be repeated.

In practical terms, at each successive interrogation the participants are given new and refined information, in the form of *opinion feedback*. This is derived by a computed consensus from the earlier part of the programme. The process continues until:

- Further progress towards a consensus appears to be negligible, or
- A bifurcation develops, with opinions that cannot be reconciled.

Even when a conclusion is arrived at, it is likely that there will be dissension. For instance, there may be two or three alternatives for evaluating a certain process, with one having a higher frequency than another. When this happens, the conflicting views are documented and presented in a form that shows the relative weight of each opinion in the group. A pattern is established; an example is presented in Figure 4.4.

Progressive refinement of judgemental opinions through successive iterations is a good way of taking some of the subjectivity out of the system. This, however, should not be done in a way that creates undesirable effects, such as one group of experts exercising dominance over the other(s). Another risk is that the panellists are subjected to a herd syndrome.

A major advantage of the Delphi method is that it requires the experts to document the opinions they give. This is one of the reasons why Delphi is well suited to credit evaluations. Iterations can target default in an effective manner through successive probability estimates. As the largely subjective quantity of counterparty risk changes, the estimate of default likelihood changes with it, whether it grows or shrinks.

- The results from the implementation of Delphi are not supposed to last forever.
- Rather, they are a snapshot of current conditions and estimates, which have to be reviewed periodically.

As this brief outline documents, scenario analysis based on the process of developing a pattern of expert opinion provides a logical string of concepts and events, which

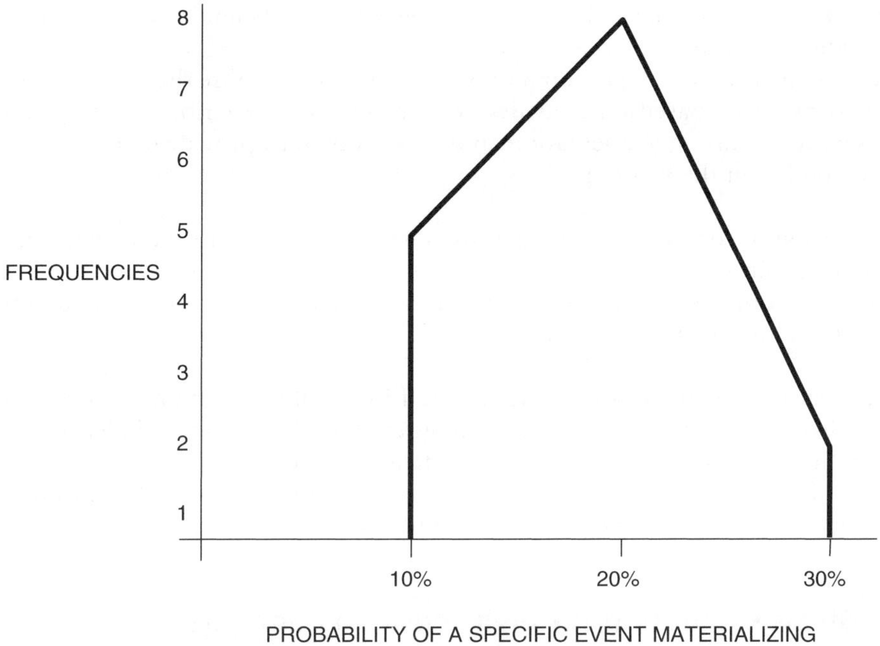

Figure 4.4 The opinions of participating experts can be presented as a pattern with corresponding frequencies

can be exploited to advantage. In actual practice, such a procedure is undertaken for one of several reasons, or a combination of them:

- Exploring a new line of thinking or of action,
- Prognosticating important developments,
- Reaching a certain convergence of opinions,
- Restructuring existing notions regarding a certain issue, or
- Making relatively abstract opinions about events (whether risks or budgets) more understandable, and
- Improving upon current policies, as well as the systems and procedures supporting them.

Scenarios and the patterning of expert advice also help in evaluating alternative courses of action, and in examining their aftermath. They also help in specifying desired change at a conceptual level, or in implementing new system configuration while taking into account the constraints of an existing legacy solution.

In an application of the Delphi method, for example, experts may be asked to undertake a country rating for creditworthiness reasons, along a frame of reference similar to the one in Figure 4.4. This evaluation will take into account not only the country, but also the instrument. For instance, foreign debt typically receives a lower rating than internal debt, because the latter benefits from the government's ability to tax its citizens.

Another dimension in which the Delphi method can make a valuable contribution is the timing of projected happenings. The term of major events is often a matter among experts. Delphi helps in explaining the reasoning behind divergent views and in providing a link to reality.

Scenario analysis and expert opinion voting correlate because the successive phases of expert feedback based on quartiles are themselves a scenario. At the same time, any scenario requires documentation, and expert opinions provide it. The strength of the method lies in the fact that:

- The elicitation of expert opinion is systematic and more forthcoming than in a committee, and
- A combination of quantitative and judgemental processes can be used through conditional probability.

In conclusion, Delphi is a powerful method for distilling opinions. The experts do not act like members of a classical committee; they have greater independence of opinion and details of their opinions are databased. This is a practical application where issues with yes/no answers are the exception. Opinions are documented, and this is critical to the proper estimation of a likely outcome.

4.7 Stress evaluation through sensitivity analysis

Estimating the likelihood of an event is one thing; evaluating whether or not that event is rational or sustainable seems to be another. However, in reality rationality and likelihood are, up to a point, interlinked, as can be demonstrated through qualitative and quantitative disclosures.

- Qualitative disclosures help in appreciating the nature of the problem.
- Quantitative metrics provide information on its magnitude and impact.

Qualitative financial disclosures offer management the opportunity to elaborate on and acquire depth in connection with statements made in quantitative disclosures, such as included in the annual report. Within the evolving regulatory framework, banks, securities firms and other financial institutions are encouraged to include an overview of key aspects of organization and structure central to their risk management and control process for all types of business activity.

Of the stress-testing methods briefly covered in Chapter 3, sensitivity analysis is primarily (but not exclusively) orientated towards the provision of qualitative information. By contrast, statistical inference (see section 4.8) is mainly, although again not exclusively, quantitatively orientated. Both can be a motor behind experimentation.

Sometimes, practitioners tend to confuse the meaning of, and roles played by, sensitivity and connectivity in data analysis. In part, this happens because of the polyvalence of tests being performed, so that the meaning of sensitivity and connectivity is confused.

- *Sensitivity* refers to the likelihood of a given presentation of financial risk, or reward, being recognized as being out of the ordinary.
- *Connectivity* shows how quickly and accurately information about a case is passed to the different levels of an organization.

This difference is significant. Connectivity should accompany all other types of stress testing: scenarios, statistical inference and drills. Connectivity is often the missing link in management's need to act and take advantage of a situation or, alternatively, to redress the situation to avoid further exposure.

In other cases, the terms scenario and sensitivity analysis are used interchangeably. This, too, is wrong. Comparing sensitivities to scenarios, discussed in section 4.5, it can be seen that they are fairly different, if for no other reason than because sensitivities usually rest on an induced change in value, rather than on opinion.

Banks may use sensitivities to estimate interest rate or equity price risk; for instance, the aftermath on their capital base by ±100, ±200, ±300 or ±400 basis points increase (or decrease) in interest rates. This is a shock that provides both:

- Quantitative, and
- Qualitative information.

Frequently, but not always, sensitivity stress testing contains symmetrical shocks up and down a given scale. Parallel yield curve shifts are also subject to sensitivity analysis. A difference between scenario and sensitivity stress tests is that, most frequently, the latter address only one well-defined risk factor.

This contrasts with scenarios that tend to target more general propositions of a wider perspective and impact. In the majority of implementations, sensitivity analysis tends to be more linear and simpler than either scenarios or statistical inference. It is also concerned with one-off events rather than patterns.

It is appropriate to bring to the reader's attention that the simpler characteristics of sensitivity analysis do not mean that it cannot be used for advanced testing. Sensitivity stress tests are more popular with interest rates and less so with equities, exchange rates, volatility and liquidity.

In contrast to sensitivity approaches, stress tests based on statistical analysis are more rigorous and open to scientific experimentation. Simpler methods, too, have their place in analysis. The downside of a method being simpler is that it tends to be less able to satisfy the goal of capturing multiple types of risk. An advantage of simplicity is that it may be able to detect changes that might be lost with a complex methodology targeting several variables, or handling non-linearities. The difference in deliverables between a linearized approach and real life is seen in Figure 4.5, which presents:

- Actual market sensitivity, and
- Linearized sensitivity to changes in interest rates.

In this and many other situations, *non-linearity* is typically more precise in the sense of representing the real world. However, over short distances, linearity could provide a good enough approximation. The problem is that many entities do not have access to the skills needed to study complex non-linear relations.

In terms of the information to be analysed and stress-tested, sensitivity analysis may work with both historical data and hypotheses. To improve the accuracy of

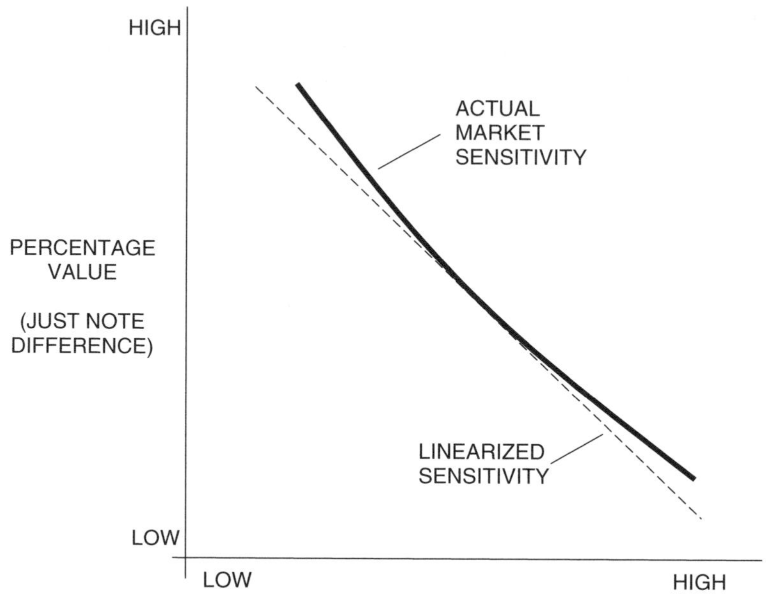

Figure 4.5 Actual sensitivity and linearized sensitivity to changes in market interest rate

deliverables, analysts engaged in sensitivity analysis must keep in mind that historical information may involve:

- Bias, and
- Recurring errors.

The presence of either or both can create deviations from what should have been objective results. Sensitivity analysis lacks the flexibility-characterizing scenarios or statistical documentation of an inference engine (see section 4.8). It is, however, feasible to use a Delphi method for data evaluation by a panel of experts.

Removing part of the data uncertainty, even through subjective methods, is important because stress tests are conducted to reveal both positive and negative aspects of a problem that are not evident with normal tests. Data uncertainty works against this objective.

4.8 Fundamentals of statistical inference

Chapter 3 outlined four methods fort stress testing. Up to a point, but only up to a point, the first three of them, scenario writing, sensitivity analysis and rigorous statistical tests, tend to overlap. At the same time, they complement one another. This suggests that all types of stress test have their place in the prognostication of unlikely but plausible conditions under stress.

Of the three, statistical inference is the most quantitatively oriented. In practice, it often has the high ground because meaningful experimentation is usually conducted on a rich base of statistics.

By definition, the primary goal of statistical analysis is that of inference between observed properties of a sample, and those of the population from which it derives. The complete set of observations upon which a statistical analysis is based is usually called a *sample of 'n'*, where *n* refers to the number of observations.

The sample of observations (or measurements) is sensed to be taken out of all observations that might be made, which constitute the *population.* A better way of looking at the population is as a universe of potential observations that are not available to us. We try to learn about the characteristics of that population through sampling.

- Any subset of a population is a *sample* of that population, but for statistical inference, significant samples must be used.
- One of the most important problems in statistics is to decide what information about the distribution of the population can be *inferred* from the study of a sample.

By *study of a sample* is meant that from the sample mathematically meaningful information about the population under investigation can be obtained. Measurements of both the population and the sample are distributed from a minimum to a maximum value. These data are referred to as a *distribution.* Different forms of distributions can be distinguished, for example:

- Normal, or bell-shaped,
- Leptokyrtotic,
- Poisson,
- Hypergeometric.

As shown in Chapter 7, the normal and the leptokyrtotic distribution differ from each other in terms of the processes that they describe and the likelihood of some of the events. While they may both have the same mode, the density function of the leptokyrtotic distribution is distinct from that of the normal distribution. At one of the leptokyrtotic distribution's legs, the Hurst coefficient suggests that tail events will duplicate themselves over time.

With reference to the normal distribution, sample values, referred to as *statistics*, are *estimates* of the population values which are unknown. The (unknown) population metrics are the *parameters*, and they are the true values.

The statistics are an estimated description of true values, qualified through *explanation*, provided by *experimental* or *non-experimental* means. An explanation of experimental data includes methods such as randomization, tests of significance, regression analysis, and analysis of variance and covariance.

- Typically, statistical testing is done on the assumption that statistics and parameters form a normal distribution.
- Stress testing, by contrast, concentrates on tail values, with statistical inference orientated towards outliers and extreme events.

In both cases, scientific methodology requires that the researcher properly defines the larger system (population), determines process dynamics, states the objectives of experimentation, states the hypothesis to be tested, executes the sampling procedure, analyses sample statistics, and accepts or rejects the hypothesis, based on the outcome of the test.

Let us take a stock index as an example of normal statistical testing and stress testing for inference reasons. Normal testing with NASDAQ, Dow Jones, S&P 500, FTSE 100 or Nikkei data streams is usually done within $x \pm 3s$ (mean and 3 standard deviations), choosing a confidence of 99 per cent or less.

This widespread practice provides limited insight, because it does not account for outliers or on-and-off extreme events. There are no explicit rules for *statistical stress testing*, but there are sound practices. Good practice is to consider:

- $x \pm 5s$, as a weak-level stress test
- $x \pm 10s$, as better frame of reference in stress testing for outliers
- $x \pm 15s$, for emulating the $14.5s$ Black Monday event at the New York Stock Exchange
- $x \pm 30s$, as the worst case, emulating the volatility of DAX options in 1998.

Practically all of these examples fall into the class of historical testing, since the information being used makes reference to past stockmarket and options market behaviour. What is sought with this approach is the study of similar events happening sometime in the future, and its aftermath. Through emulation, the test looks for:

- Outliers that, statistically speaking, are improbable but possible, and
- Extreme events that may upset the balances and turn current plans on their head.

Research along this line of reference would benefit from of tools and methods that go beyond the confines of probability theory. Examples are possibility theory, fuzzy engineering, chaos theory[5] and genetic algorithms.[6] All tests must be fully documented in a simple, comprehensive language. Contrary to what certain theorists profess, in business a method only has value if it is:

- Understandable,
- Relatively easy to use, and
- Appreciated by its users.

Esoteric theories developed by pure mathematicians turned theoretical financial experts often lack the plausibility that comes from experience. By contrast, a pragmatic stress test typically considers events that make professional sense. As such, they attract the attention of end-users in terms of their deliverables.

To emulate market disruptions, experimenters can take the following events as a reference: the East Asia meltdown of 1997, the abrupt Russian devaluation of August 1998, the LTCM bankruptcy of 1998, the Enron bankruptcy of 2001, the K-Mart bankruptcy of 2002, the Parmalat bankruptcy of 2003, and similar major happenings. *Emulation stress testing* should also consider the synergy of such events within a short time-frame, concentrating on:

- *Credit risk*, by widening various credit and swap spreads, over a number of countries linked by global investment; also on major failure(s) connected to credit derivatives, or the bankruptcy examples listed above, or
- *Market risk*, including shocks to equity prices, interest rates, exchange rates of major currencies or events connected to derivative instruments, with their associated volatility and illiquidity, or
- *Operational risk*, such as Herstatt risk, where one counterparty executes its obligations, while the other (defaulting) party does not; also, operational risks due to the laws of two different countries being heterogeneous regarding the treatment of recovered assets.

Another example of stress testing based on statistical inference is that of the aftermath of the eleven consecutive interest rate decreases by the Federal Reserve, in 2001, in an effort to revive the US economy and the stockmarket, versus the six consecutive increases in interest rates during 1994, which led to a bond market crash and concomitant shocks to equity prices, forex and swap rates.

Finally, co-ordinated use of the Delphi method and statistical stress testing can assist in experimentation under extreme conditions at the junction of qualitative and quantitative approaches. In today's dynamic, and therefore unpredictable, markets, there is a steadily growing need for this type of evaluation, which can be made more sophisticated by including volatility spikes and liquidity constraints.

Notes

1. A. Einstein, *Essays in Science*, Philosophical Library, New York, 1934.
2. W. Tucher and K. Tucher, *The Dark Matter*, William Morrow, New York, 1988.
3. J.B. Burry and R. Meiggs, *A History of Greece*, Macmillan, London, 1975.
4. D.N. Chorafas, *Reliable Financial Reporting and Internal Control: A Global Implementation Guide*, John Wiley, New York, 2000.
5. D.N. Chorafas, *Chaos Theory in the Financial Markets*, Probus, Chicago, 1994.
6. D.N. Chorafas, *Rocket Scientists in Banking*, Lafferty Publications, London, 1995.

5 Worst case scenarios and drills

5.1 Introduction

Every situation, no matter how bad it may be, can have a *worst case*. This worst case is not necessarily a catastrophe but, invariably, it leads to a salient problem; one to which senior management must devote its full attention. The objective of this chapter is to present how worst cases develop, how they can be simulated and what solutions have been found to confront them.

5.2 Worst cases happen when chance meets unpreparedness

In business, industry and government, a worst case is generally an event of low probability, but very high impact. It is something that, if it happens, would upset the most carefully laid out plans. One of the interesting aspects with worst cases is that we may be wrong in thinking this is the *worst* thing possible. 'The singular feature of the great crash', John Kenneth Galbraith once suggested, 'was that the worst continued to worsen.'

Worst case drills are what the military calls *War Games*. They are real-life simulations that revolve around the interplay of human decisions and a real-life grand test. In terms of hypotheses, scenarios and procedures, the financial industry has learned a good deal from war games, and from mistakes that happen both in real life and in simulated exercises, because of an unforeseen nasty event.

Tragic as it was, World War II *Operation Tiger*, which took place on 28 April 1944, has taught us a great lesson about what happens when chance is at work, but preparedness is wanting. The cost was 441 GIs dead and missing, along with 198 Navy dead. The loss in human life came from explosion, fire, being locked in lower compartments of ships attacked unexpectedly by German torpedo boats, and sinking in a cold, agitated sea.

This exercise, which took place at Slapton Sands, in the south of England, had to be done. It was a dry run of the invasion of Normandy. But the precautions that were taken were substandard, leaving the gates open for a large amount of risk. The similarity of this tragic event to what sometimes happens in financial operations is striking. Soldiers and sailors boarded, with their armour, light ship transports (LSTs), a special unit in World War II which played a major role in landings both in the Atlantic and in the Pacific.

But the abbreviation LST also stands for long slow target, because the ships are slow and difficult to manoeuvre. This, plus the fact that the English Channel was patrolled by German E-boats operating at speeds of 34–36 knots, heightened the need for:

- First class communications, and
- Plenty of naval support, plus training all soldiers on how to swim, and how to wear their life-jackets. Failure to do so was an inexcusable mistake.

Disaster is what happens when an enemy attack meets lack of preparedness. Although they defended a common cause, the US and British armoury and communications systems were not integrated. Insufficiency also characterized Army/Navy communications, in both the American and British ranks.

As the support provided to the LSTs by the navy was, at best, wanting, all the ingredients were there for turning the landing's dry run into a nightmare scenario, when the German E-boats struck. Post mortem, historians said that the boys did not die for nothing. Although it ended in catastrophe, the Slapton Sands exercise taught the military valuable lessons, and led to an overhaul of Operation Overlord, the landing in Normandy. Perhaps the most valuable lessons are that:

- In war as in business, *detail* matters a great deal, and
- The readiness, not just the active involvement of different sorts of players, is what distinguishes a successful enterprise.

This lesson taught at Slapton Sands has a great impact on finance. It was a nightmare scenario. With derivatives, the worst case scenario and the nightmare scenario are not the same thing, but both can happen. As Alexander Lamfalussy, former general manager of the Bank for International Settlements (BIS) and the European Financial Institute, said: 'There might never be a problem. But, and it is a big but, if there were, it would be a very big problem'.

Attention to detail is the alter ego of the need to know about a very big problem, even if it has a very small probability of happening. This need is an integral part of a sound governance policy in any and every walk of life. Only by anticipating the worst case, in an informed, well-studied and holistic way:

- Are we in a position to take the necessary measures to confront adversity, and
- Are we able to master our resources in such a way that we succeed in our task.

A drill, or dry run, goes beyond the confines of statistical inference (see Chapter 4) and seeks to obtain evidence of what actually happens when a catastrophe occurs. A worst case drill has no use for the normal distribution: it is concerned only with extreme events towards the end of the long leg of extreme events, as shown in Figure 5.1.

A drill can be conducted, for example, to determine what would have happened if the collapse of Long-Term Capital Management (LTCM) had been accompanied by a default on the part of three or four big banks which were, at the time, on shaky ground; and if, simultaneously, Thailand, Indonesia and South Korea were going bust, which they had done a year earlier.

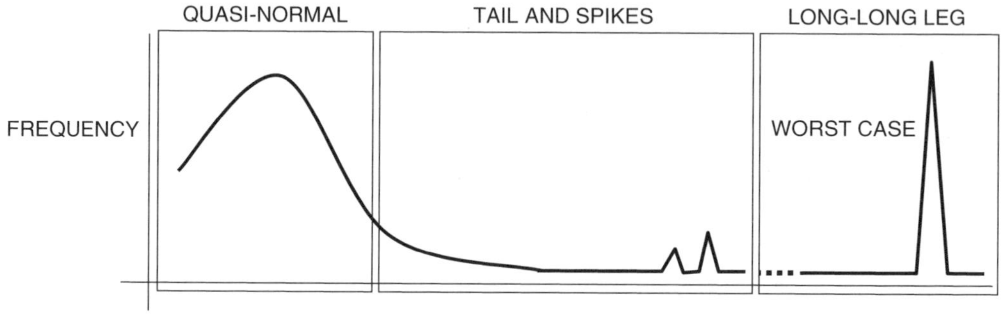

Figure 5.1 Distribution of risk events along a triple frame of reference

A drill based on such a historical scenario could be instrumental in stress testing the combined effects of the bankruptcy of big companies' global commitments, such as Enron, WorldCom and Parmalat, along with the collapse of a couple of major credit institutions, which financed them, and major insurers that had covered Enron's prepays. What if these meltdowns had occurred simultaneously? Such a drill is a useful way of:

- Studying systemic risk, and
- Projecting on the aftermath that this would have on a particular institution.

'The complexities and interdependencies inherently associated with multilegged positions are such that a sudden failure of a major market participant might disrupt the financial system', stated a joint Federal Reserve, Federal Deposit Insurance Corporation and Office of the Controller of the Currency report on 'Derivative Product Activities at Commercial Banks', in 1993. In the years that have elapsed since that date, exposure to derivatives has increased by more than one order of magnitude.

The common aim of nearly all worst case scenarios and drills is to identify the weak links in a chain of command, and instigate capital damage control procedures, so that problems that can be corrected before a catastrophe hits. As such, worst case drills are relatively new in testing. The best among them are both qualitative and quantitative. They are becoming popular at the higher level of stress testing.

5.3 A bird's-eye view of worst case analysis

As discussed in the preceding four chapters, stress testing is based on both conceptual premises and mathematical models. The interest in worst case analysis, by both regulators and clear-eyed commercial or investment bankers, has increased in proportion to the fact that a global economy is characterized by high leverage, an inordinate amount of risk, and on-and-off illiquidity. This is leading many experts to worry about:

- The risks of high global asset prices, and
- The after effects of persistently low long-term interest rates.

How critical liquidity can be in times of crisis is exemplified by the fact that the morning after the 11 September 2001 terrorist attack on the World Trade Center and the Pentagon, the Federal Reserve injected US $38 billion into the money market, compared with the normal $5 billion. In addition, the central banks of Europe and Japan pumped another $80 billion into the financial markets on Wednesday 12 September, to assure liquidity at a moment when the financial markets were on the edge of panic.

However, excessive liquidity has many negatives, not least that it increases by leaps and bounds the risk appetite of investors and speculators. The presence of other factors, such as sky-rocketing oil prices, disappointments with quarterly earnings and financial scandals, adds to the stress scenario.

A drill aims to establish

- How bad a situation may be, because of synergy of negative factors, and
- How well we may be prepared to face the challenge, given that the negatives may overwhelm some positions.

A worse case *stress test* may contain simultaneous moves in different *risk factors*, which affect a particular institution directly and indirectly; in the latter case because of the effect they have on the economy. Whether the object is derivative instruments, equity prices, interest rates or currency exchange rates, the worse case test will integrate a highly unfavourable event that:

- May occur in the foreseeable future, or
- May repeat itself unexpectedly.

The invasion of Kuwait by Iraq in August 1990 provides an example. When the Chief Executive Officer (CEO) of Bankers Trust received the news, via the institution's general manager in Hong Kong, it was past midnight in New York; but, at the time, Bankers Trust had one of the best technologies available in the banking industry, which made it possible to:

- Put together in record time a global virtual balance sheet,[1]
- Run a worst case analysis on balance sheet positions, and
- Reposition the bank, before its competitors were able to assess their wounds.

In fact, the worst case test established that the Iraqi invasion of Kuwait caught Bankers Trust's investments on the wrong side of the balance sheet. By being ahead of its competitors in information technology, the institution was able to reposition itself on the right side of the balance sheet. Done a priori, a drill would have a similar effect.

Another example of a drill is that of human resources. Take as an example the sudden loss of key personnel, as well as of a big chunk of technological infrastructure, as a result of a terrorist attack (like that of 11 September 2001, against the twin towers of the World Trade Center in New York), or the loss of a whole major subsidiary, its branch offices and accounts, similar to the one suffered by ABN, the Dutch global bank, when religious fanatics took over the government in Iran.

The extraordinary events referred to in all of these cases are real, and they may happen again; hence the wisdom of being prepared for them through worst case scenarios and drills. While the timing of their reappearance is hypothetical, if it happens it will result in significant twists or in catastrophe.

Alternatively, the worse case stress test (with worst case being the limiting condition) may be based on a plausible market event, an expected outlier that has not yet taken place. This is essentially a *'what if' hypothetical stress* scenario, where the 'what' is something exceptional.

There may also be hybrid worse case cases for stress testing. The bankruptcies of the Bank of New England and Continental Illinois are no direct precedents in global banking because, while both were superregional, neither was a truly global player. Both events, however, can be extended to a global banking perspective, with:

- The Bank of New England providing a precedence on failure due to a real-estate bubble, and
- The case of Continental Illinois contributing to a worse case stress test because of concentrated exposure in the oil industry.

Other historical examples that can be adapted to a worse case stress scenario fall into a domain that can best be described as 'the contribution of adversity'. British Petroleum (BP), one of the oil majors, provides an example. In 1992, when Lord Browne, then head of the company's oil exploration division, known as BPX, set out to restructure his area of operation, BP was close to bankruptcy. The choice was to:

- Initiate radical change, or
- Fall prey to a predator, as the best of possible alternatives other than restructuring.

Radical change carried the day, redrawing the horizontal and vertical boundaries of the entity to increase strategic focus. With this came the task of creating relatively small subunits within the organization, endowed with significant decision-making power; as well as a significant reduction in the number of management layers.

5.4 Impaired claims, credit risk and worst case

Credit institutions classify a claim as *impaired* if its book value exceeds the present value of cash flows expected in future periods. This calculation includes interest payments and scheduled principal repayments. This is a fairly general algorithm which evidently accounts for liquidation of collateral if and when available.

Loans are classified as *non-performing* where payment of interest, principal or fees is overdue by more than ninety days. Regulatory authorities sometimes ease this restriction, but do not waive it. To be ahead of the curve, a bank needs to determine the carrying values of impaired claims on a consistent, fair-value basis. This is a particular challenge for impaired loans for which no market value estimate, or benchmark, exists for likely recovery value.

At the same time, however, new regulations ensure that marking to market is a cornerstone to the valuation of assets. The *fair value* of an asset is the value agreed between a willing seller and a willing buyer under conditions other than fire sale. One of the better strategies in fair value estimates is that each case is assessed on its merits, with particular attention being paid to:

- Capital that has been invested,
- Discounted cash flows, and
- Recovery of funds from the investment.

Worst case analysis becomes particularly important when credit is easy because, on the one hand, the expansion of credit is the grease of the wheels of a market economy. On the other hand, leveraging through easy credit contributes to the build-up of imbalances in the financial system because it often leads to misallocation of capital. Examples are provided by major bad credit events such as the collapse, and near collapse, of significant market players.

Banks that depend for a good deal of their business on loans are well advised to test for interest rate risk through worst case scenarios, such as the ± 400 basis points discussed in Chapter 4. Worst case tests must also be conducted for credit risk in an environment of cheap, plentiful debt, which companies have been able to use for deals, such as throughout 2005 and part of 2006.

Even if bankers are reluctant to say, in the 2005/06 time-frame, that there is a *credit bubble*, there have certainly been signs of one. For instance, it has been easy to raise money even if leveraging cuts a borrower's credit rating. As a result, credit quality started to slip, a fact that should be tested to its limits. Standard & Poor's (S&P), the independent rating agency, noted that:

- The number of AA-rated issuers slid from thirty-nine to twenty-three from 2001 to 2006,
- While the number of much riskier BB credits doubled.

Moreover, listed acquirers had to dig more deeply to compete against private-equity rivals flush with debt. The direction of worst case tests has been provided in 2006 by investment bankers. Concerned about the credit bubble, they actively looked for creditworthy borrowers, stress-testing the debt companies on their balance sheets.

A high level of debt in the balance sheet when liquidity is high is a prescription for financial trouble, on the borrower's side, when liquidity dries up. An extraordinary growth in liquidity resembles an inverse pyramid structure:

- Ample liquidity helps to solve one problem,
- But it also creates new challenges, several of them in domains containing many unknowns.

A growing number of supervisors in Group of Ten countries now believe that the availability of liquidity under stress has not been fully tested. Therefore, it is uncertain how the use of leverage can turn the markets under conditions of a simultaneous failure of two or more big institutions.

Practically every issue described in the preceding paragraphs provides opportunities for stress testing. For example, if the bank's strategy with non-performing loans is based on a foreclosure, then the portfolio of mortgage loans must be subjected to a test based on the long leg of a loss distribution, derived from receivables from forced liquidations and related costs.

For commercial exposures, if recovery is likely to be successful, then enterprise value is determined from an assessment of expected cash flows from future operations. Alternatively, if bankruptcy proceedings are to be initiated against the borrower, what should be taken into account is the loss distribution derived from the remains of the liquidation value of the borrower's assets, after subtracting legal costs.

As these examples demonstrate, for a number of common financial instruments there exists an established method that supports some generally accepted basis for testing. The problem is that this method is largely based on high-frequency cases, which are by no means representative of extreme events. Hence, there is a need to:

- Enrich the existing methodology with tools that permit evaluation of different levels of worst cases, and
- Provide methods and tools enabling worse case credit risk events to be forecast, rather than only analysing their aftermath post mortem.

In addition, tools for worse case analysis need to be developed that can handle non-legacy-type exposures; for instance, currency exchange risk, as far as it affects the main currencies, in which transactions in debt financing, global trade and derivative financial instruments are denominated. Another area of analysis in need of worse case studies at different thresholds is that of alternative investments.[2]

Of the current methods, the one that could be adapted to stress tests and worse case scenarios is discounted cash flows. All future cash flows considered recoverable must be discounted to present value on the basis of International Financial Reporting Standard principles.[3] Once this has been done, provisions should be computed for unexpected losses on the assets in question, taking 5, 10 and 15 standard deviations from the mean.

The $60 trillion question is: '*What would happen if one of the mammoth financial organizations blew up?*' This kind of worst case stress testing needs to be done at both the microlevel and macrolevel of exposure.

5.5 Why are worst case drills important?

One of the author's professors at UCLA taught his students that if we prepare ourselves for the worst case, then we have really nothing to fear. Preparing means studying, analysing, conditioning and positioning one's assets so that when confronted by worse case events it is still possible to hold the high ground. This strategy is aimed at:

- Minimizing panics,
- Preserving resources, and
- Preventing a domino effect when a wounded entity pulls its counterparts into the abyss.

If something is judged to be possible, albeit unlikely, then it must be studied all the way to identify what sort of an extreme event it may be. As Operation Tiger, in section 5.2, documented, nothing is negligible, because low-frequency events are likely to:

- Involve many unknowns, and
- Have a relatively high impact, which can be destabilizing.

Drills for low-frequency, high-impact events must include the psychology of markets and their players. They should also account for collateral damage, and reflect the aftermath of a sudden change for the worse in market behaviour. Credit derivatives are a case in point.

On 28 February 2006, Timothy Geithner, president of the New York Federal Reserve Bank, gave a feature speech to the Global Association of Risk Professionals, in New York City. Geithner focused on derivatives, especially credit derivatives: 'They have not eliminated risk. They have not ended the tendency of markets to occasional periods of manta and panic. They have not eliminated the possibility of failure of a major financial intermediary. And they cannot fully insulate the broader financial system from the effects of such a failure'.

According to the president of the New York Federal Reserve Bank, the scale of the over-the-counter derivatives markets is very large, approaching $300 trillion in notional principal amount. In case of a financial earthquake this may represent $60 trillion in real money. Geithner emphasized that were one counterparty derivative to fail, and have to leave its contracts, the process of:

- Closing out those positions, and
- Replacing them

could add stress to markets and intensify direct damage. He then pointed out that credit derivatives are written on a much smaller base of underlying debt issuance. Practically, for each $1 in a corporation's debt, banks could write up to $10 in credit derivatives, to insure the debt. Therefore, in the event of a default, credit derivatives would magnify the risk of adverse market dynamics. This order of magnitude difference makes worst case drills much more important than they would otherwise be.

By no means is this a lonely opinion. A few weeks before Geithner's talk, on 7 February 2006, in an address to the European Financial Services Roundtable in Zürich, Switzerland, Malcolm D. Knight, general manager of BIS, pointed to a dangerous disconnection, which should also be part of a worst case test. The disconnection Knight spoke about is between:

- Major macroeconomic risks present in the global economy, and
- The financial markets' perception of a benign risk environment, as indicated by parameters such as prevailing risk premiums and volatility indices.

Between them, these two important references to the health of the financial system provide an excellent landscape for drills. While worse case analysis is still an art in the process of development, and nearly every financial institution has its own way of going about it, there is a body of knowledge available that permits some meaningful results to be obtained.[4]

The best way to confront the polyvalence of the outlined risks is to borrow a leaf from modern science, which signified the arrival on the scene of the:

- Possible,
- Probable, and
- Relative in terms of impact.

Adverse impact may be most severe for the macromarkets, including trades and investments connected to them. Therefore, the drill should involve all factors connected to and influencing the behaviour of global market players. Such behaviour will be found in the junction of globalization, deregulation, technology and innovation which, among themselves, have created growing business opportunities, but at the same time a significant amount of embedded risk and uncertainty.

5.6 A catastrophe drill undertaken by the International Monetary Fund in 2002

As discussed in section 5.5, catastrophe drills are used to investigate not only processes but also the responses of players to extreme market events. The strength of such drills lies in the fact that they are closely linked to real life and, as such, they make it feasible to explore the implications of alternative strategic or tactical decisions, or plans, as well as responses to extraordinary conditions. Obtained results

- Permit evaluation of the utility of certain moves,
- Provide a ground for testing and co-ordinating procedures,
- Constitute a baseline from which the potential of projected solutions can be judged.

On 5 May 2001 Japanese government sources revealed that Group of Seven (G-7) nations, together with other major economies, had agreed to conduct the 'first joint field of co-ordinated measures aimed at minimizing panic and preventing a domino effect when megabanks and huge hedge funds collapse'. This was reported in *Japan Times* on 7 May 2000. While details of the exercise had not yet been fixed, and G-7 and related institutions had not yet indicated exactly what they would do, analysts believed that:

- The scope of the drill would centre around measures to be taken if a global financial meltdown were to occur, and
- One of the major objectives was to study what it takes to put together again a financial fabric torn apart by the failure of major credit institutions and megafunds.

At the time, available information suggested that this joint drill had been planned at the Financial Stability Forum held in Washington, DC, a few months earlier. Market players saw this as the 'first international attempt to establish a policy coordination framework to deal with the risk of cross-border economic crises', the *Japan Times* reported. It looked as if participants to the drill were set to test how they could co-ordinate measures to deal with a megacrisis. Other key objectives were how to:

- Facilitate communications among central bankers,
- Supply emergency funds to curb contagious failures, and
- Co-ordinate disclosure methods to the public, so that panic can be avoided.

Rumour had it that participating G-7 governments and central bankers, as well as supranational institutions, also wanted to experiment by using public funds to bail out all sorts of collapsed private big financial entities. In the scenario presented, these ranged from commercial banks and investment banks, to different funds and insurance companies.

Critics of the equity market bubble of the late 1990s and of the high-liquidity, low-interest rate policy of central banks, said that all this came none too soon because with hit-and-run instruments such as structured derivative products and collateralized mortgage obligations filling the portfolio of banks and institutional investors, nobody could tell in the old approximate way:

- When the next systemic crisis would occur, or
- What magnitude it may reach on the financial Richter scale.

To appreciate more fully the sense of this contemplated megatest, it should be recalled that the Financial Stability Forum was founded in the wake of the 1997 financial crisis in East Asia, and 1998 bankruptcy of the highly leveraged LTCM hedge fund with its $1.4 trillion exposure. Hence, a drill on a hypothetical global financial catastrophe was an issue well within its scope and jurisdiction.

With time, it was revealed that what really happened on 22/23 March 2001, at the Financial Stability Forum's meeting in Washington, is that central bankers of the G-7 and leading supranatural institutions had agreed on the need to conduct the first field test of co-ordinated measures:

- Aimed at minimizing panic and preventing a domino effect, and
- Involving worst case scenarios of megabanks and hedge funds collapsing.

The drill was proposed by William McDonough, then chairman of the New York Federal Reserve Bank, and the central banker credited with the salvage of super-leveraged LTCM without using taxpayers' money, as is usually the case. Clear-eyed executives of central banks looked at this as the first international attempt to establish a policy co-ordination framework, to deal with cross-border crises.

A year later, the catastrophe drill was carried out, but not by the Financial Stability Forum. In 2002, the International Monetary Fund (IMF), in collaboration with central banks and big commercial and investment banks, took the initiative of the global worst case study. In the UK, for example, the drill was co-ordinated by the Bank of England.

Banks were given crisis-type data by the IMF, and they were asked to study what would have happened to their institution if there had been an instant disaster. In discussions with the author about the IMF drill, commercial bankers said that this initiative was very good and it provided an interesting insight. Their only reservation was that the time-span being covered by the drill was just one year, not far enough into the future.

- Big banks, senior financial executives said, do not fail in one year.
- According to this opinion, it takes several years of poor governance and lightly controlled risk to bring a major institution to its knees.

Other senior bankers agreed with the aforementioned thesis, stating that the main challenge posted by financial catastrophes, which should be reflected through drills, is not just the short term but the likely aftermath in a ten-year time-frame. Their thesis was that:

- Financial problems due to exposure and illiquidity take time to unwind.
- Banks die over years, not overnight, even if the untrained eye sees only the sudden effect.

According to other experts, however, although it may be difficult to materialize an instant meltdown, in the longer term it may be catastrophic. Evidence to that effect is provided by the Japanese banks. Since 1991, for at least fourteen years, big Japanese banks have been locked into a process of longer term crisis, the effect of massive bad loans originating in the bubble years of Japan's rise to stardom (1980s).

5.7 The Federal Reserve's 'new bank' and the carry trade

Whether we talk of one bank's worst case scenarios, or of a global drill by IMF or the BIS, advanced tests conducted under this wider risk perspective require plenty of preparation. They also call for a good deal of educated guesswork, expressed by means of hypotheses and scenario settings. Such hypotheses must be instrumental in representing stress conditions, so that:

- Undesirable results of a crisis are unearthed,
- Unintended consequences are highlighted, and
- Monetary policy makers, as well as regulators, are provided with an emulation of extreme real-life events.

A clear advantage of this experimental approach to the study of adversity is that it promotes *proactive management*. Two examples are presented in this section, extending on the discussion in section 5.5; that of the aftermath of piling up credit risk, and the effect of very low interest rates over an extended period.

One of the earliest pieces of evidence available on a government and central bank orchestrating massive transfer of liabilities from the private banking sector to a new entity dates back to the early 1990s. From November 1992 to April 1993, as the Scandinavian banking crises widened, the Swedish krona went into freefall, losing 20 per cent of its value. In March 1993, S&P slashed its credit rating on Sweden's $14 billion debt.

It was not the Kingdom of Sweden that risked bankruptcy. Rather, the credit crisis centred on some of its bigger and better known banks, in sympathy with similar events in Norway, Denmark and Finland. Not unlike their Japanese colleagues in the 1980s, Swedish bankers had overplayed their hand.

All three major Swedish banks, Skandinaviska Enskilda, Nordbanken and Handelsbanken, were hit hard by non-performing loans, and by some of their investments which had turned sour. To save the day, the Swedish government appointed a task-force to analyse Nordbanken's (the former PK Banken) loans portfolio, and associated investments including real estate, and then to propose a remedy.

The government focused on Nordbanken because it was partly owned by public interests. The solution was *Securum*,[5] incorrectly nicknamed by financial analysts as a 'bad bank'. Securum was not a bank; it was a holding, a government-owned enterprise capitalized with 66 billion Swedish krona.

- That money was paid to refinance Nordbanken.
- In exchange, Securum took over all of Norbanken's non-performing loans, most holdings and all real estate.

The mission given to Securum by the Swedish government was to manage these holdings and slowly liquidate them. In a fire sale such assets might have brought between 30 and 40 per cent of book value. Through excellent asset management, supported by high technology, Securum did much better than the 75–80 per cent recovery target which (according to experts) it had been assigned by the government.

Securum's lesson has not been lost on central bankers and governments. In the first quarter of 2006 came a fairly bizarre announcement that with the support of the Treasury and the Federal Reserve System, the bond industry was setting up an emergency back-up bank. Its purpose was to step into the breach if one of the two clearinghouse banks for US Treasury bonds and bills sales failed.

These US banks were said to be faced with severe problems. (In New York, rumour had it that the Bank of New York or Morgan Chase might need support.) This *New Bank*, as it has been called, existed mainly on paper, but it was ready to move in and take over the operations of banks that might not be able to clear their overnight positions. In this case, the New Bank:

- Will be operating from the damaged institution's physical headquarters,
- Will be using their employees, and
- Most importantly, will be supported by Federal money.

That is not exactly how Securum did its business, but neither is it a totally different model. The concept is basically the same, that of a new entity which, like *deus ex machina*, lifts a fallen institution, rather than allowing it to drift towards the abyss.

On 28 February 2006 an article in the *New York Times* stated that this had merely been a precaution in case of a terror attack, or similar catastrophe. However, it also mentioned that such takeovers could be triggered by sudden legal problems or a severe credit downgrade. At Wall Street, insiders suggested that the treasury and

Federal Reserve really targeted the preliminaries of a major banking crisis, probably triggered by:

- The collapse of one or two major hedge funds, or
- Some other catastrophic event, such as the near collapse of the three major banks of Iceland in early 2006 because of the *carry trade*.

This is the second example of being ready for an extreme event that may precipitate a crisis. For starters, conceptually the carry trade is a rather straightforward global transaction. Hedge funds, speculators and investors borrow fresh liquidity at zero or near zero interest rates, available on the Japanese yen, and then channel it into any kind of high-yield, high-risk assets. When interest rates rise, this house of cards collapses.

A massive global carry trade has been one of unintended consequences of zero interest rates in Japan, in the late twentieth and early twenty-first century. For some time, this was a prosperous enterprise for those who engaged in it, but in 2006 negative reports by Fitch, the rating agency, pointed to Iceland's 'unsustainable current account deficit and soaring external indebtedness'. This created a stampede, with speculators trying to get out through the same door, and the country's banks crashed.

- All profits from the Icelandic carry trade over the last two years were eliminated in just two days, and
- As foreign capital flows reversed, they put the country's three largest credit institutions in an impossible condition.[6]

Since the bursting of the equity bubble in 2000, very low interest rates have, also, characterized the dollar and the euro. In this case, one of the unexpected consequences has been that, starved for yield, pension funds, insurance companies and other institutional investors, as well as consumers:

- Significantly increased their risk appetite, shrinking the interest rate premium for junk bonds to a bare minimum, and
- Went in a big way for alternative investment through structured financial products, with all that this entails in complexity of investments and high risk.

It would have been proper that before keeping interest rates at their lowest level in the last five decades, and doing so over many years, the Federal Reserve as well as the European Central Bank had undertaken a drill to study the longer term aftermath of such a decision. All stakeholders – governments, bondholders, stockholders and bankers – should have participated in this drill, and for every class of stakeholder risk and return should have been examined.

5.8 The nature of worst case drills is polyvalent

In his foreword to *The Art of War Gaming*, Admiral Thomas B. Hayward says that, during World War II, Admiral Nimitz exhorted the value and utility of war games, as they applied to the ultimate execution of the Pacific War. A major reason for Nimitz's appreciation of strategic war gaming was the fact that a certain scenario of action could be repeated a great many times before being put to the test.[7]

Paraphrasing the famous remark of Charles Wilson, former CEO of General Motors and American Secretary of Defense ('what is good for GM is good for the USA'), what is good for the military in terms of simulation and experimentation is good for industry, business and finance. Some real-life cases are examined in this section, starting with insurance. The theme is what could go wrong with simulation.

In 1994, the Northridge quake laid homeowners' losses on insurers that greatly exceeded what computer models had told them to expect. Yet, the intensity of that quake was mild compared with a worst case scenario typically run for California. Critics who looked at this exercise said that the failure was in accounting for compound effects.

What many model developers, as well as insurers, do not always understand is that a truly terrible year in insurance coverage is not conditioned by one type of risk. Worst case scenarios must have polyvalence. This has been taught on many occasions, particularly by hurricanes, such as Katrina and others in the second half of 2005. Not just one, but a tandem of hurricanes ravaged Louisiana, Mississippi and other states of the south-eastern USA. Experts advise that in the insurance business coverage is not a possibility but a certainty:

- The only real question is when the catastrophe will occur.
- Therefore, experimentation should be on timing, with coverage provided for a supercatastrophe, a fact that is not yet widely appreciated.

A similar statement is valid about systematic risk, leading to major financial losses for a single institution. Tandem event coverage is not typically embedded into the artefact by model makers. Yet, not only the likelihood of an event, but also the tandem of similar events, should be carefully examined, along with sources of cash needed to cover claims.

Experimenting on cash for coverage presents complexities of its own. In the insurance business, the assets that will provide necessary cash flow may be liquid but subject to market risk. Asset allocation is the key. Based on statistics by Swiss Re,[8] Figure 5.2 shows that in the USA:

- Life insurance companies have only a very small part of their portfolio in equities, while in the UK this share is an order of magnitude higher.
- However, US life insurance companies have smaller annual losses than UK life insurance companies. Still, capital losses continue to be a present danger.

In the 1990s, across the G-7 nations, booming stock markets created very favourable financial conditions for life insurers. Companies with substantial equity investments prospered. By contrast, the global equity decline of 2000–2002 abruptly changed this environment. The bursting of the equity bubble:

- Created extraordinary capital losses for some life insurers, and
- Hit particularly hard the British firms who held large equity positions.

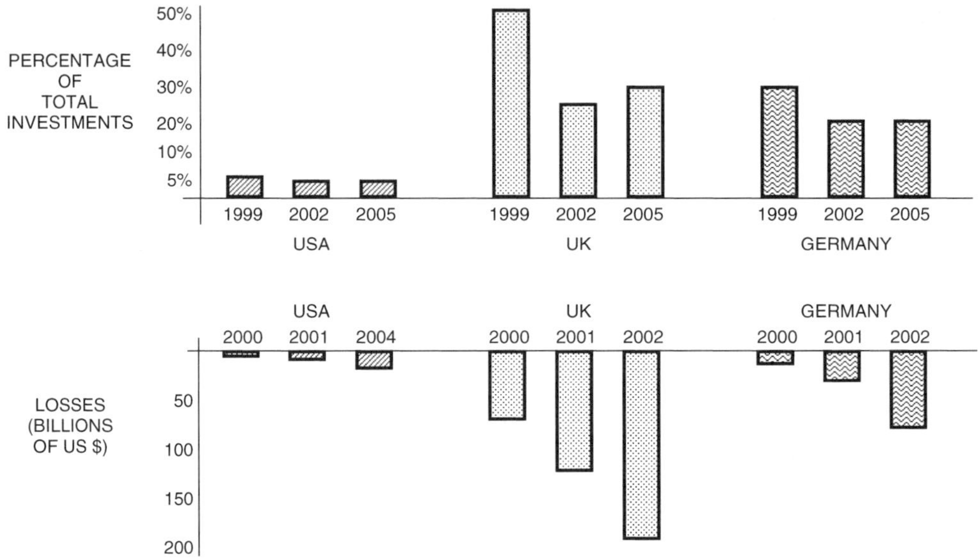

Figure 5.2 Investments in equities and losses faced by life insurers (statistics by Swiss Re)

An a priori drill on equity risk might have saved a torrent of red ink, because whether losses were large or small, no life insurer was left unscathed. Yet, companies continued betting on the stockmarket year after year, time and again being burned. This is an ideal environment in which to apply worse case analysis, with data based on real life.

The insurers' equity investments are not the only capital at risk. Traditionally, insurance companies invest a large chunk of their assets in real estate and most of the rest in debt instruments. While bonds in the portfolio can be sold fairly easily, usually without major discount, property comes in lumps and can be hard to unload to pay claims due to a natural or human-induced disaster. Therefore, insurance companies should all have an interest in conducting worst case drills that test, at the same time:

- Concentrations of risk,
- The likelihood of catastrophic events, and
- The pattern of liquefaction of assets.

Account should also be taken of correlation effects associated with exposures, which are often introduced by a policy of balancing different types of risk. The evaluation of risk factors should include expected and unexpected losses, recovery rates, interest rate risk, foreign exchange risk, historic default rates and other factors associated with credit risk. As Figure 5.3 suggests:

- The risks confronted by the modern enterprise are expanding.
- Today, practically every portfolio has concentration risk, even if senior management assures the stakeholders that there is practically none.

A recent example on concentration exposure is provided by the market for home mortgages by banks that cater to high-risk borrowers. The Mortgage Bankers

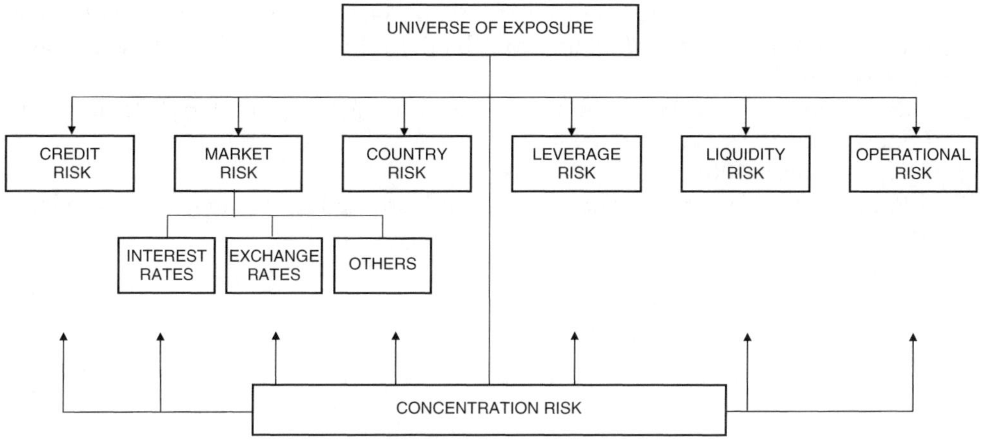

Figure 5.3 The risks confronted by the modern enterprise keep on expanding

Association reported that at the end of June 2005 an estimated 13.4 per cent of US home mortgages were contracted to borrowers considered most likely to default. Since the size of the US residential mortgage market is $7.6 trillion, this means that $1.09 trillion on home mortgages are likely to default.[9]

Those who would be hurt the most are not necessarily the banks who issued such loans, because most mortgages are packaged into securitized pools, with bonds issued against them. Published statistics indicate that the number of bonds backed by these high-risk loans more than doubled since 2001, to $476 billion. A worst case drill should address the aftermath of two types of leverage:

- The home mortgages themselves, and
- The bonds issued against the pools of mortgages; therefore, the losses to be suffered by bondholders.

Manufacturing companies, too, have much to gain from worst case drills. At General Electric, which in 2001 saw earnings grow 11 per cent, to $14.1 billion, CEO Jeffrey R. Immelt expressed concern that the downturn could still affect the company: 'We are doing our business planning as if 2002 is going to stay tough the entire year',[10] he said. In the background to this statement was the fact that a tough year is always a useful reference.

Notes

1. D.N. Chorafas, *The Real-time Enterprise*, Auerbach, New York, 2005.
2. D.N. Chorafas, *Alternative Investments and the Mismanagement of Risk*, Macmillan/Palgrave, London, 2003.
3. D.N. Chorafas, *International Financial Reporting Standards and Corporate Governance. IFRS and Fair Value Impact on Budgets, Balance Sheets and Management Accounts*, Butterworth-Heinemann, London, 2005.

4. Committee on the Global Financial System, *A Survey of Stress Tests and Current Practice at Major Financial Institutions*, Bank for International Settlements, Basel, February 2001.
5. D.N. Chorafas and H. Steinmann, *Database Mining*, Lafferty Publications, London, 1995.
6. EIR, 31 March 2006.
7. P.P. Perla, *The Art of War Gaming*, Naval Institute Press, Annapolis, Maryland, 1990.
8. Swiss Re, Sigma No. 1/2006.
9. EIR, 30 December 2005.
10. *BusinessWeek*, 25 February 2002.

6 Technology strategy for advanced testing

6.1 Introduction

This chapter summarizes a spectrum of concepts that affect information technology (IT), and the support it can provide to an advanced testing methodology. The text explains why leadership in technology is now looked upon as a means of survival of the fittest; the reasons we should move forward as the epochs of IT continue to change; what is meant by a real-world enterprise architecture, and how to develop it; and the contribution of strategic planning to IT's deliverables.

6.2 Managing a successful technology effort

Chapter 1 introduced the reasons why only high technology can effectively support advanced testing. Developing successful IT solutions is a challenge that extends far beyond classical approaches with information systems. Ask any head of finance, research, engineering, manufacturing or new venture development whether he or she can operate successfully without having a state-of-the-art technological infrastructure. Many questions loom on the horizon of IT re-engineering:

- Where does one begin?
- How should one decide on which technology to invest in?
- What is the best way to marry critical business choices with the right technical choices?

The solution to a horde of problems can be approached through different angles. Therefore, a thorough study of alternatives is necessary. Guesswork is not acceptable, because very often the high priests of technology make totally wrong guesses.

'I think there is a world market for maybe five computers', said Thomas Watson Sr, IBM's founder, animator and chairman in 1943. 'There is no reason anyone would want a computer in their home', suggested Ken Olsen, president, chairman and founder of Digital Equipment Corporation in 1977.

Conversely, judgements on the effects of IT on corporate life are often tremendously optimistic. 'By the turn of this century, we will live in a paperless society', predicted Roger Smith, chairman of General Motors, as late as 1986. By contrast, other prognostications are very pessimistic. 'There is not the slightest indication that nuclear energy will ever be obtainable. It would mean that the atom would have to be shattered at will', Albert Einstein said in 1932.[1]

Here are some other examples of misjudgement by experts and by companies for which they work. 'This telephone has too many shortcomings to be seriously considered as a means of communication. The device is inherently of no value to us', stated a Western Union internal memo in 1876. Seven decades later, in 1949, the *New York Times* commented, 'The problem with television is that the people must sit and keep their eyes glued on a screen; the average American family hasn't time for it'.

These and more quotations from well-known people and firms document that there are no *self-evident truths* in IT. Every advanced system has to be conceived, designed, evaluated and tested for reliability, cost and performance; and every study should be analytical, factual and documented.

In IT, analysis should be followed by design. To a considerable degree, system design is a process of problem solving and, as such, it requires orderly thinking. Training in orderly thinking starts with the right priorities. Questions to be asked and answered in an able manner in order to set priorities include:

- What is the problem?
- What is the salient issue associated with this problem?
- What is aimed at by the solution to the problem?
- What are the critical factors in this problem?
- How do these factors vary with the intensity of sought-out solutions?
- How many resources (time, money, personnel, equipment) should be committed?
- What will be the return on investment (ROI) from this commitment?
- Can we accelerate ROI if we change the priorities?

Distinguishing between high and low ROI is an important ingredient of good governance. It is also a test of the soundness of the company's enterprise information system design. The job of evaluating ROI can be performed in an able manner if there is:

- A clear understanding of business dynamics, and
- A properly chosen corporate strategy, which should be served by IT.

Focused queries similar to those of the above eight bullet points have to be asked and answered in any design work, and in every product development effort. Among themselves, critical queries confirm the fact that, in the coming years, more intellectual effort will be organized:

- Around the problem to be solved,
- Than in connection with traditional functions, such as production or marketing.

Technology can be instrumental in supporting the search for answers. Therefore, if we do not invest in new technology we will not compete successfully in a rapidly developing market. If for no other reason, this is true because our competitors do not stand still. Technology investments in the financial industry have more than one purpose; among the most important are:

- The management of risk,
- Improved business processes,
- Enhanced products and services, and
- Low-cost, far-reaching delivery of services.

Properly used, technology assists in steady quality improvement, and this promotes effective use of testing tools, by increasing their effectiveness. High technology also supports the use of detailed methodology for study and research, as well as for evaluating the performance of testing tools.

Fifty-three years of work with communications and computers since 1953 at UCLA suggest that information systems should not be seen as a heap of sand, its grains being software routines and hardware devices. Neither should the IT solution be designed as discrete islands of applications. The keywords are:

- Integration, and
- Seamless pass-through.

Integration and seamless pass-through will not happen by chance. They have to be designed from the IT's drawing board. This is the function of the enterprise architecture, which is covered in section 6.6. Moreover, the architectural design should be prepared by the user organization, not by the vendor, and it must be followed by decisions on technology sourcing.

- What are the real system requirements needed to sustain a first class technology base?
- How can we ensure that the realized solution fulfils the desired qualities for advanced testing?
- Where will we acquire the technology products needed to remain competitive in the future?
- What are the prerequisites to continue strategic management of our IT supply chain, in today's rapidly changing markets?

It is likely that the sought-after technology will lead to a complex system. Contrary to complex models, however, which are still at early stages of development (see Chapter 1), over the past fifty years experience has been acquired on how to design, implement and maintain complex computers and communications systems. The ability to overcome complexity is now looked at as a test of survival of the fittest.

6.3 Innovation and survival of the fittest

In 1859, Charles Darwin published his famous book *On the Origin of Species*, in which he practically stated that only those able to adapt to the environment will survive. In 1872 Darwin improved upon his theory of survival of the fittest by taking a holistic approach. What he said on the second occasion about survival can be applied to market behaviour, because the market resembles a biological system.

The difference is that in nature evolution in action takes millions of years to bear fruit. By contrast, a modern economy evolves not in million of years but in weeks, months and years, with innovation acting as the accelerator. In terms of competition, the ability to create value brings both an organization and a person ahead of the curve. Keys for survival are:

- Steady innovation,
- Technological prowess, and
- Effective control of risk, to avoid falling off the cliff.

Product innovation in the financial industry must be both imaginative and rapid. It should also be accompanied by an advanced methodology to control exposure, and by first class technological support, as mentioned in section 6.2. Progress in the use of technology should target both the enlargement of business opportunity, through innovation, and the control of risk.

The emphasis on creativity and a novel design strategy is not limited to financial products or computer systems. Practically all fields of endeavour are open to it, if, and only if, a person or a company has the right culture. In 2006, the World Economic Forum in Davos, Switzerland, included an unprecedented twenty-two sessions on innovation. Some themes were:

- Building a culture of innovation
- Making innovation real, and
- What creativity can do for you.

The highlight of these conferences has been *thinking for a living*, which fits hand in glove with both finance and technology, but also extends to a myriad of other domains. This new emphasis reflects the fact that companies with a need for cultural change can no longer generate value by competing only on:

- Cost, and
- Quality.

To be ahead of competition, they need a new customer-centric and design-based management methodology. In turn, this requires *changing mental models*, as part of a strategy of business transformation. It also carries with it the need for a change in the nature of tests being performed:

- From traditional,
- To advanced, with the possibility of still moving forward.

It should also be appreciated that at no time is innovation and change a once-only affair. If evolution is prerequisite to fitness, adapting to a process of change is a cultural issue that has a great deal to do with survival of the fittest. This runs contrary to the legacy approach, followed by people and companies intent on conserving the past.

Quite often in IT applications, renewal of 'this' or 'that' subsystem is much more constrained than forward looking, stressing present pressing needs rather than opening perspectives to the future. This is counterproductive, because it results in longer term advanced applications being overlooked. To avoid the trap of falling behind in IT, self-respecting companies have to invest a greater degree of energy than ever before in anticipating developments in the marketplace:

- Applications should be marked by the ongoing rapid change in machines and software, and
- In a rapidly changing market environment, it is prudent to prognosticate developments and implement changes for the future.

Living in the past almost cost IBM its life. After being one of the most well-to-do companies of the 1960s and 1970s, IBM fell hard. In the 1980s, the slide was hidden because the company was still making annual profits of US $8 billion to $9 billion a year.

The year 1990 was capped by $11 billion in profits. This seems to have blurred the vision of John Akers, IBM's chief executive officer (CEO). He could not conceive that the era of the mainframes was over. Yet, financial analysts had pointed out that if Akers did not do something soon in repositioning his company, IBM's profits would be zero the next year. Indeed,

- Profits were zero in 1991,
- Profits were minus $9 billion in 1992,
- Profits were minus $5 billion in 1993, and
- In the next four years IBM lost a total of $23 billion, more than any US corporation had ever lost, except for General Motors.

IBM has been able to turn itself around only because Lou Gerstner, its new CEO, knew how to manage change.

There is also a counterexample, where innovation has kept profits streaming into a company's coffers. Coca-Cola is a company that, many people think, has made nearly all of its fortune from a single unvarying product for more than a century. This is untrue. Coca-Cola is relentlessly innovative and able to diversify its bets among different product lines:

- Its management does not think that creativity has to be just in the arts and sciences, and
- For this reason, it encourages creativity in staffing, strategy, branding and the diversification of business processes.

Whether they are in technology, finance, pharmaceuticals, beverages or any other sector, well-managed companies appreciate that innovation is a style of corporate behaviour. To be innovative, one must be full of new ideas, embrace change, take risks and accept that there will also be failures. Seen in this perspective, innovation permeates a wide swath of organizations, and it makes a difference in terms of deliverables.

Contrary to what many people think, innovation is not just spending money, on research and development (R&D) or on trying to find the latest gimmick; the culture of innovation correlates poorly with R&D spending. For some financial analysts, the relation between R&D dollars and perceived innovation is downright perverse. As a research project by the author in mid-1990s revealed:

- Pharmacia Upjohn was spending over 18 per cent of revenues on research, more than almost any manor company in any industry,
- But in terms of deliverables, in 1996 that high research spending pharmaceuticals company ranked 339th in innovation.

While without investments there will be no new products in the pipeline, throwing money at the problem produces no commendable results. The reason is that the R&D budget may be misdirected, products stay too long in the laboratory, competitors decream the market or the whole corporate climate may be unsupportive of innovation.

Good ideas are kept in the time closet when a new creative culture espoused by the CEO conflicts with an outdated managerial approach, still embraced by large sections of the company, and the board does not have the guts to clean out its house. When he became Chrysler's CEO, while the company was sliding into bankruptcy, Lee Iaccoca was mindful of this possibility; therefore, he was set on executive renewal.

- Chrysler had thirty-five slow-moving vice-presidents when Iaccoca took over.
- Of these, only one was left two years later, as a result of a profound staff turnover, which brought in new blood.

Mirage Resorts of Las Vegas provides another example of how far brilliant ideas go. What made it a star in innovation and in overall reputation in its heyday was CEO Steve Wynn's simple but creative ideas. 'When someone walks into the Mirage, you can never tell if he is going to drop $500 at the tables, or $100 000', said Wynn. His $475 million Treasure Island casino hotel was the first designed to generate more revenue from non-gambling sources than from gambling. It was run on an enviable 99.4 per cent occupancy rate, which was an innovation in the hotel business.

Innovation in information system design uses the latest and most cost-effective hardware and software to improve the efficiency of deliverables and swamp costs. A study by this author for a global financial institution in the early 1990s documented that the cost of acquiring a Teradata computer was about equal to the monthly cost of an IBM mainframe including DB2 rental. This efficiency was obtained for equal storage capacity, but with the added advantage that:

- Teradata provided for greater reliability in imagining information elements,
- Whereas DB2 was a plain relational database management system, a big consumer of cycles, but a provider of no redundant data images.

At about the same time, in two other financial industry companies, mainframes were replaced by client-server solutions.[2] At the time, this was an innovative system design. In the aftermath, the reliability of the aggregate was increased, while (in total budgetary terms) costs dropped by an impressive 82 per cent. The lesson these references teach is that cost-effectiveness should dictate the nature of IT solutions and of innovation.

6.4 A phase-shift technology strategy

The examples given in the last paragraphs of section 6.3 have been a phase shift in system design. *Phase shift* means a radical change in the characteristics of a given processor system or in a person's behaviour. A simple example from physical sciences is when ice melts or water turns into steam. A more complex example is the infrastructural change necessary to face market forces, which is often a phase shift.

For instance, airports had to be thoroughly restructured for jet travel, the rapid increase in the travelling public and the requirements of a service economy brought about by rapid transport. Similarly, there are fundamental phase shifts in finance and economics, such as the change from a regulated business environment to a market economy.

The proper study of phase shifts is an integral part of the management of change. For example, analyses connected with the behaviour of people include behavioural information indicating clinical phenomena to be observed in the foreground, as well as infrastructural changes in the background. All studies on phase shifts should incorporate an outline of:

- How the unfolding of an ongoing process is expected to lead to business opportunities, and
- What constraints may be forecast, conceivable risks and ways to keep them under control.

One of the curious aspects of business life, which impacts on innovation and on the company's ability to deliver, is an inability to manage change, which increases the risks.

A repetition of the past will not necessarily generate income in the future. This is a fundamental business principle that is not really observed in information science, where sometimes:

- Thirty years of experience in computer applications
- Is nothing more than one year of experience repeated thirty times.

The so-called *legacy solutions*, which can still be found in the majority of IT shops, are deadly when the company wishes to follow a course of product innovation and a policy of advanced testing. By contrast, a phase-shift IT strategy will leverage the skills of information scientists across the enterprise, by designing systems for the future.

Designing for the future means anticipating end-users' technological requirements and meeting them *ex ante*. It also involves scaling advanced technology and releasing it in increments, rather than one large chunk that is too far removed from the way in which the bank's own professionals, and its clients, currently think and work.

As far as innovative design is concerned, attention should be paid to the effect of changes at a systems level. Modifications to software and hardware may range from relatively modest alterations with respect to current operations, to grand, ambitious goals. The keywords with system changes are:

- Predictability of aftermath, and
- Thorough training of both system specialists and end-users.

An integral part of the training should be to appreciate that, contrary to what has been thought to be the case over five decades of computer use, the main object of computing is foresight, insight, analysis and design. It is not the automation of numerical calculation, which is secondary objective.

This, too, is a phase shift in thinking. Foresight and insight lead to better decisions, and to more timely responses to ongoing challenges. In three short sentences, Alfred P. Sloan gives an excellent example on the need to be ready and react quickly, when describing how General Motors avoided the aftermath of the Depression of 1929–1932 suffered by other companies:

- 'No more than anyone else did we see the depression coming',
- 'We had simply learned how to react quickly',
- 'This was perhaps the greatest payoff of our system of financial and operating controls'.[3]

This is also the most important payoff of modern management, because it provides technology, and advanced technology is the best friend of timely and accurate financial control, all the way from auditing to stress testing. At every level of the organization, managers and professionals should be supported by technology that is ahead of that of their competitors.

Based on a research project undertaken by the author in the mid-1990s with a major international bank, Figure 6.1 shows the way in which the IT budget was allocated at the three basic structural levels of the organization, before the study (left-hand scale). The board decided that this had to change, but that those who decided which solution to follow should be the end-users, not the IT specialists. This was the scope of the study. On the right-hand side of Figure 6.1 the new allocation of IT money is shown:

- Over a transitional five-year period, and
- As a goal after the transition has been completed.

The lesson to retain from this study is that the status quo in money allocation for IT, and in the whole system's infrastructure, must be challenged. Challenging the foundation of our experience and know-how is a rewarding enterprise. 'History shows that the premise on which the phone system was built is now being challenged', said Robert Kahn, one of internet's fathers. 'Its whole design is based on the typical call being about three minutes long'.[4]

This is the often encountered aspect of legacy solutions. As the user environment changes and new technologies move in, they become technical aberrations. With

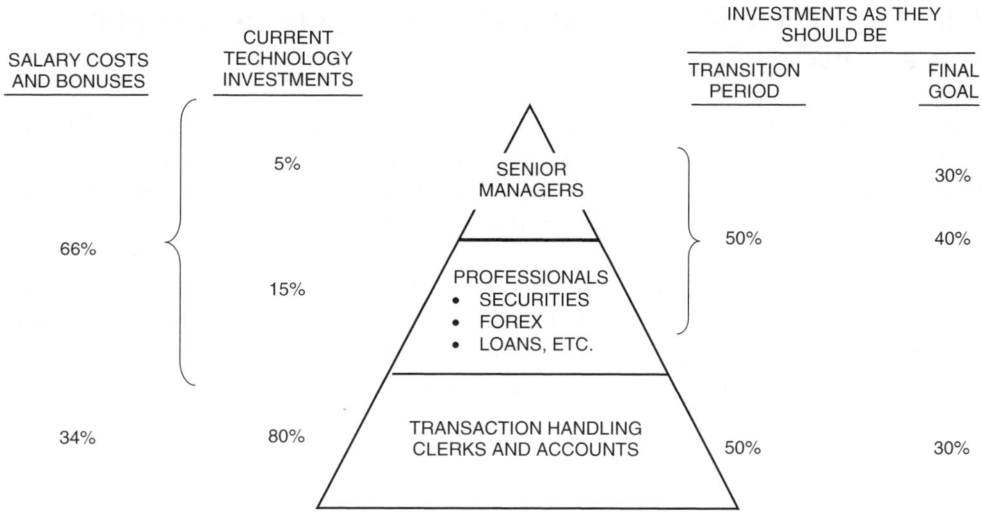

Figure 6.1 Capital allocation for information technology by major organizational level

the internet, users may be staying on the line for hours. Therefore, the demand for local dialling bandwidth is increasing sharply. There is no way that the telephone companies can recover investments in new facilities to handle it, while continuing to invest in, and run, the existing plant.

The best remedy is to create imaginative but unconventional solutions. This issue recurs time and again. In the late 1880s, one of the drivers of AT&T's research and development in long-distance telephone technology was the imminent expiry of key patents in 1894. AT&T had foreseen that by the end of the 1890s there was going to be intense competition in telephony and this did, indeed, occur.

However, even the right sort of foresight can be in one channel, neglecting other channels of development. For instance, the telephone pioneers did not foresee the profound effect that their new medium would have on *sociability*. They envisioned it as something of limited aperture, like Thomas Watson Sr thought about the computer (see section 6.2). In fact, the old internet also looked that way.

- Today, the internet is being used for terrorist content, such as posting on websites 'Paris burns'. (After the uprising in Paris suburbs in October/November 2006, French and other fundamentalists posted pictures of burning cars, shops, depots and schools on the internet.)
- Tomorrow, every device with an electricity supply in it will be connected to other similar devices, through the web.

Brian Arthur thinks that the rise of the railways can tell us a great deal about what is happening with the internet. It can alert us to how information superhighways are changing the whole topology of society, and the impact on countries, by connecting markets and permitting new levels of regional specialization. As a result, many new small centres of innovative expertise are emerging, and with them new sorts of content from daily life, such as 'Paris Burns'.

6.5 Re-engineering information technology is not an option; it is a 'must'

Thomas Edison invented the lightbulb in 1878, but it was not until the 1920s that many factories with all-electric lighting were built. Similarly with IT, companies migrated to a more rational use of computers and communications not in the 1950s when the business use of computers started, but in the mid-1980s, which was a long time lag.

When they first established a computer centre, many companies preferred to operate in ways emulating processes already known from electrical accounting machines and punched card equipment. Much later, as their operations became more complex, firms who were well managed changed their approach. They:

- Moved away from centralized mainframes, towards distributed client-server environments, and
- Revamped their software solutions, improving the productivity of analysts and programmers, and incorporating knowledge engineering artefacts.[5]

Since the mid-1980s, the choice of application domains with knowledge engineering support has included mapping the expertise existing in the organization; providing for data analysis and interactive presentation, to increase the span of control; serving as 'assistant to' artefacts tracking personal productivity and performance; restructuring legacy applications with the aim of making them more efficient and up to date; and opening up new fields for the implementation of computers and communications, which legacy approaches could not tackle.

By the late 1990s, a thorough reorganization of software solutions, along with the use of knowledge-enriched tools, became the mark of distinction, in IT, of top-tier firms. One thing to be retained from the meeting between this author and Dr Gordon Bell (and there has been many an interesting hindsight) is his statement that the new technology that will have a major effect on the economy for some time is simply not there. This can be seen from projects in the laboratories. By contrast, Bell said, companies have a great deal of work to do in:

- Pre-architecturing their applications, and
- Developing new, competitive, intelligence-enriched and trustworthy solutions.

This is not yet in the general conscience, which is a pity because IT money is spent on pseudoproblems. Yet, given the present position in computers and communications technology, almost everything currently required can be achieved by establishing a real-time basis for:

- Tracking transactions,
- Managing risks, and
- Doing advanced testing procedures.

Any company wishing to achieve a competitive advantage, and obtain good IT ROIs, must remove the old legacy constraints. Simply stated, the problem of modernizing IT solutions needs to be solved. To do so, means a return to the fundamentals. In the 1950s, data processing meant:

- Punched cards, with eighty columns, and
- Electrical accounting machines.

This eighty-column constraint passed into the Univac, IBM's 701, 702, 650, then Systems 360, 370, and so on; and it is still present, particularly with mainframe installations. For this reason it is estimated that only 5–10 per cent of disk storage is being used effectively. Much of the rest is spoiled, because legacy software still uses punched card images.

By no stretch of the imagination does it make sense to repair thirty-year-old applications software, or even older routines. Yet, this is precisely what a horde of companies continues to do. In a meeting with a major British bank, the client information officer (CIO) said that he has to use twenty-five-year-old graduates to maintain programs written before they were born. He then added that an able solution to IT's renewal must start with:

- New concepts that bring along with them new departures,
- A new system design that is flexible and adaptable to changing customer requirements.

The British bank's CIO added that the requirements posed by these two bullet points can be satisfied only through cultural change. The fact that renewal of the IT infrastructure is a 'must' needs to filter down through the organization.

This took place in the USA in the late 1990s, and began happening in Europe with a delay of nearly ten years. A 2006 study found that over the next two years between 40 and 60 per cent of European fund managers (but not all firms at large) will be:

- Changing their IT, and
- Re-engineering their back office.

One of the basic reasons is that during the go-go 1990s most investment banks only did some patch work for the year 2000 (Y2K) problem. Then, they distributed their profits to partners and shareholders, rather than reinvesting in their IT. Finally, it became evident they cannot afford to fall behind in technology forever. In order of importance, the main costs they are faced with are:

- Restructuring of procedures,
- Rebuilding of IT system capabilities, and
- Contingency planning for IT-based business disruptions.

Figure 6.2 provides a bird's-eye view of the most important issues around which the re-engineering effort centres. The better managed firms no longer do patch work;

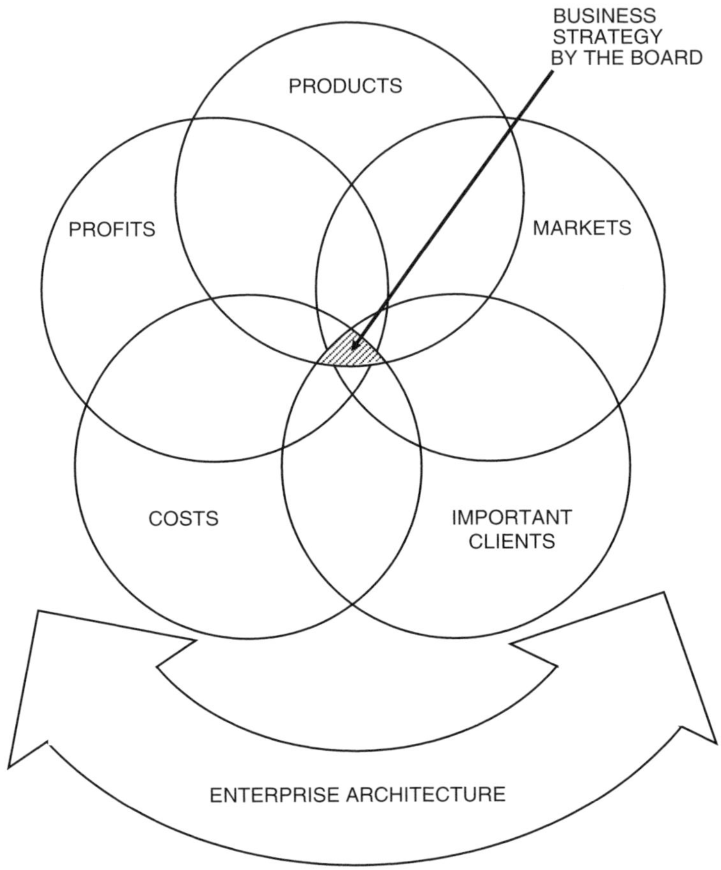

Figure 6.2 Re-engineering must be both holistic and detailed, and the resulting system should support the firm's business strategy

instead, they focus on the real origins of serious IT problems. The Y2K problem of the late 1990s provides an example. Contrary to widespread belief:

- It was not *primarily* a problem with obsolete software and old computers.
- It was a broad systems issue, which haunted companies for several decades, but it was kept in the time closet because technology was mismanaged, while lavishly financed.

Even today, billions of lines of computer code are running simultaneously on top of successive layers of heterogeneous machines. This is true all the way from high-level applications to low-level operating systems, database management systems and teleprocessing routines.

Incompatible systems fail to work together in a stable, predictable fashion, and new solutions work badly in tandem with the old. The result is plenty of errors, system interruptions, low effectiveness and client dissatisfaction. The 2004 failure of IT systems at British Airways (BA) provides an example. In mid-September

2004, the introduction of new computer programs at BA's engineering operations resulted in:

- Aircraft being unavailable at the start of the day, and
- Supply chain breakdowns, which held up routine overnight maintenance and turned flight schedules on their head.

In the aftermath, BA cancelled 966 flights at London Heathrow until the end of November 2004. This has not been the only computer glitch at BA. In September 2003, software failures, also at Heathrow Airport, ended in:

- Luggage being misdirected and lost for three days, and
- Flights delayed for up to four hours, leading to a torrent of passenger complaints.

While these examples characterize failures resulting from a mix of new and old computer programs, other notable software failures occur in the aftermath of new developments that have not been stress tested. A case in point is what currently happens in autoelectronics. Technological progress has meant that embedded autoelectronics has become a hot issue, but:

- Software problems are reaching epidemic proportions, and
- Dealers are very often unable to trace the causes, particularly those of intermittent error messages.

For example, a brand new Citroën spent a full three months back with the dealer following sudden and unexplained battery drain, intermittent failure of telephone and entertainment systems' voice control, and failure of some of its warning instruments. Lawyers are now involved in a messy, unpleasant case in which there will be no winners.[6]

Studies conducted by the German Centre for Automotive Research point to electronic glitches as being the main reason why cars break down. This does not happen only with automotives. It is a widespread problem because classical software tests are not able to debug sophisticated programs. Advanced tests are necessary, just like the stress-testing procedures necessary for risk control.

6.6 Projecting and implementing an enterprise architecture

As stated in section 6.5, it often takes a long time for financial and industrial companies to switch to new information system solutions, characterized by the latest advances in engineering; and it takes even longer to revamp systems and procedures. Does that mean that this text takes a pessimistic view of IT prospects? Not at all. The fact that leaders move ahead and laggards pay the price of their failure to change their culture is everyday business. As Figure 6.3 demonstrates, over time:

- The leaders move ahead and they reap all of the benefits.
- In contrast, the IT laggards pay all of the costs.

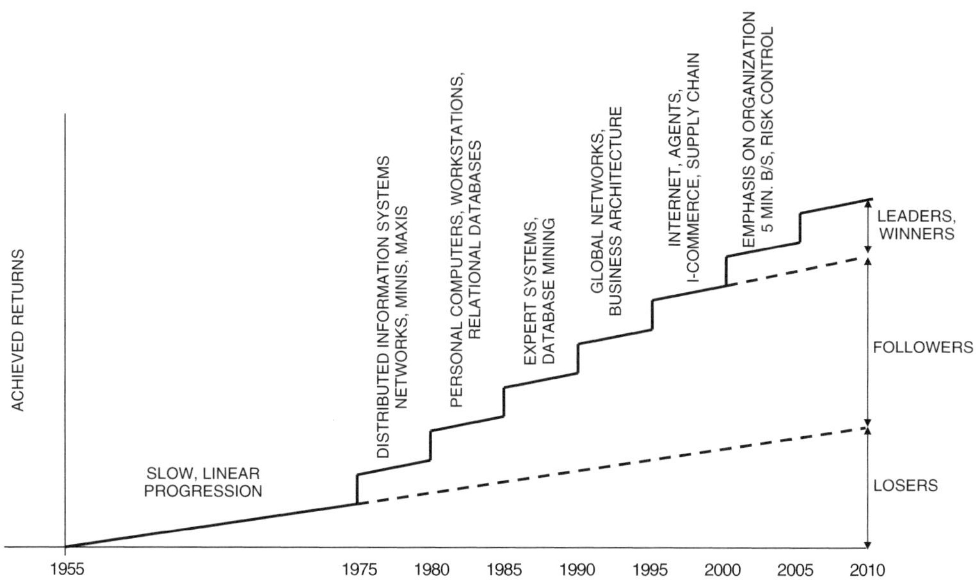

Figure 6.3 Only the leaders capitalize on the advances of technology. The laggards simply pay the costs.

An integral part of this perspective is the fact that today's technology makes feasible solutions that were not even dreamed of in the mid-1960s, when legacy systems grew roots. Any information in the world can be digitized, from accounting books to financial results and engineering files. Then, it can be effectively analysed. This is part of the bigger, better IT picture. The bottleneck is in two places:

- The obsolete IT culture, and
- The inflexible system architecture characterizing most past and current solutions.

The architectural reference is important, as the following paragraphs will demonstrate. No company should accept the vendor's architecture as its own, as happened in the past with system network architecture, system application architecture and many others. User organizations should design their own architectural solution, which fits in a flexible way their own information results.

This need for flexible and effective custom-made approaches can be satisfied by the design and implementation of an *enterprise architecture*. Among successful firms, the goal assigned to an enterprise architecture is to permit not only current results, but also an ongoing adaptation of the IT infrastructure to:

- Changes taking place in the business environment, and
- Internal organizational restructuring, necessary to confront market forces and senior management needs (a practical example is given in section 6.7).

In this sense, the enterprise architecture serves as the framework for improved computing and communications services. Typically, a focal point of such services is to address the information needs of managers and professionals who, in the past, received too little, too late, in IT support. Figure 6.1 presents an example on the difference between ongoing and best practices. The enterprise architecture's key products are:

- Structural flexibility, and
- Adaptability to changing information conditions.

Over the past fifteen years, conditions characterizing the input, throughput and output of information systems have changed quite rapidly, as the sophistication of support required by end-users has increased in leaps and bounds. Sustaining market competitiveness requires a landscape of advanced technology implementation, which offers extended business opportunities, from new product design to greater market appeal and holistic risk management. As Dr Gordon Bell remarked, many applications:

- Are not a computing problem,
- They are a database mining problem; *who got what*.

Crucial issues are both the availability of rich databases and instantaneous responses provided in a user-friendly manner. A change towards greater flexibility and better accuracy in data-mining is important because so far many companies do a miserable job tracking business opportunities, and they are even less successful in controlling risk. Hence, there is a need for designing and implementing the company's *personalized enterprise architecture*. This is usually done at one of two levels:

1. One approach, which is more common but less exciting, is that of a tactical method focused on handling mainly transactions.

Its objective is to operate in a more or less structured environment, assisting middle to lower management, and other personnel, by taking over routine jobs, thereby improving their productivity. With this approach, the support provided to senior managers and top professionals is limited.

The reason for this restricted view is largely historical. Years ago, when systems architectures were developed, the focal point was transactions. Even at this lower level of complexity, however, implementation and maintenance of an enterprise architecture require our company's current and projected *business strategy* to be clearly stated, including answers to critical questions: What is our company's value-added advantage? What do we commoditize? How do we bring our products to the market?

2. The other approach to enterprise architecture addresses the unstructured information environment, and has as its principal objective first class support to senior management.

This architectural approach is more sophisticated, and it provides a more significant contribution to the company and hence a much better return on IT investments. An advanced architectural solution positions a firm on higher ground than its competitors, by:

- Capitalizing on its value-added advantages in terms of products and services, and
- Making feasible a policy of dynamic planning, which itself requires models, experimentation and real-time interactive reporting.

Based on design breakthroughs attained by the Oxygen project at the Massachusetts Institute of Technology (MIT), Figure 6.4 shows the frame of reference of a modern enterprise architecture. The concept underpinning its design is polyvalent, and every one of the axes of reference is crucial in terms of obtaining commendable results.

Apart from flexibility and adaptability to changing conditions, a focal point of the enterprise architecture should be that of making *knowledge work productive*. This is the great management mission of the twenty-first century. Experience in knowledge-enriched system solutions suggests that the best approach to the able management of skills and know-how is to:

- Provide the necessary infrastructure: networks, data-mining, expert systems and training programs,
- Enable people to find for themselves what they need to know to improve their effectiveness, and
- Track individual performance in mental productivity, as IBM does by profiling its 50 000 consultants.

Moreover, another principal role of an enterprise architecture must be that of aligning the implementation of technology with a company's *business strategy*. This

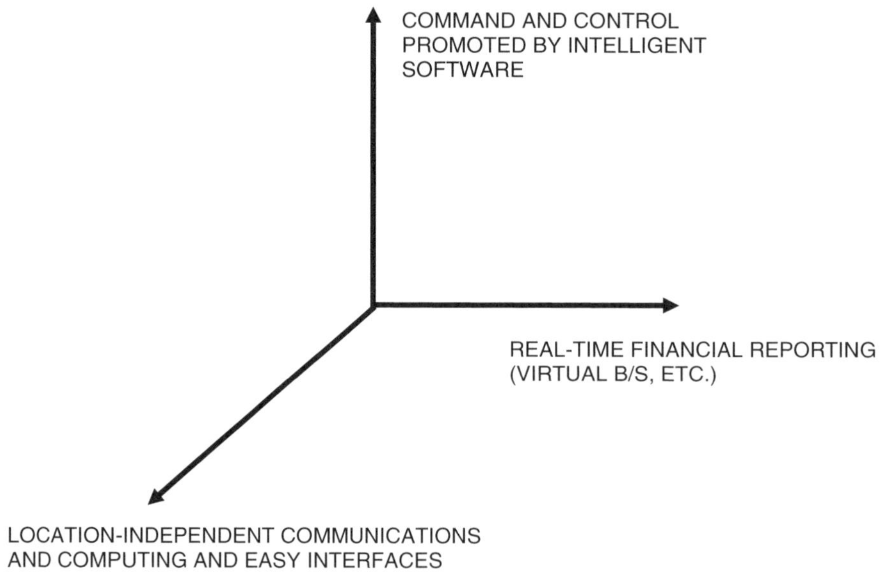

Figure 6.4 Frame of reference of the new enterprise architecture that may result from schemes such as MIT's oxygen project.

can be effectively done when technological investments target pragmatic problem solving and use state-of-the-art solutions.

Another key objective set by well-managed companies is to make technology serve *innovation economics*. Properly studied and implemented, architectural solutions help in the use of dynamic planning to transform the enterprise. Entities with experience in this endeavour suggest that this means two things at the same time:

- Being able to define and redefine the enterprise architecture of the firm in a business environment in full evolution, and
- Providing life-cycle management of IT, and of all other investments that target the firm's ability to stay competitive.

As with any enterprise, there are also architectural risks. Therefore, it is important to draw the attention of system designers to the practical limitations of theoretical approaches, which do not account for technological risk in an adequate manner. This is particularly important in connection with operational environments that must be trusted, but evidence on their dependability is thin.

In addition, because technology advances so quickly, the knowledge of designers, developers and users must increase dramatically over time, to reflect such rapid evolution and take advantage of it. Even though the fundamentals do not change as quickly, many system components do. This adds to system complexity.

- In theory, system complexity can be hidden from view,
- In practice, inadequate understanding of new and exceptional cases, which may happen, can result in disasters (see section 6.5).

New risks associated with system design come up steadily, largely because of a lack of understanding of the idiosyncrasies of architectural solutions, a variety of mechanisms and human interfaces, and also the way in which technology is used, and surrounding administrative chores that must be considered part of the overall system.

6.7 Strategic planning should account for information technology's deliverables

In the author's professional experience, over nearly fifty years, with regard to competitiveness and ROI the best results are obtained when the board and CEO spell out in clear terms the risk of falling behind in IT. Laxity by senior management increases that danger. Therefore, the CEO must establish in no uncertain terms:

- The IT strategy of the entity, and
- The timetable for deliverables, as well as the expected quality level.

Under no condition should the board and CEO accept a timetable dictated to them by the CIO, or any other person in a position to put the brakes on IT developments. In addition, IT strategy should serve first and foremost the *corporate strategy*. For instance, in today's business environment supply-chain integration has become a necessary feature, and the same is true of message-based integration, which has led to the development of messaging architectures. Among other important references:

- Core business values have taken the high ground,
- There is very much a trend towards back to basics,
- No new killer technologies are in sight, and
- High-performance applications have become a cornerstone to being a successful business player.

An example of a successful application of an enterprise architecture, the concept of which was discussed in section 6.6, is *enterprise risk management*. This is a relatively new concept, and is still largely under development, but tier-one financial institutions have begun to implement it. For instance, a properly designed enterprise architecture is the infrastructure for aggregating operational risk information:

- Channel by channel,
- Region by region, and
- Legal entity by legal entity, across the firm.

Centralized risk management and enterprise risk management are different concepts, but the latter can assist in making the former more effective. As the Basel Committee points out, many banks and complex financial institutions have centralized the responsibility for risk management in a single group or legal entity.[7] This organization is responsible for:

- Developing policies for credit risk,
- Monitoring credit risk exposures across the whole firm, and
- Reporting on credit risk wherever it occurs in the institution.

To be carried out effectively, this activity requires information that is accurate and available in real time, as well as models and tools that permit analysis and response in a matter of minutes. Providing such information on any instrument, desk, business units and area of operations, is a mission performed by the enterprise architecture.

The CEO and his or her immediate assistants also derive other benefits from the enterprise architecture, cost control and ROI being examples. Return on investment increases when, for instance, there is synchronization between IT activities and the firm's marketing strategy which is, in many cases, one of the top preoccupations of senior management. A crucial question is: What is our marketing strategy in promoting new competitive products? Figure 6.5 provides options along three lines of reference:

- Niche products, where innovation and analytics are king,
- Unique products where, quite often, advanced technology helps to decream the market, and
- Mass-market products, where the crucial factor is low cost, and therefore the company must be a very efficient designer, vendor and distributor of products and services.

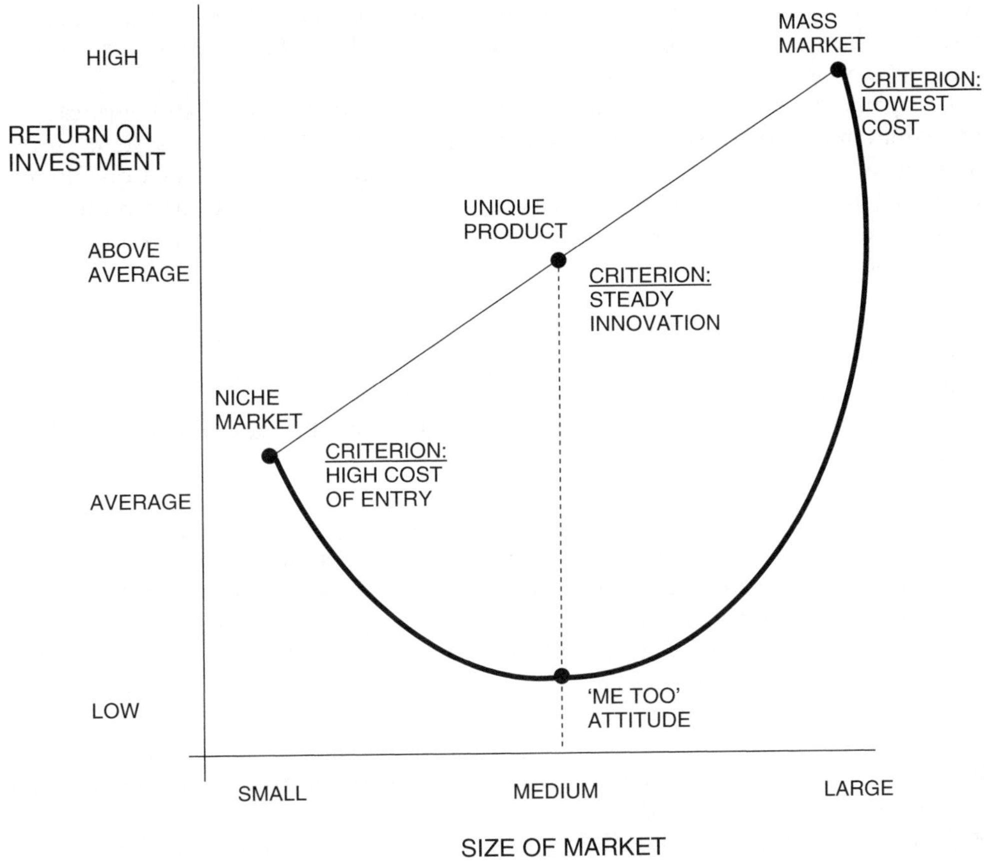

Figure 6.5 The omega curve for achieving results in product leadership

As Figure 6.5 shows, the least rewarding strategy is the 'me too' attitude, which has too many followers among poorly managed firms. 'Me too' is the wrong strategy for any company, in any place and at any time; it is on a par with the failure to capitalize on high technology, in spite of significant investments that the firm is making in IT.

Moreover, as noted in the previous sections, at no time should strategic planning for IT underplay the importance of ROI. Areas of attention that are currently fuelling IT investments, and where first class solutions provide opportunities for ROI, include:

- New value creation,
- Corporate customer care,
- Regulatory compliance,
- The control of risk, and
- Stress-testing procedures.

Still other areas with opportunities for a good ROI are leveraging of existing channels through any-to-any networks, supplier consolidation, consolidation of banking relationships and cost containment. All things being equal, IT projects targeting short-term tangible returns provide more rewarding financial benefits than the rather vague long-term projections on potential benefits.

Companies that are careful in developing and implementing an IT strategy also pay special attention to treasury management. They revamp the treasury system, throw home-grown software out and bring in top-tier packages. Beyond treasury operations, plenty of the security orientations of IT applications in the twenty-first century are expected to emphasize *identification* (ID). In finance, the ID challenge is an ongoing trend. The goal is to identify:

- *Risk*, per instrument, counterparty, transaction, desk and trader,
- *Cost*, per unit of production and distribution,
- Profit and loss of each *customer* relationship, and
- *Recognized*, but not realized, gains and losses for every business unit and any desk, as well as the entity as a whole.

In terms of risk identification, an effective enterprise risk management solution must be highly disciplined, aligning strategy, policies, systems, processes and people, with the goal of evaluating assumed and inventoried risks anywhere in the world. This requires an advanced enterprise architecture (see section 6.6), as well as a high degree of system integration. It should come as no surprise that among tier-one firms today, between 60 and 80 per cent of new technology implementation is in system integration, aiming to:

- Provide a sound platform for further product promotion, risk control and account management functions, and
- Be the core of capital allocation, profit and loss accounting, and longer term survival in a highly competitive market.

The message from these two bullet points is that the top goal in IT is not just applications, but *solutions*. Today, market leaders are characterized by solution development and implementation, as well as by *solution selling*. This goes beyond the value-added concept, because differentiation is based on the ability to use not only machines but also people's intelligence to the full extent.

Research conducted in the first years of the twenty-first century confirmed earlier projections that IT specialists would have to work harder. A market compensation study on IT by the Gartner Group found that technology departments should expect workloads to increase by 50 per cent in the coming years.[8] They did.

There is no alternative to working smarter and harder. As reported in the *Chicago Tribune*, a survey of 1400 CIOs across the USA showed that only 15 per cent intended to add staff, while 4 per cent would reduce staff. This has been the lowest net increase in personnel in the survey's seven-year history, while the IT work to be done went up significantly. The same survey also found that the safest jobs were those whose work history demonstrated contributions to the bottom line.

Demonstrable contributions to the bottom line are never provided by following the beaten path. *Imagination* and *alternatives* are the answer. Therefore, every manager, as well as every designer, should ask him- or herself: 'What are *my* alternatives?'

The search for alternative solutions stimulates the imagination and provides different channels to reaching the target. Able solutions in system design require *insight* and *foresight*. These are also the criteria promoting a well-done job in stress testing.

Notes

1. *Communications of the ACM*, March 2001.
2. D.N. Chorafas, *Beyond LANs. Client-Server Computing*, McGraw-Hill, New York, 1994.
3. A.P. Sloan, *My Years With General Motors*, Sidgwick and Jackson, London, 1965.
4. *Fortune*, 3 March 1997.
5. D.N. Chorafas and H. Steinmann, *Expert Systems in Banking*, Macmillan, London, 1991; D.N. Chorafas and H. Steinmann, *Intelligent Networks. Telecommunications Solutions for the 1990s*, CRC Press, Boca Raton, FL, 1990.
6. *European Automotive Design*, September 2004.
7. Basel Committee, Joint Forum, *Regulatory and Market Differences: Issues and Observations*, BIS, Basel, May 2006.
8. *Communications of the ACM*, February 2002, Vol. 45, No. 2.

PART 2

Stress testing probability of default, loss given default and exposure at default

7 Models and procedures for the study of volatility patterns

7.1 Introduction

The objective of this chapter is to introduce *volatility* and its aftermath. Volatility underpins many stress tests associated with creditworthiness. After defining volatility, and underlining the need to keep it in perspective in all financial analyses, the text provides references to sophisticated volatility models, but also draws attention to the prevailing algorithmic insufficiency and procedural insufficiency. Among the practical examples provided is a case study with General Motors Acceptance Corporation (GMAC).

7.2 Volatility defined

Volatility is the quality of being changeable, flighty, explosive, diffusing, unstable, erratic, mercurial, temperamental or unpredictable. Whether talking of credit risk, currency exchange risk, country risk, interest rate risk or any other exposure, the amount of risk and return increases in volatile markets. A particular feature of volatility developments in prices and yields of assets is that they are both:

- Stress factors, and
- Stress indicators.

They are stress factors because volatility underpins the dynamic evolution of dispersion of asset price movements. Within relatively tight bounds, such a dispersion of price movements can be seen as 'normal'. Nothing moves in a straight line. By contrast, high volatility leads to outliers, extreme events and stress patterns. A more practical definition of *normal volatility* than that of tight bounds is that fluctuations in prices are taken as normal if kept within a formation characterized by investor expectations regarding their future dispersion. This is true of:

- Equities,
- Debt instruments,
- Currencies, and other assets.

Volatility is measured by the extent to which asset prices fluctuate over a given period. Typically, this is expressed by means of the standard deviation, or beta, of changes of logarithmic asset prices. Alternatively, volatility is computed using an exponential weighted approach, which results in more recent observations receiving higher weighting.

Beta is a frequently used volatility metric. It is a measure of a dependent variable, for instance a market's sensitivity to the movement of a defined independent variable. The independent variable is often a well-known index such as S&P 500. The movement in either direction, up or down, over a given period, is important. For example, a beta of 1.2 means that a given equity's volatility moves 20 per cent more than the S&P 500, up or down, over the period being measured.

The fact that volatility underpins a portfolio's profits and losses tends to mask the effect of portfolio management. For this reason other ratios have recently been introduced as metrics. By targeting a specific asset's contribution to a portfolio's added value, these aim to abstract from the volatility characterizing the overall market. These metrics are known as:

- Alpha, and
- The information ratio (IR).

Both are measures that break down portfolio returns into their most important components, quantifying the value added after removing any effect of the portion of returns generated by correlations.

- Alpha measures the average return added after removing the effect of correlations (through betas) with stocks and bonds.

One way to think of alpha is as the metric of correlation-adjusted excess return. Essentially, this is seen as the return from the portfolio manager's skill only, with the return from the market removed.

- The IR is the ratio of this alpha divided by the residual analysis, volatility, also known as tracking error volatility. This is obtained from a regression analysis.

What the IR essentially provides is a risk- and correlation-adjusted measure of value added. A positive level of IR tends to indicate that value has been added to the portfolio. Experts suggest that, as studies of active managers show, IRs greater than 0.5 are indicative of top-quartile active management in long-term investing, but not in all types of trade.

Volatility also characterizes credit risk. Indeed, *credit volatility* is inseparable from the way in which the market works. It is a function of prevailing market conditions and of credit rating upgrades or downgrades (practical examples with credit volatility are presented in sections 7.7 and 7.8). In principle:

- Credit derivatives help in providing a better insight into credit volatility through the separation of credit risk from market risk,
- At the same time, however, credit derivatives do not do away with the synergy existing between credit risk and market risk, and resulting correlations.

A good example is the boom–bust cycle of the economy, when bankers start worrying about credit quality and overlending. When economists and analysts see more volatility ahead, banks start to regret lending some of the money, especially money lent to hedge funds where the collateral is often illiquid derivatives.

To a significant extent, but not always, credit volatility can be viewed as the result of differences of opinion among market players. Because different market players look in different ways at the *creditworthiness* of a given entity, credit derivatives can also be used as a means of price discovery for what many specialists consider to be pure credit risk, because:

- Their price is derived from the underlying price of an asset, and
- The underlier may be a pool of loans, plus the credit volatility factor.

What the issuer does with loans securitization is to swap the default of partial or full payout, if the pooled assets fail. Credit guarantors reduce the default probability embedded in credit derivatives. But guarantors cannot prevent the synergy of credit risk, market risk and their volatility factors, which influences ratings through its impact on exposure.

Central to all of these processes is the notion of *credit assessment*: establishing creditworthiness and a repayment pattern, on the basis of information about the client. An additional element is that the synergy of credit volatility and market volatility demands predictions on both:

- General economic and market indicators, and
- The debtor's specific risk in repaying the debt.

Predictions require measurements and models. In the general case, volatility outside what might be characterized as normal limits creates *stress conditions* in financial markets. This is described as pressure exerted on economic players by uncertainty, and changing expectations concerning profits and losses. The level of financial market stress ultimately depends on the:

- Degree of vulnerability of the financial system,
- Scale of the shock producing uncertainty regarding future losses,
- Change in risk appetite brought by high volatility, an increase in bankruptcies, a sharp drop in value of a major currency, and other factors.

Different metrics are used to measure volatility. One of them is *realized volatility*, constructed by summing squared changes; for instance, of the overnight interest rate calculated for each five-minute interval between 9 am and 6 pm. For technical reasons, this exercise focuses on the logarithm of this measure, whose strength and weakness is that it is based on statistics derived from events that have happened, but are in the past.

Past volatility is an important statistic inasmuch as a look at time series characterizing past years helps in makes estimates about future events. For instance, the time series may have a cyclicity, thereby showing that sharp upswings in volatility may occur as an accompanying feature of particular stress situations in financial markets.

For this reason, as mentioned in the opening paragraphs, the pattern of fluctuations in asset prices is both:

- A stress factor, and
- A stress indicator of what may take place.

For monetary policy, investment and other reasons, it is important to know *future volatility*. As a proxy in gauging the degree of uncertainty prevailing in markets, and providing information on future volatility expectations, *implied volatility* is used.

Bloomberg defines implied bond volatility as a series representing nearby implied volatility on the near-contract generic future, rolled over twenty days before expiry. This means that twenty days before the expiry of the contract, is made a change in the choice of contract used to obtain the implied volatility:

- From the contract closest to maturity,
- To the next contract.

Theoretically, in bond and equity markets implied volatility should tend to rise when a business cycle expansion moves into a mature phase. At that stage, uncertainty begins to increase about coming monetary policy tightening. In addition, the onset of rising interest rates typically leads to higher volatility, because of growing uncertainty about future interest rate increases. By contrast, implied volatility for foreign exchanges may increase for many reasons, country risk being one of them. It can also be affected if business and interest rate cycles are not synchronized.

Unlike measures of implied volatility derived from options prices, realized volatility does not impose restrictive assumptions on the distribution of volatility measurements. In addition, unlike other possible metrics of fluctuation in prices, realized volatility is independent of the mean level of the overnight interest rate, its downside being that, as stated, it is not forward looking, although it can serve for inference purposes. It may:

- Underestimate the risks of possible valuation corrections, and
- Downplay the reappearance of high volatility.

At the same time, a level of volatility that mirrors the fundamentals is a hallmark of efficient financial markets. Its pattern tends to reflect the intensity of change in underlying fundamentals, and the resulting assessment uncertainty regarding future developments. In this sense, the role of volatility is polyvalent, and stress tests help to uncover some of the secrets of volatility.

7.3 Keeping volatility in perspective

Section 7.2 stated that *volatility* is the quality of being changeable, temperamental or unpredictable. It also defined what volatility means in terms of market risk and credit risk. Moreover, reasons have been provided as to why volatility is not altogether unwanted. While wide price swings in a day, or a week, are unsettling, along with them come profit opportunities. This duality means that regulators, financial analysts, investment advisors and investors must:

- Always keep volatility in perspective, and
- Focus on both the opportunities and the risks associated with periods of market uncertainty.

One of the mistakes that many investors make in evaluating market volatility is thinking only in terms of points, rather than both points and percentage price changes. A 100-point decline in the industrial average in 2006 does not mean the same as it did in 1988, because the market is so much higher. A 100 per cent point correction, from a high of 2722, represents a decline of 3.7 per cent in the Dow. In early 2006, a 100-point drop from the 11 000 level would have represented only a 0.9 per cent decline.

Investors should also keep in mind that daily corrections of 1 per cent or more, and weekly corrections of 4 or 5 per cent or more, in a stockmarket index are not unusual. Taking the Dow Jones as an example, since World War II there have been several periods in which the industrial average declined by 10 per cent. The mean volatility during this period was approximately 25 per cent. It takes courage to buy stocks in a down market, but:

- The best buying opportunities often come during the market's downturn;
- However, during market corrections the majority of investors are frightened away.

In a way fairly similar to the less than factual appreciation of market volatility, investors have a lag in accounting for changes in credit risk volatility (see section 7.2). When the market is on the upside, credit ratings tend to improve, but on the downside they have a nasty habit of deteriorating rapidly. This is not always embedded in investment decisions.

Both measuring and prognosticating the volatility in financial markets is one of the pillars of good governance. The use of knowledge engineering helps in improving portfolio performance. As Figure 7.1 shows, a volatility forecaster is one of the most important modules of assets and liabilities management (ALM); just as important as the liquidity forecaster, and a stress-testing component which helps in making realistic estimates of annualized returns.

Good use can be made of the Chicago Board of Trade Volatility Index (VIX), which measures share movements implied in stock index options. However, it should be kept in mind that, as with all models, VIX is not full proof. In 2005 and the first four months of 2006, VIX was at record lows:

- In early May 2006, it predicted that S&P 500 would move by less than 1 per cent, up or down, over the next month.
- Then came the hecatomb of equities and commodities in the week of 15 May, and VIX was proved wrong by an order of magnitude.

There are reasons for such occurrences, not the least being the fact that financial models are still in their infancy. At a meeting in London, Fitch, the independent credit rating agency, drew attention to the fairly complex background of market risk volatility, its estimate and its projections.

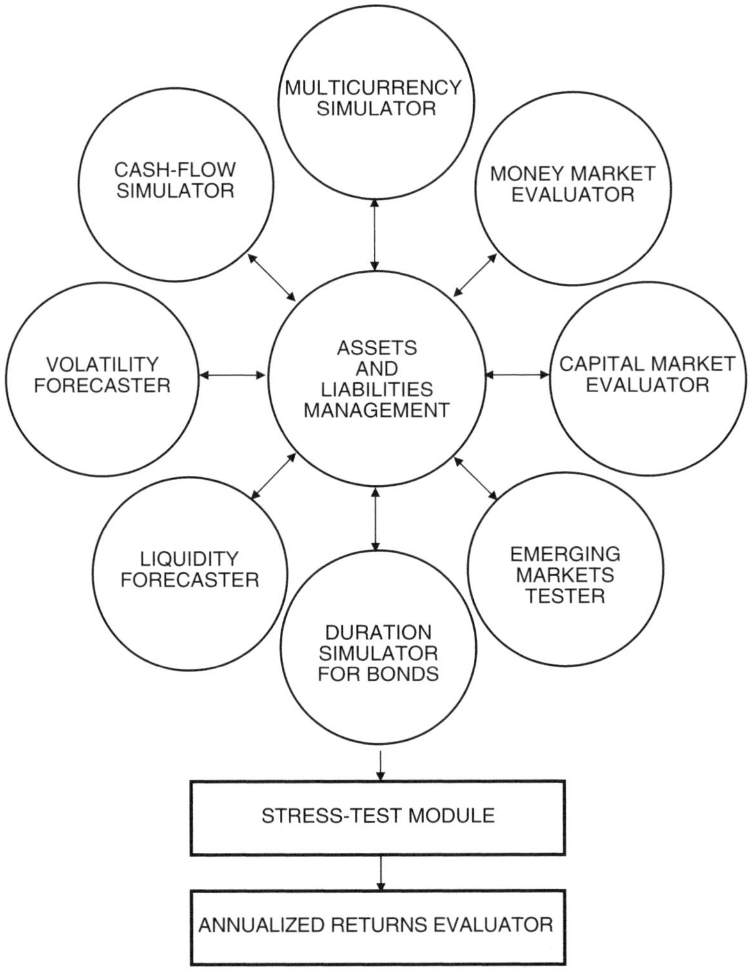

Figure 7.1 A family of portfolio management models for ALM

One of the commercial banks subsequently visited by the author also stated that, according to its research, because market volatility varies by instrument, its impact on a fixed income portfolio is uneven, depending on the portfolio's composition. For instance, an institution may have more standard interest rate swaps than structured instruments, because standard interest rate swaps are much more liquid.

Still, in spite of model risk, whether focusing on credit risk or market risk, volatility ratings are very important. A good way to think about them is that they are largely subjective. In the general case, they are financial opinions addressing the relative sensitivity of a security's price and cash flows to market conditions. Bonds, for instance, have two main determinant factors:

- Changes in interest rates, and
- Changes in creditworthiness of the issuing entity.

As with all scoring systems, volatility ratings do not constitute recommendations for financial transactions. Volatility ratings take no position regarding the adequacy of market prices or suitability of a given security for any given investor. Rather:

- They are opinions regarding the relative sensitivity of the total return to a range of market changes.
- Many factors, including market liquidity, interest rates, spreads and foreign exchange rates, affecting market conditions enter into such ratings.

It is also important to appreciate that volatility ratings do not predict the direction or magnitude of changes under different market conditions. Nor do they show the extent to which any particular security will perform in the future. What they do indicate is the likelihood of variations given the instrument's fundamentals.

As far as the instrument's fundamentals are concerned, usually but not always, securities with low market risk perform consistently across a range of interest rates, and are taken to be comparable to short-duration treasuries. Securities rated as having moderate market risk,

- Perform rather consistently across a range of interest rate scenarios,
- But they experience interest rate risk comparable to long-duration treasuries.

Securities with moderate to high market risk show a significant variation in performance across a range of interest rates. Therefore, they have considerable interest rate risk. In many cases they also exhibit negative convexity. Securities with high market risk are speculative, and show several risk characteristics, as well as:

- Great sensitivity to movements in interest rate and equity indices, and
- A most significant volatility in the aftermath of extreme events taking place in the market.

Extreme events and associated *unexpected spikes* due to exceptional movements triggered by unique circumstances are of great concern. The after effect of extreme events contrasts with the common notion of volatility in terms of average observed fluctuations when attempting to derive expectations regarding future volatility. Protracted phases of especially high volatility are often preceded by negative extreme events.

Extreme events are usually low frequency but high impact. As discussed in subsequent chapters, they generate market tensions and need to be qualified regarding their potential. Significant market movements have greater stress potential than sharp changes in individual share prices. While both could become the focus of investors' attention, in their perception of the market's health, sharp changes in individual share prices do not lead to a panic until they spread market-wide.

Many economists and financial analysts have tried to develop models aiming to prognosticate not only volatility but also its aftermath. As one theory has it, extreme share price slumps are frequently followed by phases of increased price fluctuations on the equity market. This is known as the *ripple effect.*

In addition, an after effect of extreme events is sharp price swings exhibiting a tendency to cluster. In such cases, market price movements are characterized by a leptokyrtotic distribution with fat tails. Also known as Hurst's coefficient, kyrtosis ensures that events at the end of the tail repeat themselves with greater frequency than a normal distribution would suggest (see also Part 1).

There is also the likelihood that extreme events, for instance in the S&P 500, will be followed by marked countermovements and phases of increased price volatility. Also present are negative tail events, such as days when the share price index falls by more than 3 per cent. These tend to be concentrated during certain periods, which is what the Hurst coefficient suggests.

Although the exact pattern tends to differ from one index to another, European and American stock indices showed pronounced spikes in the number of negative extreme events in 1987, 1998, 2002 and 2006. These years were associated with:

- Stockmarket crises, and
- Protracted phases of greatly increased volatility.

These crises were triggered by Black Monday in October 1987, the Russian crisis and descent into the abyss of the Long-Term Capital Management (LTCM) hedge fund in 1998, and accounting scandals in 2002, such as Enron, Global Crossing, Adelphia, WorldCom and others. The week of 15 May 2006 has seen major losses in all stockmarkets and commodity markets, particularly so in emerging markets and some commodities, for example copper.

7.4 Improving volatility models through heteroschedasticity

Many bankers and investors, as well as some analysts and experts in financial engineering, tend to define risk in terms of an investment's price volatility, but this is a simplistic approach that does not account for the many factors entering into credit risk and market risk. Differences in approaches and theoretical background mean that models addressing volatility have been built based on different grounds, some of which became inadequate as the:

- Globalization of market players altered the rules of the game,
- Increasing sophistication of financial instruments meant that simplistic approaches are unrealistic, and
- Big structural changes in the financial industry made earlier models of commercial banking, or other single industry sectors, obsolete.

With regard to basic mathematical tools, a valid approach to estimating the volatility is general autoregressive conditional heteroschedasticity (GARCH).[1] The terms 'autoregressive' and 'conditional' do not need explaining, whereas 'heteroschedasticity' looks like an esoteric, convoluted concept. What *heteroschedasticity* means is that the data streams, or samples of financial information:

- Do not have the same standard deviation.
- This difference in second momentum provides some interesting opportunities for analytics.

Market volatility is characterized over time by change in variance over time. Patterns of clusters known as conditional heteroschedasticity are relevant to every analytical effort aimed at prognostication, because price swings generally occur in clusters. Since volatility fluctuates over time, prognostications about future volatility should be derived using a dynamic solution.

An exponentially weighted historical volatility is frequently computed as the root of average of past fluctuations with exponentially declining weights for observations of the more distant past. Another indicator of market volatility connected with adverse price movements in equities is the level of share price index as a percentage of the maximum that is reached in a previous reference period. This is known as the CMax index.

CMax is a *stress indicator*, which is particularly useful in an environment of falling asset prices. Because the reference period includes current value, this indicator can reach a maximum level of 1. Price slumps are associated with a particularly low value. Other metrics, too, have been used as stress indicators; for instance, an increase in yield premiums on junk bonds.

Non-traditional financial research capitalizes on higher data frequency and heteroschedasticity. By contrast, lacking a sophisticated approach, classical financial analysis assumes constant volatility, which is unrealistic. Because, however, procedures and tables based on homoschedastic (same standard deviations) assumptions already exist, rocket scientists have developed devolatilization models, with *intrinsic time* τ.

- Intrinsic time, or business time, is different from clock time.
- In dynamic markets, traders have rapid responses and work without interruption. Therefore, they pack in, say, an extra thirty minutes of activities than when intrinsic time moves slowly.

There are other challenges. They come from the fact that high-frequency financial data are often negatively autocorrelated, although beyond a point autocorrelation decreases as frequency increases. One of the hypotheses is that this happens because of noise. (By definition, noise is any unwanted input.)

Heteroschedasticity is particularly found in turbulent market periods, with large and frequent changes in quotes. Turbulent periods tend to be followed by quiet periods, with small and infrequent quote adjustments. What are the origins of changing schedasticity? Hypotheses vary widely:

- Some experts consider it location specific.
- Other experts say that it is cross-locational.

Certain projects have demonstrated that schedasticity often characterizes volatility dependencies in the foreign-exchange market. The conditional heteroschedasticity, which is synonymous to volatility clustering across time, is another issue dividing experts. Basically, it implies that over a given period T:

- There is variable, heterogeneous volatility, and
- This contrasts with the classically followed model of homogeneous variance.

The GARCH approach addresses heteroschedasticity by estimating the conditional variance from historical data. In recent times, this process has been extensively used in modelling financial times series, but forecasting remains difficult. Moreover, account should be taken of the role played by:

- The noise component, and
- Sampling procedures.

Sampling is crucial in statistical design, as well as in experimentation. Other things being equal, almost all projects in financial analysis, and more generally in scientific studies, stand or fall on the quality of the samples that they use. It should therefore come as no surprise that the sample space is a major issue in the realm of this discussion. Ideally, in financial analysis and other studies, large samples are targeted, but:

- Heteroschedasticity tends to become more severe as sampling frequency increases, and
- This poses considerable difficulty in modelling financial time series and/or the aftermath of volatility.

This interaction between the need for large and frequent samples, which can be satisfied through high-frequency financial data, and the effects on heteroschedasticity has posed interesting challenges for many projects. Researchers have to account not only for tradeoffs, but also for the negative after effect of a contemplated approach. The shortcoming of the classically used equally spaced time series is that:

- Information is insufficient for analysis purposes when the market is highly volatile, but data streams are coarse grained,
- Whereas equally spaced time intervals can be redundant at times of low market activity. It looks like a no-win situation.

A reasonable conclusion from the message conveyed by these two bullet points is the desirability of a time series with more data at times of high volatility and fewer data at other times. Although no financial time series are recorded today as a matter of course in this manner, the availability of high-frequency data permits the sampling of subsequences that have equal or near equal volatility, a process essentially amounting to devolatilization.

7.5 Procedural insufficiency among financial institutions and individual investors

For every entity and for each investor, risk is what one makes it. This is true of all banks, other financial institutions, institutional investors and individual investors. Both the algorithms and the procedures followed for risk control are important for the control of exposure, but both of them are often characterized by insufficiency.

As will be shown in section 7.6, in spite of tools such as heteroschedasticity, many risk control algorithms currently used are too elementary, particularly so when confronting complex credit risk and market risk situations. Before examining the algorithmic insufficiency, however, the procedural insufficiency should be considered, because it comes first in terms of priorities.

Practical experience suggests that the right risk control procedures start with the entity's or investor's global outlook. This should range for at least the next five years or, even better, the next ten years. Such an outlook has multiple purposes. Among the more important to this discussion are that:

- It provides a view of the fundamentals underpinning market developments, and therefore investment choices, and
- It tends to use this view as a strategic framework, to aid in the disciplined evaluation and selection of business opportunities that hold promise in the future.

Outliers aside, big companies are not opportunity constrained but, in a large number of cases, they are not patient and disciplined in carefully evaluating the prospects of volatility, or in assuming and managing risk. A basic reason for this attitude is that they suppose that their financial strength and asset base will ensure their survival when adversity hits. The fate of most Japanese banks over sixteen years after the Japanese economy crashed in 1990 provides evidence that this is not true.

Even if a disciplined approach to credit volatility and market volatility estimates has existed, it is likely that it would be shattered in the aftermath of a wave of mergers. The same is true of the system of risk control that prevailed in one of the merger entities but did not fit the bigger firm. Because no two organizations have the same:

- Business strategy,
- Risk appetite, and
- Procedure of checks and balances,

a rapid succession of mergers leads to disruptions in systems and procedures, with the likely result being procedural insufficiency, from which it takes a long time to recover. *Procedural insufficiency* can be severe as far as control of exposure is concerned. (See in section 7.6 what happens postmerger with different value at risk versions.)

J.P. MorganChase, America's third largest bank by market capitalization, provides an example of merger mania. It is the product of mergers among 550 banks and other financial institutions, including twenty in the past fifteen years.[2] Bank One was its latest acquisition of a major credit institution, preceded by that of Chase Manhattan and of Manufacturers Hanover Trust by Chemical Banking, which is essentially the surviving bank under a different label.

Procedural insufficiency results from the fact that a big system is not a small system that just grew up. Big risk control systems have tough prerequisites, and they are increasingly in demand. Consolidation in American banking meant that in 2005 the top ten banks, out of about 8000, controlled 49 per cent of total banking assets in the USA. This is 169 per cent up from a share of 29 per cent in 1995. At the same time, the wave of megamergers ensured that:

- Diverse procedural solutions for risk control take time to integrate, and
- This happens at a time when banks, and other market players, are worried about deteriorating credit quality and overlending in the years 2002–2005.

It is the thesis of this book that stress testing can fill some of the gaps (although not all) in procedural insufficiency. Because they take a rigorous approach to the control of risk, stress tests highlight exposures that filter through normal tests because of gaps in risk control exposures.

A similar process of procedural insufficiency is present with individual investors, but for totally different reasons from those just explained in connection with banks. The large majority of individual investors are unaware both of the procedures that need to be followed for risk management, and of the fact that, in reality, risk has just as much to do with the investor as with the investment. How risky an investment is depends on:

- The price when bought, and what price the investor achieves when he or she sells,
- His or her financial staying power in waiting for a better price, and
- Whether the investor bothers to look at the daily and intraday price changes, making buy/sell decisions that profit from volatility.

The lack of a watchful eye is a procedural gap. Meltdowns happen because of the greed of market players (entities and individual investors) looking for unsustainable, high rates of return. This most important factor of speculation is included neither in current procedures nor in current models, which fail to account for:

- Lust and its effects, and
- Market phase shifts that impact on prices.

Typically, both risk management systems and the models underpinning them assume that bankers and investors are using money to do 'what is right', and accept a reasonable rate of return. This does not happen in the real world; therefore, it is not surprising that procedures and models are not developed in such a way that they can deliver on their promises.

7.6 Algorithmic insufficiency: a case study with value at risk

The search for metrics to measure exposure is just as important as the need to measure volatility in a way that is helpful in investment decisions. *Value at risk* (VAR), introduced as the model for regulatory reporting with the 1996 Market Risk

Amendment to the 1988 Capital Accord, is an example of *model insufficiency* in regard to measuring and controlling risk.[3]

There are several reasons why VAR provides a good background for a case study on algorithmic insufficiency. Although it came in two modes of computation, parametric and simulation, it has always been a one-size model, providing a limited market risk perspective and being based on the normal distribution.

- Short of biasing the whole concept underpinning its background, VAR cannot be extended to tail events, and this is a serious shortcoming.
- Yet, as Figure 7.2 shows, in real life the distribution of risk is leptokyrtotic, not normal, and high-impact risk events, those that really matter, find themselves at the long right leg of the risk distribution.

Value at risk is one of the better examples of algorithmic insufficiency. Part of the reason is historical. Value at risk was originally developed in 1991 by the Morgan Bank at the explicit request of its chief executive officer (CEO), as a means of informing top management about the bank's exposure, every day at 4.15 pm. It was an eigenmodel intended to serve a specific top management request, not to serve as a global standard for market risk control.

The second reason reflects the state of the art in model making in 1991. At that time, rocket science was at its beginning and, as a result, the level of simplification in financial model making was relatively high. This means that VAR is a weak model and most financial institutions have developed their own improved versions, such as GARCH-VAR and Delta/Gamma Neutral VAR, which are not regulatory. The aim

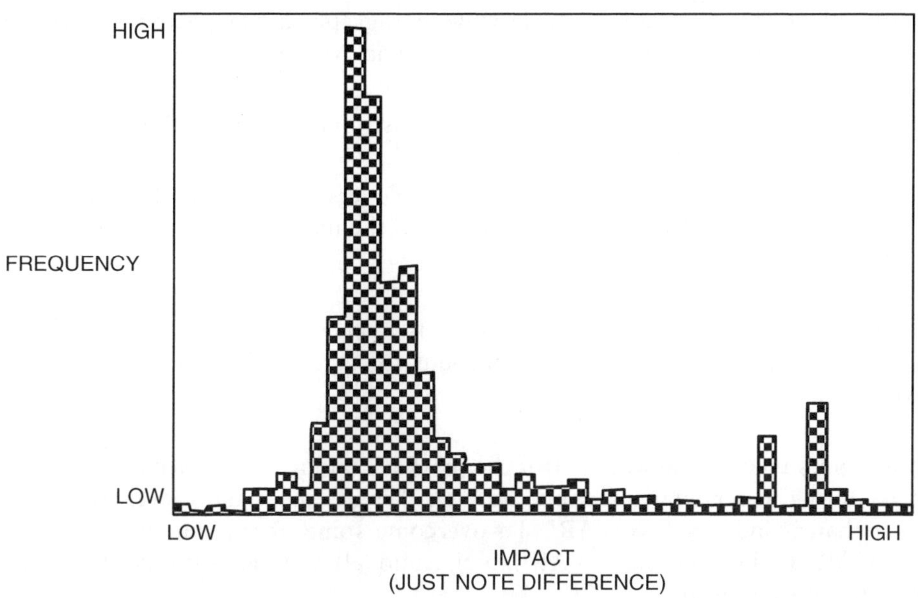

Figure 7.2 A practical example from real-life risk analysis: distribution of risk events with long leg and spikes

of such developments has been to improve upon VAR's deliverables, and this is most welcome. The negative side is that:

- Comparison between results from different VAR versions is not meaningful, and
- Companies often find themselves confronted with a sea of heterogeneous VAR models, which they continue to support and test, but from which they derive little benefit.

For instance, after the merger of Citibank with Travelers and its Salomon Smith Barney investment bank, the Federal Reserve of New York wanted Citigroup to test some seventy different VAR models for the past five years. Among other shortcomings of VAR, which have to be addressed, is the fact that:

- The model's results do not correlate with actual exposure.

In 2004 the exposure of half a dozen big and best known banks, as measured by VAR, jumped by 50 per cent over 2003 figures. Was this an indication that these financial institutions had loaded themselves with so much risk over just one year? 'No', said senior executives from a couple of these banks, 'VAR does not say how much more risk has been assumed. Other factors than pure exposure affect VAR'.

According to a 2006 article, over the past two years the amount of Goldman Sachs' value at risk on a really bad day has risen strongly. The investment bank's trading desk has more losing days than any of its Wall Street rivals.[4] Yet, overall, Goldman Sachs' trading desk makes significant profits. This is not reflected in VAR, because the model has no integrative ability.

Putting the references made in the last two paragraphs in perspective, a reasonable conclusion is that VAR is not a reliable risk metric. Moreover:

- VAR shows exposure connected with those instruments that it addresses.

This is a serious shortcoming, because it only covers between a half and two-thirds of financial products and services, depending on the institution and its business line. In addition,

- VAR says nothing about the economic consequences of exposures that it is supposed to measure, and it does not account for the likelihood of spikes and tail events.

'VAR gives incorrect assessment of the market', said a senior executive of Merrill Lynch, during a personal interview, adding, 'We see a lot more event risk in the market than is indicated by VAR'. To overcome some of the limitations, Barclays uses a GARCH distribution of VAR (an eigenmodel) and also subjects the outcome to a series of stress tests.

In the opinion of an executive of Moody's Investors Service, VAR is a rather good system, but it is not perfect in providing a single number of exposures.

During a meeting with the author, this expert pointed out two caveats connected with VAR:

1. It lacks sensitivity to events in data streams

Whether using historical information or running a simulation, such as Monte Carlo (with non-parametric VAR), an alert may not be sounded. An example is exposure to Russia in late July 1998, some three weeks before devaluation. The oncoming event could not be prognosticated through historical data. 'Intuitively one saw it coming', said the Moody's executive, 'but the model did not tell about it, putting management on guard to reallocate capital'. Yet, business in Russia had become perilous because of loans and counterpart exposure in derivatives and other deals.

2. The 99 per cent level of confidence used by VAR tells us nothing about fat tails

The 99 per cent level of confidence is utterly inadequate. The fat tails of the risk distribution may lie in the omitted 1 per cent, as so many bankers and investors discovered when market sentiment went suddenly south, as happened in the week of 15 May 2006.

Stress testing and simulation could help in this respect, but for a consistent approach to stress testing, senior bank executives must be well acquainted with stress testing and the change that it brings to the credit culture. They must also have a good background in statistical risk management rules and procedures, and have access to a rich database of historical information.

A different way of making this statement is that to improve upon current metrics of exposure, bankers and investors must pay attention to the need for a new credit culture, which is very important and is not part of VAR. In 1998, too many banks saw LTCM as market risk, not credit risk, yet credit risk loomed large. The same is true of the Russian and South Korean meltdowns, as most of the banks in the two countries, in mid-1998 and late 1997, respectively, could not deliver on their obligations. In addition:

3. VAR has been very badly misused as a sort of credit risk model in its capital at risk (CAR) and $VAR_{99.97}$ incarnations[5]

Credit VAR versions rest on weak hypotheses of similitudes, with the result that estimates are usually approximations of extremely low accuracy in computing counterparty risk. Another major fault with the credit version of the VAR model is that information on the influence of factors such as the economic cycle, geographical location, industry sector, loan maturity upon default and recovery rates is poor.

Neither CAR nor $VAR_{99.97}$ incorporates estimates of credit correlations, and this introduces more approximations. Another reason that credit VAR-type models using normal distributions do not meet requirements is that credit returns tend to be skewed. There are also miscarriages in deliverables because holding periods differ widely. They range from:

4. A comparatively short time-frame for marketable securities,
5. To much longer ones for non-marketable loans held to maturity

This magnifies VAR's algorithmic insufficiency, and it complicates the task of parameter setting. Supervisors have good reasons to be reserved when considering the suitability of VAR models for simulation of credit risk. Credit VAR is incapable of handling the profile of an institution's counterparties, yet this profile is very important in determining the appropriateness of marking-to-model credit risk.

In conclusion, the models used for volatility measurement and prognostication of trends in the nature and size of exposures are not perfect, and sometimes they are misused. Models available for the measurement of market risk are not reliable in credit risk terms. Instead, new models are necessary, such as stress probability of default, stress loss given default and stress response at default (see Chapters 9 and 10).

7.7 The volatility of credit ratings: a case study with General Motors and General Motors Acceptance Corporation

Independent rating agencies have developed volatility ratings for market risk, particularly interest rate risk, because there was market demand for this kind of product. By contrast, less effort has been expended towards model development to handle credit rating volatility, one of the reasons being that until now this was not a hot issue. This attitude has, however, changed with credit derivatives.

- If we are going to trade pure credit risk,
- Then we need an index, a rating and volatility metrics.

A credit volatility index should be able to identify securities with the same or similar rating, but from dissimilar obligors entering a pool. The pool's assets may move in the same direction and magnitude under changing market conditions, or they may exhibit their own pattern of change. Tools are necessary to highlight such differences.

A credit volatility scale is also important to high-yield bond funds, which are particularly sensitive to changes in credit risk. Such metrics and measurements started to become important after LTCM's debacle, and the concerns it raised about counterparty risk even among entities which, for several years, rated highly in their industry.

As with market risk, the challenge faced by new metrics and measures is algorithmic insufficiency. Financial instruments such as credit derivatives, which are trading on credit risk volatility estimates, require algorithmic solutions that are rigorous but also fairly complex. When credit becomes a self-standing commodity, it is wise to assign it a separate volatility factor that can be measured on a scale:

- From investment grade,
- To non-investment grade securities.

With this fairly wide range, each rating must be characterized by its own volatility distribution. It is also important to investigate when, and how, credit volatility and market volatility correlate. Based on the premise of a correlation, risk models, and early warning indicators, which take account of the prices in various markets, as well as macroeconomic variables, are becoming a 'must' for risk managers who labour to assess credit risks.

Today, rating agencies are increasingly using market price-based risk models in their investigation of default probabilities. The downside of this approach is that although market prices and credit ratings tend to correlate, they also tend to diverge. This requires rating agencies and other users to adjust their grades every time:

- New information regarding the financial situation of an issuer becomes available, and
- The volatility behind an entity's market exposure changes.

Experts believe that a risk control policy that is based on these two parts will lead to a significant change from current practices, where rating is only altered when the new credit outlook is supported by a change in the entity's creditworthiness due to structural reasons rather than to cyclical effects.

The plus side of the current practice is that it assumes a certain degree of rating stability. As such, it prevents rating changes having to be revised too frequently. However, such ratings cannot be used for stress testing unless they are reverse engineered to their fundamental elements. Reverse engineering is not a straightforward process because rating agencies base their credit ratings on a wide range of information that is not necessarily available in the public domain. Hence, several hypotheses need to be made at elementary component level to arrive at fairly documented rating changes.

Based on current trends, it can be stated that the joint evaluation of credit and market risk is, in all likelihood, the way of financial analysis in the future. On 12 December 2005, an article by the *Wall Street Journal* on the contemplated purchase of GMAC, the jewel in the crown of General Motors (GM), by third parties, had this to say on the projected transaction:

> ... So the winner of the GMAC auction might not be the party who can write the biggest check, but the one with the brains to put all these moving parts into one smooth-running vehicle.

According to the opinion of rating agencies expressed at the end of 2005, if GMAC had been independent from GM it would have qualified for an AA-rating rather than the BB junk status assigned to GM, and by extension to its auto credit subsidiary. This opinion was reflected in a Merrill Lynch study, which showed that expected default recoveries were much higher at GMAC than at GM:

- Recoveries for GMAC bondholders could exceed 90 per cent, given a near-term bankruptcy filing.
- By contrast, recoveries for GM bondholders were found to be significantly lower, below 50 per cent in all likelihood.

What might have been GM's financial gain by selling GMAC? According to estimates by investment banks made as 2005 came to a close, the suitors' bids seem to have hovered around \$11 billion, the GMAC stake's book value, calculated by subtracting a company's liabilities from its assets. Critics said that this was an incomplete measure:

- On the one hand, GMAC's profits have grown for ten consecutive years.
- On the other hand, such a transaction involves tricky legal and financial questions with many unknowns.

For instance, any bank that bought the GMAC controlling stake would need to bolster significantly its loan-loss reserves, as a result of capital adequacy rules by regulators. The irony is that capital adequacy does not apply to hedge funds, which are not regulated. Therefore, hedge funds purchasing a controlling stake do not need to bother about the volatility of credit.

If a bank bought the 51 per cent stake of GMAC, it would be expected to consolidate on its balance sheet, according to US Federal Reserve regulations. That would require billions of dollars in fresh capital to meet reserve requirements, and make it difficult for a credit institution to take on all of GMAC's share to be sold by its parent company.

This is not true of hedge funds and private equity players. Non-regulated funds could own all or part of the 51 per cent stake, in the latter case helping a regulated commercial bank in sidestepping capital requirement when it adds GMAC's assets to its books.

What about GM's probability of default? According to a 22 November 2005 Merrill Lynch study, 'Our analysis leads us to conclude the probability of a default at GM is over 30 per cent within the next 2 years... This is because the issues facing GM will likely need to be addressed within the next 2 years or so, which is what we would see as an assumed "inflection point" for the credit'. In late 2005, several analysts had been saying that:

- For GM (and possibly others) to avoid eventual bankruptcy, material changes were needed to both revenue drivers and cost structure, and
- To recover from financial difficulties GM must produce better products, which it is able to sell without the use of aggressive incentives, as well as maintain a stable market share.

It was also stated by financial analysts that a bankruptcy court filing by GM would damage the value of GMAC's car-loan business. Credit risk problems would immediately morph into market risk. In addition, there is the looming presence of the US government's Pension Benefit Guaranty Corporation (PBGC), the federal agency that backs private pension plans.

Based on counterparty grounds, the PBGC could make a claim on GMAC assets to help to shore up the car maker's massive pension liabilities. Analysts saw this move as quite likely, particularly because PBGC's fund had been devastated by massive bankruptcies in the air transport and other industries. This led to the statement that:

- For each problem fixed in the eventual GMAC sale,
- Another one crops up that may have devastating effects on the car maker's finances.

This was the position taken by financial analysts mid-December 2005. In what way had GM's creditworthiness changed five months down the line, in mid-May 2006, when this chapter was written? On the positive side, GM received much needed good news on 8 May when the Securities and Exchange Commission (SEC) approved some accounting tweaks that turned a $323 million 2006 first-quarter loss into a rare $445 million profit. But:

- GM's losses on its North American automotive operations, although halved, were still a painful $462 million, and
- GM faced a looming strike at Delphi, its bankrupt parts supplier, and former subsidiary, which could have disastrous knock-on effects for GM.

To redress the company, Delphi management was demanding big pay cuts from its American workforce. By contrast, the United Auto Workers were preparing to authorize a strike should the courts approve Delphi's request to scrap its existing labour agreements. Such a move could quickly lead to parts shortages that would halt GM's US assembly operations and car deliveries.

Moreover, by mid-May 2006 analysts expressed the opinion that while GM likes to give the impression that all its woes result from high labour, pension and health-care costs, forced on it by the unions over the years, it is management problems that have led to the current situation. One piece of evidence that management was not up to standard is the severe loss in US market share. The pension and health-care burden could be borne more easily:

- If GM had held on to the 33 per cent share of the market it enjoyed in the mid-1990s, rather than the current 25 per cent, and
- If its products appealed more to the US and foreign markets compared with those of its competitors.

By May 2006, the general opinion among analysts was that the longer GM's problems remained in the news, and the louder the murmurs grew of looming bankruptcy, the more consumers were liable to walk away. Financial analysts, investors and clients do not like companies that may eventually have to seek court protection from creditors.

Neither has the sale of GMAC gone as planned. Both of the big banks, Citigroup and Wachovia, who circled around, dropped out of competition. This left GM with only one option, that of selling 51 per cent of its financial unit, to a conglomerate led by Cerberus Capital Partners, a large hedge fund.

Immediately after the announcement on 3 April 2006 of a preliminary accord with Cerberus, the three major credit rating agencies said that they would not change GMAC's current junk-bond rating.[6] This knocked down GM's stated purpose in planning the sale: enabling GMAC to escape GM's deep-junk debt status. In addition:

- General Motors is receiving just $7.5 billion for the majority share of GMAC, universally estimated in late 2005 to be worth $11–15 billion.

One of the reasons for disenchantment by rating agencies and analysts has been that Cerberus grew to huge asset size in just a few years, as a leveraged global private equity firm. It is not the kind of major bank or financial services institution to which GM wanted to sell control of GMAC, in order to obtain cash and at the same time improve GMAC's credit rating.

In the aftermath of this announced sale, both the stocks and the bonds of GM dropped sharply in value, with GM thirty-year bonds reaching a low of 71.75 cents in the dollar. However, on 8 May 2006, GM's stock rebounded after the aforementioned favourable ruling by the SEC. But for how long will they remain so?

7.8 Risk estimates based on volatile probability of default

One of the basic reasons why stress tests of creditworthiness are so important is that, as economic and financial history teaches, the probability of default is volatile. This is true of all levels of credit rating and it can be well demonstrated through statistics pertinent to rated bonds. Typically, speculative-type bonds have both a higher probability of default and a much greater volatility, but volatility is also present with investment-type bonds. Therefore,

- Measuring the volatility of the probability of default of borrowers is important, and
- Of particular importance is volatility at a given point in time, which might be illustrated post mortem by the actual default rates in a pool of bond issuers.

As explained in section 7.2, for reasons of sound management of investments, the future volatility of probability of default is sought, using as a proxy default rates that are representative of prevailing economic conditions. Knowing the status of economic conditions helps in reflecting the short-term survivability of borrowers.

- To a reasonable extent, default rates tend to follow the evolution of business cycles, and
- A rise in default tends to coincide with economic slowdowns, while peaks in default are found at times of outright crises.

Using analytics, database mining and model technology it is possible to estimate the potential impact of volatility on default rates at large, as well as on borrowers and their instruments included in a specific portfolio. Comparisons can be made by considering sample portfolio structures, with ratings assigned to borrowers.

For inference of implied default probabilities a good proxy is the credit default swaps (CDS) market. For instance, in the case of GMAC (see section 7.7), analysts have been looking at the implied default probabilities using CDS pricing levels in the parent company. Assuming a recovery of 40 per cent, securities pricing at the close of a business day in mid-November 2005 indicated an implied cumulative default probability of:

- 20 per cent within one year, and
- 35 per cent within two years, more stringent than the figures provided by an analysis of cash in hand.

While such calculations have an element that is subjective given the variables involved such as recovery rates, they are a useful tool for investors. Just as important is the fact that, as this study has shown, the CDS curve continues to be inverted at GM. This finding is consistent with what typically happens with many troubled credits.

Tools such as CDS pricing levels were not meaningful with Basel I. Credit institutions using the standard approach at the 8 per cent level of capital requirements, which stays constant over time, had no reason to apply sophisticated approaches. The 1988 Capital Accord does not account for loans portfolio composition, whether this is characterized by:

- Diversification, or
- Concentration of credit risk.

In contrast, with Basel II,[7] credit institutions adopting the advanced internal rating-based (A-IRB) method should analyse and quantify their probability of default estimates. They must also account for the effects of diversification and concentration of credit risks. When this is done, the result tends to be a curve that is highly sensitive to assumed counterparty risk, in contrast to the straight 8 per cent capital requirements of the Basel I method.

Approaches aimed at compensating for accumulation of credit risk, and its volatility, beyond the confines of linear solutions, are typically non-traditional as far as the banking industry is concerned. However, they are becoming increasingly popular. In mid-2001, the CEO of a money centre bank announced that his institution had devised a risk management process that:

- Analyses of all the bank's long and short global positions, and
- Simulates a 2 standard deviation negative change in those positions.

This risk control model expresses the output in earnings per share for the bank's senior management, making available quantitative results to be reviewed on a daily basis.[8] Corrective measures can then be taken by senior management. Figure 7.3 presents, as an example, the translation to the right, hence to higher impact values, of a credit risk distribution.

One of the benefits that can be provided through experimentation based on the shifting of the risk distribution curve towards higher impact values is the study of different levels of limits to commitments in connection with risk transfer mechanisms, as well as to associated pricing structures. Typically, in banking and insurance entities take on nearly unlimited commitments,

- As the commitment impact threshold is raised,
- Management is provided with evidence on why it should call the whole concept into question.

A similar notion applies to risk transfer. In its Progress No. 42 Bulletin of December 2005, the Geneva Association has this to say on risk transfer in connection with reinsurance: 'A limitation of the risk transfer stands for a distribution of risks which

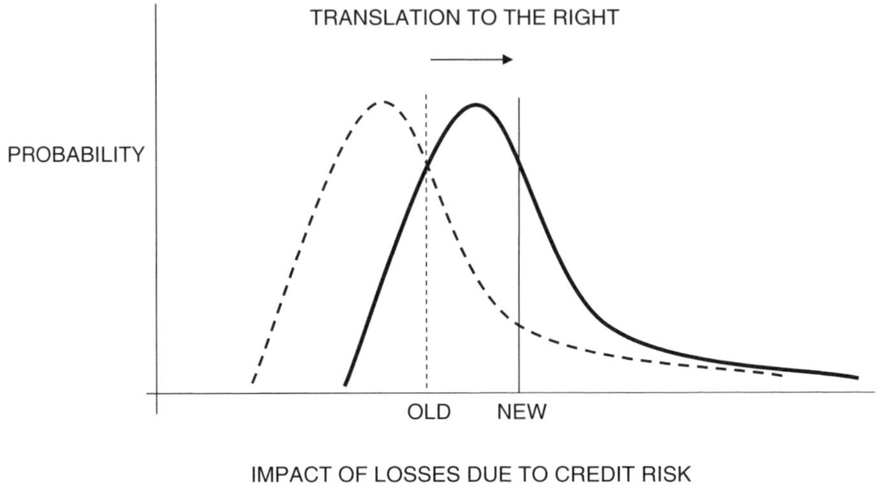

Figure 7.3 Translation to the right of the credit risk distribution increases the impact at each level of frequency, and could approximate unexpected losses

ensures the supply with adequate reinsurance protection... finite reinsurance contracts are characterized by a limitation of risk transfer'.

The thesis advanced by the Geneva Association, which is the research arm of the insurance industry, is that risk management solutions cannot be implemented properly if reinsurance contracts are always characterized by unlimited commitments. The reason is that the latter run counter to the companies' efforts to implement rigorous risk control. In addition:

- A lot of capital would have to be bound with such commitments, and
- This capital would have to bear adequate interest to satisfy investors, which would be expensive for policyholders.

As with practically all trades and investments, the big question is how to put finite reinsurance into effect in a way that enlarges business opportunity while keeping risk under lock and key. The article in the aforementioned Geneva Association publication presents three findings worthy of being highlighted:

- Contracts with a limited risk transfer should not be held responsible for individual cases of inadequate corporate governance.
- These individual cases of inadequate corporate governance should not have a negative effect on the supply of effective reinsurance protection, and
- A crucial element (in finding the right risk and return balance) is adequate accounting, because financial statements are the numerical pattern of an entity's financial status, and transparency enhances market discipline.

Notice that the issue underpinning the first two points is corporate governance, while the third point asks for rigorous and transparent accounting practices. These are helped by the recent International Financial Reporting Standards (IFRS).[9] Among themselves, these issues promote the able management of credit risk by placing on corporate governance the responsibility for keeping its volatility low.

Studies along the line of reference made in this section can offer significant possibilities for experimentation on credit risk and its volatility. The day is approaching when tier-one banks will use experimental approaches to establish and quantify the level of credit risk that they wish to assume, and thereby set well-documented limits. In all likelihood, such experimentation will be based on:

- The current composition of their loans portfolio by area of operations, industry and type of counterparty, and
- Projected developments in credit markets within prevailing (and projected) global, regional and local economic and financial conditions.

No two credit risk patterns are equal, because no two portfolio compositions are the same. In a recent experiment, the lowest capital requirements were approximately 50 per cent below the highest, a difference that can also be more than two to one. What is similar for different sample portfolios is the tendency for capital requirements to vary over time, because of different economic conditions. It is only evident that economic conditions add volatility to capital requirements, and models constructed for risk control should take them into account.

Notes

1. D.N. Chorafas, *How to Understand and Use Mathematics for Derivatives, Volume 2. Advanced Modelling Methods*, Euromoney Books, London, 1995.
2. *The Economist*, 20 May 2006.
3. For a thorough evaluation of VAR's insufficiency and misgivings see D.N. Chorafas, *Modelling the Survival of Financial and Industrial Enterprises. Advantages, Challenges, and Problems with the Internal Rating-Based (IRB) Method*, Palgrave/Macmillan, London, 2002.
4. *The Economist*, 29 April 2006.
5. D.N. Chorafas, *Economic Capital Allocation with Basel II. Cost and Benefit Analysis*, Butterworth-Heinemann, London, 2004.
6. *The Economist*, 13 May 2006.
7. D.N. Chorafas, *Economic Capital Allocation with Basel II. Cost and Benefit Analysis*, Butterworth-Heinemann, London, 2004.
8. *AIMA Newsletter*, No. 48, September 2001.
9. D.N. Chorafas, *International Financial Reporting Standards and Corporate Governance. IFRS and Fair Value Impact on Budgets, Balance Sheets and Management Accounts*, Butterworth-Heinemann, London, 2005.

8 Stress testing creditworthiness

8.1 Introduction

Credit risk and its impact are issues that have been discussed in practically all of the preceding chapters, but it has been left until this chapter, halfway through the book and just before practical examples on stress testing creditworthiness, to take a holistic approach to credit risk and default likelihood, and also to define expected and unexpected losses, which is the theme of Part 3. Special themes in this chapter are power curves, distance to default, the A/L algorithm used by the Federal Reserve and European Central Bank (ECB), unwillingness to perform and loss of creditworthiness.

8.2 Credit risk defined

Credit, dictionaries suggest, is honour for an achievement; belief that something is true; entry in an account for a sum received; an attribute characterizing an entity or person as credible, believable in the affirmation being made and obligation(s) being taken. *Creditworthiness* means that, almost certainly, such obligation will be honoured at its maturity. By contrast,

- *Credit risk* is the probability that the counterparty in a transaction (whether entity or person) will default, or
- Otherwise, will not honour assumed obligation(s), a practice that invariably leads to *reputational risk*.

Credit risk is well embedded in banking practice, with its origins dating to the Code of Hamurabi, a Babylonian emperor, circa 1700 BC. Basically, credit risk means exposure to accounting loss, measured through a credit rating assessment that is taken into account when establishing the pricing of *loans* or other debt instruments such as *bonds*.

All banks that respect themselves and their clients carry out credit risk assessment of their counterparties. In the globalized market, however, this has become increasingly the duty of independent rating agencies, which regularly revise their ratings. Table 8.1 provides an example with six ratings, out of about twenty featured by independent rating agencies.

Table 8.1 Example of average cumulative default probabilities (per cent), as a function of number of years since rating

Initial rating	Number of years since rating was given 1	2	3	4	5
AAA	0.00	0.00	0.07	0.15	0.24
AA	0.00	0.02	0.12	0.25	0.43
A	0.06	0.16	0.27	0.44	0.67
BBB	0.18	0.44	0.72	1.27	1.78
BB	1.06	3.48	6.12	8.68	10.97
B	5.20	11.00	15.95	19.40	21.88

- The first four, AAA, AA, A and BBB, are investment grade.
- In contrast, BB and B are non-investment grade. Debt instruments rated BB or worse are known as junk bonds.

In Table 8.1, the probabilities of default associated with each rating demonstrate that credit grades have a nasty habit of deteriorating over time. The usual case is that there are more downgrades than upgrades, in the long term. An AAA rating, the highest possible, represents zero probability of default in one year, but 0.24 per cent in five years. A B rating has an appreciable 5.20 per cent probability of default in one year, and nearly 22 per cent in five years.

Since the 1980s and the development of a rocket scientist culture,[1] credit risk has been subjected to rigorous mathematical analysis that revolutionizes the management of credit exposure. At the same time, as already mentioned, the use of credit derivatives has led to a reshaping of lending practices as a whole, which is sound practice. Experience teaches that:

- In the longer term, an investor can make more money from taking credit risk than from market risk.
- This, however, is conditioned by the validity of the risk control system used and the investor's risk appetite.

Part and parcel of a sound credit risk control system is *risk-based* pricing,[2] which underpins the advanced internal ratings-based (A-IRB) method, discussed in Chapter 7. Risk-based pricing is also highly recommended because investors are becoming increasingly preoccupied with *risk-adjusted earnings*. This requires a fundamental study of single transaction exposure. Risk-adjusted pricing of loans and bonds:

- Aims at reshaping the concepts and algorithms used in connection with supply and demand for credit, and
- Through its able and consistent usage, leads to restructuring of the pricing equation.

As the reader will see in Part 3, such restructuring introduces a new and important classification of losses, according to the likelihood of prognosticating them.

The capital adequacy framework of Basel II, by the Basel Committee on Banking Regulation, has formalized the distinction that always existed but was not formally appreciated, between:

- *Expected losses* (EL), which can be found in the body of the credit loss distribution, and
- *Unexpected losses* (UL), which reside at the long tail of the loss distribution and are subject to spikes.

A graphic form of the message conveyed by these two bullets is presented in Figure 8.1. In a nutshell, expected losses are reflected in the profit and loss account, as a matter of course. Typically, the bank's reserves provide a capital buffer to protect against expected losses. This is not true of unexpected losses, which require special reserves, and can make good use of instruments for risk transfer. Unexpected losses may be due to failure on the part of any:

- Customer,
- Correspondent bank,
- Sovereign, or
- Other counterparty,

in terms of fulfilling obligations assumed towards *our* bank. By and large, major credit risk uncertainties include the default point (DP) of the counterparty; value of collateral's recovery rate; correlation along defaults; synergy of defaults and credit cycles; obligor's correlation to exposure embedded in the rest of the portfolio; inadequate accounting of expected losses, which can morph into the unexpected; as well as frequency and impact of unexpected losses. Also, most importantly,

- Obligor probability of default (PD) derived from internal or external obligor rating
- Transaction loss given default (LGD), which is mainly a function of seniority and collateral
- Transaction exposure at default (EAD), which represents the bottom line in outstanding losses, and is subject to limits.

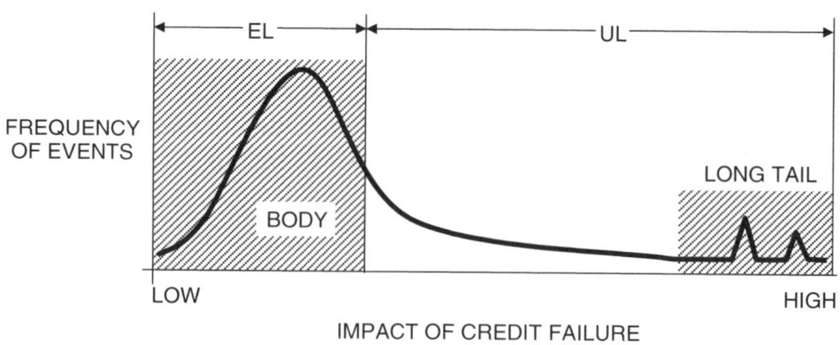

Figure 8.1 Expected losses, unexpected losses and the long tail of the loss distribution

In the original release of Basel II the algorithm for expected losses was:

$$EL = PD \cdot LGD \cdot EAD \quad (8.1)$$

In October 2003 this expected loss equation was practically dropped, because commercial banks argued that they already account for expected losses through long-established procedures for reserves. Subsequently, equation (8.1) was transformed into equation (8.2), addressing unexpected losses, where stress testing plays a crucial role:

$$UL = SPD \cdot SLGD \cdot SEAD \quad (8.2)$$

In this algorithm, SPD stands for stress PD, SLGD for stress LGD and SEAD for stress EAD. Chapters 14 and 15 describe how these factors are calculated, and the role that they play in stress testing unexpected losses.

8.3 Credit standards and default likelihood

Theoretically, credit ratings (of which a sample was shown in Table 8.1) should strengthen the hand of bankers and investors in their decision(s) about granting a loan or buying a debt instrument. Practically, however, this discriminatory ability does not work so linearly because credit ratings are usually interpreted not in absolute terms, but in conjunction with:

- Supply and demand for credit,
- Prevailing overall economic conditions, and
- Risk appetite, and other factors influencing loans and investments.

In addition, *credit standards* change over time. This complicates the process of making decisions in terms of the weight to be given to the counterparty's creditworthiness. Depending on the business climate and on the obligations it has assumed, a debtor's creditworthiness may be subject to downgrading. At the same time, also as a function of these variables, the banker's risk appetite may be tightened. For instance, banks feel less at ease in granting mortgages in the case of worsening housing market prospects.

For corporate lending, the better managed banks are keen to evaluate and incorporate into their judgement the quality of governance of this prospective debtor. Typically, this is done both in absolute terms and within the overall credit rating perspective. Quality of management is a very important reference. In the 1980s, a Kodak study demonstrated that six consecutive years of mismanagement are enough to bring a prosperous firm to its knees.

Creditworthiness is one of the major reasons why creditors are well advised to establish and follow a systematic framework for reviewing governance practices, and their effect on credit quality. Fitch, one of three major independent rating agencies, identifies the following key elements of corporate governance that are most relevant for bondholders:

- Board independence and quality,
- Integrity of the audit process, and
- Executive compensation relative to company performance.[3]

Fitch, and other rating agencies keen to evaluate the quality of management on the debtor side, correctly believe that a company's corporate governance can have a material impact on its creditworthiness. However, loans officers and bondholders tend to disregard this important criterion of governance and, therefore, downplay credit exposure.

Quality of management is indeed a basic qualitative criterion, which has an impact on credit decisions. This element, however, in no way diminishes the need for accuracy and precision in the analysis of financial information. Analysis of twenty years of balance sheets and income statements of counterparties provides both absolute and relative information on exposure. For instance, it can tell:

- *How much* better a borrower is than another, and
- *Why* this entity is 'better', in connection with established quantitative criteria.

In credit risk measurement, accuracy is more important than precision. Indeed, this is true of most quantitative business factors. Greater precision requires sharp tools and a rich database of financial information. Greater accuracy can be obtained from less quantitative detail, with the help of knowledge-engineering artefacts that steadily mine the database to:

- Determine the correlation of the obligor with the rest of the portfolio, and
- Allocate economic capital to customers to measure customer profitability.

A focal point of attention for every loans officer, and for every investor, is the likelihood that the counterparty defaults. A *default* occurs when a person or a company fails to meet a principal or interest payment of a rated obligation, unless made up within a period of grace; or, alternatively, if the entity or person files (or is filed) into bankruptcy.

Statistics show that relatively few issuers of debt instruments default early in their rated history. Sometime later on, however, some go through distressed finances, and distressed finances are also considered defaults. Financial commitments may turn into defaults if the debt holder is offered substitute obligations or securities with:

- Lower values,
- Longer maturities, or
- Other financial terms judged by the lenders to be diminished.

For instance, in late May 2006, while negotiating with banks that financed it to convert their loans into equity, Eurotunnel offered its bondholders significantly diminished terms. In exchange for a debt of €9 billion (US $11.43 billion), a heavy burden for a company that performs poorly, it proposed:

- New securities of €4 billion ($5.08 billion), and
- €1 billion in convertible bonds, without any guarantee on equity price.

This is an example of outright default, according to Moody's definition that default is any missed or delayed disbursement of interest and/or principal: bankruptcy, receivership and distressed exchange rate are practically synonymous as far as their financial aftermath is concerned, even if the exchange taking place has the objective of helping the borrower to avoid default.

Basel II defines default as any one of four different events or a combination of them: ninety days past due, write down, placement on internal non-accrual list and/or outright bankruptcy. By contrast, impaired loans are not all due to defaults. They are assets whose losses are probable and estimable. Loans are *impaired* when the book value of the claim exceeds the book value of cash flows in future periods. Such cash flows are computed accounting for:

- Interest,
- Principal payments, and
- Collateral.

Fitch Ratings points out an interesting anomaly in default practice: the principles of default likelihood do not apply on equal terms to all industry sectors. There is a difference between bank failure and bank default. As defined by Fitch, a bank has failed if:

- It is kept going only by state support,
- It is acquired by another entity,
- It requires injection of new funds from shareholders to continue operating, or
- It has defaulted.

By contrast, a bank has defaulted if it files for bankruptcy, or for bankruptcy protection; it fails to make timely payment of interest and principal; its credit is written down, as ninety days past due; or it undertakes distressed restructuring, such as offering diminished structural or economic terms. As Figure 8.2 shows:

- In manufacturing and merchandising the characteristics of failures and of default are practically the same.
- In banking, depending on the jurisdiction, default is often averted because the government is throwing good money after bad.

In the late nineteenth century (but not in 1995) the Bank of England saved Barings from bankruptcy. In the USA, too, some banks like Continental Illinois were too big

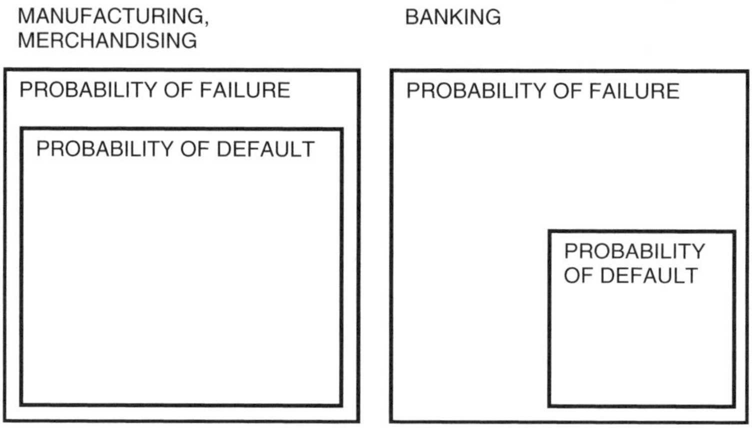

Figure 8.2 In the banking industry the probability of default is a subset of the probability of failure

to fail; while the Bank of New England (BNE) and Long-Term Capital Management (LTCM) were too loaded with derivatives, creating systemic risk problems.

Saving banks from bankruptcy using other people's money is seen, most frequently, as a continental European and Japanese practice. There are several reasons for government intervention: tens of thousands of employees (Crédit Lyonnais, Bankgesellschaft Berlin), too big to fail (Resona, and other Japanese banks), heavy deposit insurance payments (Crédit Lyonnais, Bankgesellschaft Berlin, Continental Illinois, Bank of New England) and often systemic risk. Other reasons for unwarranted salvage are the psychological effect on public confidence, politics (Crédit Lyonnais, Bankgesellschaft) and major problems in derivatives markets (BNE, LTCM).

8.4 The discriminatory ability of power curves

Etymologically, *power* means authority, capacity, capability, competences, faculty, potential or potentiality. Other meanings are command, control, clout, dominance, energy, gift, influence, might, sway, vigour and weight. Several of these terms fit *power curves* well because their reason for being lies in their capacity for differentiation in decisions related to creditworthiness.

To appreciate this statement, it is appropriate to think that nothing walks in a straight line. In practice, a credit rating of AA means that this is a central value and the entity's creditworthiness may vary between AA+ and AA−, but with a low likelihood at the extremes. There are reasons for these intervals.

- Rating is both quantitative and qualitative, and hence subjective,
- The data on which the analysts base their opinion might have been less than reliable,
- The time elapsed between when the rating was made and today might have changed the financials, and
- A new management may be more (or less) rigorous than its predecessor.

Moreover, the case has been already made that business considerations and economic conditions change the risk appetite of lenders and investors. This means that the interpretation of the counterparty's creditworthiness does not exactly correspond with that party's credit rating.

If everything were perfect, and none of these exceptions was present, one might expect that a credit rating would have nearly one-to-one correspondence with a counterparty's underlying creditworthiness, along line A in Figure 8.3, which excludes the corresponding percentage of defaulters. However, as in every other business, this ideal situation is not attainable.

Nevertheless, we do not wish to be confronted with zero predictability of creditworthiness. This is the case of the diagonal line E in Figure 8.3. Between the ideal case A and zero likelihood to foretell credit risk, comes the family of power curves B, C and D. The first of them provides better discriminatory power than the other two.

Power curves are based on histories of different defaults, distilled to their essentials. Their discriminatory power is based on Pareto's law: a small part of one factor (for example, companies) accounts for a large part of another factor (for example, defaults).

In Figure 8.3, power curve B offers the possibility of fairly good segregation between possible defaulters and non-defaulters. The whole purpose of this and similar analytical approaches is to improve upon the predictability of default and the level of results that could be expected.

The power curve maps the fraction of all companies with the value, or score, relating to the chosen top factors affecting survivability. Power curve models typically

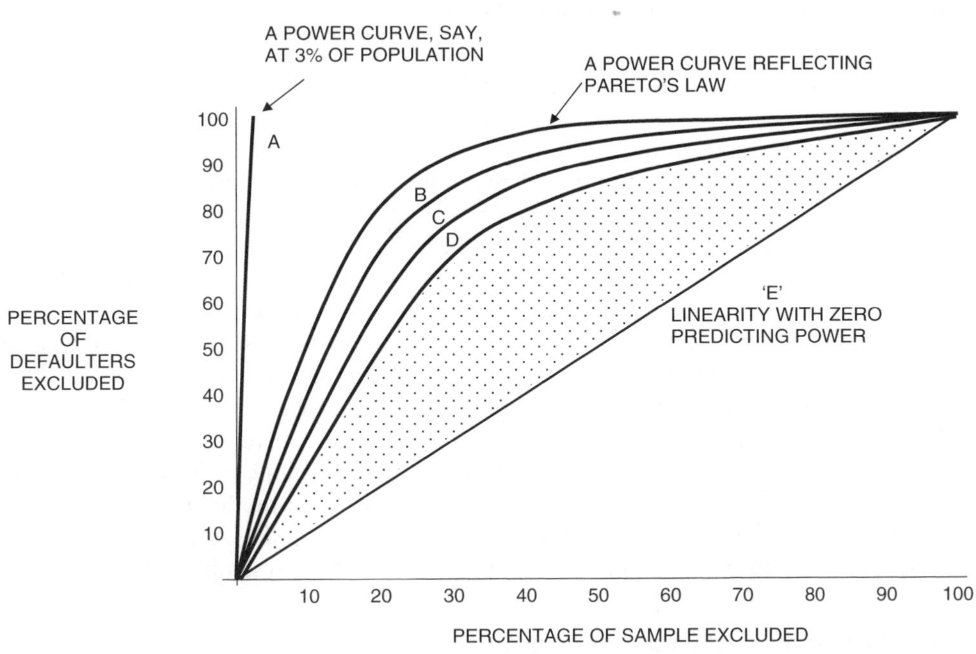

Figure 8.3 Power curves help to predict defaulters according to chosen criteria of creditworthiness

use a rigorous trapping routine that searches for negatives due to a variety of defined reasons. Typically, these reasons are found in financial statement and accounting principles. In so doing, power curve processing does not try to solve the negatives, but simply records them and moves forward with them. This process is based on:

- Statistical inference,
- A generous amount of financial information, and
- The potential of models to provide forecasts on well-defined issues.

In general, in business prognostication is based on chosen critical factors, credit risk being an example. An effective model uses historical evidence to project on the survivability of a company. Alternatively, it tells us how well a given organization manages its business so that it can confront adversity. Factors entering the model may be (in order of importance):

- Level of leverage,
- Profitability,
- Cash flow,
- Liquidity,
- Innovation,
- Cost control,
- Sales growth,
- Diversification, and
- Size of the firm (not always a positive factor).

In the calculation of power curves, significant attention is paid to the model's forecasting ability. Notice that, in Figure 8.3, the relation between estimated default frequency in the ordinate and the absolute value (or ratio) in the abscissa is not linear. Neither is it that estimated default and the value in reference always correlate in a positive way. Such characteristic relations should be reflected in the model.

The scientific method permitting analysis of the pattern of default, and documentation (up to a point) of the underlying factors, is part of the science of *stochastic analysis*, mapping what seems to be random behaviour of humans into mathematical models. Originally, the target was inanimate objects and processes with characteristic behaviour, but more recently attention has focused on human effectiveness.

An example is provided by IBM's profiling of 50 000 consultants whom it employs. At IBM's research centre, north of New York City, a forty-member team of scientists, which includes data-miners, statisticians and knowledge engineers is scrutinizing the personal profiles of some 50 000 IBM consultants. Instead of modelling machines and patterns, or credit risk networks, the analysts are building models of their colleagues.[4] Subsequently, based on these mathematical profiles, expert systems can:

- Pick the best team for every assignment,
- Track each consultant's contribution to the project's progress, and
- Rate each person's work performance hour by hour.

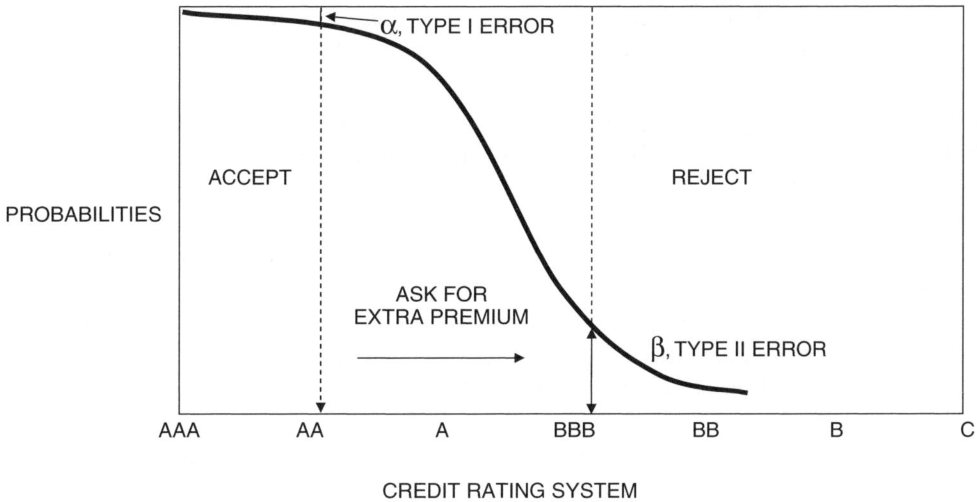

Figure 8.4 An operating characteristics curve for credit risk based on a rating system

Power curves and operating characteristics (OC) curves are the twin output of the same *discriminatory analysis*, as can be seen by comparing the power curve of Figure 8.3 with the OC curve of Figure 8.4 (taken from a credit risk evaluation project). The now classical risk-adjusted return on capital (RAROC) system is based on OC curves and the concept of an area of increased risk premium between accepting and rejecting a loan.

8.5 The predictive power of distance to default

Reference was made to the default point (DP) in section 8.2. A critical parameter in any credit analysis is the *distance to default* (DD), which represents the standard deviations of asset value away from the DP. This distance is calculated using option pricing theory, to solve for:

- Unobservable market value of assets (A), using capitalization as proxy,
- Volatility of observable capitalization, and
- Leverage relative to the firm's liabilities (L), which are taken at book value.

The DP is the point at which an entity's market value is equal to that of its liabilities. This very important ratio in the analysis of creditworthiness brings into perspective the negative side of leverage:

$$\frac{A}{L} = \frac{\text{Assets}}{\text{Liabilities}} \geq 1 \tag{8.3}$$

If the A/L is smaller than 1, then the company is insolvent. The probability of default is related to indebtedness measured by the equity to debt ratio. Leverage has a price, which is often severe. In the distance to default model by Moody's KMV,[5] implied volatility is an estimate of volatility of the stock.

- Movements in implied volatilities are proxy for asset risk.
- As Warren Buffet put it, 'It is only when the tide goes out that you see who's swimming naked'.

The Federal Reserve and ECB use equation (1), supported by Moody's KMV model, for policy decisions. From what is publicly known, in both cases the numerator is market capitalization as proxy for assets. Some difference seems to exist in the denominator; the Federal Reserve is reportedly using current liabilities, while the ECB counts all outstanding liabilities. It is evident that:

- If equity value drops, while liabilities remain the same, then distance to default shortens.
- If the proxy for assets remains invariant, but the entity's liabilities increase, then, too, the distance to default shortens.

Stockmarket volatility matters, because of its impact on capitalization. Management may try to lift the equity's price by beautifying the numbers, or through stock buybacks. Both, however, have a transitory effect (unless there is fraud connected to the numbers). More lasting is the control of liabilities, which not all companies care to do.

As a metric of financial health and stability, A/L is an ideal tool for the board and the chief executive officer (CEO), because good governance starts at the top. As section 8.3 emphasized, good governance is important to all *stakeholders*. Members of the board and the CEO are trustees and safekeepers of the entity, as well as of its financial staying power.

- Increasingly, in Western countries the responsibility for assessing risk lies squarely with the audit committee and the board.
- The board and CEO are also responsible for ensuring that appropriate internal controls are in place, and the integrity of financial information is not compromised by anyone, at any time, in any place.

Such responsibilities are more pronounced in the financial sector than in any other, because banks are not only selling products and services, but also managing other people's money, whether these are deposits or investments. This increases the banks' public vulnerability, and creates issues of systemic importance. For good governance reasons, the CEO, executive directors and board members would be well advised to require daily reports on A/L ratios, not only of the bank itself, but also of:

- The most important correspondent banks,
- Top-of-the-line loans customers, and
- The most exposed counterparties in derivative financial instruments.

The class identified by the third bullet point deserves particular attention because derivatives exposure has become the largest contributor to long-term financial liabilities by credit institutions. In Euroland, for example, during 2003–2005 the dynamics of long-term financial liabilities by credit institutions (excluding capital and reserves) zoomed.

In 2005, the annual rate of growth of long-term financial liabilities held by banks stood well above 9 per cent, as a result of growing demand for longer term instruments by Euroland investors. This is evidence of an ongoing inclination to invest in riskier financial instruments with longer life cycles, with the result of:

- Reducing the A/L ratio, and
- Correspondingly shrinking the distance to default.

Therefore, this constitutes a field with significant potential for stress testing. Moody's KMV uses *cumulative accuracy profile* (CAP) curves to make visual assessments of model performance. CAP plots are power curves, which are discussed in section 8.3, representing the cumulative probability of default of a population, subject to type I and type II errors, as explained in Part 1.

To plot CAP, companies are ordered by score, from riskiest to safest. The resulting curve is constructed by calculating the percentage of the defaulters on the ordinate y, whose risk is equal to or lower than the one for fraction x of companies plotted on the abscissa. Plotting CAP requires a choice of a *look-forward* term of three, six, nine or twelve months, or more. In regard to the evaluation of debt issues, Moody's default forecasting model includes six variables:

- Percentage of the corporate bond universe rated speculative grade,
- Percentage of the speculative grade universe rated Ba or below,
- Real industrial production (IP) trend (IP deflated by the producer price index),
- New speculative-grade issuers,
- Ten-year US Treasury (nominal) yield,
- Treasury bond-bill spread (ten years, ninety days).

The risk of default is at a maximum when the success of the enterprise is most uncertain. The model also accounts for ageing effects. The hazard rate of default is a function of time in the market for new issuers. To ensure that a given risk weight is appropriate for a particular credit risk assessment, the Basel Committee recommends that regulators evaluate the *cumulative default rate* associated with all issues assigned to the same credit rating.

8.6 The risk of unwillingness to perform

Bankruptcy is not the only source of credit risk. An equally important reason, although much less frequent, is plain *unwillingness to perform* on obligations that a counterparty assumed by entering into a given transaction. As a starter, here are two examples of unwillingness to perform from the South Korean meltdown in December 1997.

J.P. Morgan had a major derivatives contract with SK Securities, one of the better known local investment banks. With the South Korean economy going to the abyss, J.P. Morgan won a derivatives bet it had with SK Securities, to the tune of a rumoured $480 million. Although SK was not bankrupt in the aftermath of the South Korean crisis, it refused to perform owing to its alleged precarious condition. This case went to court, and from there, as far as existing evidence is concerned, into the time closet.

The virtual bankruptcy of SK in late 1997, and several of its conglomerates, stemmed from market risk that rekindled into counterparty risk and led to reputational risk. A second case, at the same time and in the same place, involved two well-known banks, one South Korean and the other British, which had entered into a major currency exchange contract in derivatives.

- This derivatives contract stipulated that if the exchange rate of the Korean won to the dollar fell below a specified barrier, then the British bank would be winning an all-or-nothing bet.
- But, to protect itself with regard to interpretations, the British bank had imposed a clause specifying that the reference would be the exchange rate published by the South Korean central bank.

With the country's bankruptcy, the won sank, but at the same time the South Korean central bank stopped publishing the won's exchange rate. Reportedly, the Korean bank counterparty to this deal found the lack of an officially published exchange rate as an excuse, informing the British bank that its unwillingness to perform was fully justified because of this technicality.

In the background of both examples lies the fact that organizations are made of people and *reputational risk* is not always at the top of their priorities. This being the case, they try to find any excuse to avoid discharging their obligations, at least to some of the stakeholders. A 2005 case is the unwarranted (not to say unethical) handling of bondholders in connection with the hedge fund takeover of TDC, the Danish telecommunications company (telco), which is studied in section 8.7.

The difficulty in testing a priori *unwillingness to perform* is that independent credit rating agencies focus on credit risk, not on reputational risk. The same is true of banks with regard to their internal credit ratings. Basel has not yet addressed reputational risk. Under current conditions, the only possible indicator is the growing attention paid to good governance, which is part of a firm's reputation.

- One indicator rests on the fact that good governance and attention to reputational risk correlate.
- Another indicator can be developed on the basis of the behavioural histories of a counterparty's board members, CEO and executive vice-presidents.

A precedence, in regard to this second bullet, is provided by the Securities and Exchange Commission (SEC) and New York Stock Exchange (NYSE). One of NYSE monitors is Automated Search and Match (ASAM). Upon receipt of information pertaining to suspect transactions, ASAM begins to match files. The system compares the names of the broker's customers (including data that it already may have on them) with information on currency executives, investment bankers and others with connections to the firm whose stock behaved oddly.

NYSE, and other exchanges, process such information through a suspicion-ranking program. People who conduct the trading analysis belong to the Inter-market Surveillance Group (ISG). Its members get together periodically and share information, which sometimes uncovers a pattern of trades by someone whose buying or selling on a single exchange may not ring an alarm.

ISG automated its pooling of information to create a unified audit trail of stocks and options. The Intermarket Surveillance Information System Database contains historical trading information from all exchanges. Computers manage the data, putting together, for example, a complete list of all trading activity by a given company on the exchanges, with a listing of all trades:

- By time, and
- By participants in the trading.

While the reason for being of ASAM and the Surveillance Group is not companies' unwillingness to perform, they do incorporate activities that lead to reputational risk. Reputational risk tracking can benefit from such a precedence.

In a globalized economy, the procedure briefly described in the preceding paragraphs should be established and followed by regulators, in a way emulating the action of the Basel Committee in regard to credit risk, market risk and operational risk. The global market has no frontiers and this can mean that opportunities for unwillingness to perform multiply.

Another precedence, which can teach a lesson on reputational risk tracking, also comes from the USA. The SEC is encouraging stock exchanges to compile, upgrade and exploit thoroughly databases for *pattern recognition*, which can become a basic tool in reputational risk control.

For example, the SEC investigates suspected cases of insider trading (brought to it by one of the exchanges), by comparing the zip codes of people who bought a given company's stock. While the input may have come, for instance, from NYSE, these may not be New Yorkers but residents of Dallas, Sacramento or another country, who may have received a tip, even in casual conversation, to buy a particular company's equity.

The investigators may suspect that leaks have come from insiders who live in the same neighbourhood, or have maintained college friendships from long ago. Their worries may come, for example, from NYSE's blue sheets indicating suspicious trading and requesting chronologies. A *chronology* is a list of people and events associated with a merger, an acquisition or another important activity that can move stock prices. This list generally includes:

- Management,
- Lawyers,
- Accountants, and
- Investment bankers.

An interesting case dates back to 1990, when the SEC used the pattern-recognition method to detect insider trading in the acquisition of the US drug company Rorer Group by France's Rhône-Poulenc in January of that year. Having been tipped off by heavy trading in Rorer options, the SEC filed suits against investment groups in Switzerland, Monaco, Greece and Lebanon.[6] France also launched a probe, but in the end it was French politicians who were found to be involved in this case.

In order to track insider trading and identify wrongdoers, since the early 1990s SEC has developed a rich database that includes not only company executives, bankers and traders, but also members of their family and roommates they had in fraternities and sororities. Expert systems exploit this database when a suspicious case arises. The control of reputational risk requires a similar solution.

Data-mining, knowledge engineering, pattern analysis and scenarios based on its findings, are the best means for protecting investors and other counterparties in the global market from unwillingness to perform. Important lessons can be learned from the use of technology in SEC's enforcement job.

- Before the aforementioned development, all investigation had to be done by sorting through trading records by hand; a slow, difficult and inefficient process.
- Now, data-mining and profiling is done through knowledge models, relieving investigators from trivia.

Another reference in the same vein is that SEC monitors the exchanges by conducting periodic inspections of their systems. SEC surveillance people conduct audits, review the exchanges' procedures and look up enforcement files to ensure that:

- Their parameters are reasonable,
- Their inspections are well documented,
- Their internal audits are complete and timely, and
- Sanctions are brought against violators.

In a globalized economy, the control of unwillingness to perform and of reputational risk must be done by a supernational authority, otherwise globalization would receive a black eye, because some countries and many people have a lot of power without responsibility. Reputations take a lifetime to build and can be destroyed in a matter of days.

8.7 Case study: the stakeholders of TeleDenmark

Starting in 2005, and sensing many weak firms among the former telecom monopolies, hedge funds and private equity companies have been playing for position in the European telecommunications industry. In December 2005 they snapped up their first

European incumbent, throwing Danish kroner 95.5 billion ($12 billion, €10 billion) at Denmark's TDC (TeleDenmark). According to experts, this has been:

- The largest private equity buyout since the $25 billion purchase of RJR Nabisco in the USA in 1988, and
- The largest ever in Europe, although the volume of assets recently managed by hedge funds and private equities outfits may mean that it is soon surpassed.

At the time of writing, all signs point to more private equity pouring into the telecoms sector in 2006 and beyond. Targeting telecoms and media companies, private equity firms are circling around plenty of possible candidates for takeovers that their buyout teams have studied.

For this reason, what has happened with TeleDenmark, formerly the country's flagship telco, makes an interesting case study. The takeover was done by the Nordic Telephone Company (NTC), a new company established by Apax Partners Worldwide LLP, the Blackstone Group International, Kohlberg Kravis Roberts (KKR), Permira Advisers and Providence Equity Partners.

Although a newly formed entity, NTC has obtained exemptive relief from the provisions of Rule 14-5 under the US Securities Exchange Act of 1934, as amended. This relief permits NTC, and financial institutions behind it, to make purchases of TDC shares outside the Tender offer, from and after the first public announcement of the tender until the end of the offer period. This is manna from heaven, as it permits NTC to bypass the tender and buy TDC shares.

- In the open market at prevailing prices, or
- In private transactions at negotiated prices.

Starting at the beginning of December 2005, the price of the tender offer represented a premium of approximately 39 per cent over TDC's average share price on 16 August 2005, a boom to the stockholders, but as we will see the bondholders paid the price.

According to NTC that offer was over 117.0 per cent relative to the share price in SBC Communications' sale of 51 351 981 TDC shares as of 10 June 2004. That sale had represented a good chunk of TDC's share capital. No wonder the board of TDC agreed to these terms and conditions, recommending that shareholders accept the tender offer. However, as shown later on, TDC's board took absolutely no care regarding the interests of the company's bondholders, yet:

- Bondholders are stakeholders like shareholders, and
- The board has a fiduciary duty over all stakeholders' interests.

Indeed, among several issues raised by critics of that deal has been that TDC's board practically dumped those investors who had trusted it and the company by purchasing its debt. The fact that bondholders' interests were neglected, while shareholders thrived, turned on its head the financial theory that:

- Stockholders are in the frontline in case of bankruptcy.

In addition, several experts pointed out that one of the curious issues associated with this takeover is that, as the tender offer announcement stated, NTC and its hedge funds dealt with a counterparty that presented itself as a public company. When this happened, TDC was no longer a public firm, but insisted on dealing on this status, thereby:

- Hiding some of its responsibilities under the thick skin of public bureaucracy.

The tender offer for TDC provides the scenario for stress testing companies with current, or projected, significant exposure in debt instruments, as far as the safeguard of bond investors' interests is concerned. Not only telecoms, but all utilities loaded with debt constitute a fertile field for testing:

- Future willingness to repay, and
- Reputational risk associated with downgrade of their debt after a takeover.

This stress test should be extended to cover conflict of interest, as attested by the fact that TDC's board members saw nothing wrong in abandoning the bondholders of 'a public firm' to the plight to which they were brought by the acquiring interests, in terms of capital losses. The TDC board allowed NTC to do whatever it deemed 'necessary or appropriate in respect to the existing debt of TDC', which is plain abdication of fiduciary duties, an unwillingness to perform according to one's responsibilities.

The bondholders' exposure connected with TDC's takeover can be best appreciated if the risks associated with it are put in the context of what happens with European telcos at large. The so-called incumbents, which are essentially former regulated state monopolies run by bureaucrats, do not have the culture or the people to implement the strategy that they are aiming at in connection with cross-border mergers and acquisitions. It follows logically that:

- If they cannot hold the high ground,
- Then they will be the victims of LBOs.

As 2005 came to a close, the bond market was reeling from declining credit ratings. The bonds of even France Telecom and Deutsche Telekom, the biggest telcos in Euroland, fell to the brink of junk status. By late 20 December 2005, as Telefonica, Vodafone and TDC planned to raise more than $45 billion in 2006, mostly in bonds (the first two to pay for acquisitions), yields of corporates were rising at their fastest rate since 2000, compared with government debt.

An interesting study for investment purposes is stress testing the synergy of takeovers and credit downgrades. Statistics are provided by leveraged telcos. Investors demand extra yield to hold Telefonica's 5.125 per cent euro-denominated bonds maturing in February 2013, rather than government debt.

- With the Spanish telco's O2 deal in the making, by the end of December 2005 the spread jumped to 67 basis points, and
- The annual cost of insuring €10 million of Telefonica debt through credit default swaps reached €54 000, the highest in more than two and a half years.

'The memory is on investors' minds of what happened in 2000', Sajiv Vaid, who helps in managing $21 billion of fixed income assets at Royal London Asset Management, said in an interview on 8 December 2005. 'The concern is that you get a frenzy and they go do stupid things'.[7] This is indeed the case with nearly all highly leveraged deals and predatory pricing of securities on which investors had bet their retirement or their children's education.

8.8 A lesson for stress testers: loss of creditworthiness has many fathers

Mergers and acquisitions picked up 'more than we were expecting and at a faster pace than we had expected', said Duncan Warwick-Champion, head of High Grade European Credit Research at UBS in London, as quoted in a Bloomberg News release. With this in mind, in mid-November 2005 UBS lowered its recommendation for European telephone company bonds to *underweight*, having started the year at *overweight*.

For its part, Standard & Poor's (S&P) let it be known it may lower credit ratings on nine telephone companies in Europe, including British Telecom, Cable & Wireless and Portugal Telecom, almost half the total number of entities it follows. A sign of the times is that:

- As the population of debt issuers among telecoms increases,
- S&P is more inclined to downgrade than keep unchanged their ratings.

A good example of the aftermath of 'underweights' and 'downgrades' is how the market treats the telecom debt. Bonds sold by TDC lost more than 13 per cent of their value in the three and a half months before it agreed to be bought by NTC. This proved that having being abandoned by TDC's board, bond investors became afraid that TDC debt could be reduced to junk status, as happened with many other LBOs.

On 30 November 2005, a short time after NTC's move, Moody's Investor's Service stripped TDC of its investment-grade status. That was about the time when Copenhagen-based TDC officially announced its LBO, proof that loss of creditworthiness and junk status of debt,

- Can come with an LBO,
- In a way similar to the after effect of bankruptcy.

The spread on TDC's 6.5 per cent bonds due in April 2012 almost tripled in the months leading up to the acquisition, widening to 315 basis points on 8 December 2005, from 111 in August of the same year.

While the privatization of dormant European telecom monopolies was originally welcomed by many experts, their subsequent dismal performance put in doubt the benefits of privatization, and LBOs made a bad situation worse. The prevailing opinion now is that current and projected acquisitions of former government-run telephone services will not only deteriorate their spreadsheets, but also affect the way in which old and new services are delivered, including:

- Quality of service, and
- Cost to telephone users.

Private equity firms and hedge funds do not buy the telcos for kicks. What is in the works is the build-up of a huge monopoly that will depend more and more on mobile networks, where the profit margins are. Hedge funds are renowned for putting money from mispriced credit markets to work. Portugal Telecom, Dutch KPN, Telecom Italia, Telecom Austria and media companies such as Peasons and Kluwer are said to be the next in line for LBOs.

Behind the risks involved in the new monopoly-in-the-making lies the fact that hedge funds and private equity firms typically invest for the short term; that is, between three and five years. During that time they hope to take out a lot more than they put in. The telecoms industry, on the other hand, is not renowned for short-term solutions; neither is it known for its ability to create value. Moreover:

- There is uncertainty over telcos' longer term performance in stemming declines in cash flow,
- While incumbent telephone operators are losing revenues to competitors, cheaper IP connections and new technologies used by start-ups.

These factors have an evident impact on creditworthiness, which needs to be stress tested from different viewpoints. Section 8.5 introduced the reader to distance to default and DP. However, it is wrong to believe that:

- Default is the aftermath of only one factor, a balance sheet that turned on its head.

In fact, it is likely that the balance sheet turned upside down because of other factors, such as those discussed in section 8.7 and this section.

When the Basel Committee's SPD, SLGD and SEAD are introduced in Chapters 9 and 10, the reader should think of TDC and of NTC. To improve their profit prospects, hedge funds and private equity firms with an LBO strategy for telcos have to cut corners, which works against quality of service and creditworthiness.

Another interesting aspect that should be examined in a stress test is the distinction often made between populations of investors. US residents are usually excluded from this curious invitation to deposit their wallets with the raiders. The NTC offer does not specify what will happen with the TDC bonds held by US citizens, but expert opinion is that they will probably end up in the same pot as other TDC bondholders. Fear will ensure that they sell them at a huge discount.

- By changing the TDC bonds' covenants, including redemption price and protective clauses,
- NTC can ensure that the LBO's aftermath is no different from that of a bankruptcy.

Beyond all this, there are plenty of unanswered questions: What kind of legal resort do the bondholders have? Against whom? NTC in Norway, or TDC in Denmark? It is ironic that the hunted TDC was itself a hunter, seeking significant leveraging to fund its projected acquisitions before falling to NTC. This has been the best that ex-bureaucrats turned entrepreneurs without know-how could do:

- As governments privatized the telcos and sold their stakes, telephone industry managers began to concentrate on growth by acquisitions, instead of steady cash flows, and
- Moreover, the privatized telcos spent about $100 billion in 2000 and 2001 buying licences to provide third generation wireless services, borrowing to pay for most of these purchases.

After the telephone industry crashed in 2001, telco managers should have learned the hard way that mergers and acquisitions business is no evidence of good governance; but this is not evident. The 2005/06 wave of telco takeovers demonstrates that the 2000/01 disaster, which caused chaos even among the biggest and best known telcos (and some, including the Dutch KPN and Finnish Sonera, had to be saved with taxpayers' money) did not make telco executives wiser. This is also true of the raiders.

As a feature article in *Total Telecom* aptly suggested, 'There's simply nothing in the private equity sector's moves so far to suggest that telecoms company board directors have anything to fear, or their long-suffering shareholders anything to cheer. More likely, the private equity sortie into major telecoms management will degenerate into farce, leaving the new masters looking for all the world like circus clowns'.[8] The clown test can be one of the best stress tests possible.

Notes

1. D.N. Chorafas, *Rocket Scientists in Banking*, Lafferty Publications, London, 1995.
2. D.N. Chorafas, *Economic Capital Allocation with Basel II. Cost and Benefit Analysis,* Butterworth-Heinemann, London, 2004.
3. Fitch Rating, *Evaluating Corporate Governance: The Bondholders' Perspective, A Special Report*, London, 2005.
4. *Businessweek*, 23 January 2006.

5. D.N. Chorafas, *Economic Capital Allocation with Basel II. Cost and Benefit Analysis,* Butterworth-Heinemann, London, 2004.
6. *Businessweek*, 6 February 1990.
7. *Blooomberg News*, 20 December 2005.
8. *Total Telecom Magazine*, January 2006.

9 Stress probability of default

9.1 Introduction

Risk management models are evolving rapidly. Adopted by the financial industry as a means for improving internal credit risk management, probability of default (PD) is the *alter ego* of distance to default, discussed in Chapter 8. The Basel Committee recommends that banks test the stress probability of default (SPD), reporting obtained results to their regulators. In compliance with Basel II, credit institutions sort PDs into buckets; however, the better managed institutions are also keen to examine the confidence that can be placed in PD and SPD tests.

9.2 Probability of default and liquidity stress testing

Probability of default focuses on obligor's defaulting rather than the obligations that default. It is a fair assumption that all of an issuer's debt instruments will go into default at the same time as he or she files for bankruptcy, or is filed into bankruptcy. Hence, theoretically, they all have the same PD. Practically, however, covenants ensure that there is a difference in quality of obligations by the same issuer. Therefore, it is wise to:

- Rate separately multiple obligations of a given obligor, and
- Assign different ratings to each of them, reflecting their seniority, if such a difference is warranted.

For example, an independent rating agency might rate an obligor's secured debt BBB, senior unsecured debt BB, senior subordinate debt BB– and junior subordinate B. Such differences in rating do not reflect different PDs on the obligor's side. Rather, they account for the fact that because of differences in seniority, default losses will not be the same.

PDs are largely based on credit ratings, whether internal to the bank or by independent agencies; but there are also other factors. The evaluation of covenants and seniorities used to be done manually. Nowadays it is in large part performed by knowledge engineering artefacts. It may be recalled from Part 1 that expert systems benefit from knowledge acquisition among experts:

- They are flexible and powerful models, and
- They can contribute a great deal in incorporating into their judgement the different factors influencing PD, including liquidity.

An entity's liquidity risk is an important counterparty variable, beyond credit rating. If an obligor has high liquidity, then the one-year PD will be lower because liquidity is more important in the short term. Liquidity will be weighted more heavily in the one-year model than in the two- or five-year PD model.

The all-important *liquidity risk* arises from a variety of sources and, if left unchecked, it has the potential to damage a firm's reputation (see Chapter 8). Liquidity risk may be due to informal factors or to major changes in the macroeconomic environment, or both. An entity, although solvent:

- May not have the financial resources needed to face its immediate obligations, or
- May be able to secure them at excessive cost, which puts its future solvency, and hence its creditworthiness, in peril.

Liquidity risk and credit risk (and therefore PD) correlate. The PD is both influenced by and impacts on liquidity. Ratings downgrades lead to a loss of market confidence, with after effects on the firm's ability to refinance its current debt obligations. As stated, liquidity risk also rises from events external to the entity, in the majority of cases; however, assumed exposure is the determinant factor.

'In the short run [Gerald] Corrigan [then president of the New York Federal Reserve] argued, there was no way to tell the difference between just short term liquidity problems and outright insolvency'.[1] Liquidity crises are often tail events, and they must be stress tested. A May 2006 survey by the Basel Committee indicated that, in financial groups, the primary transaction- and product-driven sources of liquidity risk involve:

- Derivatives,
- Other off-balance sheet instruments, and
- On-balance sheet insurance contracts with embedded optionality.[2]

In the early 1980s, the Federal Reserve permitted American banks to write *off-balance sheet* certain instruments, mainly derivatives, because of their minor weight. Today, in many institutions the weight of the off-balance sheet exceeds that of the balance sheet.

The same Basel study indicated that the most significant sources of liquidity risk in banking are over-the-counter derivative transactions and repurchasing agreements; such transactions, particularly in cases where sharp and unanticipated market movements, or events such as bankruptcies, default or ratings downgrades, could cause demand for additional collateral from counterparties, creating liquidity risk.

The Basel Committee study underlines that, 'Off-balance sheet exposures also contribute to liquidity risk at banking firms during times of stress. Off-balance sheet products than can give rise to sudden material demands for liquidity at banking firms. [These] include:

- Committed lending facilities to customers,
- Committed backstop facilities to commercial paper conduits, and
- Committed back-up lines to special purpose vehicles'.

Hence the need to perform stress testing[3]. A deliberate decision was made to prioritize liquidity stress tests over default point stress tests (see section 9.4), because the former are a moving gear of the latter. *Liquidity stress tests* can be performed at headquarters, at business units, or at both levels. Entities that stress test centrally and at the periphery do so because they believe that they are better able to consider contagion effects across the firm, and to assess potential movements of available liquidity to wherever it is needed group-wide.

Both with regard to PD and for liquidity risk purposes, stress-testing scenarios must be firm specific and market sensitive. The Basel survey documented that many entities create a firm-specific scenario that reflects a two-, three- or four-notch downgrading in their creditworthiness rating, by an independent rating agency. However, the key factor determining the severity of the stress tests:

- Is not just the number of notches by which the firm is downgraded,
- It is its consequence for the balance sheet and cash flows resulting from credit downgrading.

To account for such consequences, market stress scenarios for liquidity reasons involve changes in the macroeconomic environment at input and output level. They do the same relative to disruptions in the market. Changes in interest rate levels, equity prices, market liquidity and inflation rates are macroeconomic factors affecting the provision of and demand for funds that are thoroughly tested.

An interesting aspect of the Basel Committee survey is the finding that about one-third of participating commercial banks test the impact of a firm-specific event within an unsettled market environment; and approximately two-thirds simulate a firm-specific event occurring during a time of market stress. Participating institutions also added that, in the longer term, other factors may also steer the performance of stress tests.

The Joint Forum, which conducted the 2006 survey, advises that the outcomes of stress tests across firms should be interpreted carefully in light of differences in their nature across and within three sectors that were examined:

- Commercial banking,
- Investment banking, and
- The insurance industry.

Other studies have documented that the modelling of PD must also take account of possible anomalies characterizing a company or industry. ‘In forecasting a bank’s default probability, we take into account the degree of support by the regulator’, said a senior executive of one of the major independent rating agencies. There are many institutional and other factors deciding what the central bank is going to do.

Crédit Lyonnais was salvaged, but it was a big bank. The bank of France let smaller banks fail. In the UK, Barings folded in 1995, although it was rescued by the Bank of England at the end of the nineteenth century. As covered in Chapter 7, the debt of both General Motors and General Motors Acceptance Corporation (GMAC) was rated by independent agencies as junk. But when in January 2006 Citigroup and

Bank of Wachovia expressed interest in acquiring a controlling share in GMAC, the discount the market had accorded to the latter entity's bonds shrank.

In summing this section, not only creditworthiness, but also liquidity and other variables mean that PDs must be assigned individually. Industry averages do not contribute more than a sense of direction, which is interesting but inadequate for investment decisions.

Even behind averages it is important to distinguish the crucial PD factors, particularly when the PD is of some size. According to Tim Kasta of Moody's KMV, in the first years of the twenty-first century the average American company had a 4.4 per cent chance of default. This was more than four times the average in the 1990s.[4] A critical reason was leverage. Among financial analysts, a major concern has been that:

- Even as their market capitalization was falling,
- Companies continued to add debt and, by increasing their gearing they were bringing closer their default point (DP), which is the *cross-over* of assets and liabilities shown in Figure 9.1.

Both for the investor's own protection and for reasons of systemic risk, it is necessary to track the PD of every company, study its liquidity position and analyse the creditworthiness of its debt instruments. This is true for every financial product connected with a counterparty, whether loans, investments or derivatives. Stress probability of default can provide much needed prognostication, as shown in section 9.4.

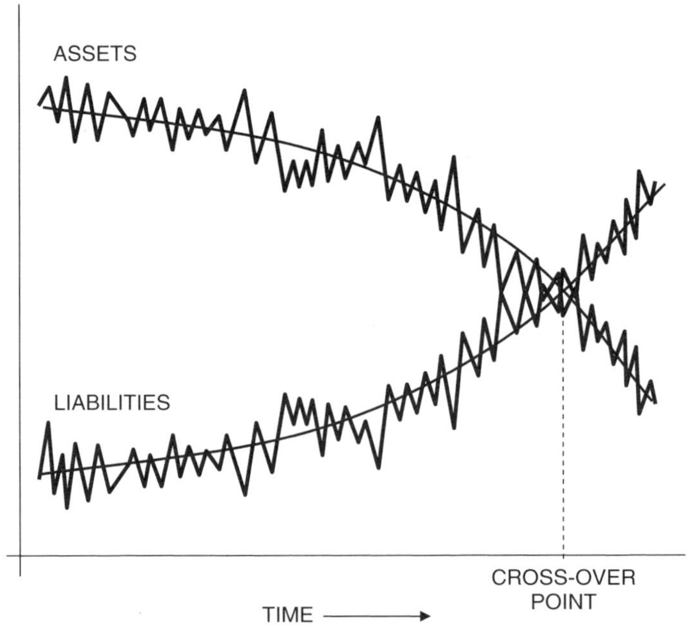

Figure 9.1 Exogenous and endogenous factors affect the calculation of the default point

9.3 Concentrations of exposure and credit risk measurement

The basic objective of developing credit risk measurements is to facilitate prudential management of exposure by establishing counterparty limits, as well as by identifying the sources giving rise to risk concentrations. Most often, this is done under simplifying assumptions, such as the binary model: default/no default, whereby the credit manager is interested in evaluating the probability that the counterparty will default over a specified time interval. The best estimate of exposure to the counterparty will depend on:

- *Probability of default* (PD, a percentage),
- *Volatility* of PD estimates,
- *Loss given default* (LGD, a percentage),
- *Volatility* of LGD estimates,
- *Exposure at default* (EAD), which is the amount of money involved,
- *Effective maturity* (M) established at the discretion of national supervisors.

M is crucial because the risk weight of sovereigns, banks, corporates and other counterparties depends on effective maturity. A uniform maturity of two and a half years can be assigned at national discretion, or give way to a maturity adjustment.

As noted in section 9.2, the PD is inferred from counterparty rating, liquidity characteristics and other crucial factors. In Chapter 8 it was explained that the computation of the DP is increasingly being based on Merton's option algorithm, which uses current information on the firm's capitalization and book value of its liabilities.

When approaching their DP, many companies try to pull themselves up by their shoelaces by means of a *salvage plan*. For instance, in early 2006, Thomas Middelhoff, chief executive officer of the embattled German retailer KarstadtQuelle, came up with a new salvage plan. This consisted of selling the company's real estate properties to repay its €2.8 billion ($3.3 billion) debt that banks were no longer willing to finance.

Analysts, however, were sceptical about the scheme because, as in many other salvage plans, it did not represent a viable solution. According to some expert opinions, if Karstadt sold and leased back its ninety properties (which it finally did), then it would be converting a financial debt liability into a lease obligation, while remaining as leveraged as before the transaction.

- Property investors are likely to demand a rental yield of around 7 per cent, on Karstadt's underinvested collection of stores, and
- The market judged this financial cost to be about the same level as the average interest on Karstadt's outstanding debt.

Creditworthiness, critics said, might even be damaged in this multibillion-euro real estate deal, because this transaction would imply additional operating costs of €210 million per year for Karstadt while, according to several estimates, year-after-year operating cash flow does not exceed €200 million by much.

In this and similar cases, the negatives associated with a chosen restructuring became more evident when the PD is put under stress. As explained in section 9.2, some of the

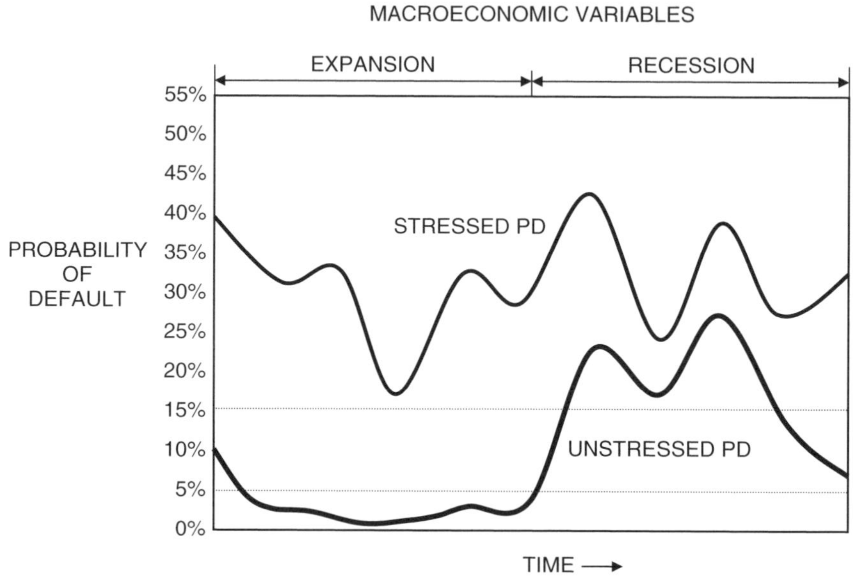

Figure 9.2 Unstressed and stressed probability of default, over time (based on a study by the Basel Committee on Banking Supervision, *Studies on the Validation of Internal Rating Systems*, BIS, Basel, February 2005). Macroeconomic variables include a growth or downturn in gross domestic product, exchange rates and market psychology

stress conditions may be endogenous, while others are exogenous, such as a downturn in the business environment, where macroeconomic variables call the tune.

Figure 9.2 gives a snapshot of stressed and unstressed probability of default during two economic cycles: expansion and recession. In good times the stressed probability of default acts as a prognosticator of the unstressed PD in case of recession. Among other purposes, this prognostication can be instrumental in determining the amount of *collateral* that should be posted. The weighting of this collateral should follow the rules of Basel II.

The limits of PD are 0 and 1. The problem is often that ratings are not sufficiently responsive to changes in economic cycles, resulting in a certain overestimation or underestimation of likelihood of default over different periods. By contrast, the approach presented in Chapter 8, based on option pricing, is a better proxy to marking to market credit risk, but it is volatile.

Loss given default is also bound between 0 and 1. The value of 1 implies that the lender will recover all money in case of default by the counterparty, whereas the lender will recover nothing with 0. As shown in section 9.2, LGD measurements are not linear because of covenants and seniority, as well as the fact that collateral may be a combination of:

- Debt instruments,
- Equity assets, and
- Different derivatives.

Collateral may also be new debt or modification of the terms of old debt. All this makes the measurement of recovery value quite difficult. Moreover, effective recovery may take several months, or even years if court action is involved. Further, under protection of bankruptcy laws there may be severe haircuts. Terms vary:

- In different jurisdictions, and
- In specific credit risk situations.

All of these factors lead to an LGD volatility. A reliable approach to stress loss given default (SLGD) should capitalize fully on the effect of different levels of volatility. Ongoing research on LGD presents some interesting statistics on LGD volatility connected to bonds. In this connection, reference should be made to a study by the European Central Bank, which examined the volatility connected with:

- Senior secured bonds,
- Senior unsecured bonds, and
- Subordinated bonds.[5]

Just like the PD, LGD must be stress tested under hypotheses of both external and internal development unfavourable to the firm, in terms of its creditworthiness. A similar statement is valid in connection with stress exposure at default (SEAD) (more on SLGD and SEAD in Chapter 10). Following the January 2004 directive established by the Basel Committee on Banking Supervision, capital adequacy based on the internal ratings-based (IRB) method covers only unexpected losses (UL). The algorithm is:

$$\mathrm{UL} = \mathrm{SPD} \cdot \mathrm{SLGD} \cdot \mathrm{SEAD} \tag{9.1}$$

What is not covered either by this algorithm for unexpected losses, or by approaches to the calculation of expected losses, is the effect of aggregation of risk. Aggregation is very important because concentrations of exposure across sectors and risk types are happening more and more frequently. In general,

- Entities continue to find it difficult to aggregate risk across sectors, and
- They are particularly confronted by some of the challenges faced in aggregation, such as intragroup exposures and heterogeneous risk types, including credit, market, legal, technology and other operational risks.

One of the defying issues is that common definitions, let alone metrics, for risk concentrations across risk types are not currently available. Neither is there a generally accepted definition of risk concentration. Moreover, the amplitude and scope of the risk concentrations domain have widened in recent years to include:

- Large exposures to one obligor, product, region or industry, and
- Multiple exposures of different member firms of the same conglomerate, to one counterparty.

A recent study by the Basel Committee points to Enron as a typical example of events that have changed thinking about risk concentrations. It also points out that while the focus is often on the asset side of the balance sheet, risk concentrations are highly relevant to the *liability side* of the balance sheet, and to derivatives exposures.

Aggregation, the Basel study says, also raises issues related to correlations. Not only are the data needed to estimate correlations often limited or unavailable, but also correlations are susceptible to change under stress scenarios, thereby affecting the results of stress tests.

Correlation assumptions are an important consideration in the setting of concentration limits, especially at the top level of a conglomerate. Miscalculation of correlations can turn on its head the effort of setting limits on risk concentrations by obligor, product and history. Moreover, it can invalidate reliance on the entity's managers' market expertise, when it comes to determining vulnerability to risk concentrations.

This May 2006 study by the Basel Committee's Joint Forum[6] further points out that, to remedy this situation there has recently been an increase in employing secondary markets to manage risk concentrations. For instance, the use of credit derivatives is widespread among banks, although the reason for engaging in derivative contracts varies across industry sectors.

- Banks tend to be net protection buyers.
- By contrast, insurers operate as protection sellers.

Many risk managers have come to appreciate that concentration in derivative financial instruments has plenty of risks of its own, and it may weigh heavily on aggregation of counterparty risk. Credit risk mitigation (see Chapter 11) is by no means an approach providing only benefits. The control of exposure is further handicapped by the fact that, as the aforementioned Joint Forum study underlines:

- Currently, there is no common cross-sectoral framework of definitions or metrics for dealing with risk concentrations, and
- There is no common approach for aggregating risk concentrations across risk types.

To close the gap, several entities continue to work on improving techniques for identifying and managing risk concentrations, while supervisors show interest in models developed by credit institutions. Altogether, this is an excellent opportunity for new developments that can revolutionize risk management by stress testing concentrations rather than only individual conditions.

9.4 Probability of default and stress probability of default

In the Merton approach to modelling credit risk, to which reference has been made several times, it is assumed that a default happens if the value of an obligor's assets falls short of the value of debt. This provides financial analysts with the ability to forecast future, or *implied*, credit risk using information available at the current time. On a firm-by-firm basis, this is an important component of modern credit risk management. At times, when market-priced asset values are not available, insolvency rates are taken as proxies for default rates. In either case:

- Default probabilities address points in time, and solvency thresholds associated with them.
- Their contribution is that they help to quantify the likelihood of an obligor's assets falling short of a given threshold, and associated default correlations given the values of risk drivers.

The inclusion of macroeconomic risk factors improves the prognostication of default probabilities, by driving loss distributions to the upside. Section 9.3 gave an example with a general market trend due to deteriorating macroeconomics. As can be seen in Figure 9.2, negative factors ensure that:

- The asset value is diminished, and
- There is an upward trend in liabilities, with the result that the assets to liabilities ratio becomes negative.

Deteriorating economic conditions, as well as reasons pertinent to an individual company, in short, general and specific credit risk, lead to stress scenarios that significantly impact on both pooled and obligor-specific PD. Probabilities of default that do not incorporate stress assumptions are likely to change rapidly as prevailing economic conditions and asset liability ratios change, tending to:

- Fall during business upturns, and
- Rise during economic downturns, as well as other adversities affecting the business cycle and/or the individual firms.

By contrast, as shown in Figure 9.2, SPDs tend to remain relatively stable over a business cycle compared with classical PDs. During economic expansion the unstressed PD declines and the obligor receives a higher rating; but during economic recession the unstressed PD increases, closely approximating stressed PD, and the obligor receives a lower rating.

As far as stress scenarios associated with obligor-specific PDs are concerned, these should incorporate information relevant to assessing the obligor's ability and willingness to repay its debts, beyond information about the economic environment in which lender and obligor operate. Two classes of data are useful in forecasting defaults, and can be the subject of stress testing.

- Aggregate information shared by many obligors, including macroeconomic variables

This requires estimating correlations between borrowers, based on points in time and thresholds. As stated in section 9.3, this is by no means a straightforward task. Asset correlations should be modelled as a function of co-movement in asset values, covering the balance sheet, insolvency data and risk drivers. In principle, the inclusion of variables correlated with the business cycle improves the prognostication of credit risk.

- Obligor-specific data unique to a particular borrower, both static and dynamic in character, including obligor's leverage

This information should include all balance sheet and off-balance sheet items. Notice that information pertaining to these two bullet points may be correlated. In addition, both will usually include embedded assumptions about future economic conditions, implicitly or explicitly, which will find their way to *stress scenarios* based on extrapolation from current conditions.

Stress scenarios will typically involve an aggregate of assumptions about future economic conditions and obligor-specific developments. Some of these may be low frequency, but they will usually tend to lead to high credit losses if they occur. The following definitions by the Basel Committee sum up the aforementioned notions:

- An *unstressed PD* is an unbiased estimate of the likelihood that an obligor will default over the next year, given all currently available information, including static and dynamic.
- A *stressed PD* (SPD) measures the likelihood that an obligor will default over the next year, using all available information, but assuming adverse economic and lender-specific conditions for the stress scenario.

Because SPD makes use of dynamic obligor characteristics, the results that it provides will change as an obligor's individual characteristics change. By contrast, for reasons already explained, it will tend not to be highly correlated with the business cycle, whereas the SPD is cyclically neutral.**7

The fact that the SPD moves as the obligor's particular circumstances change, while it is less responsive to changes in overall economic conditions, is a major benefit in terms of the ability of a stress scenario to prognosticate the likely effect of endogenous risk drivers. At the same time, however, the Basel Committee underlines that both of these probabilities of defaults, PD and SPD, represent ideal cases.**8

One of the shortcomings characterizing PD and SPD is that, so far, neither has been subjected to the discipline of confidence intervals. The quantitative result is only a mean value. (More on this later.)

Some management experts suggest that, in real life, estimated PDs may lie between two values, one incorporating dynamic obligor-specific information and the other macroeconomic data. Others are of the opinion that normal and stress scenarios help in creating, correspondingly:

- A floor of reduced PD inspection, and
- A ceiling of tightened PD likelihood under adverse conditions.

The estimation of obligor-specific and pooled PDs can be realized through the three different approaches discussed in section 9.5. With each approach, the one-year and longer term time-frame is elaborated through the historical default method. A variance of this approach is industry centric rather than company specific, with an industry under investigation characterized by its own risk drivers.

9.5 Estimating probability of default through probability of default buckets

Under Basel II, an IRB bank must assign obligors to *risk buckets*. The principle is that all obligors assigned to a given bucket should share the same *credit quality*, to be assessed by the institution's internal credit-rating system.[7] The Basel Committee does not say so explicitly, but it is evident that each credit quality bucket is characterized by:

- A mean value, and
- Variance in credit standing.

In regard to the first bullet point, for each bucket into which obligors are grouped, the bank must calculate a *pooled PD*. This will guide credit risk capital charges associated with each obligor's exposure. Notice, however, that while the June 2004 revised capital adequacy framework establishes minimum standards for IRB banks' internal rating processes, it also leaves open a great deal of latitude in determining how:

- Obligors are assigned to buckets, and
- Pooled PDs for those buckets are computed.

In relation to the variance in credit standing, which is bound to exist with every pool, all banks have an interest in establishing a level of confidence at 99.9 per cent ($\alpha = 0.001$), even if Basel does not explicitly require it. This would relieve the reservations associated with mean value, mentioned at the end of section 9.4.

Moreover, banks with experience in the implementation of Basel II rules suggest that, to apply the method of PD buckets properly, user organizations should provide themselves with the means to continue drawing a distinction between the concepts of:

- A default probability linked to an individual obligor, and
- The pooled PD assigned to a credit risk bucket.

As a reminder, a PD associated with an individual obligor is a metric of the probability that this obligor will default during a one-year credit assessment. By contrast, the pooled PD assigned to a risk bucket is a measure of the average value of the PDs of obligors in that bucket. This raises the following important questions:

- How should pooled PDs be derived that reflect the PDs of obligors assigned to each risk bucket in an accurate manner?
- How should deviations from the pool's mean value be accounted for and presented?
- How should PD bucket mean values and variances in credit risk, among individual pool members, be stress tested?

There is no clear guideline on how this pooled PD could or should be stress tested. For reasons that have been already explained, a rational approach would be to consider not only the mean value of the pooled PD, but the whole distribution, shifting to the right, towards higher PD values, as shown in Figure 9.3.

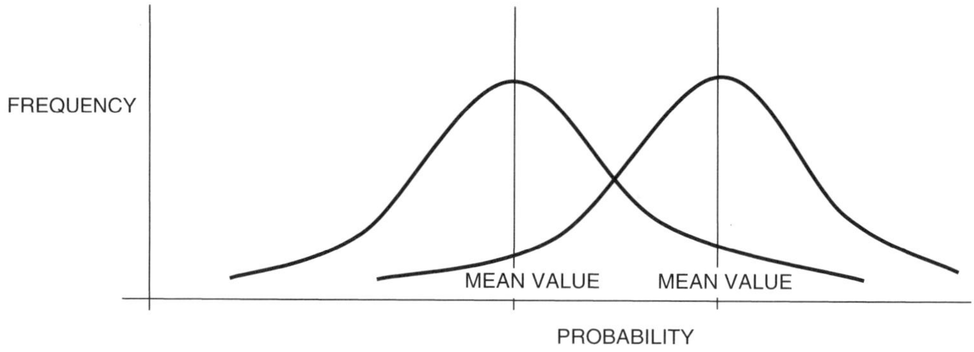

Figure 9.3 Shift of a distribution of credit risk in a grouped probability of default (PD), to a higher PD value

- This can be done by 1, 2, 3 or more standard deviations, and
- As a result, the higher the variance in the grouped PD, the greater the mean value of the shifted risk distribution.

This distribution shifting concept, for stress-testing reasons, is a more solid basis for experimentation than taking only mean risk values. Apart from its limited perspective, using only mean values raises important challenges for PD validation. By contrast, a method based on risk distribution brings attention to the dynamic properties of pooled PDs, which depend on each bank's particular approach to rating obligors.

According to the Basel Committee, the *default probability* assigned to each obligor depends strongly on the type of rating methodology and quantification techniques being used. Moreover, individual bank approaches impact on the method of using stressed rather than unstressed obligor-specific PDs to determine the pooled PD for a risk bucket (more on stressed PDs later).

Eventually, regulators will come up with a more homogeneous approach than is presently available. But at this time, there are different methods for quantifying pooled PDs. Under all of them lies the assumption that certain parameters accurately reflect the average level of obligor-specific PDs within a risk bucket, and that these parameters can be estimated from available data. The principal methods are:

- Common pool of historical defaults,
- Median of individual statistical models, and
- External-to-internal mapping of risk drivers.

In a nutshell, the revised capital adequacy framework specifies that under historical default, the pooled PD for a risk bucket is estimated using historical data on the frequency of observed defaults, among obligors who have been assigned to that bucket. Both one-year and longer term default frequencies are important in this connection. In connection with the historical default method, the *default frequency*

(DF) for a credit risk bucket is defined as the observed default rate for the bucket over a fixed assessment horizon, which is usually one year. The algorithm is:

$$DF_t = \frac{D_t}{N_t} \tag{9.2}$$

where D_t = number of defaults observed for a bucket over year t, and N_t = total number of obligors assigned to that bucket at the beginning of year t.

As an alternative, predictive statistical models are used to estimate a default probability for each obligor currently assigned to a bucket. The bucket's pooled PD is then calculated as the median of obligor-specific PDs. According to its proponents, this approach to individually quantifying pooled PDs can produce accurate estimates of credit exposure, endowing itself with an important advantage over the historical default alternative. It can also be used to:

- Quantify stressed pooled PDs, and
- Quantify pooled PDs that tend to vary significantly over the business cycle.

The downside of median statistical models is that the solution that they provide is only as accurate as the underlying default prediction model. Because of this, the challenge for bank supervisors, and for risk managers of individual banks, lies in verifying that this model produces accurate estimates of each particular type of obligor-specific PD.

The external-to-internal mapping approach establishes a system that links each of a bank's internal risk buckets to external grades established by independent rating agencies. Pooled default probabilities for external grades are calculated from external credit data. Then they are assigned to the bank's internal grades through mapping.

In a way, the external-to-internal mapping of risk drivers appears the simplest of the three quantification methods. The reason is that with this approach a bank simply establishes a mapping between its internal rating system and an external scale by Standard & Poor's, Moody's, Fitch or another well-established rating agency. Essentially,

- The bank calculates a pooled PD for each external grade using an external credit risk reference.
- Then, it assigns the pooled PD for the external grade to its internal grade through mapping.

The negative factor associated with this approach is that it poses some difficult validation problems, with associated challenges for supervisors and risk managers. Both must first confirm the accuracy of the pooled PDs connected with external ratings, as well as the precision of the bank's mapping between external and internal grades.

Another important query connected to pooled PDs is the impact of *economic conditions* on individual pool members and, by consequence, of pooled PDs values. Analysis conducted by the Basel Committee also suggests that the long-run average default frequency for a *through-the-cycle* (TTC) bucket (see Chapter 10) does not provide a good approximation of that group's unstressed pooled PD, because the latter tends to be:

- Lower than the long-run average default frequency during cyclical peaks, and
- Higher than the long-run average default frequency during cyclical lows.

The unstressed pooled PD for a risk bucket is essentially an *ex ante* forecast of the one year ahead *ex post* observed default frequency for that bucket. Computational approach should account for the fact that default events are generally correlated across obligors. Therefore, it is unlikely that in any given year a bucket's pooled PD will closely match its observed default frequency.

Last but not least, a common downside of the aforementioned approaches is that a one-year time-frame is too short for credit events to materialize. A realistic credit estimate requires the computation of longer term default frequency for a credit risk bucket. It is generally thought that estimates could be expected to converge towards the longer average unstressed pooled PD for that bucket; this, however, should be proven experimentally, not by words. Although the Basel Committee does not say so, it is necessary to account for credit risk deterioration over time by means of stressed PDs.

9.6 Errors in probability of default estimates and the role of benchmarking

Like any other metrics of counterparty risk, whether addressing an individual company or a pool of loans, the PD is unavoidably subject to error. An *error* should be viewed not as an extraneous or a misdirected event, but as an important, integral part of the process under investigation. Modelling and estimation of probabilities of default and correlations remain an art, not a science. Errors result from the fact that:

- Hypotheses underpinning credit exposure are often incorrectly taken as if they were certainties.
- The criteria used for rating counterparties are not always crisp, or homogeneous among institutions.
- Resulting parameters are rarely tested *ex ante* and *ex post*, to allow their critical evaluation, and
- Empirical evidence is not always used for backtesting, to provide a certain level of certainty. Yet this is always necessary.

Take the way that default probabilities are computed as an example of references made in these bullet points. Typically, for each credit grade a default rate is determined and it is assumed that all borrowers within a grade exhibit equal default probabilities. The hypothesis underpinning this approach is that calculation of historical averages is enough to provide needed evidence. This is a false hypothesis. Even at the high end of investment grade rating,

- Each assigned grade fluctuates in value, and
- While the given rating has a higher possibility of being true, other neighbouring ratings are also possible, albeit at a lower possibility.

In practice, no matter which institution makes them, the estimates of PD for a given individual entity, followed by the procedure characterizing a rating system, will differ from default rates actually observed in real life. A crucial question, therefore, is whether such deviations:

- Are purely random, or
- Occur systematically.

Random errors are less of a problem, as long as they cancel themselves out. But any systematic underestimation or overestimation of PDs merits critical assessment. Experience suggests that double-checking should be done by establishing whether the credit institution's computed capital requirement will be adequate to cover the risk that it is incurring.

One of the significant results of Basel II is that credit institutions have become aware not only of the importance of capital adequacy, but also of the level of confidence to which this should be computed. For AA rating by independent agencies, this level of confidence stands at 99.97 per cent ($\alpha = 0.0003$), which is very high indeed.

One of the major sources of uncertainty in computing capital requirement, and therefore in assuring low PD and higher credit rating, is the bias associated with the estimation of correlation coefficients, where one of three directions is mainly followed:

- Default correlations between two borrowers are computed directly by assuming two-dimensional, correlated, friction-free (Brownian) motion for the returns on the values of the firms' assets that trigger defaults, or
- Correlations are established by calculating borrowers' exposures to common risk factors. More or less, the Basel II model follows this approach by assuming the existence of one non-observable contemporaneous risk factor that is responsible for correlation(s), or
- The board arbitrarily decide that correlations will be set at, say, 25 per cent. This is an irrational but frequent practice. It is a potentially very expensive bias, which will not be described further in this text.

The methods described in the first two bullet points are based on assumptions that may or may not be correct. If the hypotheses being made are properly tested, it makes sense to construct a statistical test based on the binomial distribution, for assessment of estimated PDs.

A basic issue in this regard is defaults per rating grade, which are taken as being statistically independent. If this were true, then the actually observable number of defaults per rating grader, after one year, would be binomially distributed. But,

- If major differences are evident between the default rate and estimated PD of the rating grade,
- Then the hypothesis of binomial distribution must be rejected, because the rating model is poorly calibrated.

An evident weakness of the binomial test is the assumption that the borrowers' defaults are independent events. In life, the defaults are *correlated* because of cyclical moves by bankers in granting loans, and other influences. Moreover, the true value of correlations is not known; it is only guessed, and still taken as being right, while it may well be (and often is) wrong.

Another assumption often used with extraordinary frequency is that, in probabilistic terms, the default event is random. While attempts to quantifying credit risk try to determine the *probability* of the default event within a given future period, the randomness hypothesis:

- Makes a mockery of what happens in real life, and
- Evidently leads to results that are far from being dependable.

A better approach to statistical validation of PDs is the use of *benchmark portfolios*. For instance, benchmark portfolios can be constructed through external data from correspondent banks and rating agencies. Because it provides a way of verifying estimates, this comparison through benchmarks is becoming fairly widespread.

The target is the tracking of systematic deviations of the bank's internal estimates, from estimates in the benchmark portfolio. In this sense, benchmarking can serve as a useful complement to post-mortem testing and post-mortem validation, but its usefulness depends very much on the choice of:

- Appropriate benchmark subjects,
- Suitable benchmark data, and
- The accuracy with which endogenous and exogenous factors are accounted for.

Satisfaction of requirements posed by the third point requires sophisticated modelling approaches because risk factor drivers for default often work with a time lag. For instance, in debt instruments of non-investment grade (BB+ and worse), an increase in the Central Bank's interest rate will lead to an increase of default probabilities in *the following year*.

The likely effect of changes in interest rates on debt instruments, and on borrowers, should be studied both *ex ante* and *ex post*. Modelling and estimation of default probabilities and default correlations are central to modern financial analysis. Post-mortem benchmarking is done through backtesting, which involves comparing the estimated quantities with observed results. For instance,

- Probability of default
- With actual defaults statistics.

In principle, this would make it possible to test a credit institution's internal quantitative validation of credit risk exposure. In addition, *quantitative* validation methods have to be complemented by *qualitative* approaches, which serve to safeguard the applicability of quantitative methods. Usually, qualitative analyses test four main issues:

- Hypotheses underpinning credit rating,
- Design of credit rating processes,
- Quality of data for credit rating,
- Consistency and effectiveness of the internal use of rating in the granting of credits.

Observance of requirements posed by the item depends greatly on management policies and on quality of governance of the enterprise. What is most often wanting is the quantitative validation of the database suggested by the third bullet. As for the first issues, the hypotheses being made and the process of assigning ratings must be not only factual but also transparent.

9.7 The many aspects of confidence placed on a test

Although it has not been stated in black and white, existing evidence suggests that the approach taken with Basel II starts with *unconditional PDs*. Basel does not prescribe how to model unconditional PDs, but the implementation of IRB requires that unconditional PDs are modelled, within the capital adequacy framework, in a way that:

- Generates asset returns,
- Accounts for risk drivers, and
- Results in an estimate of default probability.

To face the challenge posed by the transition from unconditional to conditional estimates of default probabilities, no matter what may be the exact nature of risk drivers, a testing procedure that can be handled with confidence is needed. This is likely to call for a fairly sophisticated approach. Classical types of risk analysis are at a disadvantage because:

- The degree of complexity characterizing the current operations of companies is much higher than the old business model,
- Failure to analyse not only the most apparent but also underlying reason(s), as well as motivation for assuming credit risk, can be fatal,
- New requirements posed by financial and commercial relationships, between their various subsidiaries and their sister companies, continue to morph into risk drivers, and
- The location of significant operations or subsidiaries in other jurisdictions, with more permissive or more stringent regulatory regimes and legal requirements than in their country of origin, alters assumptions based on models of linear behaviour.

Many of the elements entering into these bullet points relate to corporate governance rather than to the instrument itself, but they do have a major impact on this discussion. The reasons underlying risk factors amplify their effect when management is not quite in charge. In fact, risk drivers associated with management action and inaction are at the top of the list of those examined by private equity firms when they circle around a company for takeover.

Confidence in the underlying ability of a model to map a real-life situation increases when the stress scenario is based on real-life events, which although outliers, have a probability of taking place. Real events provide the necessary ground for a detailed analysis of:

- The hypotheses underpinning the conceptual and structural aspects of a model,
- The algorithms themselves, using number theory, statistics and complexity theory, and
- The information elements from data feeds and databases, which can themselves be tested.

For instance, an important part of having confidence in an algorithm is whether it has been examined thoroughly by traders and analysts, the *ex ante* tests, as well as validated by *ex post* tests based on current market events. No entity that uses models should forget about the need for *ex ante* and *ex post* continuous testing.

- Modelling today is an important discipline in finance, and
- What has just been stated is applicable to all models. With stress testing, it is a 'must', and it also increases the end-users' confidence in the results.

A stress scenario on PD can benefit by transposing situations that have taken place in other companies, and their aftermath, to our firm. What if our company falls victim to hedge funds and private equity joints, as happened in late 2005 with TeleDenmark, the former state telecommunications company in Denmark? This has been a stress test on an entity's governance.

- Until that leveraged buyout, TeleDenmark was a rather well-to-do telecommunications company,
- But it had a weak management, which was ready to sell out irrespective of what this meant to stakeholders such as bondholders and employees.

Clear-headed financial analysts are aware of the importance of analogous thinking, and the same is true of the tier-one financial press. On 5 January 2006, under a cartoon of a shark drinking through a straw from a goldfish bowl, the *Wall Street Journal* described how private equity firms take companies over. The technique, particularly applicable when management is not worth its salt, is to:

- Buy a company, and
- Make it take on a load of debt.

Then the takeover artists pay themselves large fees and dividends, out of the loan, before any of that money is used to benefit the newly acquired firm. On the contrary, hobbled with debt, the acquired company is often sold again.

A stress scenario for a particular company can be developed out of Apax Partners' buying of Intelsat, and then immediately taking out a loan for the company. Right afterwards, the partners of Apax paid themselves US $350 million in dividends. For its part, the Blackstone Group bought Celanese Corporation for $650 million up front, for the $3.4 billion price. Within nine months Blackstone took a return of $1.3 billion in dividends, a 266.66 per cent return on an annualized basis. The private equity firm that bought Warner Music:

- Put up $1.25 billion in equity, and
- Within a year it took four dividend payouts totalling $1.45 billion, 16 per cent more than the initial investment.[9]

These are statistics based on real-life events; they are not hypotheses. Therefore, they make good case studies on which to base 'what if' stress scenarios for other firms. Huge loans assumed immediately after the leverage buyout have an evident after effect on the creditworthiness of entities that become the target of hedge funds and private equity specialists.

There is a common thread in these cases: the qualitative aspect of these deals holds the upper ground. This is not a one-off affair. In 2005, researchers at Georgetown University postulated that:

- To understand currencies
- We have to study the thinking and behaviour of their traders.

The model elaborated by the Georgetown University researchers focuses on market-makers. Market-makers take orders from a mix of clients with beliefs about currency exchange rates as diverse as their motives. Typically, foreign exchange orders:

- Reflect diverse and often contradictory opinions,
- But they are backed by money, which is an important real-life component.

For this reason, the mix of orders taken by market-makers conveys useful information about what their clients believe, and how strongly they believe it. The market-maker is practically following the hypothesis that the economy runs on dispersed bits of incomplete and frequently contradictory knowledge.

Scattered insights are communicated to everyone through shifts in market prices. Theoretically, it could be said that this scattered pattern provides a fuzzy picture. Practically, however, this fuzzy picture makes the market and, therefore, it is serious business. When real money, rather than gearing, enters a trade, the confidence placed on a test increases.

Notes

1. B. Woodward, *Maestro: Greenspan's Fed, and the American Boom*, Simon and Schuster, New York, 2000.
2. Basel Committee, Joint Forum, *The Management of Liquidity Risk in Financial Groups*, BIS, Basel, May 2006.
3. *The Economist*, 27 July 2002.

4. S. Ramaswamy, Setting counterparty credit limits for the reserves portfolio, in C. Bernadel et al. (Eds), *Risk Management for Central Bank Foreign Reserves*, European Central Bank, Frankfurt, 2004.
5. Basel Committee, *Joint Forum, Regulatory and Market Differences: Issues and Observations*, BIS, Basel, May 2006.
6. Basel Committee on Banking Supervision, Working Paper No. 14, *Studies on the Validation of Internal Rating Systems*, BIS, Basel, February 2005.
7. *EIR*, 13 January 2006.

10 Stress loss given default and stress exposure at default

10.1 Introduction

The probability of default (PD) is a very interesting statistic in guiding the hand of loans officers, and in customer handling. By itself, however, it does not tell us much in terms of capital at risk. Whether computing expected or unexpected losses, PD has to be completed by loss given default (LGD) and exposure at default (EAD). The theme of this chapter is stress testing both LGD and EAD. In addition, TTC PD is defined, and stress-testing procedures for legal risk and other operational problems are described.

10.2 Loss given default and exposure at default

Loss given default (LGD) is a percentage expressing the loss associated with an EAD on a credit facility. The LGD of non-defaulted loan(s) is *ex ante*, whereas the LGD of defaulted loan(s) is *ex post*. To a large extent the measure of LGD is based on subjective approaches, and these are methods that largely rely on expert judgement. Objective methods exploit LGD databases, and they may be:

- *Explicit*, using reference data sets (RDSs), or
- *Implicit*, derived by measuring total losses.

Another dichotomy regarding LGD metrics is between market values based on price differences, and discovery involving historical experience derived from the cost of losses in default cases. The latter is based on two methods known as:

- *Workout LGD*, resting on discounted cash flows, and
- *Implied historical LGD*, which is mainly used with retail portfolios.

Because of simplification in modelling, LGD is often approached through a linear perspective. Linearity in LGD is a poor approximation of the real world, and it can be misleading because losses incurred because of default(s) are not a linear function; hence, the interest in testing loss estimates by means of *stress loss given default*

(SLGD). The underlying concept is that of computing LGD under stress conditions, assuming, for instance, that:

- Collateral prices have fallen sharply (see Chapter 11), or
- Certain extreme events impact on the distribution of risks associated with lending.

In its instructions for the Quantitative Impact Study 5 (QIS 5), published in July 2005, the Basel Committee said that for better credit protection banks should allocate exposures according to the nature of collateral held against credit risk. Eight categories have been specified for that purpose:

- Two unsecured, and
- Six collateralized.

The unsecured categories address subordinated and other types of debt. One of the collateralized categories concerns receivables; two target real estate, commercial and residential; one targets gold; one other physical assets; and the final category loans supported by financial collateral, including cash, equities on a main index, government securities and other securities.

- If the exposure is fully unsecure, then banks should allocate the full amount to the unsecured class.
- If the exposure is collateralized by financial assets or gold, then they should enter the collateralized portion after specified adjustments.

An important category is that of subordinated loans. These are a facility expressly subordinated to another facility; by the foundation internal rating-based (F-IRB) method, where regulators set the appropriate values for banks to follow, all subordinated claims on corporates, sovereigns and banks will be assigned a 75 per cent LGD. Moreover, at national discretion, supervisors may choose to use a wider definition of subordination. For instance, they may include economic subordination, as in cases where:

- The facility is unsecured, and/or
- The bulk of the borrower's assets are used to secure other exposures.

A methodology based on stress testing will focus on outliers in LGD, rather than the most often used average LGD figures. This is a new and forthcoming regulatory requirement. However, even without the supervisors asking for it, banks would be well advised to examine carefully the aftermath at *the tail* of any LGD distribution with which they are confronted.

Once the SLGD culture has been acquired, its use does not need to be limited to the risk arising from loans. Other banking channels where the concept underpinning SLGD can be applied are proprietary trading; capital raising services, including equity and debt underwriting; derivative financial instruments, including convertible bonds; currency derivatives; index arbitrage and other programme-trading activities;

interest rate products; and most evidently leveraged finance, including high-yield and distressed debt and non-investment grade loans.

Still other areas where risk management can be improved by learning from SLGD, and from stress exposure at default (SEAD), are margin lending; market making in securities and options; trading of syndicated, defaulted, distressed and other loans; real-estate activities, including financing real estate and real estate-related products; risk arbitrage in equity securities of companies; securities lending and repurchasing agreements; as well as the expanding perspective of structure products, including asset-backed securities, such as collateralized debt obligations.

As far as stress testing the risk from loans is concerned, EAD consists of two parts: the amount currently drawn by the obligor, and the estimate of future drawdowns of available but untapped credit. As shown in greater detail in section 10.5, both quantities are important and they should be subject to stress testing.

Even more than is the case for PD and LGD, stress testing EAD focuses on how the relationship between lender and borrower evolves in adverse business conditions. To a substantial extent, EAD is largely influenced by decisions and commitments made by the credit institution before default. In general, these are taken as basically depending on:

- The type of loan, and
- The type of borrower.

This fairly widespread approach is technically correct but incomplete, because it does not account for the impact of novel instruments, from securitization to other derivatives that alter the classical way of treating loans, and tend to abstract from the typical notion of the borrower. Neither does it consider other factors vital to EAD.

Any loans transaction has associated with it a number of characteristics qualifying the credit given to a client. As a result, several variables affect EAD, including type of loan, type of borrower, obligor-specific references, current use of loan commitments, covenants attached to the loan and time to maturity. Other factors are:

- Fixed versus floating interest rate,
- Revolving versus non-revolving credit,
- Conditions in case of restructuring, and
- The obligor's alternative ways and means of financing.

Just as important factors, to be subjected to a stress test, are estimates of potential future drawdowns by the obligor. These are known as credit conversion factors (CCFs) and, in general, they are the only random variable of EAD to be stress tested. (More on CCFs in section 10.5.)

10.3 The challenge of computing stress loss given default

Loss given default (section 10.2) is a percentage expressing the loss associated with EAD on a credit facility, if the obligor defaults. For a defaulted credit, LGD is *ex post* loss expected. Realized LGD can be calculated , if there is complete and accurate information on all losses related to a facility. Otherwise, *ex post* LGD is a random variable that:

- Can change significantly under different volatilities.

As with PD 5 (see Chapter 9), even if the mean estimated value remains the same, the distribution of LGD values, characterizing a given position, flattens as volatility increases. Figure 10.1 illustrates this point. Therefore, a credit institution must have:

- A rigorous and well-documented process for assessing the effects of volatility, as well as of economic downturn conditions, on recovery rates.

Basel II ensures that senior management is responsible for producing LGD estimates consistent with changed market conditions for each supervisory asset class. Because national regulators have degrees of freedom, this must be done at the specific level of documented computation and comprehensive presentation defined within each jurisdiction.

Examples of adverse market conditions affecting LGD are no different from those connected with other financial variables; for instance, periods in which observed historical default rates have been relatively high for a portfolio of exposures representative of the bank's current portfolio. A common risk driver affected by adverse macroeconomics is collateral. A downturn impacts upon both:

- Default rates, and
- Recovery rates.

The richness of risk drivers means that the domain for stress testing on LGD is very fertile. Adverse dependencies are typically identified by a comparison of average recovery rates with recovery rates under stress; statistical analysis of relationships

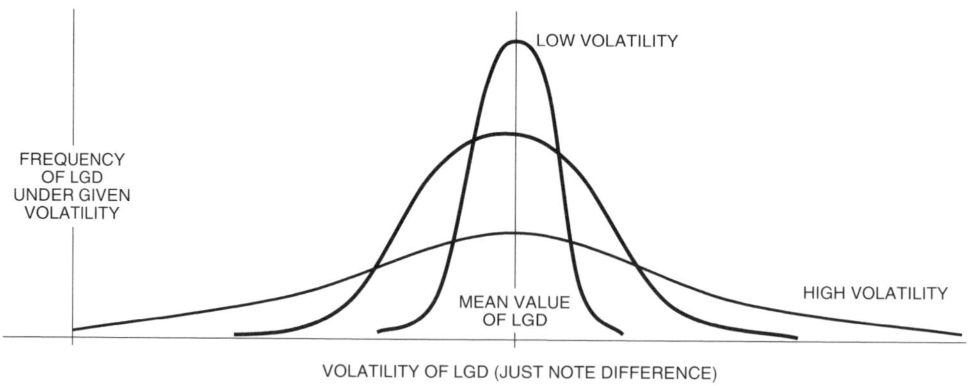

Figure 10.1 The value of loss given default (LGD), as a percentage, significantly changes under different volatility distributions, characterizing a given position

between observed default rates and observed recovery rates over an economic cycle; and, for secured exposures, comparisons of recovery rate forecasts derived from:

- Models that use classical assumptions about collateral value changes,
- Against models sensitive to the increase in market volatility and advent of downturn conditions.

Section 10.2 also drew attention to the fact that different methods are used by the banking industry to assign an LGD to non-defaulted facilities, and these can be subjective or objective, with the latter classified as explicit or implicit.

With an *explicit method*, LGD is estimated for each facility using an RDS of defaulted facilities. This is known as a realized LGD. *Implicit methods* are not based on realized LGD on defaulted facilities contained in an RDS. Rather, LGD is derived by means of measuring total losses, applying PD estimates. For instance, the implied market LGD method derives LGD from risky bond prices using an asset pricing model. A stress test would capitalize on using bond prizes associated with B-rated instruments, or worse.

The concept described in the preceding paragraph has evolved since the first draft of Basel II in July 1999. With the revised capital adequacy framework an implicit method for obtaining LGDs for retail portfolios uses the experience of total losses in the portfolio to derive an implied LGD approach known as *implied historical LGD*.

Basel II's revised framework specifies that the LGD estimates must be grounded in historical recovery rates. However, there is also another way of classifying objective approaches to LGD estimates. This consists of distinguishing between 'market values' and the 'recovery and cost' historical experience.

- *Market values* are based on price differences if there are RDSs, and credit spreads if there are no RDSs.
- *Discovery and cost experience* is based on discounted cash flows (the 'workout LGD') and implied historical LGD (for retail portfolios). Both, however, need RDSs.

A stress test will simulate RDSs, including outliers and extreme events, from historical evidence, or, alternatively, testing values chosen for their impact on LGD, under stress:

- Macroeconomics,
- Industry conditions,
- Individual borrower financial status, or
- A combination of these factors.

A stress market LGD will be based on prices of traded defaulted loans. By contrast, an implied market LGD is derived from non-defaulted bond prices processed by means of an asset pricing model. Well-managed institutions should ensure that both methods are used in parallel and their results compared. Experimental design and analysis of variance[1] should be the order of the day in stress testing.

A typical market LGD depends on the market price of a defaulted facility, usually thirty days after the date of default. Most rating agencies use this approach in recoveries. Results obtained through this method are useful, since prices reflect the investor's assessment of discounted value of recoveries, but this metric may not be appropriate if:

- Markets are illiquid, or
- They are driven by shocks unrelated to expected recoveries.

A workout LGD will rest on the discounted cash flows after default. An implied historical LGD reflects the experience of total losses and PD estimates. With workout LGD, value loss is associated with a defaulted facility and calculated by discounting the cash flow(s). This approach should include costs resulting:

- From workout,
- From date of default,
- To the end of recovery process.

The timing of cash flows, as well as the method and rate of discount, are critical in the approach that has been briefly discussed. Furthermore, it is important to use the appropriate discount rate, chosen from different possibilities on how to treat zero or negative LGD observations in reference data. It is just as vital to ensure that measurement and allocation of costs associated with workouts are realistic.

Some senior managers in charge of LGDs faced by their institutions have developed their own method leading to appropriate completion of workouts. They have done so because they appreciate that every one of the approaches examined so far has its strengths and weaknesses. The computation of workout LGDs, for example, involves issues relating to:

- Different types of recoveries: cash and non-cash,
- Direct and indirect costs of recovery, and
- The definition of when the recovery process is over, including treatment of repurchases.

The default definition used for LGD calculations has to be consistent with the one used when estimating PDs. This is necessary to obtain sensible values for economic capital and expected losses. In addition, it makes little sense to perform direct benchmarking exercises on LGDs, among banks, portfolios or at different moments of time, if different definitions of default are being used.

10.4 Stress loss given default and ability to perform

In conclusion, SLGD should be the output of a polyvalent validation process involving all the elements necessary to produce dependable LGD estimates under adverse conditions. Stress testing should include all assumptions made during LGD computation, involving higher up percentiles at the leg of the loss distribution, rather than the median or mean. Emphasis must always be placed on bad years and bad debtors, otherwise the SLGD results will be half-baked. As a minimum, SLGD should:

- Cover at least a business cycle,
- Reflect on relevant drivers of losses,
- Include stress estimates of all risk parameters, and
- Incorporate cash/non-cash recoveries by the bank.

Non-cash types of recovery can result in an amount significantly less than what had originally been expected. Such recoveries are rather difficult to track, and they must be treated case by case. Experienced analysts appreciate that the costs involved in recoveries are another risk factor. Appraisal of recovery value may involve both third party costs and overheads. For example, there may be a significant fee for appraisal of collateral or of a recovery value. There are also indirect costs necessary to carrying out the recovery.

Stress tests should pay full attention to all costs and discount factors, because a major component of both LGD and SLGD is the level of recoveries that the financial institution might obtain following counterparty default. The computation must provide a realistic measure of the net, rather than gross, amount that will be lost in the event of default.

The level of recovery in default is often derived from historical statistics. As with PD, historical recovery information may be obtained from the bank's own past experience and/or from data supplied by independent rating agencies, including recovery experience. This leads, however, to the case where another risk factor in SLGD estimates is the gap between:

- Historical discount rates, and
- Current discount rates.

Current discount rates are fixed on each date when LGD is estimated, and are often higher than historical discount rates. The type of obligor is also an important variable. Historical discount rates are usually characterized by *willingness to perform*, which should also be stress tested.

As noted in Chapter 8, unwillingness to perform is real, and it has always been a complex issue that can impact significantly on both counterparty risk and legal risk, as Figure 10.2 suggests. (More on legal risk in section 10.7.) A rotten law enforcement mechanism, corrupt judiciary and political factors,

- Increase the risk of unwillingness to perform, and
- Offer themselves to 'what if' scenarios for stress testing.

As far as *ability to perform* is concerned, it is likely that the bank can expect to recover a greater percentage of amounts due from senior secured creditors than from

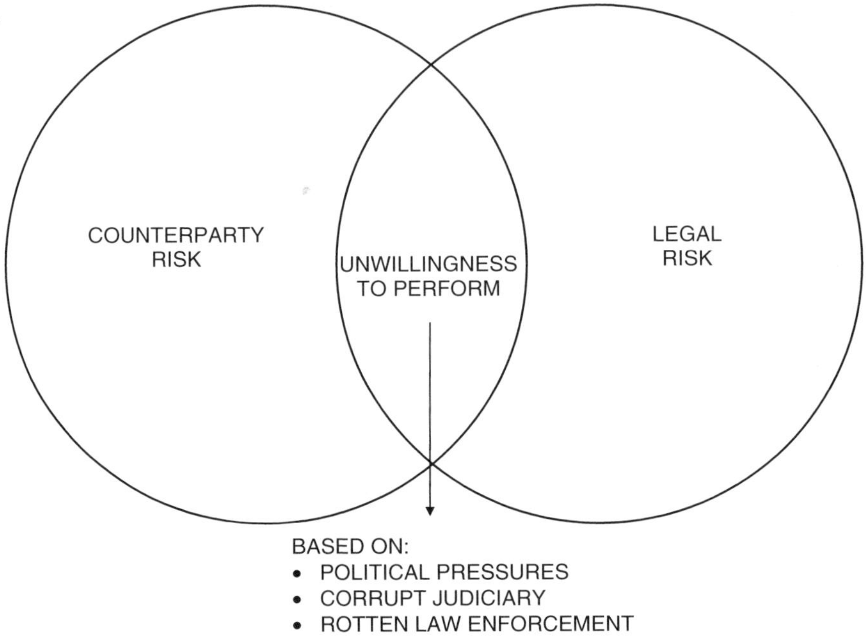

Figure 10.2 Stress testing should focus on the grey area where counterparty risk and legal risk merge

senior unsecured, subordinated or junior subordinated creditors. It worth noting, however, that according to historical evidence:

- Secured and senior unsecured creditors also face the largest variance in recoveries, and
- This factor, too, is provided plenty of opportunity for stress testing.

Another ground for stress testing is the residual value assigned to the assets of a company in bankruptcy that enables creditors to receive (usually) partial repayment of amounts due at the conclusion of bankruptcy proceedings. Much depends on the clauses of the loans contract, or alternatively on specific structures characterizing derivative financial instruments, and on the nature of client relationships. For instance,

- Collateralized derivatives are classified as senior secured claims,
- Whereas most non-collateralized derivatives are classified as a senior unsecured claims.

A further important classification with an impact on stress tests regards the economic and account treatment of potential losses due to credit risk. A distinction should be made between economic loss and accounting loss. As defined in the revised capital adequacy framework by the Basel Committee, economic loss is not the same as *accounting loss*. Loss used in estimating LGD is economic, and it must include:

- Material discount effects, and
- Material direct and indirect costs associated with collecting on the exposure.

Economic loss can be determined using the different methods outlined as explicit or implicit in section 10.3, with particular attention paid to the method's component parts and procedures being used in stress estimates of all risk drivers. These references document the importance of *loss calibration*, in connection with both expected and unexpected losses. Indeed, unexpected loss (UL) calibration is a key reason why the requirements for internal LGD calculation in the advanced internal rating-based (A-IRB) method had to be rewritten.

Theoretically, but only theoretically, the LGD parameter can be seen as an average, default-weighted, loss ratio. This loss ratio is often taken as not being associated with a particular economic scenario. However, in connection with the LGD distribution under different market volatilities,

- This is an oversimplification, and
- It is disconnected from real business life.

In daily banking practice, particularly in connection with unexpected loss estimates, the risk weight describes the loss that occurs if a systemic risk becomes significant, owing to adverse economic conditions. This is embedded into a stress probability of default (SPD), and also affects in an important way the method to be followed for SLGD estimates.

In addition, to take account of systemic risk, the input PD must be converted into an SPD, by applying an appropriately adjusted UL risk-weight function (to be prescribed by supervisors). As far as SLGD is concerned, the downturn scenario must be studied at different levels of stress, entered into the UL risk-weight function. This essentially leads to three LGDs, each with its own risk distribution:

- *Mean LGD*, taken as the lower level of exposure,
- *Expected LGD*, which accounts for exposure associated with the current economic environment,
- *Downturn LGD*, taken as exposure at crisis time, hence one of the SLGD options.

The mean LGD is practically a lower limit for the downturn LGD, which can be calculated from LGDs in periods characterized by large credit losses. With Basel II, downturn LGD is applied to non-defaulted loans, both when determining UL and when determining expected losses (EL). This is a simplification that permits banks to use only a single estimated value of LGD to determine regulatory capital requirements. Such an estimated value is computed for each individual category of assets and collateral.

10.5 Stress exposure at default

Under the A-IRB method, banks are permitted to use their own estimates of expected EAD for each facility. As section 10.2 brought to the reader's attention, typically EAD is considered as consisting of two parts:

- The amount currently drawn, and
- An estimate of future drawdowns of available but untapped credit.

Both should be subject to stress testing. The estimates of potential future drawdowns are known as CCFs. For each obligor transaction, CCF is the only random variable of EAD, therefore estimating EAD is almost synonymous with estimating the applicable CCFs.

Moreover, a loans transaction has several characteristic issues qualifying the credit to the client. This makes it necessary to qualify those qualifying factors, in a way that complements the type of loan and type of borrower.

The most important, which should reflect themselves into SEAD, are:

- Obligor-specific references,
- Current use of loan commitment, and
- The obligor's alternative ways and means of financing.

There are also additional factors, at the point of qualification and quantification of a loan commitment. Every loans officer and every EAD model should incorporate:

- Covenants attached to the loan,
- Time to maturity (see Chapter 11),
- Conditions in case of restructuring,
- Fixed versus floating interest rate, and
- Revolving versus non-revolving credit.

Beyond the type of borrower and obligor-specific references, a realistic estimation of earnings at risk should take into account the history of the borrower with the credit institution, as well as with other institutions. Part of this history concerns the ability to perform and prompt payments. Another part is obtained from the study of longer term balance sheet structure and customer profitability.

- Positive values in these two variables are likely to improve the estimation of EAD.
- This is similar to the statement made in regard to default point (DP) projections, discussed in Chapter 8.

Estimates of qualitative factors may be biased, and the balance sheet cooked. Enron's equity was at peak value in mid-2000. Liabilities were hidden because of prepays and the different shell subsidiaries that the company controlled. Therefore, the DP algorithm looked very comfortable, and this affected the estimated earnings at risk. However, if a worst case test had been done in mid-August 2000, big banks would have saved a lot of money lost in the Enron bankruptcy:

- J.P. MorganChase $3.3 billion
- Citigroup $3.0 billion
- Bank of New York $2.4 billion
- Bank of America $1.0 billion, and so on.

At Wall Street, it is rumoured that after this experience J.P. MorganChase used stress testing with its $17 billion exposure to WorldCom, and that it has been able to reposition itself in the aftermath of stress-test results. Good governance requires that stress testing becomes a bank's (or any other lender's) basic policy with EAD.

Contrarians to an EAD policy answer that there is scarcity of default data on high-quality borrowers, and this does not allow clear-cut evidence as to how different obligor characteristics influence EAD. Others suggest that a lack of critical data also limits documentation on covenants to be written to a loan.

By and large, these are lightweight excuses, by people who do not want to do a clean job. Simply stated, an important obligor must be very closely watched, with every move and every piece of news analysed in terms of impact. If it were the case that critical data for covenants are usually missing, then no covenants would be written to loans, which is simply absurd.

If the obligor experiences payment difficulties, or is in default, credit restructuring is more linear if its likelihood has been reflected in the borrower's loan conditions. Well before restructuring, a careful watch should have resulted in stricter covenants, as well as in making the obligor less likely to use the unused portion of a commitment.

- A golden horde of ifs provides the background for testing EAD.
- The compilation of the ifs list should benefit from both historical and hypothetical events, the latter characterized by low frequency but high impact.

This practice is not totally new to the banking industry, often being used in writing covenants. In principle, obligor-specific covenants should practically always be associated with a loan or credit line. Yet, this is not the general case, although there is evidence that the drawdown of a credit line at the time of default tends to decrease with:

- The quality of borrower's credit rating at the time of the commitment, and
- The nature of stringent covenants associated with a loan, when this loan was granted.

While a bank is more likely to require covenants for borrowers with lower credit quality, 'dear clients' have the muscle to escape stringent covenants. This works contrary to the bank's interests. Appropriate covenants help in restricting future drawdowns in cases where credit quality declines.

- Contrarians mention one of the prevailing hypotheses, that while covenants can lower EAD, this may come at the cost of higher PDs.
- This is a senseless argument, comparable to saying that a borrowing escapes bankruptcy thanks to our bank's generosity.

Not only are covenant-type stress tests of EAD a 'must', but also the loan should be stress tested within its proper time-frame, as explained in Chapter 11. Other things being equal, the longer the time to maturity, the greater the probability that the obligor's credit quality will decrease. This is likely because the obligor has both:

- An increased opportunity, and
- An increased need to drawdown the remaining credit line.

The fixed versus floating rate of a loan also has a role to play in EAD as well as in SEAD. Exposure at default with floating rate credits is more difficult to predict. Quite crucial is also whether the loan represents a revolving or non-revolving credit. Revolving credits often have normal utilization rates that are different from normal utilization for non-revolving credits. This impacts on EAD and it should be the subject of SEAD analysis.

Experts believe that the way in which the loan commitment is currently used is also likely to affect EAD. The Basel Committee suggests that one of the key factors perceived to influence, and/or explain, EAD is market volatility. Last but not least is the case of alternative means of financing available to the obligor. The existence of alternatives has a positive effect on EAD. Other things being equal, the more the borrower has access to alternative sources and forms of credit, the lower the EAD is expected to be. Hence, a form of SEAD is to limit the possibility of borrower financing to only our bank.

10.6 Point-in-time and through-the-cycle probability of default

Section 10.5 connected EAD estimates with the rating of obligor's creditworthiness. Two different approaches are used to describe the dynamic characteristics of rating systems: *point in time* (PIT) and *through the cycle* (TTC). Point in time attempts to produce ratings that are responsive to changes in current business conditions. Through the cycle tends to create ordinal rankings of obligors that usually remain static over the business cycle.

- Point-in-time results focus particularly on the current conditions of an obligor,
- Through-the-cycle results concentrate on an obligor's likely performance at the low of a business cycle, or during adverse personal conditions.

Banks whose ratings are used primarily for underwriting purposes are likely to implement TTC systems, because TTC tends to remain more or less constant. By contrast, institutions that aim to track current portfolio risk are more likely to implement PIT ratings, as PITs adjust more quickly to a changing economic environment.

Between these two lie hybrid rating systems that embody characteristics of both PIT and TTC. For instance, the method used by Standard & Poor's for corporate ratings primarily reflects longer run assessments of credit quality, a TTC approach. However, these ratings are permitted to vary to a limited extent as current business conditions change, which is a PIT solution.[2]

Theoretically, obligors with the same PIT grade are likely to share similar unstressed PDs. Practically, however, an obligor's rating can be expected to change rapidly as its economic prospects change in a way characterizing an entity, not a bunch of firms in an industry sector. Other things being equal, PIT ratings will tend to:

- Fall during economic downturns, and
- Rise in the course of economic expansion.

An interesting contrast between theoretical notions and pragmatic results characterizes obligors with the same TTC grade. Theoretically, obligors with same TTC are likely to share similar stressed PDs. Practically, an individual borrower's rating will change when his or her dynamic credit characteristics change, although the distribution of ratings across obligors may not change significantly over the business cycle. Viewed in this light,

- Under a PIT rating system, all obligors in a credit risk bucket may share similar unstressed PDs.
- Under a TTC rating system, all obligors in a bucket should share similar stressed PDs.

Hybrid TTC and PIT systems are more difficult to implement, but present advantages in the sense that EAD default probabilities can be described as either unstressed or stressed. The former provide a rather unbiased prediction of the likelihood that an obligor will default, while the latter predict the likelihood of default conditional on adverse stress-scenario assumptions about the:

- Macroeconomic environment, and
- Change in the obligor's own creditworthiness.

The logical conclusion from this discussion is that both the PIT and TTC characteristics are important. A similar statement is valid of other metrics having a significant impact on the whole range of factors, ranging from percentages expressed through PDs and LGDs to money at risk estimates provided by EAD.

Other metrics are also important, including correlation coefficients between important factors of exposure. For instance, there is always a correlation between default risk and recoveries. While lenders and investors know that recovery rates vary over the credit cycle, only rigorous studies that account for prevailing correlations between different types of assumed exposure and for market volatility can effectively upkeep the estimation of expected losses.

Whether they follow the PIT or TTC approach, currently many banks arbitrarily reduce the computed correlation coefficients, because higher correlations lead to capital. Concerned about this happening, several regulators consider recalibrating the correlations used by banks in their jurisdiction.

Because of an increasingly complex and changing business environment, recalibration of correlation coefficients is always necessary in order to increase the precision of capital adequacy estimates. As Figure 10.3 suggests, precision and complexity relate to each other in a non-linear fashion. The purpose of adequacy in capital is that of resisting stress condition. When market stress increases, it is only normal that capital requirements also go up.

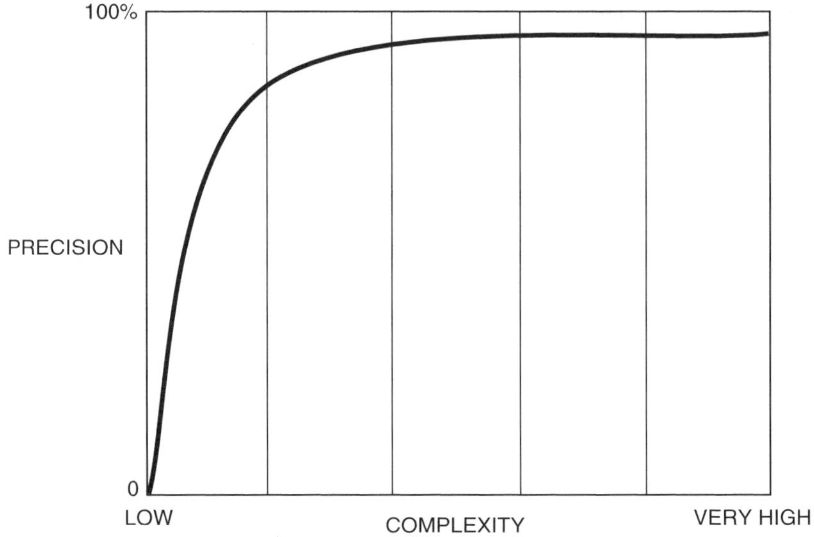

Figure 10.3 Precision and complexity correlate in a non-linear way

10.7 Stress testing legal risk

Basel II addresses two main areas of exposure: credit risk, significantly improving the 1988 Capital Adequacy (Basel I), and operational risk. A most important component of the latter is legal risk, which can be present in all instruments, transactions and execution processes.

In the investment banking business, legal risks include disputes over the terms of trades and other transactions in which a financial institution acts as principal; and potential liability under securities laws, for materially false or misleading:

- Underwriting,
- Actions of placement agent, or
- Financial advisory activities.

Still other types of legal risk are potential liability for fairness opinions, and other advice provided by the institution to participants in transactions, disputes over the terms and conditions of complex trading arrangements, action brought to court in connection with sales and trading practices, and disputes concerning the adequacy or enforceability of documents relating to some of the transactions.

Moreover, an institution is subject to claims from disputes with employees for, among other things, discrimination or harassment. A bank also faces the possibility that counterparties in complex, or risk trading, transactions will claim that it improperly failed to inform them of the risks; or that they were not authorized or permitted to enter into these transactions, and that their obligations to the banks are not enforceable; or that the bank mishandled their interests, and therefore should pay them damages.

Italy's Parmalat, the hedge fund with a dairy product line on the side that went under in December 2003, sued Citigroup and Bank of America for more than $10 billion each, claiming that they played a role in its bankruptcy. That is more than Bank of America's first half 2004 pretax income of $9.7 billion (at the time when the court action started). Both banks have contested the suit.

Banks seek to minimize legal risk through the adoption of compliance policies and procedures. They are also active in the continuing refinement of internal controls over business practices. However, the risks outlined in the preceding paragraphs:

- May be difficult to assess or quantify, and
- Their existence and magnitude often remain unknown for substantial periods.

In addition, institutions operating in many different jurisdictions face the risk that changes in laws, rules or regulations affect their operations in more than one way. Apart from making adaptation and compliance more difficult, their management and legal counsel may fail in proper interpretation or enforcement of such laws, rules and regulations. As a result, the bank may be materially affected by:

- Regulations applicable to it as a financial services company, which it did not properly understand, or
- Conflicts among regulations in different jurisdictions where the bank operates, and between them and those prevailing in home country.

Legal risk is omnipresent and its management requires paying significant attention to it, as well as first class skills. As shown in Figure 10.4, in the USA, in some domains such as settlement of securities class actions, it has increased by a factor of

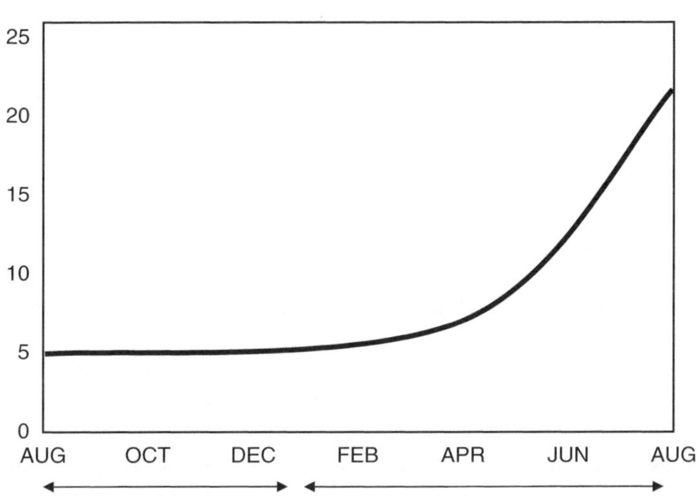

Figure 10.4 In the USA, in 2005, the settlement of securities class actions was characterized by an exponential rise

four within one year, and it is still growing. The law of unintended consequences can often be stronger than the law itself.

A decade ago, in 1995, the US Private Securities Litigation Reform Act was meant to curb frivolous class-action suits in the domain of securities. But tort lawyers raised their stakes and, as a result, the unintended consequence of the 1995 Act is that it has contributed to a new era of:

- Big lawsuits, and
- Very big settlements.

Some experts now suggest that the new 2005 Class Action Fairness Act, which seeks to curb frivolous class-action lawsuits against companies in areas such as product liability and labour law, may have a similar effect. Instead of curbing, it may be spreading tort in new domains such as business to obligors, who may sue for being put in distress when banks find it necessary to:

- Call back loans,
- Ask for tougher covenants, or
- Simply put a tap on drawdowns by borrowers at the edge of bankruptcy.

The spike that came in 2005 under the umbrella of the 1995 Act gives food for thought. At the high end, tentative settlements included $7.1 billion made by banks and other parties linked to Enron, $6.1 billion in pending settlements by WorldCom and related parties, and a $2.5 billion pending settlement by Time Warner agreed on 3 August 2005. By all evidence, instead of putting the tort lawyers out of business, the 1995 Act forced them to think longer term, and cultivate the parties that they would need as clients; for instance, in the securities domain, the public pension funds.

The likelihood of legal risk spreading into matters concerning PD, LGD and earnings at default should be taken very seriously, and it must be subjected to stress testing. Class actions have happened in the past, and there is no reason why they will not happen again in connection with obligors, when hundreds of millions of dollars are at stake in settlements.

Even the cultivation of class actions has become a sort of business practice. On 18 May 2006, senior partners of Milberg Weiss, the law firm, and the company itself, were indicted by a grand jury in California for criminal charges including racketeering, fraud and conspiracy.[3] What is interesting about this case is that:

- It does not address the economic damages of litigation in which some law firms specialize,
- But focuses on *how* lawsuits, which end up in mega-settlements, are begun; who pays who to start them; and who the beneficiaries are.

Experts suggest that one of the most disturbing issues revealed by the grand jury is the number of beneficiaries from this sort of law case. Quoted in the aforementioned article by the *Economist*, professor Jonathan Macey, of Yale Law School suggests this much. For instance, some of the beneficiaries are insurers who have experienced a dramatic increase in demand for legal protection contracts.

Who is to say that clauses included in the 2005 Act will not be exploited to include all ends associated with debt instruments, from bread-and-butter loans to securitizations, credit derivatives and other forms of capital market financing? This will bring legal risk to the heart of PD, LGD and EAD calculations, just as today legal risk is at the heart of liability insurance, since what is insured is the policyholders' legal liabilities.

In an economy that relies heavily on companies conducting their business along free-market principles, it is inevitable that firms will assume various degrees of legal risk that could result in disputes and losses connected with compliance to rules and regulations, or with the interpretation of legal issues associated with market functioning by tort lawyers and courts.

A sign of a well-governed institution is that it considers the possibility that, similarly to liability insurance, debt insurance will become a cornerstone to the modern economy. Liability insurance became popular because of a sharp escalation in judicial awards. The most common types are those purchased by businesses, along the following lines:

- Commercial general liability,
- Product liability,
- Professional indemnity,
- Directors and officers liability,
- Private personal liability.

To its proponents, a well-functioning liability regime allows a rational assessment of potential third party risks, contractual costs, terms and conditions. It also offers assurance of *ex post* financial protection to policyholders, in the event of loss, without which several business activities may not have been undertaken. It could well be that, less than ten years down the line, as credit derivatives are on their way to becoming scandal ridden, similar considerations will prevail with debt instruments.

10.8 Stress testing other operational risks

Legal risk is by no means the only operational risk requiring special attention to its substance, repeated appearance and financial aftermath. There are also many other operational risks which, briefly defined, are the risks of loss resulting from inadequate or failed internal processes, people and systems, or from external events. Fraud, for instance, is an event with both internal and external origins.

Until Basel II established capital requirements for operational risk, many operational risk problems escaped management's attention.[4] One of the challenges with this type of risk is that normal tests will not necessarily reveal their existence, let alone their importance. To face this challenge, stress tests are needed, such as those conducted by the Federal Reserve in 1998 and 1999, with two drills involving the US banks' preparedness to face the year 2000 problem.

A first step in keeping operational risks under lock and key is the early identification and monitoring of such exposures. This should be followed by the recording, assessment, prevention, correction and mitigation of operational risks, in a consistent and steady manner, appreciating that:

- Operational risks are inherent in most aspects of banking activities, and
- They comprise a large number of disparate exposures, some of them are age old and others fairly recent.

Moreover, while market risk and credit risk are often taken for prospects of gain, operational risk is accepted as a consequence of doing business. It is plainly a cost. Added to this is the fact that, in comparison to market or credit risk,

- The sources of operational risk are difficult to identify comprehensively, and
- The amount of operational risk is intrinsically difficult to measure.

Effective management of operational risks requires penalties for its presence and rewards for its absence. Such merits and demerits must be directly connected to the manager responsible for the relevant business process, and his or her personnel. Also necessary is a network of procedures with precise responsibilities, within each individual business area or unit.

Basel II states that operational risk must be funded. The best way to confront capital requirements is the advanced measurement approach. This is based on the identification of a number of key risk scenarios that describe all of the major operational risks faced by a bank.

Senior staff must review each scenario and discuss how likely it is to occur, as well as the probable severity of loss if it were to happen. Internal and external loss data, along with internal control factors and risk indicators, should be used as significant input into these scenarios.

Based on the input to be obtained from the aforementioned evaluations, each business unit must define the severity of a loss distribution due to operational risk or risks. Insurance mitigation may be included in the capital assessment, where appropriate, by considering the level of insurance protection for each scenario and level of impact. Sometimes, the impact of operational risk may be very severe indeed, as documented in the following example.

Mizuho, Japan's second largest bank, provides an example of the severity of operational risk losses. Its management must have regretted not having done its homework in terms of controls connected with its securities trading system and its linkage to trading software of the Tokyo Stock Exchange (TSE). On 12 December 2005 trading system malfunctioning prevented Mizuho Securities from quickly cancelling a botched order. That trade:

- Cost the brokerage one-third of a billion dollars, and
- Raised questions about who is responsible for the financial fallout of operational risk.

According to Mizuho, the bank racked up a stock-trading loss of at least $333 million, caused when a broker made an error inputting an order to trade shares of a small job-recruiting company called J-Com. When Mizuho noticed the input error just minutes after the opening of TSE, only several thousand shares had actually been sold to buyers. Still, although this was a fraction of the 610 000 shares that Mizuho had mistakenly offered to the market at a bargain price that was too good to be true, it was a very costly operational error.

This is one of the best examples that can be found in terms of the magnitude that operational risk can take. Who was responsible for the $333 million dollar loss? Mizuho, whose broker made the original mistake? Or TSE, because of its failing computer system? If the TSE's order-cancelling software had functioned properly, the amount of the loss would have been nil or, at least, much smaller. Both parties were at fault:

- The brokerage firm that mistakenly offered to sell 610 000 shares of the J-Com for 1 yen each (0.8 of 1 cent), while it had intended to place an order to sell one share at 912 000 yen ($7500), and
- The stock exchange, whose controls were out of function, thereby allowing this error to slip through.

Exercising damage control, Mizuho bought back a majority of the trade, but 96 236 shares, which was more than six times the number of J-Com shares outstanding, were purchased by investors. According to the terms of securities laws, these investors were owed stock certificates by the bank.

As a post mortem, Japan Securities Clearing Corporation, a trade-clearing body affiliated with the TSE, said that, in accordance with its emergency procedures, the brokerage arm of Mizuho Financial Group would pay 912 000 yen ($7560) in cash for each share of J-Com, instead of delivering actual stock certificates. In the aftermath, Hirofumi Gomi, Financial Services Agency Commissioner, commented that TSE must improve its procedures, noting that the exchange had had to halt trading for almost a full day a month earlier (in November 2005), during another trading glitch.[5]

Notes

1. D.N. Chorafas, *How to Understand and Use Mathematics for Derivatives, Volume 2. Advanced Modelling Methods*, Euromoney Books, London, 1995.
2. Basel Committee on Banking Supervision, Working Paper No. 14, *Studies on the Validation of Internal Rating Systems*, BIS, Basel, February 2005.
3. *The Economist*, 27 May 2006.
4. D.N. Chorafas, *Operational Risk Control with Basel II. Basic Principles and Capital Requirements*, Butterworth-Heinemann, London, 2004.
5. *Wall Street Journal*, 13 December 2005.

11 Counterparty credit risk, transfer of credit risk and wrong-way risk

11.1 Introduction

As the number of risk factors multiplies, and total exposure is the product of partial exposures, stress testing probability of default (PD), loss given default (LGD) and exposure at default (EAD) increasingly depends on the accuracy of each test. This means that risk factors have to be revised regularly to provide an effective model that contributes to the control of risk. These issues are the theme of the present chapter, which includes the notions of counterparty credit risk (CCR), expected positive exposure (EPE) and other methods, the very important concept of maturity parameter, netting, collateral, haircuts and new approaches to credit risk mitigation (CRM), as well as general and specific wrong-way risk.

11.2 Counterparty credit risk

Since Chapter 1, the term *counterparty* has been used to denote a party to whom a bank has an on-balance sheet or off-balance sheet credit exposure, or potential credit exposure. In the way that regulators view the issue of CCR, such exposure may take the form of a loan of cash or securities, securities posted as collateral, or a commitment under an over-the-counter (OTC) derivatives contract.

Counterparty credit risk is the *bilateral* credit risk of transactions with *uncertain exposures*. The characteristic of such exposures is that they can vary over time with the movement of underlying market factors. Specifically, the term CCR refers to the likelihood that the counterparty to a transaction could default *before* final settlement of the transaction's risk flows. This is also known as Herstatt risk.

Counterparty credit risk contrasts with the institution's exposure to a loan, because in the case of a loan credit exposure is *unilateral* and only the bank faces a risk of loss. In a way, this notion can be extended to the capital market, as the risk assumed by bondholders. Bondholders are loan givers to the entity whose debt instruments they buy; an issue discussed in Chapter 8 through a case study on TeleDenmark.

The importance of the risk of loss being bilateral comes from the fact that the market value of the transaction can be positive or negative to either counterparty. This issue is as old as banking, but its regulations were not well established. Rules have been set out in an amendment to the 1988 Basel Accord. Basel II updates the treatment for transactions booked in either:

- The trading book, or
- The banking book.

Regulatory action has also become necessary because ongoing innovation in financial instruments, and evolution in trading procedures, have provided novel types of mechanisms for transfer of credit risk. These range from securitization of loans and receivables to credit derivatives such as collateralized debt obligations (CDOs). Sections 11.6 and 11.7 address CRM techniques.

Credit risk mitigation has both pluses and minuses. At the positive end, credit derivatives provide market players with a number of trading, hedging and arbitrage strategies. Developments such as the introduction of standardized credit default swap (CDS) index tranches have led to greater price transparency because:

- Market prices are set continuously, and
- This makes market assessment both easier and better documented.

At the negative end, however, credit transfer mechanisms have brought credit risk challenges to the door of entities and investors with very limited knowledge of what credit risk is, and how it should be managed. Trading advances achieved with new instruments have influenced the development of risk management practices across different sectors, but not everybody has benefited from them.

Among the better managed institutions, developments referred to in this chapter have led a growing number of financial specialists to look at credit risk under a new light: an instrument that can be traded as a commodity, a process that reveals new types of exposure with different characteristics from older instruments and processes and, therefore, different risks. A good example is wrong-way risk, a new term identifying synergy in credit exposure (see section 11.8).

- *General wrong-way risk* arises when the PD of counterparties correlates positively with general market risk.
- *Specific wrong-way risk* is the result of exposure to a particular counterparty, which correlates positively with the counterparty's PD.

In conclusion, credit risk practices in the last couple of decades of the twentieth century, and the early years of the twenty-first, have moved a long way from the classical nature of credit risk associated with commercial and financial transactions, codified in about 1700 BC by Hammurabi, the great lawgiver and ruler of the first Babylonian dynasty.

The first known legislation and administration of justice are also credited to the same period, 1700 BC. Laws have evolved over time to keep pace with changes in society, albeit with considerable time lag. Rules and regulations should be proactive rather than reactive. Counterparty credit risk, and the way that it contrasts with the more classical form of credit exposure, should be seen in this aspect.

11.3 Methods for handling counterparty credit risk

Basel II advances treatments for CCR of repurchasing-style and other transactions. The existing treatment of OTC derivatives, known as the current exposure method (CEM), is based on a method reflecting potential future exposure (PFE), calculated by applying a weighting factor to the notional principal amount of the derivatives contract.

Because the risk sensitivity of this treatment appears limited, particularly with regard to the internal ratings-based (IRB) method, supervisors have enhanced this treatment for OTC derivative transactions by introducing a new procedure for securities financial transactions (SFTs). The April 2005 consultative document by the Basel Committee advances three methods for calculating EAD, or exposure amount for transactions involving CCR in the banking book or trading book. The alternatives are:

- An internal model using EPE,
- A new standardized method, and
- Existing CEM.

These alternatives represent points in a process of sophistication in risk management, and they aim to provide incentives for banks to improve their handling of CCR, by adopting more accurate approaches. (Expected positive exposure and other methods are discussed in section 11.4 in connection with cross-product netting.)

An integral part of more accurate approaches to the measurement and control of CCR is the development of metrics associated with stress tests and their deliverables. Because the subject is complex, it is wise to remember that models rely on a number of assumptions to make their calculations or predictions, and to explain their deliverables. It is likely that the best approach will be based on two pillars:

- One qualitative, and
- The other quantitative.

Qualitative disclosure requirements, regarding derivatives and CCR, include the methodology used to assign economic capital and credit limits for counterparty credit exposures, policies for securing collateral, policies for establishing credit reserves, and policies with respect to wrong-way risk exposures (see section 11.7), as well as discussions on the impact of the amount of collateral the bank would need, to provide itself with protection in case of a credit rating downgrade.

Quantitative disclosures address items such as gross positive fair value of contracts, netting benefits, netted current credit exposure, potential future credit exposure, collateral held (see section 11.5), net derivatives credit exposure and notional value of credit derivative hedges. Current and potential future exposures to CCR, in notional value, are segregated between:

- Use for the institution's own credit portfolio, and
- Use for its intermediation activities.

Compliance with Basel II requires that financial reporting includes the distribution of credit derivatives products used, broken down by protection bought and sold, within each product group. This underlines the fact that an important case of CCR, which rapidly becomes mainstream banking, is credit derivatives.[1] As buyers of credit derivatives, bankers or investors are making a payment in exchange for a potential payoff. If they buy credit protection, then they gain in case the underlying reference credit defaults.

- In this transaction, the investor shorts the credit and benefits if the credit deteriorates.
- The underwriter sells the credit protection, and therefore becomes long on credit risk and benefits if the credit improves.

There are several variations of credit derivatives, generally having as an objective hedging credit risk. As with all instruments, however, these can fail. Credit derivatives are not always a viable risk reduction approach. Many of the different transaction types require negotiation with investors and/or other dealers who:

- Hold the opposite view of a given credit, or
- Face no credit capacity constraints, at least theoretically.

Dealers may buy credit forwards or sell credit options but, to price their instruments correctly, they must be aware of the counterparty's current credit difficulties and constraints. This is information that a counterparty generally prefers to keep confidential, whether this party is a bank or any other lender.

There is always a synergy among different quantitative and qualitative tests, as well as between them and associated regulatory reporting. Care should, however, be taken to avoid the often found inclination towards a classical type of test, disregarding the benefits to be derived from stress tests. Stress tests on CCR should be conducted at:

- Business unit level,
- Corporate level for the whole entity, and
- The junction of credit risk and market risk.

In addition, cultural factors tend to limit the breadth of tests. For instance, qualitative stress tests performed through scenario analysis and the Delphi method are often run contrary to management's inclination to depend almost exclusively on numbers. Yet, qualitative stress tests can provide good insight into the forces that cause an economy, or an entity, to sway in one direction or another. The principle in stress testing CCR is no different from that in any other case: both the *issues* and the *numbers* are important. What is vital is for people to think systematically about:

- What they believe has changed,
- How market behaviour evolves, and
- In what way instruments and players alter their standards of risk and return.

In the author's practice, he has found that a qualitative stress test approach is, at first, upsetting to several attendees at seminars on risk management who had expected more of an emphasis on numerical factors. The numbers are still provided, of course, but it is important to give the listeners insight and foresight. A qualitative analysis under extreme conditions gives muscles to numbers that otherwise may be unintelligible and meaningless.

11.4 Expected positive exposure and cross-product netting

Section 11.2 made reference to two new methods proposed by the Basel Committee, as replacements for the existing CEM for measurement of CCR. One is a standardized approach and the other is EPE. Expected positive exposure is one of a family of measures for managing CCR exposure, which includes:

- Potential future exposure (PFE)
- Expected exposure (EE),
- Expected positive exposure (EPE), and
- Effective expected positive exposure (EEPE).

Briefly defined, PFE is the maximum exposure estimated to occur on a future date, at a relatively high level of confidence. Credit institutions often use PFE when measuring CCR exposure against counterparty credit limits. Expected exposure is the probability-weighted average exposure estimated to exist on a future date, and EPE is the time-weighted average of individual expected exposures estimated for a given forecasting horizon, which is typically one year.

Effective expected positive exposure is usually measured as an average. If all contracts in a netting set mature before one year, then the EEPE of the set is the average of individual EEPEs until all contracts in the netting set mature. For instance, if the longest maturity contract in the netting set matures in six months, then the EEPE of the set would be the average of individual EEPEs over six months. This introduces two concepts:

- Maturity adjustment (see section 11.5), and
- Cross-product netting, distinguishing between on-balance sheet and off-balance sheet.

In the revised framework, *International Convergence of Capital Measurements and Capital Standards*, the Basel Committee has this to say on *on-balance sheet netting*:

> Where banks have legally enforceable netting arrangements for loans and deposits, they may calculate requirements on the basis of net credit exposures subject to (specific) conditions.

By contrast, in regard to *guarantees and credit derivatives*, the same Basel document states:

> Where guarantees or credit derivatives are direct, explicit, irrevocable and unconditional, and supervisors are satisfied that banks fulfil certain minimum

> operational conditions relating to risk management processes, they *may* allow banks to take account of such credit protection in calculating capital requirements[2] (emphasis added).

In a way fairly similar to corporate loan exposures with maturity greater than one year, counterparty exposure on netting sets, with maturity greater than one year, is susceptible to changes in value from deterioration in the counterparty's creditworthiness short of default. Because of this, an effective maturity parameter (M) must reflect the impact of such changes in capital.

For risk management reasons, netting is used to mitigate a bank's exposure to credit risk and to CCR. However, credit institutions often cut corners in their netting practices. Bilateral netting has been recognized by the Basel Committee for the purpose of calculating capital requirements *within* certain product categories such as:

- OTC derivatives,
- Repurchasing-type transactions, and
- On-balance sheet loans/deposits.

By contrast, under Basel I netting *across* these product categories has not been recognized for regulatory capital purposes. The change that came with Basel II is that banks may be permitted by their supervisors to use a value at risk (VAR) model approach for repurchasing-style transactions and other similar operations.

This easing of regulatory rules is not necessarily for the better in terms of global level regulation. It has been advanced to give national supervisors discretion to permit banks to net margin loans executed with a single counterparty under a legally enforceable master netting agreement. Evidently such discretion creates heterogeneous approaches that make a global level playing field unfeasible. Still, there are limitations. Banks:

- Cannot net across different types of SFTs, and
- Cannot net SFTs against OTC derivatives.

Credit institutions have informed the Basel Committee that for internal risk management purposes netting among different SFTs is more common than netting between OTC derivatives and SFTs. The Basel Committee put forward proposed *cross-product netting* rules which provide, for banks that use the internal model method, the possibility of recognizing netting arrangements for SFTs, if they satisfy both:

- Legal, and
- Operational criteria.

To recognize cross-product netting for capital requirements reasons, the supervisory authority should determine whether the bank has obtained a high degree of certainty on the legal enforceability of cross-product netting arrangement(s). This legal enforceability should be guaranteed under the laws of all relevant jurisdictions in the event of a counterpart's:

- Bankruptcy, or
- Insolvency.

The satisfaction of this clause requires that credit institutions obtain and update written and reasoned legal opinions. Based on factual documentation, the bank must demonstrate to supervisors that it effectively integrates the risk-mitigating effects of cross-product netting into its risk management system.

Legal enforceability is the weak point of this regulatory approach. Stress tests should focus on the lack of legal enforceability of such transactions, or challenges associated with it, as well as on the event that the bank is shockingly exposed because of legal changes, political or legal upheavals and other factors. Operational criteria, too, should be put under stress.

- Each one of the SFTs that may be subject to cross-product netting should undergo a stress test.
- Scenarios, sensitivity analyses and drills help in ascertaining the exposures arising from ongoing business in connection with CCR.

Stress studies can also provide the best possible evidence regarding limit policies for exposures. One of the problems that remain to be solved is that of the extreme events in CCR, which stress tests need to address. Another problem is that of the blurred line of expected versus unexpected risks connected to SFTs, and their impact on the survival of an institution.

A catastrophe scenario can shed some light on what may be coming. For instance, it may focus on a crisis among counterparties exacerbated by a deterioration in general economic conditions, and cutting off of traditional funding sources. The challenge is to structure a stress test in a way that integrates the industry-wide impact of skewed risk and return estimates, which upset:

- Netting hypotheses, and
- Associated hedges.

Beyond junk bonds and the foreign debts of sovereigns and global companies, looms the vast amount of liabilities due to derivatives trades. Derivatives exposures are numbered in the trillions, while the foreign debt of Argentina, Brazil and Mexico is in billions. Once more, the lion's share of the derivatives bubble is on the side of the largest banks and other financial institutions, US, European and Japanese. The challenge is how to structure a stress test that accounts for the compound effect on:

- Individual banks,
- National economies, and
- The global economy.

This stress test should take into consideration all major risk factors: junk bonds, shaky sovereign debt and derivatives going sour, not just the better established SFTs, and it should do so both individually and in a compound manner, integrating credit risk factors under normal conditions, as well as their spikes and outliers. This will be instrumental in leading senior management away from the often assumed complacent view and towards probing questions.

11.5 Maturity parameters

One of the secrets of buying securities is properly judging their maturity. The same is true with making trades. For instance, although yield is important with bonds, the *maturity* of the debt instrument also plays a crucial role in investors' risk and return. With the exception of perpetuals, bonds are issued with a fixed date when they will mature. At that time, the issuing entity must repay the security's principal amount, usually at par value.

- Maturities of debt instruments issued by corporates can range from one year to over thirty years.
- Other things being equal, the longer the maturity the higher the yield, because the investor has to wait longer for his or her principal to be repaid.

Investors who hold their bonds until maturity expect to obtain the stated yield to maturity. If bonds are called by the issuer, the difference between *yield-to-maturity* and *yield-to-call* comes into play. Investors who obtain repayment easily may have to reinvest their capital at lower interest, if there is a downward trend in interest rates.

In trading, too, a crucial parameter is *transaction maturity*. The longer the maturity of a transaction, the greater the opportunity for a given market, price or rate to move. Market prices can only move so far in one day, but they have the potential of moving much farther in one week, one month or one year. Therefore, any effective measurement of risk must also include the *time dimension*. With derivatives:

- Maturity of the underlying exposure and maturity of the hedge should both be defined conservatively.
- Effective maturity of the underlying should be gauged as the longest possible remaining time, before the counterparty is scheduled to fulfil its obligation.

A stress test will lengthen this period of grace, or work on the hypothesis of rescheduling made necessary to allow a counterparty to perform, while currently facing illiquidity. There may also be maturity mismatches, which must be exploited to reveal their effects, by means of advanced testing.

Effective maturity (M) is defined as the greater of one year and remaining effective maturity in years. In no case will M be more than five years. The M algorithm given by the Basel Committee for an instrument subject to a determined cash-flow schedule is:

$$\text{Effective maturity} = \Sigma \text{CF}_t \tag{11.1}$$

where CF is the cash flow from principal, interest payments and fees, contractually payable by the borrower in period t.[3]

If a credit institution is not in a position to calculate the effective maturity of contracted payments, it is allowed to use a more conservative measure of M; for instance, equal to the maximum remaining time, in years, that a borrower is permitted to take to discharge fully its contractual agreement. For derivatives subject to a master netting agreement, the weighted average maturity of the transactions should be used when applying the explicit maturity adjustment, with the notional amount of each transaction used for weighting the maturity.

A maturity mismatch occurs when the residual maturity of a CRM contract is less than that of the underlying credit exposure. The Basel Committee states that where there is a maturity mismatch and the CRM has an original maturity of less than one year, the CRM approach is not recognized for capital purposes.

However, in other cases where there is a maturity mismatch, partial recognition may be given to the CRM for regulatory capital reasons, but not under the simple approach for collateral maturity mismatches. Under Basel II, hedges with maturity mismatches are only recognized when their original maturities are greater than or equal to one year.

Banks using any element of the advanced internal ratings-based (A-IRB) method are required to measure effective maturity for each facility, although national supervisors may exempt facilities to certain smaller domestic corporate borrowers from the explicit maturity adjustment. This can happen if the reported sales, as well as total assets, for the consolidated group to which the firm belongs are less than €500 million.

If the exemption is applied, then all exposures to qualifying smaller borrowers will be assumed to have an average maturity of two and a half years. This is similar to maturity used under the foundation internal ratings-based (F-IRB) method.

11.6 Credit risk mitigation: collateral and haircuts

There are plenty of CRM methods used in banking practice that have been given supervisory recognition. A classical example is *collateral*, which can be used to reduce the bank's capital charge. As shown in Table 11.1, eligible collateral under Basel II is classified into three different types depending on the capital adequacy method chosen by the bank (F-IRB, A-IRB or standardized method).

The origin of collateral dates to ancient Egypt, with King Asychis credited as its inventor. Under Asychis' reign, the Egyptians became short of money, and the king published a law that allowed citizens to borrow, using as collateral the mummy of their fathers. As expected, there was abuse, with obligors choosing to give their father's mummy to the lender rather than return the money. Therefore, a second law extended the security associated with the collateral, by making the lender the owner of the borrower's graveyard.

- If the borrower would not or could not repay his debt,
- Then he could no longer use his graveyard for himself or his family.

In current practice, collateral may be a good way to mitigate credit risk, but it is subject to market risk. Basel II advances two approaches that banks may use to determine the risk weight for financial collateral.

Table 11.1 Eligible collateral under Basel II

Internal ratings-based methods	
F-IRB	**A-IRB**
Receivables	No restrictions on the range of eligible collateral, if the institution provides reliable estimates of its value
Other forms of collateral recognized by the national supervisor	
Standardized method	
Cash	
Gold	
Debt securities (issued by sovereigns, banks and other entities rated investment grade, or above a regulator-specified minimum)	
Unrated bank debt securities, which are listed on recognized stock exchange(s)	
Equities	
Mutual fund shares	
Real estate	

F-IRB: foundation internal ratings-based; A-IRB, advanced internal ratings-based.

- The simpler way replaces the borrower's risk weight with the risk weight of the collateral for the secured part of the exposure.
- The alternative is a comprehensive approach, with the amount of exposure reduced by the adjusted value of the collateral.

This is done by means of a *haircut*, or reduction in the estimated collateral's value at the time of transaction. Typically, haircuts depend on factors such as type of collateral, assumed holding period of the underlying transaction and frequency of revaluation of the collateral's fair value. Usually, but not always, the haircut is kept at 10–30 per cent of estimated value.

Fuzzy engineering can be used effectively in connection with stress testing, to provide a much more accurate estimate of the collateral's value. Taking instruments sensitive to credit risk as an example, Figure 11.1 shows that none of the highest three grades, AAA, AA or A, is crisp, yet they are assumed to be so when haircuts are computed.

Basel II specifies how collateral should be handled, under each of the capital adequacy methods. For instance, with F-IRB, collateral is recognized through reducing LGD, while the adjusted value of the collateral is determined according to the rules of the standardized method. Standard supervisory haircuts assuming daily marking to market and remargining are shown in Table 11.2.

As a risk mitigation strategy, collateral brings into perspective the need for credit institutions to rethink how they recognize all of the instruments that are used for securing loans, including guarantees, repurchases, warranties, credit derivatives and on-balance-sheet netting. There is a significant difference between:

- The classical type of collateral, and
- Different sorts of guarantees, all the way to credit derivatives.

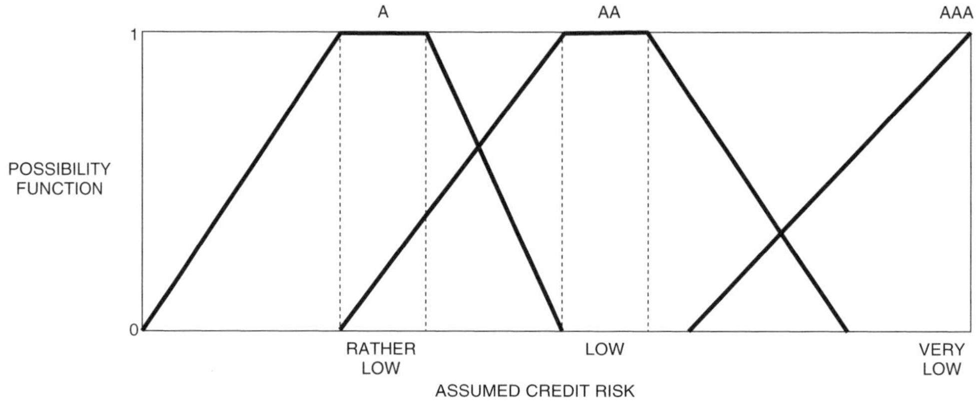

Figure 11.1 Defuzzification of the rating of collateral, taking AAA, AA and A as examples

Table 11.2 Standard supervisory haircuts assuming daily marking-to-market and remargining (figures in per cent)

Collateral	Sovereigns	Banks/corporates
Issue rating for debt securities, by residual maturity		
AAA/AA		
≤1 year	0.5	1
>1 year, ≤5 years	2	4
>5 years	4	8
A/BBB		
≤1year	1	2
>1 year, ≤5 years	3	6
>5 years	6	12
BB		
≤1year	20	
>1 year, ≤5 years	20	
>5 years	20	
Main index equities	20	
Other equities listed on a recognized exchange	30	
Cash	0	
Gold	15	
Surcharge for foreign exchange risk	8	

In the case of classical collateral the lending bank receives an asset that it can use in the event of the borrower defaulting. Under the New Capital Adequacy Framework warranties and credit derivatives are risk weighted by assigning the (lower) risk weight of the guarantor to the secured part of the loan. This is known as the substitution approach. The range of eligible guarantors includes:

- All sovereigns,
- Banks with a lower risk weight than the borrower, and
- Non-banks with a minimum rating of A– or with a certain maximum PD in F-IRB.

With Basel II, collateral is seen as one of a class of *risk mitigants*. The process of risk transfer includes several products and techniques, aiming to have a direct result in reduction of a risk. Examples other than collateral are reinsurance and co-insurance, inflation-linked bonds, securitizations and derivative instruments. In general,

- Risk mitigants can serve an important function in reducing risks and allowing for the efficient reallocation of capital,
- But at the same time, risk mitigants may create new risks, or increase a firm's exposure to existing risks.

For instance, reinsurance contracts usually introduce credit risk, derivatives introduce both credit risk and operational risk, and collateral may introduce liquidity risk and market risk. Therefore, supervisors need to be satisfied with regard to:

- The nature and extent of the risk that is actually mitigated, and
- The effectiveness of the way in which CRM is chosen and implemented.

A new aspect with Basel II is that collateral and warranties will be recognized as mitigating risk even if there is a maturity mismatch between the underlying exposure and the collateral instrument. Hence, the extent of the risk mitigation depends on the ratio of the hedge's residual maturity to that of the exposure.

For repurchasing-type transactions falling under a bilateral netting agreement with a counterparty, Basel II permits banks to make their own estimates of VAR, instead of the more classical comprehensive approach that has been frequently followed. However, supervisory approval of the VAR model to be used is necessary.

Apart from the likelihood of a decrease in the value of the collateral, there may also be credit risk because of PD of the issuer, or plain weaknesses in contractual terms. Basel II ensures that the factor applied to the collateralized portion of the exposure is 15 per cent of the risk weight of the original borrower; this is known as the *w factor*, which may be dispensed with certain types of collateral.

- With guarantees and credit derivatives, the risk weight of the protection provider is assigned to the collateralized exposure. The application of the w factor is a new element,
- But for short-term repurchasing, securities lending and securities borrowing transactions with domestic government securities, a 100 per cent collateralization is recognized if such transactions are subject to certain conditions, including daily remargining.

Basel II ensures that collateralization techniques are enhanced through a risk mitigation approach being applied even if there is a maturity mismatch between the loan and hedging instrument. The extent to which the mitigation of risk is recognized, however, depends on the length of the collateralized period in relation to residual maturity.

The handling of collateral and that of asset-backed securities (ABS) correlate. Not only ABS instruments can be used as collateral, but also other collateralized obligations, which may be liabilities based, rather than assets based. Practically all ABS are somebody else's liabilities.

Credit institutions securitizing their clients' liabilities often try to hit two birds with one well-placed stone. Through ABS transactions, they recover money that they lend out and, at the same time, they lower their own regulatory capital requirements without a corresponding reduction in the bank's credit risk in all cases. This process is known as *regulatory capital arbitrage.*

11.7 Credit risk mitigation: new techniques

With support from high technology, innovation in financial instruments has brought forward new techniques for transferring credit risk. In addition, as liquid markets develop, participants are better able to set an appropriate price for accepting credit risk. However, there is also a downside associated with leveraging through credit derivatives,[4] an issue that raises supervisory concerns. Some of the reasons are that with the more complex types of CRM transaction:

- The distribution of counterparty risk, within the financial system, becomes less transparent,
- Risk may be concentrated risk just as easily as dispersed, and
- Insurance companies, as well as other institutional investors, become increasingly involved in inventorying credit risk, since many of these credit transfer instruments are similar to insurance policies.

From a regulatory viewpoint, this morphing of credit risk exposure into a widespread commodity implies the need for very close collaboration between banking and insurance supervisors, to prevent one-sided actions or gaps in regulation, and to ensure that risks are properly monitored and priced among market players, so that new entrants, such as institutional investors, are not taken for a ride.

One of the simpler new forms of credit risk transfer is *securitization.* Section 11.6 made reference to ABS, which is a rapidly growing business line in banking. However, it is also a fairly complex field of activity for which Basel II, for the first time, provides an internationally harmonized standard for supervisory treatment. This is expected to:

- Reduce the incentive for capital arbitrage, which was a key motive for the securitization of claims in the past, and
- Enhance both risk management and refinancing activities, expected to assume a more prominent role than in the past.

Contrarians to securitizing and selling of credit risk have raised questions about the adequacy of documentation supporting such transactions, as well as their legal status. Some jurists point out that credit risk transfer instruments are ahead of appropriate legislation and, as with many recent innovations in the financial industry, legal uncertainties may only be resolved in the courts, which could take a long time. Such uncertainty can be unsettling to both:

- Clients of various risk transfer instruments, and
- Banks, known as *originators*, that securitize their own assets.

In principle, the originator's capital relief is contingent on an effective and significant risk transfer. Basel II places non-explicit limits on the volume of securitization exposures that the originator may retain, but the issue of national regulatory interpretation based on the economic impact of a CRM transaction is always present.

For practical purposes, for supervisory recognition of securitized risk transfer, the standardized and two IRB approaches are identical. The only distinction regards capital charges on securitized exposures held by originators and investors.

The standardized approach for exposure associated with securitization is modelled along the frame used for credit risk. For tranches with an external rating of less than BBB–, however, higher risk weights are applied. Unrated positions require a reduction in capital split evenly between:

- Core capital, and
- Additional capital.

With both IRB approaches, the rule for securitization exposures deviates from the general credit risk framework. This is necessary because non-internal estimates of tranche-specific PD, LGD and EAD are taken into account. Basel offers three ways to calculate the capital requirement for securitization exposure:

- External ratings-based approach (RBA),
- Supervisory formula (SF), and
- Internal assessment approach (IAA), permitted only for a limited scope of implementation.

The external RBA must be applied to all securitization exposures of IRB banks whose risk assessment involves external ratings, with risk weight assigned to each rating category. The RBA segments are finer than those of the standardized method, and there is a greater range of risk weights, accounting for seniority of a tranche.

The development of credit derivatives markets, and most specifically markets for collateralized debt swaps, moved towards increased sophistication in approaching credit risk transfer. Collateralized debt obligations (CDOs) are structured finance products with a defining feature of claims on the payment flows from the pool of assets.

- These are split into various tranches with different risk and return profiles, and
- Such tranches are geared towards individual investor preferences in terms of risk and return.

Defaults of assets from the collateral pool are initially incurred by the first loss tranche. After this tranche had been exhausted the junior or mezzanine tranches will be called upon. Losses in senior tranches occur only in the case of very significant deterioration of credit quality of the asset pool.

This particular feature of senior tranches means that they usually have a higher rating than the average rating of securitized assets. At the same time, however, they pay less interest than the riskier tranches. In the general case, the risk of a CDO tranche depends greatly on the correlation with the PD of the underlying reference pool:

- If there is a low default correlation,
- Then reference assets evolve relatively independently of each other in terms of credit quality.

This means that the probability distribution is centred on the expected portfolio loss. Depending on their degree of *subordination*, individual CDO tranches react differently to the correlation changes. Subordinated CDO tranches are financial instruments with leverage, which needs to be appropriately stress tested before commitment. Depending on the volume of the tranche and position in the loss distribution,

- Decreases in the value of reference pool have a magnified impact on exposure, and
- They can quickly lead to a considerable loss of nominal amount of the tranche.

While the investor remains exposed to the deterioration in a leveraged instrument, the originator bank usually protects itself against downgrading in credit quality by means of *credit protection* connected with assets in the reference pool. For their part, a CDS allows credit risk to be unbundled from other exposures embedded in a financial instrument and traded separately. In a CDS transaction, the buyer of credit protection pays a periodic fee to the seller of the protection. This generally reflects the spread between the:

- Yield on a defaultable security, and
- Risk-free interest rate of a G-10 government bond.

In the event that the reference entity defaults, the buyer delivers to the seller debt owed by the defaulted entity, in return for a lump sum equal to the face value of the debt. In this sense, CDS is an insurance contract protecting against losses arising from a default, and insurance companies are active in this market, but without necessarily appreciating the full amount of assumed credit risk.

11.8 Double default: general and specific wrong-way risk

Double default, of obligor and guarantor, has always been a problem in finance. Exposure is of two kinds, general and specific. This wrong-way risk was defined in section 11.2. As a reminder, the reason behind general wrong-way risk is that the counterparty's PD generally correlates with general market risk. By contrast, if exposure to a given counterparty positively correlates with that party's PD, then the bank is confronted with specific wrong-way risk.

A crucial role in the treatment of double default is played by correlation coefficients. Released in April 2005, the consultative document by the Basel Committee, *The Application of Basel II to Trading Activities and the Treatment of Double Default Effects*,[5] specifies, in connection with the probability of double default, that an extension of the asymptotic single risk factor model (ASRF) to hedged exposures requires the parameterization of three correlation factors: ρ_{os}, ρ_{gs} and ρ_{og}, where ρ_{os} is obligor sensitivity to systematic risk, ρ_{gs} is guarantor sensitivity and ρ_{og} is pairwise correlation.

The obligor's sensitivity to systematic risk, ρ_{os}, is calibrated within the revised framework of Basel II. The parameter ρ_{gs}, regarding the sensitivity of an exposure's guarantor's systematic risk subject to the double-default treatment, is given by regulators: $\rho_{gs} = 0.7$. This value corresponds to the median observed in empirical studies.

Also through empirical analyses, the Basel Committee has determined the pairwise correlation $\rho_{og} = 0.6$. This value has been set at a higher percentile as a prudent safeguard against wrong-way risk, which is of two parts: general and specific. The April 2005 discussion document addressed two issues:

- Finding a prudentially sound treatment to double default, where the risk of both borrower and guarantor defaulting on the same obligation may be substantially lower than the risk of only one of the parties defaulting, and
- Applying Basel II rules to certain exposures arising from trading activities, including treatment of CCR for OTC derivatives, repurchases and SFTs, as well as cross-product netting arrangements (see section 11.4).

A new regulatory solution being developed has been worked out jointly with the International Organization of Securities Commissions (IOSCO). This rule addresses both *obligors* and *protection providers*, and focuses on three forms of protection:

- Guarantees,
- Credit derivatives, and
- Insurance contracts.

Theoretically, obligors and protection providers are different entities. Practically, a protection provider may be a member of the same financial group as the obligor, or obligor and protection provider may be linked in some other way. For instance, the guarantor may be a supplier of goods and services to the obligor, with financial connections amplifying wrong-way risk.

- If such a connection exists, then their performance will be dependent on common economic factors.

Therefore, the new Basel rules place particular emphasis on the existence of a high correlation in the creditworthiness of the protection provider and the obligor of the underlying exposure.

Basel II not only brings into perspective a theme that has always been latent in finance and commerce, but also emphasizes its importance in estimating the likelihood of double default and, eventually, double recovery. This is done in a way seeking to reflect best practice. What the Basel Committee essentially says is that in developing the new capital adequacy framework it has been necessary to make certain tradeoffs, with guiding principles such as:

- Economic substance,
- Supervisability of the entity,
- Simplicity of capital calculation, and
- Consistency with the ASRF model.

Forms of protection addressed by the rules pertinent to wrong-way risk include protection provided through the use of single-name unfunded credit derivatives and single-name guarantees, as well as *n*th-to-default basket products subject to conditions outlined in the established operational requirements of Basel II.

By contrast, no recognition for double default will be granted to multiple-name credit derivatives (other than *n*th-to-default basket products) considered to be eligible, multiple-name guarantees or index-based products, synthetic securitizations and other tranched products. This is seen as being practical within the scope of the securitization framework and funded credit derivatives.

In addition, because of dilution risk some parties are excluded from the class of eligible protection providers. Examples are sellers of purchased receivables and parties connected to them, given the high likelihood of wrong-way risk being present. This is consistent with the fact that the rules target benefits to be obtained from the presence of credit protection, whereby both:

- The underlying exposure, and
- The protection provider

must default for a double-default loss to be incurred. In the case of double recovery, a bank or investor may recover from both the obligor and the protection provider. However, statistics that could substantiate a high likelihood of double recovery do not appear to be available and, therefore, double-default and double-recovery events are bound to be asymmetric.

Asymmetric events taking place in finance are an excellent ground for stress tests. Banks and investors who tend to forget about the likelihood of double default, do so because of complacency. Complacency is a state of mind that exists only in retrospect; it has to be shattered before being ascertained.

According to the Basel Committee's *Application of Basel II to Trading Activities and the Treatment of Double Default Effects*, for any transaction where a bank wishes to apply the double-default approach in connection with the A-IRB method, it will have to report a PD, LGD and EAD for the unhedged exposure to the underlying obligor, in the same way as for unprotected exposures under the IRB approaches.

The LGD and EAD parameters will be set by supervisors for banks using the F-IRB approach, but an IRB bank should report a PD for the guarantor and a separate EAD defined as the amount of the underlying exposure that is hedged, as well as the LGD associated with the hedged facility. For the latter, the credit institution should use the LGD of a comparable direct exposure to the guarantor.

To help to untangle complex cases of wrong-way risk, the Basel Committee has developed a simplified formula for the calculation of capital requirements regarding exposures subject to the double-default treatment (K_{DD}). For such exposures, capital adequacy is calculated by multiplying a capital requirement (K_U) similar to that for unhedged exposures by an adjustment factor:

$$K_{DD} = K_U \cdot (0.15 + 270 \cdot PD_g) \quad (11.2)$$

where K_{DD} is capital subject to double default, K_U is capital for unhedged exposure, • is an adjustment factor, and PD_g is the guarantor's probability of default.

For hedged exposures to be treated under the double-default approach, the risk-weighted asset amount must, in no case, be lower than the risk-weighted asset amount, for an otherwise identical exposure guaranteed by the protection provider. The maturity adjustment is based on the minimum PD_s of obligor and guarantor. A maturity adjustment function will use as inputs the effective maturity of the guaranteed exposure and the lower of the PD_s of protection provider and obligor.

Notes

1. D.N. Chorafas, *Credit Derivatives and the Management of Risk*, New York Institute of Finance, New York, 2000.
2. Basel Committee, *International Convergence of Capital Measurements and Capital Standards. A Revised Framework*, BIS, Basel, November 2005.
3. Basel Committee, *International Convergence of Capital Measurements and Capital Standards. A Revised Framework*, BIS, Basel, November 2005.
4. D.N. Chorafas, *Credit Derivatives and the Management of Risk*, New York Institute of Finance, New York, 2000.
5. Basel Committee, *The Application of Basel II to Trading Activities and the Treatment of Double Default Effects*, BIS, April 2005, Basel.

PART 3

Expected and unexpected losses

12 Stress testing expected losses

12.1 Introduction

Traditionally, bankers' training and experience meant that they thought only of expected losses, and they did so only in the short term. Both notions are obsolete, if not downright wrong in a globalized economy. The more severe losses are unexpected, and the medium to longer term should always be a banker's preoccupation, as this chapter demonstrates. This is itself a stress test. Other themes include the role of credit rating agencies in prognostication of credit losses, risk drivers entering into counterparty models and stress testing regulatory capital requirements.

12.2 Bird's-eye view of expected and unexpected losses

One of the key advantages of the new Capital Adequacy Framework known as Basel II is that it distinguishes between *expected* losses (EL) and *unexpected* losses (UL). This difference between EL and UL is not just a conceptual issue, but neither are we talking of two distinct populations of events. The difference is subtle, and it takes a lot of attention to appreciate it.

- El and UL are two areas of the same risk distribution function, as clearly shown in Figure 12.1.
- Where they differ is in the frequency, magnitude and impact of credit risk events.

Expected losses and unexpected losses, and the thin line dividing them, have much to do with how a bank manages its lending risks and its capital adequacy. One of the difficulties in making this simple fact understood is that different banks look at their EL from different viewpoints.

- Some see EL as an accident waiting to happen and to be covered by FMI, accounted for in pricing their loans.
- Others follow a strategy that aims to minimize EL using the best possible methods, tools and policies, assuming that this will also take care of UL.
- Still others, aware that UL happen, put aside special reserves, but do not really care to calculate the pattern and likelihood of UL, with the result that they find difficulty in managing it.

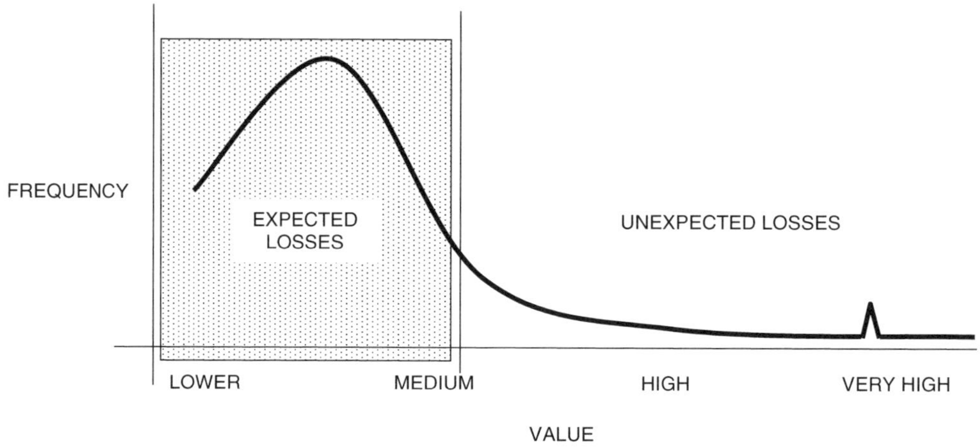

Figure 12.1 Expected losses and unexpected losses come from one risk distribution, not two

In general, more attention is paid to EL than to UL, even though the latter can be more deadly than the former. Slowly, however, well-managed banks have come to appreciate that there are problems even with EL. One of them is that many of the means that are currently popular for credit risk control are weak, obsolete or out of place in a highly dynamic market environment. They are also:

- Mathematically unsophisticated, and
- Lacking in necessary qualitative components.

Traditionally, the mathematical approach to expected loss is to take it as the average loss in market value of an asset, resulting from credit-related events over the holding period of that asset. This is basically correct but too simplistic, if for no other reason than it does not account for the volatility of EL. Unexpected losses are even more exposed to volatility than EL, which increases their impact. In spite of this difference in frequency, volatility and impact, however, UL lie in the same distribution, but beyond the level of EL.

Expressing the same distribution function in two different ways is, mathematically speaking, inconsistent. This impacts on stress testing, as shown in Chapter 13. Another inconsistency is of a functional nature. Both EL and UL are typically expressed over a one-year horizon, too short to give a valid estimate of the credit risk being assumed. Many loans are medium to longer term, and over that period:

- The obligor's credit rating may change, and
- Volatility means that, in the case of fixed interest rate loans, the bank may have assumed significant market risk.

A change in credit rating can have a negative impact on a firm and affects the estimates of EL. Statistically, there are more downgrades than upgrades of creditworthiness. In addition, while originally ratings used to be based only on probability of default (PD), now they are also based on severity loss upon default:

$$\textit{Expected loss} = \text{Probability of default} \times \text{Severity loss upon default} \tag{12.1}$$

This sensitivity of default is a function of loss given default (LGD) and exposure at default (EAD). As mentioned in Chapter 11, measurement of EL must take into account the value of collateral of an eventual guarantor, and of credit risk mitigation techniques, all of which affect the recovery rate. The equation reads:

$$\textit{Expected credit loss rate} = \text{Probability of default} \times (1 - \text{Recovery rate}) \tag{12.2}$$

Top-tier credit institutions ensure that the distribution of EL is analysed both by position and on a portfolio basis. Analytics helps to address the *risk contribution* of each position, defined as the incremental risk of the exposure of a single asset's contribution to the portfolio's total risk. For management purposes, and for the whole bank, a holistic EL equation for n positions in the loans book will be:

$$\text{EL} = \text{PD}_i(\%) \cdot \text{LGD}_i(\%) \cdot \text{EAD}_i(\$) \tag{12.3}$$

As a reminder of what has already been covered in Part 2, the obligor rating gives the PD, on a one-year time-frame. Loss given default for loans should include collateral (type, amount), guarantor (if any), recovery rate discounted in the expected time-frame, bankruptcy rate, and so on. For a snapshot on EL exposure, this information should be mined interactively from the bank's exposure database, which includes all clients.

- Primary emphasis for EAD must be placed on big client commitments, to be analysed individually in terms of credit risk and resulting EAD.
- By contrast, smaller client commitments should be pooled as if this were a case of securitization, with weighted averages computed for each pool.

This approach provides the appropriate grounds for stress testing, with particular attention paid to clients with major exposures, the population of the first bullet point. A reconciliation process at the 99 per cent level of confidence, or even better 99.9 per cent (see Chapter 1), should be applied.

In a way similar to that of equation (12.3), the stress probability of default (SPD), stress loss given default (SLGD) and stress exposure at default (SEAD) should be calculated individually for each big account, reflecting obligor, transaction (and collateral), product-specific information and other deal-specific references. For the whole institution:

$$\text{UL} = \text{SPD}_i(\%) \cdot \text{SLGD}_i(\%) \cdot \text{SEAD}_i(\$) \tag{12.4}$$

The SPD and SLGD should be individually computed for all major accounts, with particular attention being paid to covenants, warranties, other add-ons and the likelihood of spikes. The same is true for EAD and SEAD. Into EAD must be mapped drawn amount, undrawn but committed (converted to cash), a factor reflecting product type (converted to capital) and other commitments that are applicable, expressed in financial terms. Estimates must include macroeconomic factors. (More on this in Chapter 13.)

12.3 Stress testing regulatory capital requirements for expected losses

When the concept of global regulatory capital requirements was being developed and implemented, with the 1998 Basel Capital Accord (Basel I), it was specified that such capital must be backed by the bank's own funds, identified as tier one, and some other eligible funds defined under the envelope of tier two.

For internationally active banks, the 8 per cent capital requirement was a compromise that made possible the Basel I agreement. Some central bankers participating in the Basel meetings wanted to keep capital requirements low because they knew that commercial banks under their jurisdiction were not able to meet a high capital standard. This would have been counterproductive to global financial stability.

The question of how much capital, in regard to EL, should be reserved by banks for prudential reasons, was not raised in the past. Historical evidence suggests that between 1840 and the late 1870s, among European banks the average ratio of capital over assets fluctuated between 24 and 36 per cent, with a mean value slightly above 30 per cent. In the following twenty years, however, it dropped steadily and by 1900 it fell below the 20 per cent level.

Between the two world wars, the capital ratio stabilized in the 12–16 per cent range, with a much smaller volatility than in the mid-nineteenth century, but it again took a dive during World War II. In the postwar years, and prior to the 1988 Capital Accord, the *average* capital ratio held within a narrow 6–8 per cent band. This was:

- Less than a quarter of its level 100 years earlier, and
- Half of what it had been in the interwar period, which itself led to bank disasters during the Great Depression.

By itself, such an average does not mean much, since some banks are fairly well capitalized while others are very weak. Worse still, prior to Basel I there was no standard on what sort of funds are eligible to constitute a bank's capital adequacy. The 1988 Capital Accord defined regulatory capital as principally consisting of:

- Tier one (T-1), and
- Tier two (T-2) capital.

Tier one is core capital, which essentially means shareholder funds (equity), and it should constitute 50 per cent or more of capital adequacy. Within the Eurosystem, T-2 capital includes bonds issued by corporations, asset-backed securities (ABS) other than mortgages and public sector debt, and non-marketable instruments, such as bank loans, trade bills and mortgage-backed promissory notes. Other jurisdictions, however, have added more instruments in T-2. Examples are:

- Preferential shares, excluding own preferential shares,
- Liabilities represented by participation rights, and
- Longer term subordinated liabilities.

Such regulatory differences among Basel Committee members provide an enviable domain for stress testing. Both liabilities represented by participation rights and longer term subordinated liabilities are volatile, and are not universally accepted elements of a capital base.

- What if a common ground were established, eliminating them from T-2 components?
- What if other selected capital elements were to drop off the T-2 radar screen?
- What other assets can be beefed up to fulfil capital adequacy requirements?

A methodology of experimentation and stress testing should examine proactively changes in T-1 and T-2 capital, which impact upon a particular bank's capital adequacy now and in the future. Examples of 'new' capital sources added at the beginning of the twenty-first century are:

- *Hybrid tier-one* (HT-1), and
- *Tier-three* (T-3) capital.

Independent rating agencies do not buy HT-1. 'We don't consider hybrids as core capital', said Walter Pompliano, of Standard & Poor's (S&P). Some regulators, however, permit HT-1 to constitute up to 15 per cent of T-1, which turns prudential capital requirements promoted by Basel II on their head.

Hybrid tier-one is hybrid in the sense that it has some characteristics of equity, some of debt and much of leveraging. As for T-3 capital, to a substantial extent it comes from trading profits. Here again, because to a large measure T-3 derives itself from derivatives trading, it is very volatile, and it should be subject to stress testing, since, at a moment's notice, trading profits can turn into trading losses.

Nor are the aforementioned hybrids the only violation of the concept of financial staying power, inasmuch as they dilute the capital base. In the late 1990s, the Financial Services Agency, Japan's bank supervisor, unilaterally allowed the country's banks to use *deferred tax assets* (DTAs) as capital.These are a pure oracle.[1] They are also an example of the fact that since the 1988 Capital Accord, the broadly defined asset categories created opportunities for banks (and some of the supervisors) to play the system,

- Reducing their burden of regulatory capital for any given level of risk, and
- Increasing their overall exposure for any given level of capital, or both.

Over the years, plenty of financial tricks have become possible for regulatory arbitrage, despite regulators' trying to close the loopholes. The usual way of managing a portfolio, some bankers say, involves combining assets with different risks in such a way that the hazards offset each other. That might be good theory, but in practice it is a myth, which:

- Produces a great number of opportunities for creative accounting in financial reporting, and
- Opens the gates for a torrent of defaults in case of a severe crisis in the market.

One of the best known scandals in creative accounting, followed by virtual bankruptcy, is Resona's, then the fifth largest Japanese bank. When the DTAs were excluded, its capital reserves fell from 6 per cent to 2 per cent, making a mockery of international capital agreements. To save it from default, the Japanese government recapitalized Resona with taxpayers' money.

Since regulatory capital is supposed to cover EL in an adequate way, a stress test for EL is that of weeding out all capital tricks and gearing, returning to the original definition of T-1 and T-2 of the 1988 Capital Accord. Are the remaining funds able to support the bank's distribution of EL? In addition, stress testing T-1 and T-2 capital must include *time* as key variable because, as so often stated, capital requirements are always dynamic.

A sound stress testing methodology would examine T-1, T-2 and T-3 capital separately, before looking at them in conjunction with one another. A crucial question is: which allocation of assets can be maintained as T-1, T-2 and T-3 fluctuate?

- Can capital adequacy be sustained over five years? Over ten years?
- What is the likelihood of running short of capital requirements and risking disintermediation?

'We have been doing stress tests, then found them to be reality', said Rainer Rauleder, Deutsche Bank's director capital management. In a personal meeting, Rauleder and other senior bankers commented that stress testing capital adequacy simulates:

- Future growth in capital needs, and
- Problems regarding capital availability.

A properly planned stress test of capital requirements factors in business changes, regulatory rules and compliance to them, alternatives in net income planning, the aftermath of unexpected shortfalls, and ways of avoiding 'idle' surpluses. Through the results provided by stress testing,

- Capital plans can be prepared proactively, and
- Risk management is able to operate in a forward-looking way.

A bank using internal ratings-based (IRB) methods must develop a sound procedure for stress testing its computation of capital requirements, by evaluating the effect of specific adverse conditions on IRB capital, identifying likely events and changes in economic conditions with unfavourable effects on credit and/or market exposures, and moving from one year to five years, or even better ten years, in risk projections.

In conclusion, properly done, stress tests on capital adequacy provide perspective; account for unlikely events that can, however, happen; evaluate the sense of correlation between different types of exposure; reflect recession effects and macroeconomics; and confront the results of procyclicality. This is a steady business, which should address all sources of regulatory capital.

12.4 Back to basics: do we know the reason for credit losses?

Credit practices in the post-World War II years, and most particularly since the 1980s, have brought the banking industry a long way from the traditional definition of credit risk. The first major step from the ancient world's notion of *credit*, which finds its origin in the reign of Hammurabi (circa 1700 BC), took place in the Renaissance. Its promoters were banks, which acted as exchanges and clearing houses. This:

- Brought to life the practice of using a structural hub that could play the role of an intermediary, and
- Defined the functions assumed by the intermediary, altering the previous notions of credit risk because it created a mechanism to handle counterparty exposure in a way other than face to face.

It was not until after World War II years that financial instruments that restructured packaged and exploited concepts embedded in credit were invented (or rather reinvented). Reinventing is a more appropriate term because several elements embedded in modern financial instruments have been hundreds and thousands of years old.

For instance, options were originally invented by Thales of Militos (588 BC), the mathematician and philosopher who is said to have used them to corner the market for olive oil. Commercial paper and letters of credit date back to the Medicis, hence to the fifteenth century; but other credit trading instruments are more recent.

Securitization of some form first showed up in the mid-1920s. Syndicated loans are a development of the early 1960s. Other structural financial transactions, such as collateralized mortgage obligations and ABS, followed the deregulation of the banking industry in the late 1970s and the 1980s. Credit derivatives found a market in the 1990s. Notice that *credit* constitutes the common ground of these instruments, which:

- Pool assets and liabilities, and transfer all or part of the originator's credit risk to other investors, and
- Lead to disintermediation of credit institutions from the lending business, a loss that they compensate with new opportunities for profits, and new risks, on the side of the trading book.

The reincarnation of financial institutions into traders rather than safekeepers and lenders means that their exposure has been morphing, in many cases, from credit risk to market risk. However, credit risk is always present in new financial products designed at different levels of complexity, even if they aim to transfer the risk of counterparty's default.

Credit migration is a business line, not an indulgence from credit responsibility. It is of interest to the market, because more money can be made by taking credit risk than through market risk.

Contrarians say that the capital market, as a whole, does not have the same commitment to a credit relationship that a bank, the old intermediary, had. This is true, but no bank, by itself, has available the huge amounts of capital needed for modern large projects, or can assume all alone the ever-growing amount of credit risk, as:

- Rapid innovation in financial instruments alters market behaviour over time, including the introduction of a greater amount of leverage,
- But it does not change the fact that an element of credit risk exists whenever an investor buys or sells a financial product without immediate settlement, or handling through a recognized exchange.

The notion of *leverage* or gearing, nowadays exercised in hefty amounts, is one of the major changes in market behaviour, as well as morals and amount of assumed risk. It is used as a tool to multiply financial power, without having the corresponding capital. In so doing, it also multiplies the credit risk and market risk being assumed:

- In times of crisis, this may have catastrophic consequences,
- Hence the need to look at exposure in the more rigorous way provided by stress testing.

Opinions are divided as to whether an ever-growing amount of gearing is 'good' or 'bad'. Some people think of leverage as something to boast about, not as something to conceal. They believe that people who know how to gear their assets and liabilities are both clever and skilful. Other people, however, think that, to the contrary,

- High gearing is very dangerous, and
- It can lead to uncontrollable, unexpected losses.

An example of a company that willingly assumed high leverage is Long-Term Capital Management (LTCM). If it had gambled only its capital, then the dry hole that it left would have been a 'mere' $4 billion. If its leverage had been 15:1, as for other hedge funds at the time, then the loss would have been $60 billion. But by gearing up to 350:1, LTCM had a sword of Damocles of $1.4 trillion hanging over the world's financial system. This is a case study on *unexpected losses*.[2]

Leverage should not be confused with normal credit, which facilitates the way in which society lives and works. The classical notion of credit enables companies to function and makes it possible for people with modest cash flow to buy homes, cars, computers and holidays. In this way, normal credit creates economic opportunity and boosts employment, but there is always credit risk, in this case, of *expected loss* type.

Normal credit is typically secured by some type of good assets, whereas leverage is often unsecured or secured through dubious assets. Since the gearing of up to 50:1, or 350:1, is frequently seen with bank lending, EL morph into UL.

In conclusion, the answer to the question: 'Do we know the reasons for credit losses?' is that prudence in credit engagements is not synonymous with refusing most of the loans. A sound policy is first to decide on risk appetite, then to conduct research leading to better knowledge about a given transaction's credit exposure. This is the amount of credit risk taken to be priced, dividing counterparty exposure into normal or expected, to be covered by ongoing business, and unexpected, for which appropriate capital and reserves should be available. This, in a nutshell, is the difference between EL and UL.

12.5 Contribution of rating agencies to prognostication of expected losses

In a globalized economy, the more the capital markets assert their importance in issuance, trading and management of credit risk, the more they need independent rating agencies to grade the level of counterparty exposure of investors. This has become part of the role of the three major international rating agencies: S&P, Moody's Investor Services and Fitch IBCA, as well as many others that rate the creditworthiness of:

- The better known companies worldwide,
- Bonds of all types, including municipals and government debt,
- Commercial paper and medium-term notes, and
- ABS, and other issues.

Rating agencies have acquired significant power as statistical reference organizations, if not watchdogs, of credit risk in capital markets. Like regulators, they are becoming part of the global system of checks and balances, their scores used both to exercise vigilance and to fine-tune risk embedded in instruments outlined in the above bullet points.

The grading classification of independent agencies has about twenty thresholds (it varies by agency). This is a much finer grid than six to eight credit thresholds used by most banks, including the big ones, in their internal rating. A coarse classification of credit risk helps precious little in the control of exposure. The golden rule for fine-grained risk-based decisions can be expressed in seven bullets:

- Determine the purpose of the credit.
- Analyse the quality of the obligor.
- Research the underlying economics.
- Examining covenants and guarantees.
- Price the credit exposure being taken.

- Evaluate whether risk and reward are acceptable.
- Keep on re-evaluating the creditworthiness, because risk drivers and financial staying power change.

Almost all of these points can be subdivided into two or more components. For instance, embedded in the second are not only the borrower's ability to pay the interest and repay the principal, but also their willingness to do so, which is a matter of investigating the entity's management, its ethics and its character and, hence, a qualitative process. However,

- While ability to pay has much to do with economic and financial conditions,
- Willingness to face up to one's obligations is a matter of policy and virtue.

That's why the words 'leverage suggests one is clever' are misleading. A company, person or any other entity who sought the protection of bankruptcy courts to avoid facing up to its geared up obligations is likely to do it again. In terms of virtue, that party should never be viewed as a good credit risk. Notice, however, that:

- Rating agencies do not express an opinion on ethics regarding the rated institution,
- But the credit risk threshold that they assign to an entity also accounts for its quality of governance, not only its balance sheet.

Similarly to expert loan officers, independent credit agencies appreciate that there is no alternative to asking tough questions that reveal a company's strengths and weaknesses, not only in financials and guarantees but also in governance. Among these questions are the debt instrument issuer's strategy in regard to contemplated investments, and the issuer's ability to pay interest and repay the capital.

This procedure cannot be effectively followed unless the independent agency's officers, credit evaluation committee, auditors and other organs are disciplined, which is usually the case. Only then is the rating agency in a position to appreciate the boundaries of credit risk assumed by the rated institution, and its creditworthiness. Moreover, feedback in regard to the obligor's creditworthiness is a qualifying channel of great importance.

With Basel II, rating agencies are also taking a close look at the capital requirements of rated credit institutions and their adequacy. 'Since 1999, we don't believe banks to be overcapitalized', said Barbara Ridpath of S&P. 'It is rather the opposite'.[3] She makes the point that while regulatory capital keeps an institution's banking licence, 'more capital' means that the bank is safer, for its stakeholders:

- Shareholders,
- Bondholders,
- Employees,
- Lenders,
- Depositors,
- Regulators, and
- The capital market.

To make sure that no entity uses funny money, in its rating S&P excludes all hybrid funds from core capital (see section 12.8). For evaluation purposes, the rating agency has introduced its own measures: adjusted common equity (ACE) and adjusted total equity (ATE). Some, but not all, hybrid capital instruments are included in ATE. For those included, there are three conditions:

- Permanency,
- Loss absorption, and
- Cushion to debitholders in liquidation.

Standard & Poor's adjusted risk-weighted assets (RWAs) incorporate qualitative assessment of portfolio quality, credit and market risk management, use of securitization, risk mitigation techniques and concentration risk. Other basic criteria are assets and liabilities management, diversification in business activities, insurance and operational risk. Measures of adjusted capital:

- Exclude hybrid capital instruments from core capital,
- Incorporate specific assessment of hybrids' capital characteristics, and
- Make deductions for investments in unconsolidated subsidiaries.

These two sets of three bullet points each, encapsulate a good deal of the sort of stress testing that is necessary. Made for each inventoried position, the test of permanency may reveal a portfolio that is lopsided in its hybrids, as none of them qualifies under S&P criteria. For instance, if hybrid capital instruments are excluded from core capital, even if the national regulator looks the other way, then there may be no core capital left, as happened with the Resona Bank, one of Japan's largest (see section 12.3).

Basically, what a rigorous testing should look at is precisely what independent rating agencies are after: the ability to identify sufficient capital to absorb all risks through an economic cycle, particularly its low level when the market does not support replenishment. Regarding a recession scenario, the S&P capital model assumes:

- Three years without access to capital markets,
- Forced rollover of maturing loans,
- No liquidity of loans, and
- Enough capital at the end to be in the business of making new loans.

This focus goes beyond EL, although it does not necessarily cover all UL. Financial staying power is seen as sufficient capital to absorb most risks, without going cap in hand to the credit market. Cornerstone to such evaluation is the quality and makeup of the risk portfolio, and the way in which a credit institution manages its exposure.

Banks are well advised to apply this S&P evaluation model by means of stress tests. They should appreciate that there are clear advantages in improving the quality of risk management through worst case drills, not only for the stakeholders, but also for reasons of self-interest. Stress tests following the guideline of Basel II will expose, to a significant extent, existing credit risks and market risks.

This is why regulators increasingly insist on stress tests, and on the institution's process of internal control to assure that senior management is properly informed of the results. When feedback channels are open and stress test results are available to all people involved in the institution's governance, the risk of going under diminishes.

12.6 How to handle expected losses from lending

In the 1950s, the author had a professor of banking at UCLA who taught his students that a lending officer who has no bad loans is as poor an agent of the bank as one who has many bad loans. By being too prudent, he or she turns down lots of good credits. Implicit to that assumption is that some bad credits will filter through loans screening, and they will end up in EL.

The way that most credit institutions look at it, the EL from credit risk in lending is an average measure. As explained in section 12.2, the problem with this historical approach to expected loan losses is that it takes little account of volatility, macroeconomics and other reasons for extreme circumstances. Therefore, in terms of reserve capital, it needs to be supplemented by a meaningful consideration of unexpectedly adverse conditions (see Chapter 13).

As Dr Alan Greenspan, then Federal Reserve Board chairman, said at the Annual Convention of the Independent Bankers' Association of America, in Phoenix, Arizona, on 22 March 1997,

> Mistakes in lending, after all, are not generally made during recessions but when the economic outlook appears benevolent. Recent evidence of thin margins and non-bank competition in some portions of the syndicated loan market, as well as other indicators, suggest that some modest underwriting laxity has a tendency to emerge during good times.

One way of interpreting this statement is that both the borrower asking for a loan, and the bank granting it, are responsible for EL. The statement that EL tend to find their origin in good times and they are most likely to occur in bad business times is not only fair but also generally applicable wherever a bank may reside. Statistically,

- They are represented by the mean and variance on the left side of the risk distribution of credit losses shown in Figure 12.1.
- In connection with the left side of the loss distribution, capital adequacy rules are established by regulators for expected losses.

According to Basel II, and its interpretation by major regulatory agencies, capital adequacy for EL will buy the bank a licence. By contrast, the market will not be convinced that the credit institution has enough resources to face uncertainty until it sees economic capital allocated to UL, also known as signalling capital (which is the theme of Chapter 13).

In analysing a bank's ability to survive adversity, the market looks for evidence on whether its management is properly aggregating credit exposures accounting for extreme events, and sizing up appropriate capital buffers. Modern technology assists in doing a sophisticated job in aggregation along that line of reference. Models based on default probability and severity can project future losses by:

- Counterparty,
- Class of clients,
- Industry,
- Country, and
- Other criteria pertinent to the credit institution.

Stress tests must work along that line, keeping in perspective both historical and hypothetical outliers, and their real-life or estimated aftermath. For instance, if loans are given, or investments made, in a developing country, what is the likelihood that a new government will freeze repayment of foreign loans, as happened in Argentina in 2001, then take a 75 per cent haircut; or nationalize foreign investments without compensation, as in Bolivia in 2006?

- How much will this hurt?
- What will be its impact on our bank's capital adequacy?

An experimental approach that is both qualitative and quantitative helps to smooth the effect of EL, and it also provides a basis for prognosticating UL. Modelling, however, while necessary, is not enough. The bank's strategy must be that when there are generally favourable macroeconomic conditions, management:

- Takes a pause,
- Conducts stress tests to highlight weak conditions, and
- Reassesses the appropriateness of lending decisions.

This should be done in conjunction with rethinking the institution's risk appetite in the medium to longer term. Stress testing risk drivers may reveal hidden areas of exposure, and from time to time the risk drivers themselves must be assessed.

A reference to risk drivers, which should always be taken into account, can be found in the instructions for the fifth Quantitative Impact Study (QIS 5), issued in July 2005 by the Basel Committee. (See the results of this study in section 12.7.) Planning for the impact test made necessary certain changes from the previous QIS. The main issues affecting QIS 5 concerned assignment of exposure to portfolios, with eleven broad categories classified for this purpose:

- Corporate,
- Specialized lending,
- Sovereign,
- Banks,
- Retail,
- Small and medium sized enterprises,
- Equity,

- Purchased receivables,
- Securitized assets,
- Trading book, and
- Investments in related entities.

With QIS 5, particular attention has been paid to credit risk transfer (see Chapter 11). Credit derivatives and guarantees subject to double default were of particular concern. Credit protection other than collateral (such as guarantees) provided by a special purpose vehicle to securitization exposure, has been defined as not eligible for credit risk mitigation treatment.[4]

In its Newsletter No. 7, in November 2005, the Basel Committee brought additional clarification to matters regarding the handling of EL and UL, although the principal focus of this newsletter was operational risk. Such is the case of paragraph 669(b), which states that a bank may be allowed to base its operational risk capital calculations on UL alone, only if it can document to the satisfaction of its national supervisor that it is adequately capturing EL in its business practices.

The point is further made that for that operational risk capital purposes, the bank's measure of EL must be consistent with the EL-plus-UL capital charge calculated using the model approved by supervisors (in this case, the AMA model for operational risk).[5] Moreover, the bank must be able to demonstrate that:

- The estimating process is consistent over time, and
- Corresponding losses are highly predictable and reasonably stable.

An added reason why all references made by the Basel Committee to EL and UL should be paid full attention is that the original formula for EL [equation (12.3)] was abandoned with the June 2004 version of Basel II, in favour of credit loss reserves traditionally made by banks. This, however, carried the condition that the variables entering into such calculations must reflect:

- Economic circumstances, and
- The capital facility status.

For the banking industry as a whole, these issues have been revolutionizing the classical approach to computation of EL. This is also true of the use of a factor of *maturity* (M, see Chapter 11), which enters into the picture by way of RWAs; and of the fact that PDs and LGDs must be stress tested, leading to a UL algorithm under supervisory control*.

$$UL = SPD(\%) \cdot SLGD(\%) \cdot SEAD(\$) - EL \tag{12.5}$$

Stress probability of default, under adverse market conditions, SLGD, also known as downturn LGD, and SEAD are becoming basic elements in banking governance.

*While there is confusion between UL and EL in the aftermath of QIS 5 – as explained in the Warning – equation 12.5 is, and remains, most helpful in practised use.

For some of them, the die is not yet cast. For instance, supervisors will work together with banks to develop suitable methods for downturn LGD.[6] However, on the credit institution's side senior management should appreciate that the evolving SPD, SLGD and SEAD concepts and metrics are, in essence, integral parts of sound governance.

12.7 The results of the fifth Quantitative Impact Study

The careful reader will precede the study of this chapter by focusing on the remarks made in the *Warning*, regarding QIS 5 and its after-effects in 2006 and beyond.

In 2005 and 2006, the Basel Committee on Banking Supervision conducted QIS 5, with credit institutions from thirty-one countries, including the G-10 countries, except for the USA, and nineteen non-G-10 countries. The Basel Committee received data from:

- 56 group 1 banks in the G-10 countries,
- 146 group 2 banks in G-10 countries, and
- 155 banks from countries other than G-10.

As in QIS 3, group 1 banks are those fulfilling all of the following criteria: tier-one capital of more than €3 billion ($3.75 billion), diversification of assets and international banking activities.

Limited data from the US QIS 4 exercise, representing an additional twenty-six institutions, were also partly included. The Federal Reserve and other US regulators conduct, and will continue conducting, their own Basel II tests. For participating G-10 and non-G-10 banks, the QIS 5 workbooks reflected all recent changes to the Basel II framework, in particular the:

- Change in the treatment of reserves,
- Move to a UL-only basis for computing RWAs,
- 1.06 scaling factor applied to credit RWAs,
- Recognition of double default (wrong-way risk), and
- Revised trading book rules for credit institutions.

It should be noted that, for the above-mentioned reasons, a comparison of results from QIS 5 and previous quantitative impact studies is unwise. The successive QIS tests were not done on the basis of an experimental design with results based on the same regulatory rules. They took place to help in tuning the capital adequacy requirements, with the outcome that the Basel II rules have evolved considerably from one QIS to another, particularly the latter ones.

In addition, macroeconomic and credit conditions prevailing in most G-10 countries at the time of QIS 5 and QIS 4 were more benign than during QIS 3, with evident impact on needed capital. Concomitant with this is a question of data quality. While national supervisors reported that data survey quality has significantly improved since the previous QIS, the Basel Committee thinks that:

- Implementation of economic downturn LGD estimates, and
- Issues relating to trading book paper

are in need of further improvement.[7] There is also the very negative fact that supervisors of the largest economy in the world did not participate in QIS 5. This is an additional reason why the outcome of this test may be considered inconclusive. Moreover, in the Basel Committee's Madrid meeting in late 2003, which dropped the EL formula and converted it to one for UL, the argument by commercial banks was that they already have a credit risk provision for EL. The published results of QIS 5:

- Make the reference that this particular test regarded UL,
- But do not specify whether these computed capital reserves for UL are over and above the banks' classical credit risk reserves, which would be a conservative and logical approach.

QIS 5 should be interpreted with these facts in mind. The quantitative results for the G-10 countries show that minimum required capital under Basel II would *decrease* relative to the Capital Accord of Basel I. For group 1 banks, for instance, minimum required capital under the most likely approaches to credit risk *and* operational risk would, on average, decrease by 6.8 per cent, a large and dangerous drop.

To appreciate the magnitude of this most significant reduction in capital requirements, the reader should recall that when reserves for operational risk first came up with Basel II, the regulators demanded 20 per cent capital over what was required for credit risk. Because commercial banks objected, the Basel Committee settled for about 17 per cent. Hence:

- The 6.8 per cent reduction in capital adequacy for credit risk and operational risk essentially means 24 per cent less than 8 per cent required for international banks under Basel I.
- Since only half is T-1 capital, this drop is tantamount to opening Pandora's box in exposure to adversity, preparing for big bank failures, and for taxpayer's money to salvage overleveraged and overexposed credit institutions.

As should have been expected, of the two IRB approaches, the more independently minded advanced internal ratings-based (A-IRB) method shows more reduction in minimum required capital (–7.1 per cent) than the foundation internal ratings-based (F-IRB) method (–1.3 per cent). This indicates that the –6.8 per cent in capital requirements is loaded on the A-IRB side, and suggests that central banks and regulators of all countries whose banks participated in QIS 5 should conduct a stress test of the commercial banks models, before deciding on the reliability of the QIS 5 results.

In contrast to these figures, QIS 5 shows that minimum required capital under the standardized approach of Basel II would increase by 1.7 per cent for group 1 banks, but it would *decrease* by 1.3 per cent for group 2 banks. One interpretation is that this probably happens because of the higher proportion of retail exposures for group 2 credit institutions.

An interesting finding, in connection with QIS 5 results, is that among non-G-10 banks capital requirements are on average higher than in the G-10. The explanation given in the official document suggests that the reason may lie in (more conservative) judgement by bank management, market pressure, supervisory discretion or a combination of these factors.

It is likely that the choice of the correlation coefficient, ρ, also played a major role, because a great deal of difference in capital requirements is created by the choice of ρ: The lower the correlation coefficient, the lower the resulting capital requirements. This is a caveat in prudential supervision, because the methods and means for evaluating ρ, let alone controlling it, are lacking in Basel II. Hence, the way is wide open for playing the system.

In conclusion, keeping in mind that Basel I addressed only credit risk, while QIS 5 in Basel II includes both credit risk and operational risk, the outlined *decreases* in capital adequacy requirements are unsettling. Over the nearly three decades since Basel I, banks have been taking and inventorying much more risk, not less. There is a high likelihood that the Achilles' heel of Basel II is the correlation coefficients. This makes much greater the need for stress testing at large, and for stress testing of ρ in particular.

12.8 Thinking about models for credit risk

'*Thinking* is those mental processes we don't understand', said Dr Alan Turing, famous as a World War II code breaker and one of the fathers of the computer revolution. A basic kind of thinking, advised the Massachusetts Institute of Technology's 'Things That Think' project, in the late 1990s, is *perception.* A good part of the importance of focusing on perception in terms of EL and UL comes from the fact that we have shifted from being a society of *participants* to being a society of *observers.* In spite of globalization:

- Our universe of creation comes from a much smaller group of people than it once did.
- These are the main players in the international market who, among themselves, account for the majority of transactions, profits and risks.

One of the participants in the research that led to this book suggested that we must tune our perception to the deliverables that we expect to obtain from what we do. He then added that this statement applies all the way to credit risk models and the way in which we use them. Focusing on a model's deliverables essentially means that the artefact has to be evaluated both *ex ante* and *ex post.*

Take as an example on post-mortem analysis the aftermath of the third Quantitative Impact Study (QIS 3) of IRB.[8] This was the fourth testing of Basel II rules, following in the path of QIS 1, QIS 2 and QIS 2.5.

QIS 3 provided an estimation of impact regarding the changes in capital adequacy origination connected to an experimental implementation of A-IRB, F-IRB and the standardized approach. The extent to which a bank with a capital ratio of 8 per cent would have to adjust its financial resources to maintain this minimum capital ratio under Basel II, for EL, varied among the three different methods:

- From 0 per cent to +12 per cent for the standardized approach,
- To –2 per cent to +11 per cent for F-IRB, and
- To –5 per cent to –9 per cent for A-IRB.

Why these margins? Some of the variation is due to the specific economic environment in which each bank operates, possible uncertainty about the new Basel definition of default, limited availability of data needed to estimate key risk parameters such as PD and LGD and, most certainly, the choice of correlation coefficients. However, not every difference between the 8 per cent fixed rate of Basel I and models of Basel II is due to these reasons.

Within the perspective of EL, it is reasonable to suggest that other sources of differences are due to the volume of retail business characterizing a given bank. For instance, because of lower risk weights a high volume of retail business can lead to lower minimum capital requirements, other things being equal.

To ensure that minimum capital requirements are maintained, which is the goal of both Basel II and the calibration of three alternative capital adequacy methods, the Basel Committee envisaged the use of a scaling factor to adjust RWAs for credit risk. However, independently of the adopted method the most determinant factors of capital adequacy are:

- A bank's risk profile, and
- The way that this risk is managed.

Because for EL variations in creditworthiness impact on the variables entering into the model's input, this provides plenty of opportunity for stress testing PDs, LGDs and EADs. An example on impact is when, in regard to a certain class of loans or other instruments, the bank deals with a limited number of counterparties. This brings into perspective the importance of the model's structure in terms of prognostication.

- If the model for EL has been projected to capitalize on diversification,
- Then the case of risk concentration runs against its structure. Models based on risk distribution characteristics will not be able to optimize capital reserves, when encountering credit risk concentration.

A subject that comes up surprisingly often in the author's seminars is the lack of appreciation by banking, and even model developers, that models have locality. Their structure makes them suitable for a given domain. A model for credit risk will not serve in evaluating market risk, and vice versa. Even within a given domain there are specializations. A sophisticated, non-parametric model based on credit risk diversification will not be able to optimize capital reserves when encountering credit risk concentration.

Models made by supervisors, A-IRB and F-IRB being examples, are usually designed to serve in the best possible way banks with a diversity of counterparties and credit exposures. These are situations that present less correlated default probabilities when dealing with large samples of borrowers. In the case of small samples, concentrations are more likely to show up, and therefore additional safeguards must be in place.

In the background of this perception of model structure lies the fact that, in essence, the banker's job is not to avoid the risk of non-payment through some extraordinary moves, but to manage risk in a professional way. Expected loan losses represent events that have a statistical probability of materializing, and credit risk models account for this. Indeed, both bankers and insurers accept financial risks that for good governance purposes they must qualify, quantify and manage.

- For the insurer, the risk comes from compensation claims,
- For the banker, it shows up in the form of loans that are not repaid.

Therefore, in both cases sufficient premiums must be received to cover EL. The concept borrowed from insurance is that actuarial reserves are required to cushion volatility in the effective size of counterparty failures. In addition, capital adequacy is necessary to guarantee solvency. This boils down to:

- Margins, and
- Provisions.

Whether or not they use models as assistants to their decision processes, credit institutions have to show, not only to their supervisors but also to the market, that they really set aside sufficient provisions to cover EL and UL. They must also be convincing that they have done so in an effective manner.

- If there is insufficient coverage of EL, then the shortfall must be deducted from capital.
- If the EL provisions are more than necessary, then, up to a certain level, many supervisors may recognize the surplus as capital.

These 'ifs' should be subject to stress tests, at a high level of significance. This would assist management in having confidence in estimates of statistically expected losses determined by means of their risk distribution, over a certain period and for a specific loan portfolio. Crucial to this type of modelling is the right perception of risk characteristics of each individual transaction, counterparty and instrument.

12.9 Strengths and weaknesses of credit risk models

A positive result of the original 1988 Capital Accord (Basel I) by the Basel Committee on Banking Supervision is that since it has come into force among G-10 countries, provisioning requirements for credit risks have continued to rise. This has obliged a number of banks to carry out a re-evaluation of their loan portfolio, and to rethink their credit policies.

At the same time, however, market forces have meant that credit risk also continued to rise, with the aftermath that, among well-governed banks, senior management became sensitive to the need for incorporating the potential for future deterioration into its current assessment of credits. With a view to applying a proactive approach, tier-one banks decided to use technology to be ahead of the curve in providing provisions for loans.

Credit risk graduated from notional to analytical subjects by the mid-1980s. At about that time, the quantitative study of credit exposure opened up new career perspectives for physicists, mathematicians, nuclear engineers and rocket scientists.[9] A young generation of bankers, too, brought new thinking to credit risk studies. In conjunction with credit rating through a fine grid of thresholds, modelling made feasible:

- Pricing loan products according to the risks involved,
- Identifying potential problems at an earlier stage, and
- Providing a framework for active management of credit exposure assumed by the bank.

To improve the way in which they manage their credit portfolio, banks have developed tools that allow them to analyse and test credit risk drivers, instrument by instrument and counterparty by counterparty. This has been a positive development, but there are several caveats associated with it, whether for credit risk or for market risk.

First and foremost, the popular belief that models and computers can do anything is unfounded. Models and computers cannot do 'everything' and, moreover, computers can only work in partnership with good software. Developments in software, including modelling, are driving the banking revolution through more accurate and better timed control of exposure. This statement is also true about the development and on-line use of databases that:

- Are rich in content,
- Range over several decades of the series, and
- Are populated by accurate information elements that have been updated in real time.

The use of technology, however, has prerequisites that are not always fulfilled. One of the weaknesses connected to many modelling approaches associated with credit risk is the small amount of attention paid to testing data sources in terms of dependability. Yet, the figures obtained from risk analysis greatly depend on the information fed into it in the first place. Starved of reliable sources of credit and other references, the model becomes an engine of garbage-in and garbage-out.

In addition, until the model output has been market tested, and proves to be realistic as well as reliable, simulated EL may be subject to *model risk*, potential errors made in modelling and in hypothesis relating to exposure. Examples of pitfalls range:

- From loans book assumptions about correlations between reference entities and exposures
- To estimated effects of volatility on the pricing of derivative instruments, such as options.

In science, the role of mathematical models is generally to describe and predict, within a pre-established acceptable level of accuracy. As Dr John von Neumann once suggested, the sciences do not try to explain, they hardly even try to interpret; they just make models.

For credit risk control purposes, these models describe observable phenomena, with the addition of certain verbal interpretations. The hypotheses entering into such descriptions, however, come from the developers, and the developers' bias filters into the model. A common bias is the short term. Therefore, the mistake made by most credit risk models (including those by regulators) is in confining EL and UL estimation to one year, rather than considering:

- The lifetime of the loan, and
- All risk drivers entering into play over that time-span.

Some banks answer this argument by saying that a credit risk model's performance heavily depends on default rates, and a lot of ratings are not available in the longer term. Others say that modelling the longer terms is not convincing, because it is difficult to bring it down to a level that managers and loans officers can live with.

Both statements are wrong. Transition matrices available from independent rating agencies go to five and ten years. As such, they can be used to advantage to answer the first objection. Used in an able manner, and supplemented by internal ratings and other data, transition matrices can provide a ten-year time-frame in credit risk projection, by counterparty and in the aggregate of the bank's credit exposure, as shown in Figure 12.2.

As for the second argument, it is a wrong policy for the managers, loans officers and other professionals of a credit institution to be thinking only in the short term. Credit risk exposure must be considered in the longer term, not only on the basis of daily, monthly or yearly business. An estimation of necessary financial resources to face major adversity over a five- to ten-year time-frame provides the board, chief executive officer and senior management with something tangible to integrate into their decision.

- The fact these are characterized by uncertainty does not reduce their importance.
- Senior people must know how to live with uncertainty, expect the unthinkable, and be able to deal with adversity.

A weakness of the model is the bias that often exists in connection with correlation and weighting factors downsized to hide the lack of diversification in lending.

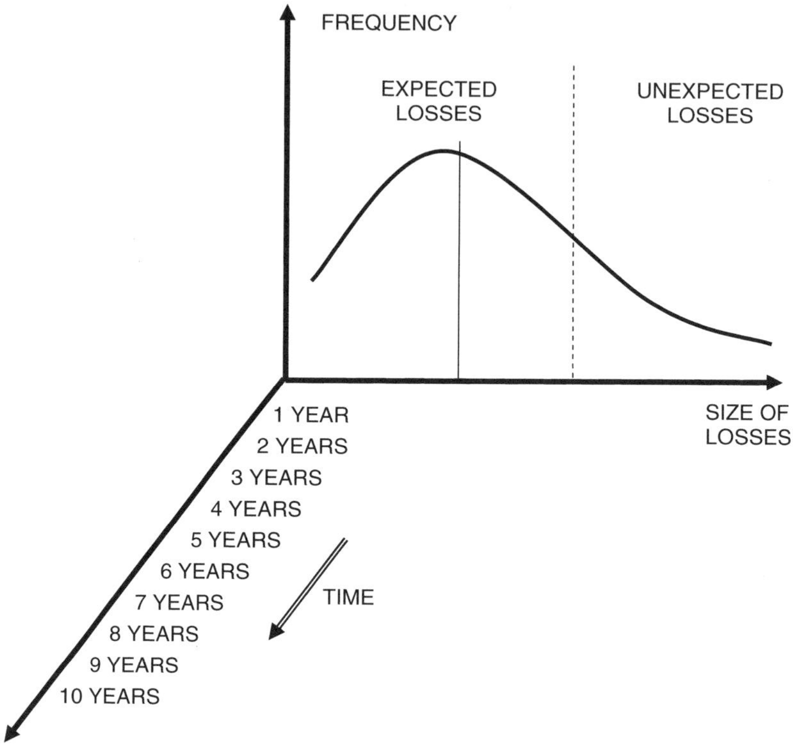

Figure 12.2 Credit projections require a longer term time dimension to become a meaningful tool

Prudence calls for *diversification*, but this term does not have the same meaning in all institutions, and indeed for some banks diversification is simply an illusion.

Credit risk modelling should not mask the facts. It should reflect real policies and procedures, whether these lead to diversification or to concentration of credit risk. Because many real-life situations are characterized by concentration rather than by diversification, this is an excellent domain for stress tests. Is our bank avoiding massive loans to, for instance:

- The same industrial sector,
- Companies in the same geographical area, or
- Entities belonging to the same holding?

Stress tests should also look into whether the bank avoids financial commitments with about the same maturity. Notice that in all of these cases the core reference is to *credit risk*, not to market risk. Still, for a globally operating bank, country risk and currency risk must be taken into account.

Apart from financial loss from market risk, if a given currency comes under pressure, currency exposure may correlate with credit risk because local companies would find it difficult, if not impossible, to honour commitments that they contracted in a foreign currency. This has happened in the most flagrant sense with dollar-denominated loans to South Korean and Indonesian firms.

In conclusion, a main issue with modern banking is the development and use of eigenmodels. Conceiving, building, testing, using and maintaining them are demanding tasks. This statement is just as valid about establishing and using a valid methodology for stress testing *regulatory capital* requirements, which was the theme of section 12.3.

Notes

1. D.N. Chorafas, *After Basel II. Assuring Compliance and Smoothing the Rough Edges*, Lafferty/VRL Publishing, London, 2005.
2. D.N. Chorafas, *Managing Risk in the New Economy*, New York Institute of Finance, New York, 2001.
3. Basel II Masterclass, organized by IIR, London, 27/28 March 2003.
4. Basel Committee, *Instructions for QIS 5*, BIS, Basel, July 2005.
5. D.N. Chorafas, *Operational Risk Control with Basel II. Basic Principles and Capital Requirements*, Butterworth-Heinemann, London, 2004.
6. Deutsche Bundesbank, *Monthly Report*, September 2004.
7. Basel Committee on Banking Supervision, *Results of the Fifth Quantitative Impact Study (QIS 5)*, BIS, Basel, 16 June 2006.
8. Deutsche Bundesbank, *Monthly Report*, September 2004.
9. D.N. Chorafas, *Rocket Scientists in Banking*, Lafferty Publications, London, 1995.

13 Analysing the reasons for unexpected losses

13.1 Introduction

For its profits and its survival, every business depends on the level of activity that it is undertaking. Expectations of potential changes in market variables that turn out to be wrong, and exposures assumed without appropriate study of risk and return, or in violation of risk-based pricing principles, lead to unexpected losses (UL). From macroeconomic factors, through individual instruments to business risk, plenty of reasons contribute to UL, and their input tends to be major. This is the theme of the present chapter.

13.2 Unexpected risks confront every enterprise

Every industrial, financial, merchandising or service firm is confronted with risks associated with rare but extraordinary events or exposures. It is likely that, because of their impact, UL cannot be effectively met only by regulatory capital. Examples are large non-performing loans, such as those given by banks to Russia, Indonesia and Korea; exotic derivative deals that go bust; major loss exposures taken for some reason or another without appropriate research and testing; the multiple faces of legal risk; mergers and acquisitions that not only disappointed but turned sour.[1]

- As described in Chapter 12, UL are the stress test of expected losses (EL).
- However, UL have their own pattern, and need customized stress tests, as shown in this chapter and in Chapter 14.

Major UL are unlikely to take place in low-intensity banking activities. This, however, is a conditional statement because it is not that easy to define what exactly is meant by 'low intensity'. Statistically, UL are represented by multiple standard deviations from the mean of a distribution of credit losses, towards the right-hand side of that distribution (more on this later). Catastrophic losses are part of UL at the long end of the tail.

The general business thinking is that UL are due to unlikely, although plausible events and, when they happen, they represent a very large sum of money. This approach is correct but incomplete. An example from the oil industry helps to explain the reason for this statement, starting with the fact that the business of energy companies depends on:

- The level of activity in oil and gas exploration, and
- Production and transportation to market sectors worldwide (see also Chapter 16 for a case study on the oil and gas industry's risk factors).

Oil and gas prices, and market expectations of potential changes in prices, significantly affect an oil firm's level of activity, but not necessarily exploration. Higher commodity prices do not necessarily translate into increased drilling. Rather, it is expectations of future commodity prices that typically drive demand for rigs, with worldwide political and economic events contributing to oil and gas price volatility. Unexpected losses can be created by numerous factors, including:

- A sudden slump in worldwide demand for oil and gas, because of poor economic conditions,
- Natural disasters leading to environmentalists demanding, and often obtaining, stringent rules for exploration and transportation,
- Work stoppages, weather interference, storm damage and unanticipated cost increases,
- Lack of major advances in exploration and development technology,
- Price and availability of alternative fuels, as well as transport facilities, and
- The worldwide military and political environment, including uncertainty or instability resulting from an escalation or additional outbreak of armed hostilities.

To these exogenous factors are added endogenous risks by oil and natural gas companies, such as fires; explosions; failures of oilfield drilling and service tools; wrong estimates of underground pressure in a formation that causes the surface to collapse or crater; dangerous pressure in forcing oil or natural gas out of the wellbore, increasing the risk of fire and explosion; pipeline ruptures or cement failures; and unwanted consequences leading to environmental hazards, such as natural gas leaks, oil spills and discharges of toxic gases.

While some of these risks may be expected, and therefore contained, the long list in the preceding paragraphs includes plenty of unexpected risks that can cause substantial losses resulting from injury or loss of life; damage to and destruction of property, natural resources and equipment; pollution and other environmental problems. In turn, such happenings lead to regulatory investigations, penalties or outright suspension of operations. There may also be major:

- Repair costs, and
- Remediation costs.

Every company in every line of business can write a list of exogenous and endogenous factors that at one time of another have led to UL. Mispricing of options and binary type derivatives are a couple of banking examples. Contrary to conditions considered to be low intensity or 'normal', the magnitude and frequency of UL may:

- Upset business practices, and
- Lead the firm towards a crisis.

Macroeconomic factors (see section 13.3) have much to do with events that are unexpected, because macroeconomics and market sentiment can change in a moment's notice. However, former outliers in business activity sometimes become 'normal' events. What would have been an extreme event in the mid-1950s, when US credit market debt stood at about $1 trillion, may be seen as a normal event in 2006, as the American credit market debt exceeds $11 trillion, an increase of more than an order of magnitude.

At the same time, new sorts of extreme events and associated losses show up. A bank may lose capital and reserves in the aftermath of a meltdown in an important industry, such as real estate, which from time to time goes into a tailspin. An example is provided by the Bank of New England in 1990. Alternatively, a severe recession may lead a large number of major borrowers to default simultaneously.

- The law of unexpected consequences always comes into play.
- For instance, each year in the USA more people die from medical errors in hospitals than from road accidents or Aids.

These examples from the oil industry, banking and medical errors suggest that many factors may be at work behind UL. Some of them are unknown to management until adversity hits. Only post mortem are the results of these factors measurable in operational and financial terms, hence the need to prognosticate them.

- Prognostication makes UL a forward-looking, *ex ante* measure.
- This contrasts with accounting for losses being incurred, which is always *ex post*.

As will be seen in Chapter 14, a good way to proceed with calibration of UL is to make it evaluate the way in which banks compute their economic capital requirements. This is quite apart from regulatory capital, but the attention that supervisors now pay to UL may mean that the notions behind regulatory capital and economic capital eventually merge. In either case, whether we talk of:

- Expected losses, hence regulatory capital, or
- Unexpected losses, and therefore economic capital,

we must be extremely careful with the distribution of risk events, and its pattern. Prudence suggests using an established statistical distribution rather than a curve drawn free hand, to describe expected, unexpected and catastrophic losses. The reason may not be self-evident. But as Dr L.M.K. Boelter, the dean of the College of Engineering at UCLA, taught his students back in 1953,

- When we map a real-life situation the curve or surface must be mathematically expressed and reproducible.
- Free-hand drawings are for the junior high-school level, not for mature scientists.

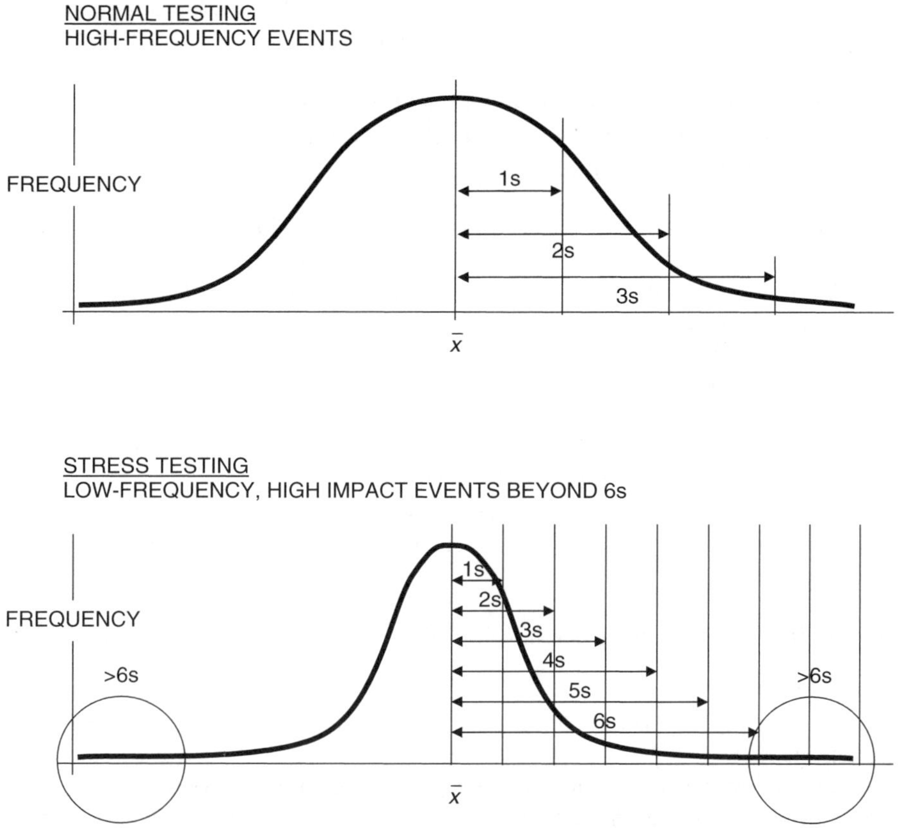

Figure 13.1 Normal testing and stress-testing distribution

Careful analysis can ensure that an originally free-hand drawn distribution, made to convey a certain concept, can be structured and decomposed into established statistical shapes, characterized by moments. This is the sense of references made in Chapter 12 and elsewhere, that EL and UL are part of the same distribution: the EL part addresses higher frequency events (within ± 3 standard deviations), the majority of which have a relatively low impact; by contrast, UL studies concentrate on the long leg, principally beyond 6 standard deviations, where the outliers can be found.

Stress testing aims to find these outliers, torture them and make them reveal some of their secrets. Figure 13.1 provides a snapshot of statistical distributions for normal testing and stress testing. (More on stress tests for UL in Chapter 14.)

13.3 Impact of macroeconomic developments

One of the main determinants of credit risk is macroeconomic developments that prove too adverse to the strategic plan of an enterprise, hence the need to study them *ex ante*. Typically, a baseline scenario of a macro stress test for the banking industry assumes that the economy will move downwards and a bank's lending, as well as its inventoried loans positions, will go through a low point.

- If the level of loss provisions remains almost unchanged,
- Then the institution navigates in a danger zone that can severely affect its profitability, or have worse consequences.

Experience teaches that tests concerning criticality thresholds are valuable in assessing an economy's ability to withstand stress, as well as the stability of the banking system. Within limits, they permit a forward-looking analysis for identifying potential risks, even if subjective elements enter into the stress tests.

For instance, with regard to equity price risk, the threshold for a stress test may be defined on the assumption of a sudden, unexpected 30 per cent slide in equity prices within a period of, say, one month, taking place simultaneously on all markets. This equity price risk must be calculated for both the trading book and the bank's own investment portfolio, at assumed market values.

Several central banks provide significant assistance in macroeconomic prognostications. Quoting from the February 2006 issue of the *Monthly Bulletin* of the European Central Bank (ECB):

> Risks to [the] outlook for price developments remain on the upside and include:
>
> - Further rises in oil prices,
> - A pass-through of oil prices into consumer prices stronger than currently envisaged,
> - Additional increases in administered prices and indirect taxes,
> - And, more fundamentally, potential second-round effects on wage and price-setting behavior.[2]

Such conditions tend to have their own line of development, which is often exogenous to the central bank and the enterprise sector. Therefore, they require not only steady watch, but also tests that might reveal the economy's secrets. As the *Financial Stability Review* of the Deutsche Bundesbank puts it:

> Macro stress tests assess the extent to which economic shocks affect the quality of a credit portfolio and whether they threaten banks' stability. [Such tests] confirm the crucial influence that macroeconomic factors exert on banks' credit risk.
>
> - A 1-percent drop in economic output may be expected to result in an 11-percent to 12-percent increase in provisions.
> - While an unexpected 1 percentage point rise in interest rates would see provisions rise by an average of around 17 percent.[3]

Different stress scenarios are simulated, by well-managed banks, over a given time horizon, for instance a two- or three-year time-frame. One of them is a permanent one percentage point interest rate increase together with overall economic growth that is half a percentage point below current level, year after year. Hypotheses based on historical evidence provide the background for this exercise. Alternatively, the two shocks outlined in the above bullets can be unstuck:

- One test concerning interest rate increases, albeit higher then 1 per cent per year,
- The other test focusing on steady interest rates, but with a 1 or 2 per cent reduction in gross domestic product (GDP), which approximates the case of Japan in the 1990s.

This type of stress testing based on macroeconomics has gained increasing acceptance in recent years, as many institutions expanded their quantitative market risk management systems into the credit business, in preparation for Basel II implementation. In this process, they developed scenarios in which risk parameters are selected from different categories of exposure, including both market and credit domains.

- The advantage of *multivariate* stress tests is that they can take an integrative approach in studying the influence of risk factors.
- By contrast, *univariate* tests (sensitivity analyses) tend to isolate the influence of one selected risk factor, in an effort to identify the weaknesses in the portfolio structure relative to this one factor.

One of the multivariate test scenarios for macroeconomic reasons combines an interest rate shock with a significant depreciation in the country's currency against a basket of currencies, and its opposite, a significant appreciation in the country's currency. Owing to the international interest rate link in financial markets, the aftermath could spill over to other countries' real economy, meaning that it slides into stagnation. A stress scenario would help to study several negative components, including:

- Permanently higher oil prices, and
- A strain on price competitiveness of enterprises in the economy under study.

The hypotheses on spillover between trading economies rest on correlations linking their productive functions, monetary policies, investments and general macroeconomic facts. As already discussed, and will be shown in greater detail, correlations:

- Are vital links in all economic studies, and they become pivot points in stress tests,
- But, contrary to correlations experimentally established in engineering and physics, in economics and finance correlations are often fuzzy, and awfully manipulated. (More on this in Chapter 14.)

The problem in connection with financial studies is that, as Dr Alan Greenspan, the former chairman of the Federal Reserve, once stated: covariance in economics is still in its infancy in the financial industry and, therefore, an ill-defined issue. Greenspan could have added that, moreover, covariance means nothing to most board members and chief executive officers (CEOs). Therefore, they do not appreciate its impact.

For starters, covariance aims to describe by means of a single number, under certain conditions (typically normal correlation), the relationship between two variables. If large values of one variable are most frequently associated with large values of the other, the two are *positively correlated*. If large values of one are most frequently associated with small values of the other, they are *negatively correlated*.

- If defaults are positively correlated with a recession,
- Then a bank's loss provisions have to increase with the downturn of the economy.

This sounds like an obvious scenario, but in mathematical analysis, the estimation of covariance is much less clear. Added to this is the fact that all models of the economy are simplifications and abstractions. Instead of a thousand factors, by necessity we make do with half a dozen, losing a large part of information that is vital in the study of correlations. At the same time, defaults have latency, while in several industries, such as banking, the heavy hand of the state can make the difference between bankruptcy and default.

13.4 Risk drivers targeted by macro stress tests

By means of stress tests, banks and other financial institutions are making in-depth analysis of critical developments in the macroeconomy, trying to prognosticate their potential implications. This permits them to expect what might have seemed to be unexpected, study ahead of time countermeasures, and be ready to react when events are happening. In connection with macroeconomic factors as in any other domain, nearly all stress tests are based on the same investigative principle:

- Find the hidden and often unexpected amount of exposure, and
- Analyse how this impacts upon the value of assets and liabilities, given an assumed shock in the risk parameters.

In the evaluation of the possible after effect of macroeconomic developments through stress testing, risk parameters that come into consideration are the projected state of the economy, and forecast changes in interest rates (see section 13.6), interest rate curves, currency exchange rates, equity prices, base metals, precious metals and other commodity prices. Changes in most of these factors can have an impact on credit risk.

Stress testing on macroeconomic factors often reveals whether in good times it is wise for banks to reduce reserves against future losses. For instance, a study conducted in late 2004 by CreditSights analyst David A. Hendler found that banks reduced their capital reserves by $800 million in the third quarter of the year, adding to earnings.[4] But as the analyst correctly forecast, with loan losses below historical norms, an uptick in bad loans became inevitable.

One of the examples of macroeconomics tests given in section 13.2 involved both a rise in interest rates and downsizing of a national product; a multivariate case. By contrast, the scenario that was subsequently examined focused on only the one or the other of these macroeconomic factors, and it was univariate.

In the multivariate scenario the loss provisions of the credit institutions increase in parallel to default risk. As lending starts and continues a downward trend as interest rates rise and economic activity enters a negative growth zone, a stress test should target an answer to whether the institution could cope relatively well with:

- An interest rate shock, and
- Prolonged weak or negative economic growth.

It is likely that such a scenario would identify problems for weakly capitalized banks with regard to their profitability and financial staying power. Much will depend on the motors behind the economic downtrend. These may be:

- *A geopolitical crisis*: geopolitical tensions exist in many locations, at different levels of global or regional impact. Such crises act as catalysts for a flare-up. Moreover, escalating frictions with a country that is a major supplier of gas or oil may cause a drag in the economy of energy-importing nations. Elections could lead to political and economic disarray in a region, as happened with Hamas in early 2006. Natural disasters and geopolitical crises occur with little or no warning.
- *A global housing bust*: economists look at a possible crisis in housing market in the USA as a much more severe event than the stockmarket bubble of 2000. A US housing bust would reverberate in world housing markets, particularly in the UK and western Europe, stifling consumer spending and increasing negative investor sentiment. At present, the US consumer accounts for an estimated 25 per cent of world GDP. More than 50 per cent of the US current account deficit is in consumer goods, as 40 per cent of what consumers buy is made abroad. If the US consumer stopped spending, the economies of Canada, Mexico and China would be hit hardest, while Europe would see a more negative impact than Asia, except for China.
- *Material deterioration in company profits, and return of overly levered corporate balance sheets*: substantially higher raw material costs and/or a deceleration in productivity would derail the profit cycle, with low-margin industries most negatively impacted. Corporate debt spreads would widen, particularly so as pressure to grow again could result in mishaps over mergers and acquisitions and deterioration in credit quality.
- *A motor in the global economy going into reverse gear*: for example, the go-go economy of China may have a hard landing, with an impact throughout the global market, particularly in commodities; or if US consumer spending dramatically falls it may hurt exports throughout the region in a big way.
- *A financial accident triggering a credit crunch*: for instance, one or more major financial entities may go under, prompting fears of a domino effect in the markets, as with the Savings & Loan and Long-Term Capital Management (LTCM) crises. Corporate bonds and leveraged companies would be negatively impacted.
- *Global spread of a contagious disease, such as human transmission of bird flu*: with this, global trade and hours worked would be likely to decline significantly. Growth would fall sharply and global liquidity seize up. The impact would vary by jurisdiction. Exporting countries would be more negatively impacted than the USA, which is a large importer.
- *A major natural disaster or terrorist attack, which would significantly affect the global economy*: a large terrorist attack in a G-7 country would be likely to have global economic ramifications. In general, government bonds and cash would

benefit over stocks, as by all likelihood there would be an immediate overreaction in global equity markets, as happened in 2001, with 9/11.

Stress analysis on macroeconomic facts should be tuned so that it clearly distinguishes between fundamental risks to the bank's *most important* themes and *disruptive surprises*. The core theme must be risks that are primarily economic and typically observable over time, such as overshooting in interest rates and critical types of exposure.

Macroeconomic stress analysis should be preceded by a planning session that develops several examples of what would cause a reassessment of economic and financial perspectives. Examples are the cases outlined in the above list. Risks should be examined to the *upside* as well as to the *downside*. Protecting against every possible downside is impossible, but this is not the objective of stress analysis. The goal is to provide an early warning and make possible damage control.

13.5 Stress testing macroeconomic risks and opportunities

The closing paragraph of section 13.4 made the reference that risks to the *upside* must be examined, which may sound odd. This is necessary because the effect of macroeconomic factors is by no means only negative. Even macroglobal imbalances provide business opportunities, and one must be prepared for them.

A stress test on the upside should account for the fact that the strength of any recovery depends on what caused the downturn. The 2001 economic environment provides a good example, because it came in the aftermath not only of the stockmarket bubble, but also of tightened monetary policy during late 1999 and 2000, particularly in the USA. Also in its background were soaring oil prices during 1999 and 2000, and the bursting of internet companies. These macroeconomic conditions triggered:

- Severe cutbacks in investment,
- Decline in demand for manufactured output,
- Accumulation of unsold inventories, and
- A significant reduction in output on a global scale.

For instance, in October 2001 the output of American manufacturers was 7 per cent below its peak in June 2000. The slowdown expanded globally, partly because the background forces were also global, and partly because between 1996 and 2000, the USA alone generated just under half of total world incremental demand.

At a macromarket level, as 2001 came to a close, the justification for optimism was that these conditions had changed or, at least, were about to change. Oil prices were down by about 40 per cent in real terms from their peak in 2000. Monetary policy eased dramatically, particularly in the USA, with short-term rates down 4.5 percentage points in less than a year after eleven consecutive rate cuts by the Federal Reserve.

Fiscal policy had also become more expansionary, at least in America, where the Bush administration pushed through Congress a multibillion dollar tax cut, and at the same time accelerated military spending. On these grounds, several economists were to comment that the industrial/military complex was back in power, sharing economic revival with consumer spending.

What these references seemed to justify, at the time, was expectations of a fairly normal recovery. Many analysts, however, suggested that the view that there would be a conventional recovery rested on the mistaken assumption that the 2000/01 events were a conventional downturn, which they were not. To them the opposite case was more likely, resting on three assumptions:

- The USA was a large postbubble economy, and it is difficult for very large economies to grow out of corrections following a market bubble.
- There would be an inverse wealth effect, such as between 1994 and 2000, when the wealth held in the stockmarket soared by $12 trillion (equal to more than six years of normal gross saving in the economy), and much of that went down the drain.
- The dependence of the global recovery on a resurgence in US demand would mean that the world economy would take time to recover.

What these estimates missed is that the rise in the American housing market kept households busy in acquiring more and more goods, tremendously easing the correction in the internal US market. Furthermore, China emerged as a new motor in global trade; indeed, for a couple of years, it was the only economy really going strong.

These events meant that the pessimistic scenarios of 2000/01 were flawed. Yet, originally, from an economic analysis perspective all points sounded reasonable. Expanding at a time characterized by market uncertainty due to a crush seemed a prescription for major losses. Hence, the case that was made for an extended period of weak growth in private demand, and therefore a limping recovery in the USA, albeit stronger than Japan's recovery in the 1990s.

The dynamism of the new economy of the late 1990s, which was short lived, was no longer around, but neither did macroeconomic events turn out the way originally projected. The remedy was a combination of military spending, tax cuts and, in particular, rock-bottom interest rates that fed the nascent housing bubble and:

- Brought the American consumer to the forefront of sustained economic activity, and
- Even expanded US consumer purchases to an astonishing 24 per cent of global GDP (see section 13.4).

Starting in 2003/04, there was a resurgence in economic activity that sustained itself so well that its pace remained strong in 2005, while large and growing financial imbalances continued to pose risks for global stability. Of particular concern to economists, and therefore an excellent subject for macroeconomic stress tests, has been the magnitude of capital flows required to finance large and growing US current account deficits. With prolonged accumulation of these deficits, there have been questions regarding:

- The willingness of foreign investors, both official and private, to increase their holdings in US securities, and
- Whether foreign exchange reserves accumulated by some Asian economies would continue to be recycled into the US bond markets.

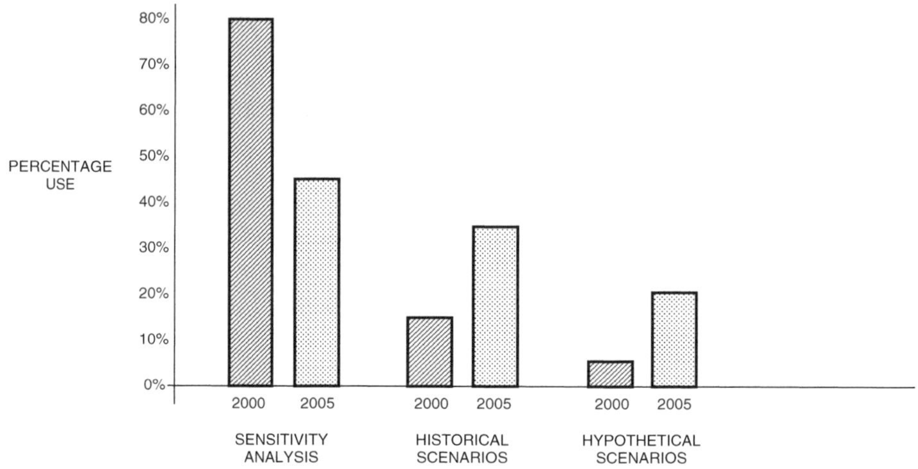

Figure 13.2 The change in the pattern of test methods among commercial banks

Macroeconomic stress based on these two points could provide answers to 'What if not' scenarios. There is no evidence that this has been done, but overall stress tests have reached significant acceptance; their overall popularity is expanding, with sensitivity analyses losing ground to more rigorous types of test.

Figure 13.2 presents cumulative stress-testing statistics in the USA, the UK and continental Europe. Notice the change in relative importance of different families of tests. In addition, there is a growing proportion of multivariate analyses. The challenge is that of the skill necessary to design and conduct such tests, as well as to provide realistic hypotheses for appraisal.

One reason why macro stress tests are increasingly being carried out by financial institutions is that macroeconomic developments are one of the main factors influencing credit risk. However, the considerable amount of input required for modelling means that, at present, only the larger credit institutions are in a position to conduct such tests. Choices in risk parameters are usually influenced by:

- The bank's experience with certain types of risk, and
- Its sensitivity to exposures that were assumed in the past.

Another difference in the way that macroeconomic events are approached among credit institutions is due to the sophistication of the risk managers and rocket scientists who they employ. An example is stress tests for interest rate risk, not only in relation to the whole yield curve, but also considering asymmetrical changes in interest rates that may pose problems for credit exposures, as will be shown in section 13.6.

13.6 Stress testing financial instruments: a case study with interest rates

In terms of macroeconomic effects, in Euroland, economists forecast that 2005/06 oil price rises and already announced changes to administered prices and indirect taxes, such as a nearly 20 per cent rise in German value-added tax (VAT), would have an upward impact on annual inflation over the coming years. Therefore, the European Central Bank (ECB) decided on a policy of vigilance to ensure that the risks to price stability over the medium to longer term would not materialize. If they did, then they would impact on a whole range of financial instruments, including:

- *Foreign exchange rates*: flight to or from the US dollar, depending on US macroeconomics,
- *Fixed income*: global tightening with a substantial increase in interest rates because of looming inflation,
- *Internal interest rate swaps*: where spreads would be widening,
- *Traded credit risk*: characterized by a likelihood of a major increase in defaults,
- *Equities*: increasing the probability of a stockmarket crash, and
- *Real estate*: possible collapse of this market because of high interest rates and a lack of consumer confidence.

Different scenarios must be considered when stress testing this outlook. Oil price rises should not simply be regarded as passing ‘volatility’; they must be definitely included in the indicators of underlying inflation. Other risk drivers are the leading and lagging indicators. However, there are uncertainties. According to an ECB study:

- There is no clear-cut answer to the question of which indicator is lagging the other, as this depends on the nature of the shocks affecting the economy, and
- The uncertainty with regard to the nature of current shocks impacting on inflation, whether they are temporary or more lasting, suggests a need for caution in interpreting the currently relatively subdued levels of some underlying inflation indicators.[6]

The ECB economists are right to be prudent. The most dramatic recent reference to inflation escaping the control of the Federal Reserve is that of the late 1970s with the second oil shock. To curb it, the Federal Reserve increased interest rates to double-digit numbers, leading to mismatch risk for long-term mortgages and eventually to huge UL for savings and loans (S&Ls) in the USA.

Stress tests of inflation and its impact on interest rates are that much more important as, during the early years of the twenty-first century, the global financial system has been marked by a continued low interest rate environment and abundant liquidity in key industrial countries. Lessons on the control of interest rates’ aftermath can be learned from the late 1980s debacle over S&Ls. With this background, their supervisor, the Office of Thrift Supervision (OTS), currently requires daily reports with stress tests, along the following axes of reference:

- Zero change in interest rates and ±100 basis points change are normal tests,
- ±200 basis points change is the reference test, and
- ±300 and ±400 basis points changes are stress tests.

Other supervisory authorities are not known to require daily stress tests from the credit institutions that they regulate. Yet, this would have been important in every country, the USA, Euroland and Japan, where the fact that key interest rates have remained at all-time lows has inevitably led to complacency. For instance, in Euroland interest rates have remained for too long at an all-time low level, while the money stock measure M3 has increased very sharply throughout the same period. This has led to:

- The creation of high excess liquidity, and
- Search for yield in riskier assets, exposing institutional and other investors to perils.

To avoid a *mismatch crisis* similar to that of S&Ls in the late 1980s, financial entities of all types, from banks to institutional investors and hedge funds, need steadily to stress test their portfolio of debt instruments against the risk driver of changes affecting interest rates and exchange rates.

Recent publications by the Basel Committee, the ECB and Deutsche Bundesbank, increasingly underline the need for stress testing along the aforementioned reference to stress-testing procedures. The sense of what is being published by supervisors and central bankers is presented in Figure 13.3. The magnitude of:

- Credit risk will be determined by the financial staying power of the institution under ± 300 and ± 400 basis points shocks, while refinancing its lending power,
- The market risk associated with inventoried positions will be determined, to a large extent, by the length of a phase of volatility in all sorts of commodity prices, and abruptness of a possible subsequent correction.

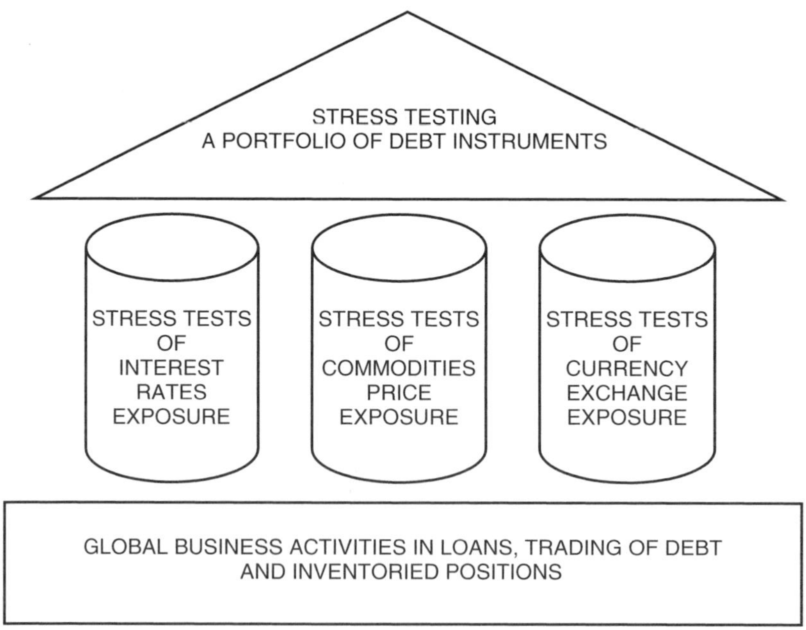

Figure 13.3 Foundation and pillars of a stress-testing project

A crucial risk driver in both scenarios is the tightening of monetary policy in the USA, UK and Euroland, and the consequent gradual onset of liquidity withdrawal. These moves typically put upward pressure on long-term capital market rates. Along with volatility, the withdrawal of liquidity presents an excellent ground for stress tests.

Specifically in connection with interest rate risk, the term structure is one of the key elements needed in stress testing. Particular problems are caused by asymmetrical changes in interest rates. Searching for criticalities, well-managed institutions assume three different types of positive and negative shifts in the yield curve:

- Twists in the curve's short end,
- Parallel shifts over all maturities, and
- Fluctuations in the middle range.

A basis points model is shown in Table 13.1. In every case the shifts are calibrated so that the stress scenario can be expected only once in a predetermined number of years. One stress-testing project followed by the author assumed proportional increases of 25 per cent, 30 per cent and 35 per cent for interest rate volatilities, exchange rate volatilities and stockmarket volatilities, respectively.

Similarly, exchange rate risk was calculated by considering an *x* per cent appreciation or depreciation in the base currency, for instance the US dollar, within one month. In this specific case, a 15 per cent scenario corresponded to the largest monthly change in the DEM/US dollar currency exchange rate, from the end of 1992 to the late 1990s.

Other stress tests have been designed to map the effects of nervous markets, which are a recurring phenomenon. In February 2006, a Merrill Lynch study pointed out: 'Markets appear to have entered a nervous zone, with investors seemingly trying to time every market top, whether in gold, oil, currencies, interest rates, or equities... [at the same time] flat yield curves globally are creating concern that economic growth will be weaker in the second half of the year [2006] and into 2007... [but] we do *not* subscribe to the belief that flat or inverted curves invariably predict a coming recession'.[7]

Whether an inverted yield curve is a predictor of recession, or only represents an imbalance between supply and demand, is an issue that has been debated by

Table 13.1 A basis points model for stress testing interest rate curves

Position	$		£		€	
	<3 months >5 years	3 months to 5 years	>5 years <3 months	3 months to 5 years	<3 months >5 years	3 months to 5 years
Twist (+)						
Parallel (+)						
Peak (+)						
Twist (–)						
Parallel (–)						
Peak (–)						

economists for many years, without having reached a factual conclusion. It is also an issue that should be subject to careful analysis, in which stress tests based on historical evidence can play an important role.

13.7 Stress testing for unexpected losses from business risk

No two people have, or are expected to have, the same notion of *business risk*. To many, business risk is practically synonymous with *reputational risk*. When Martha Stuart had problems with justice, her firm suffered greatly as advertisers cut their sponsorship short. Reputation is a major business risk driver, but not the only one.

As Figure 13.4 suggests, industry risk is another factor. In the 1980s, IBM had stayed for too long in the mainframe computer industry, whose market appeal was fading rapidly. Short of an eleventh hour turnaround, the company could have gone down the tubes like Digital Equipment Corporation (DEC). In June 2006, an article in *Total Telecom Magazine* had this to say about competition in the telecoms industry:

> Alternative network operators are threatening to take valuable revenue away from UK's mobile providers, by muscling in on the business service market.
>
> But mobile operators are set to fight back with offers of their own, designed to encourage their fixed lines altogether.[8]

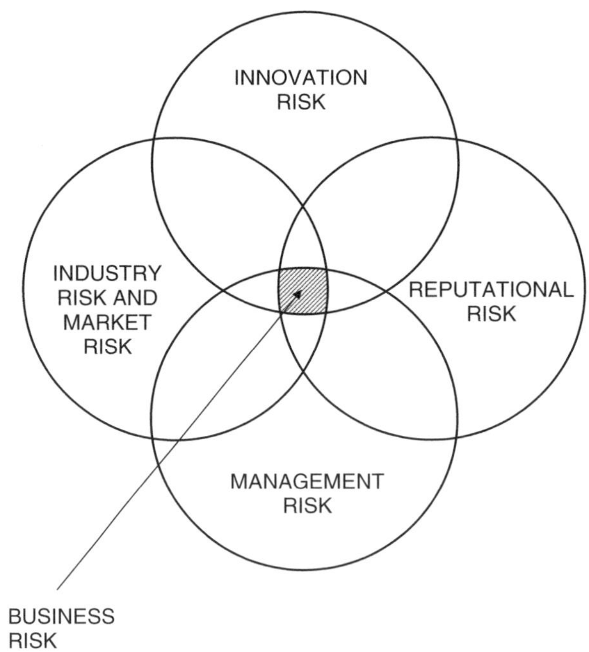

Figure 13.4 Business risk can be found at the junction of many risk drivers, with management risk at the base and innovation risk at the top

The challenges that DEC's Vaxes represented to IBM's mainframes, client-server solutions to DEC's Vaxes, mobile telephony (and cable networks) to the traditional plant of telcos, and alternative network operators to mobile telephony firms, are all part of *business risk*, which must be stress tested for UL due to market migration.

The ability to face up to the challenges is part of senior management's duties, and therefore of *management risk*, which is another crucial business risk driver to be appropriately tested. Study after study suggests that roughly one-third of companies have an effective management, in another third management is passable, but in the remaining firms management is substandard, leading them into major business risks. Exposure to poor management comes in many forms, ranging:

- From innovation, and the ability of the company to reinvent itself,
- To design, engineering, marketing and aftersales service.

Other characteristics of good management to be thoroughly tested, are keeping a lid on labour costs, keeping overheads low, prestudy and commitments such as health plans and pensions, and the ability to be ahead of the curve in competition.

Rating agencies have their own way of looking at business risk. 'We don't specifically put business risk in credit rating', said Charles Prescott, Group Managing Director of Fitch Ratings, one of the major independent credit rating agencies in London, in an interview. Prescott adds that business risk is a function of both:

- Endogenous factors which, to a significant extent, are concerned with quality of management, and
- Exogenous factors, including the business environment, economic facts, unemployment and physical disasters such as hurricanes.

In the opinion of other cognizant executives, a third factor should be added to these two basic factors:

- Spikes, resulting from events such as major frauds, adversity originating in legal risk and other crucial reasons.

For instance, in late September 2005 an American judge approved legal settlements that will return more than $6.2 billion to investors who lost money in the WorldCom accounting scandal. About 830 000 people and institutions will benefit, with the money coming from a variety of defendants. Legal risk is a major driver of business risk, and it eventually spreads into reputational risk.

Settlements connected to legal risk are on the increase. Citigroup and J.P. MorganChase, which underwrote or traded WorldCom securities, will each pay more than $2 billion. This is over and above similar amounts paid by the two banks for legal risk alone during 2004 and 2005. Time and again, such examples are providing evidence of UL connected with business risk.

Tyco is another example of a spike in business risk that hit a company because of fraud. Investors dumped the equity upon learning that Dennis Kozlowski, its CEO, had cheated New York State with sales tax on artwork. Kozlowski had also cheated his company out of $150 million, for which, in September 2005, he was condemned to serve up to twenty-five years in prison. 'Fraud is difficult to factor into ratings. We don't have all the information', said Charles Prescott of Fitch.

The lack of metrics and standards through which to judge business risk is one of the major uncertainties connected with its identification, measurement and testing. As noted in the opening paragraphs of this section, there is no convention about what exactly enters into business risk and, therefore, what it is all about. As a result, it is difficult to pinpoint in every case all of its component parts at a reasonable level of accuracy. A similar case characterized operational risk prior to Basel II.[9] In principle:

- To treat business risk through a sound approach, it has to be measurable, and
- It will become measurable only after its definition has been settled and becomes generally acceptable.

'One of the crucial queries is how far business risk, industry risk, and management risk correlate', said Alastair Graham, senior vice-president of Moody's Investors Service. Graham gave the Rover car company as an example of how far industry risk and management risk overlap. Several important factors enter into their common area, some of which are endogenous and others exogenous. Moreover, endogenous factors of one company may become exogenous factors of others.

As Alastair Graham pointed out, a significant number of business activities is characterized by *contingent risk*. When Rover went bust, hundreds of other companies suffered, particularly those not careful enough to diversify their client base. But is client diversification part of business risk? Opinions differ in this regard, which essentially means that there are many judgemental factors. These are important issues in stress testing credit risk, because business risk plays a significant part in:

- Creditworthiness, and
- Financial conditions associated with a company's debt.

When in the 1990s the Japanese economy was in intensive care, and the country's banks had found themselves at the edge of the abyss, there was 'Japan premium' associated with the loans that they could obtain. A recent example is provided by the corporate bond markets. The downgrade of General Motors and Ford, including their financing subsidiaries, to non-investment grade triggered:

- An abrupt upward movement in the interest that the two car manufacturers had to pay, and
- A corresponding loss of value for their debt instruments, which found themselves in the portfolios of institutional and other investors.

What should be retained from this discussion is the magnitude of the problem in stress testing business risk. The challenge is no different in the banking industry, where stress tests for business risk should include all product lines and income derived from each of them:

- Commissions income,
- Fees income,

- Loans income,
- Trading income,
- Net interest income,
- Income from insurance, and
- Income from ancillary channels.

Notice that, in a similar way to lists for other industries, each of these positions identifies *earnings at risk*. Stress tests should also focus on expense by channel in a crisis because, as several experts believe, on the bottom line business risk is the difference between:

- Income in a crisis, and
- Expense in a crisis.

Both must be compared with precrisis income and expense. Furthermore, one of the most important stress tests for business risk concerns its correlation with strategic risk. The covariance of the two risk drivers (see Chapter 14) depends on:

- The type of organization, and
- The market in which an entity operates.

In 2005, HSBC wrote off $5 billion connected to losses in its household finance subsidiary in the USA. By purchasing household finance, HSBC bought market share. However, the $5 billion red ink wiped out a quarter of HSBC's $20 billion profit in 2005, an excellent example of how business risk can hit both the balance sheet and income statement, with the amount depending on:

- The products being offered,
- The markets within which the entity is active, and
- The leverage factor, which is always part of the equation.

How are companies allocating economic capital for business risk reasons? Crédit Suisse reserves about 60 per cent of its intangibles, including goodwill, for business risk. Other companies have their own method, sometimes putting aside part of their economic capital.

During research for this book in London in September 2005, cognizant executives suggested that Deutsche Bank allocates 3 per cent of its economic capital to business risk; while Danske Bank, a much smaller European regional credit institution, allocates 21 per cent of its economic capital. (Economic capital is discussed in Chapter 14.)

These are figures. As always with quantitative statements, to appreciate what they mean, one has to know the qualitative criteria and allocation decisions; for instance,

- What the bank puts into business risk,
- Which drivers are guiding the allocation,
- How the capital allocation is made between competing risk factors, and
- Where the money will come from to pay for assumed business risk.

As Charles Prescott aptly stated, one needs to watch not just the numbers but also the logic behind them. Numbers alone do not tell the whole story; even if these numbers are accurate, which is not always true, their interpretation requires more insight than data alone can provide. As in so many other domains where we try to understand the risks involved, business risk can be confronted only through a quantitative and qualitative approach.

Notes

1. D.N. Chorafas, *Strategic Business Planning for Accountants: Methods, Tools and Case Studies*, Butterworth-Heinemann, London, 2007.
2. European Central Bank, *Monthly Bulletin*, Frankfurt, February 2006.
3. Deutsche Bundesbank, *Financial Stability Review*, Frankfurt, November 2005.
4. *BusinessWeek*, 6 December 2004.
5. European Central Bank, *Monthly Bulletin*, Frankfurt, November 2005.
6. Merrill Lynch, *RIC Report*, 14 February 2006.
7. *Total Telecom Magazine*, June 2006.
8. D.N. Chorafas, *Management Risk. The Bottleneck is at the Top of the Bottle*, Macmillan/Palgrave, London, 2004.
9. D.N. Chorafas, *Operational Risk Control with Basel II. Basic Principles and Capital Requirements*, Butterworth-Heinemann, London, 2004.

14 Economic capital and algorithms for stress testing unexpected losses

14.1 Introduction

'In theory', said a senior executive of Standard & Poor's (S&P) who participated in this research, 'if a bank were to substantially reduce capital under Basel II, all else remaining the same, we could lower the rating'. In practice, changes in capital policy will be gradual, as banks incrementally adapt to Basel II principles, and account for market response to their improved capital reserves.

In addition, more and more credit institutions will learn how to deal with unexpected losses (ULs). ULs require much more than loan-loss provisions, a staple item with expected losses (EL). The allocation of economic capital is one of the recent solutions promoted by the market's watch. Its downside is algorithm insufficiency in computing necessary capital resources. Unreliable correlation coefficients magnify this insufficiency. Some relief may be provided by qualitative scenarios, one of the tools that banks need for estimating UL.

14.2 Economic capital for credit rating and unexpected losses

While preparing for the implementation of Basel II, particularly the advanced methods, the better managed banks have done a great deal of work in learning how to deal with *economic capital* and its allocation to their business units (BUs). Typically, this is done according to the exposure that each BU assumes, with the driving force being UL. Independent rating agencies look at economic capital as *signalling capital*, telling the market that:

- The bank is here to stay, and
- It has financial resources to take care of more than classical credit risk.

Allocated at BU level, economic capital is a financial buffer for extreme events connected with counterparty risk, as well as major market exposures due to interest rates, currency exchange, business risk, low margin profits and other factors that may have unexpected consequences on the bank's own credit risk and rating. Good governance looks at economic capital as required risk capital. To emphasize this approach, Belgium's KBC has instituted a new book: available financial resources (AFR).

According to management policy, AFR must be about 20 per cent larger than otherwise computed risk capital, because of strategic reasons, evolving business opportunities, effects of procyclicality, information latency, model risk, and more. In the opinion of Tim Thompson, head of economic capital at Barclays Bank, economic capital is basically risk capital representing a whole family of exposures in:

- Retail markets,
- Wholesale markets,
- Fixed assets,
- Private equity,
- Insurance,
- Pension funds, and
- Certain residual value.

Under the enquiring eye of independent rating agencies, a growing number of credit institutions put economic capital at the top of the list in enhancing their credit rating. For Holland's Rabobank, the capital base for regulatory requirements is pure tier one: equity and retained earnings; economic capital goes beyond that. It is evident that rating agencies appreciate this prudent policy. A good question is: 'How much more capital does a credit institution need beyond regulatory capital for AAA over AA credit rating?'

- Should this difference be 10, 20 or 30 per cent, or more?

There is no unique answer to this query. Apart from the factors already mentioned, the amount of economic capital that should be on hand depends on assumed risks, internal controls, quality of management and macroeconomic conditions (see Chapter 13). *Solvency standard* should be the guide. Figure 14.1 provides a snapshot based on:

- Level of confidence (α), and
- Amount of capital at risk.

In addition, credit rating agencies look not only at regulatory and economic financial resources, but also beyond capital; for instance, at management decisions, actions and results being obtained; corporate outlook, risk appetite and risk control; access to funding; franchise; stock buybacks; diversification, and changes in risk profile.

Any one of the aforementioned factors may not allow AA credit rating. The rating process has a lot to do with dynamics of the company and of the market. In addition, independent rating agencies have good experience in the discovery of weak spots that can damage what currently may look like a good balance sheet.

As these examples document, both quantitative and qualitative factors play a significant role in financial staying power and, therefore, in credit rating. It should, however, be noted that similar critical issues also apply the other way round, to downgrading. Specifically in regard to risk capital, some rating agencies suggested that:

- If a credit institution has only regulatory capital to cover credit risk,
- Then it may be a BBB or BB bank, because it has no provision for UL.

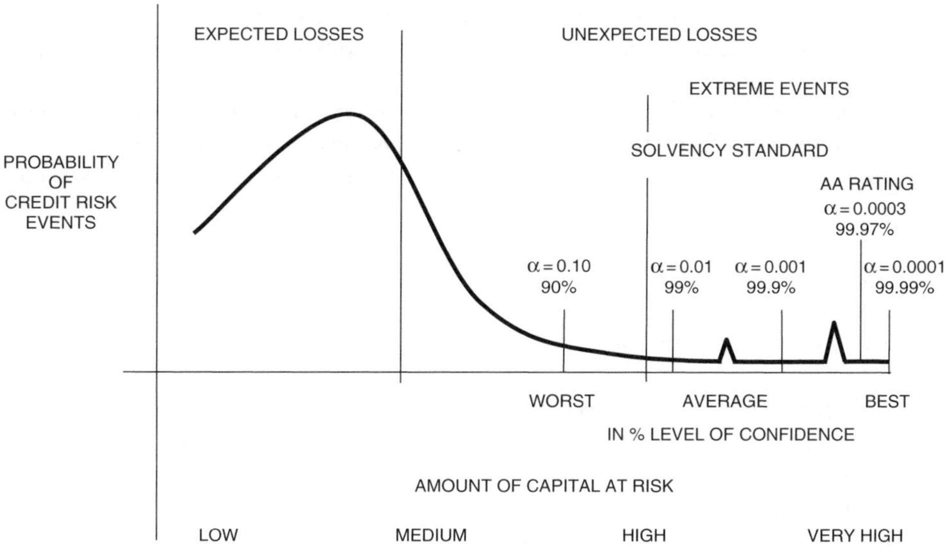

Figure 14.1 Capital at risk as a percentage of unexpected losses, spikes and extreme events

Since Basel II started to change the capital adequacy structure, as well as the culture associated with it, several banks found it necessary to target AA credit rating. The effort to ensure AA or better credit grade from independent rating agencies is an imaginative business, and it is not an easy one.[1] As an AA, and even more so an AA+ or AAA entity, the bank must have more economic capital than otherwise. It should also appreciate that the target rating:

- Is global, and
- Can be a financial burden.

A high credit rating attracts customers and lowers interbank lending costs. Another basic characteristic of target rating is that it constitutes a moving target, since it is a lagging indicator depending on assumed risks (credit, market, operational), the mitigation of risk(s), business cycle, quality of management (see Chapter 13) and financial resources earmarked as economic capital.

Economic capital should not be kept as a lump sum, but allocated by senior management to business lines and transactions. No two banks have the same capital allocation system; however, several have common principles associated with creditworthiness. For instance:

- Transactions with lower credit quality should be allocated more risk capital, and
- Transactions with greater correlations and concentration risk should also be the subject of more economic capital.

The second bullet point is based on the principle that economic capital allocation should take account of *true* diversification effects, and benefit from variable small correlation coefficients. This is easier said than done. By and large, concentrations of risks are a mind set, and correlation coefficients are high, requiring higher capital amounts.

Risk sensitivity in the allocation of economic capital is crucial not only because of this long list of exposures faced by an institution, but also because, faced by an institution, this is capital of last resort. Some companies divide signalling capital into two major classes:

- One addressed to *catastrophic events*, intended to cover extreme losses that could destroy the institution,
- The other covering more generally *UL* and EL shortfall.

Thus, there is a significant synergy between economic capital allocation and risk management. A factual and documented basis for economic capital allocation is a major improvement in risk control; it is not a new religion.

Economic capital allocation is also an exercise in compliance. The senior vice-president of a money centre bank emphasized that, 'As the new regulatory requirements come out, they restructure our portfolio. We can comply with anything. It is just part of the cost of doing business. We have already reduced the credit risk in our portfolio by shifting to higher credit rating'.

14.3 Capital beyond loan-loss provisions

A basic reason why regulators, credit rating agencies and the market at large watch carefully after capital adequacy, and loan-loss provisions able to withstand severe shocks, is that banks play a key role in the process of monetary policy transmission. Therefore, changes in their financial situation:

- Can signal potential risks to financial stability, and
- Will probably have important implications on economic activity.

As plenty of examples in the preceding chapters have shown, Basel II is an improvement over past methods for calculating capital adequacy. First, it reinforces a trend firmly in place among the better institutions in the banking industry, which already use advanced credit risk management approaches. Secondly, the fact that it places increased emphasis on stress testing is welcome.

However, there are some drawbacks. The internal ratings-based (IRB) method is good, but its growing complexity overwhelms smaller banks, who do not have the human resources and necessary technology. Therefore, they are condemned to stay with the less sophisticated standardized approach (and in America with Basel I). At the same time, the regulators need additional resources to face the ongoing evolution of Basel II.

Then, there is the case of model risk, augmented by the fact that several credit institutions, and some regulators, are not ready to handle the intricacies associated with models, let alone develop eigenmodels. As a result, they use *any* model they come across, right or wrong. (More on this in section 14.5.)

In addition, currently available models pay no attention to the macroeconomic level of exposure which, as shown in Chapter 13, is critical even for EL. Neither do current models provide provisioning for cyclical downturns; yet, downturns magnify the impact of economic cycles on banks' risks, income and capital.

There are also structural factors that account for higher loan losses than is provided by the classical type of bad loan reserves. This leads some regulators to regret that the EL algorithm has been abandoned by Basel. The risk of shortfall in loans reserves exists even with:

- The use of better risk management techniques than those in the past, and
- The availability of opportunities for larger banks to offload part of their credit risks, through securitization and credit derivatives.

Credit derivatives themselves are subject to EL and UL, with the latter represented by spikes in spot market value, or a persistent downward trend. For risk management purposes, such losses must be projected under stress conditions, on the basis of hypotheses about default (or unwillingness to pay) of different major counterparties over the same periods, using:

- The lower estimate of recovery rate, and
- The higher estimate of default probability.

Unexpected credit losses must be tested through factors that reflect the counterparty's behaviour under stress conditions. Within a certain margin of error, this helps in defining the amount of allocated capital at risk, money at the edge of being lost after bankruptcy proceedings.

There are also cases where even the classical bad loan reserves are dwindling because of expediency. For example, the 2004 Q3 quarterly banking profile by the Federal Deposit Insurance Corporation (FDIC, one of the three main American regulators) showed that US banks had been drawing down their reserves. In Q3, the big banks' loan-loss provisions covered only 93 per cent of their write-offs. On 21 February 2004, an article in *BusinessWeek* pointed out that Detroit's Comerica had the largest 2004 drop in reserves:

- The bank failed to add money in Q4, and
- It extracted \$21 million from loss reserves adding it to income, to beat analysts by 10 cents per share.

Shortfalls in loan-loss reserves of other banks are shown in Table 14.1; invariably, they work counter to profits shortfalls. Companies dread profits shortfall, because missing analysts' estimates damage their credibility on Wall Street. At the same time, however, playing with the rules in loan-loss reserves opens up a path to much greater dangers than a downgrade from 'buy' to 'hold'. To be in charge of risk control, senior management should:

- Clearly define which channels and BUs are more sensitive to capital allocation for UL purposes,

Table 14.1 Banks mentioned in a *BusinessWeek* article on fall in loan provisions*

	Fall in loan-loss provisions (millions)	Contribution to earnings per share	Beat consensus estimate by
Citigroup	\$807.0	15¢	1 ¢
Fifth Third	\$28.6	5¢	2 ¢
Associated	\$6.0	5¢	5 ¢
Compass	\$4.1	3¢	2 ¢
First Horizon	\$3.6	3¢	1 ¢

* *Source: BusinessWeek*, 21 February 2004.

- Set standards to be observed by all channels and BUs in terms of loan-loss provisions, and
- Ensure the collaboration of BU management in the avoidance of 'reporting freedoms' taken with provisioning.

This mission can be fulfilled more successfully by focusing on one objective. After a sound reporting system has been designed, its implementation should start with a couple of BUs that are willing to co-operate. Then, a pilot project with stress tests should be undertaken. Other things being equal, banks that pay attention to an orderly approach to risk control will position themselves for survival in a market that is tougher than ever. This is particularly true when:

- Risks are measured in real time,
- Longer time horizons are observed in risk measurement,
- Not only mean value, but also confidence intervals are computed (see Chapter 1), and
- Correlation assumptions as well as all types of weights are tested against real-life statistics, and appropriately corrected.

Stress testing can be of invaluable assistance in connection with all of these points. Honesty in stress testing results is the best policy, particularly when accompanied by corrective action. Management should keep in mind that no credit rating is immune to a downside. As Figure 14.2 documents, the global ratings distribution of credit institutions is deteriorating over time. Upholding a credit rating takes a lot of effort.

A good way of avoiding this drift towards lower credit ratings is rigorous handling of both EL and UL. Along with this comes the notion of dynamically aggregating counterparty exposures, rather than simply adding them together.

Basically, a dynamic aggression of assumed credit risks finds its place in the leg of the credit risk distribution that has been examined so often in this book. Measured in standard deviations (s) for stress-testing purposes, the author's experience suggests that:

- $s = 5$ is almost trivial (as suggested in Chapter 13, $6s$ is the minimum deviation from the central value that should be considered),

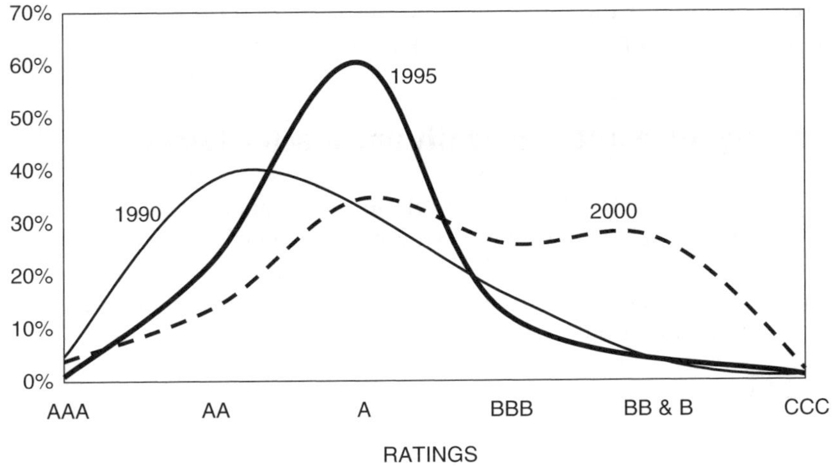

Figure 14.2 Ratings distribution of global banks according to Standard & Poor's (by permission of Walter Pompliano, S&P)

- $s = 10$ is realistic, and
- $s = 15$ is conservative, but also more likely to reveal hidden extreme exposures.

In terms of pitfalls, much can be learned and avoided, in computing capital charges, from failures that have taken place in the past. An example is provided by the space shuttle Columbia disaster. A blue-ribbon committee, appointed by the American government, said that there were six major problems. The first was that the shuttle's budget had decreased by 40 per cent, because the spaceship was considered a 'mature product'. High technology has no mature product to start with; practically everything needs developing and sustaining.

The second mistake was a life-cycle uncertainty. Originally projected for 2005–07, the shuttle's replacement slid to 2012–15, and then to beyond 2020. The third reason for the Columbia disaster is one often found in banking. The maintenance and test equipment for the shuttle was twenty-two years old, way out of date. The same is true of the software, medieval mainframes and other information systems gear used by most banks.

Fourthly, poor data quality played a key role in the disaster, by keeping reasons for oncoming failures opaque. Fifthly, with poor data sets and flawed judgement came overdependence on simulations, which is an aberration because simulations need first, not third class data. Simulation, like derivatives, is a useful tool when used within limits. Dependence only on simulation is one of the aspects of *model risk*.

Finally, as in most bank failures, in Columbia's case, mismanagement was found to be a key factor. At the space agency, the blue-ribbon committee said, managers had no understanding of how their organization worked, and were lulled into complacency by the shuttle's successes.[2]

The same attitude underpins the actions of many executives and professionals in the banking industry, particularly those blessed with successful deals and high commissions, who become less careful and lose their hand. A case in point is the often stated wrong estimations of correlation coefficients characterizing risk drivers.

14.4 Wrong correlations magnify unexpected losses

Chapter 13 stressed the importance of correlations in financial studies, but also the risk of inaccuracy and misrepresentation associated with their estimation. To appreciate this statement, remember that a *coefficient of correlation* is computed by dividing the *covariance* characterizing two populations X and Y by the product of the standard deviations of these two populations:

$$\rho_{xy} = \frac{s_{xy}}{s_x \cdot s_y} \tag{14.1}$$

where ρ = correlation coefficient, s_{xy} = covariance, s_x = standard deviation of X domain values, and s_y = standard deviation of Y domain values.

Also to be recalled is Dr Alan Greenspan's statement, quoted in Chapter 13. The former chairman of the Federal Reserve said that the study of covariance in finance is still in its infancy. This has evident aftereffects on the confidence to be placed in correlations. In addition, in many cases the term *correlation* is loosely used.

- Implicitly, it contains the notions of synthesis, interpretation and analogy.
- In practice, it also adds to these notions the concept of a common relation, and of complementarity.

In physics and engineering, the mathematical meaning of correlation is precise. In banking, the term is used in a broader but imprecise sense; often, it is used to mean *synergy*. Theoretically, the computational engine should be the algorithmic result of covariance between values characterizing two populations; for instance, market risk and credit risk, or business risk and legal risk. Practically, bankers take many freedoms with *estimating correlation*.

Mathematically, historical data and events are typically used to compute correlation coefficients. Often, however, historical correlation assumptions do not hold up because market factors, which were reflected in them, have changed in the meantime. There is also intentional misuse of correction measurements, not infrequently owing to a lack of appreciation, or conflicts of interest.

Some advice, given to the author over fifty years ago by his professors at UCLA, can be of help in using correlations in finance and banking. This advice is general, but it applies closely to correlation coefficients: when reading statistics, one should watch out for a switch somewhere between:

- The raw figure, and
- The conclusion.

Often what is missing in a quantitative presentation, including correlations, is the factor that caused a change to occur; this is a factor of critical importance. In other cases, results are biased because the time series that are used may be incomplete, obsolete, misleading or simply irrelevant. For these reasons, correlations do not always mean what one thinks they do.

For instance, in a recent meeting, the chief risk manager of a major bank said that in one of its divisions he found a correlation of 68 per cent between credit risk and market risk. Immediately, this raised the question: What might have caused such a correlation? Then, after investigating the background reasons for such ρ, two other questions came up. Given the particular circumstances:

- Is $\rho = 68$ 'too high' or 'too low'?
- Is this 68 per cent correlation 'good' or 'bad'?

Answers that help in making decisions can by no means be limited to quantitative results. Interpretation requires qualitative analysis, and this is based on assumptions. This is where conflicts of interest may come in. Assumptions about correlations are often structured in a way that reduces capital requirements, but fail to take into account the likelihood and magnitude of tail events. This is a basic reason why the validity of an economic capital model may be questionable. The principle is that:

- If risks are correlated,
- Then a change in one influences total exposure.

- If they are independent,
- Then the influence of the larger one is diminished.

A challenging problem associated with the handling of correlated risks is that beyond that point, arbitrary manipulation of correlations leads to serious aggravation of exposure. Correlated risks are complex systems. 'The relative impact of correlations', said a senior executive of S&P, 'is that the further we look in the tail, the greater is the impact of correlations'. A basic law of finance is that:

- Unexpected financial shocks happen at the long leg of risk distributions, and
- At the tail of a risk distribution, the picture of losses is broader, and more representative of market realities.

While, at least in theory, diversification helps to reduce correlations, specifically in terms of co-movement and dependency of risk drivers on one another, in practice diversification of risk is a very sophisticated business, and it is more often fiction than fact.

Neither does credit risk mitigation (see Chapter 11) reduce correlations under every possible condition. Regulators have introduced correlations to make bankers aware that different risk factors may move in the same way. Therefore, since day one, the Basel Committee has emphasized that:

- Credit institutions must validate their assumptions about correlation through analysis, and
- The correlation coefficient they use must be tested and proven.

Central bankers follow the advice that they have given to commercial bankers. In 2005 a study by the Deutsche Bundesbank, with regard to financial stability, found that the sharp rise in the correlation of trading results during 2004 called for increased vigilance: 'As a mean of the pairwise correlation of the daily trading results of twelve German banks with their own market risk models, co-movement at the end of 2004 was even higher than the level during the stress situation surrounding 11 September 2001'.[3]

Other studies have shown that often lightly reached conclusions about correlations are the result of cherry-picking financial data, of using 'this' or 'that' arbitrary and undocumented assumption, or of using heterogeneous models. The computation of unexpected credit losses (UL), which is the theme of this chapter, provides an example.

A couple of years ago, the German Banking Association worked with Deutsche Bank, Dresdner Bank, Commerzbank and Hypovereinsbank to evaluate UL eigenmodels. The finding was that the resulting EL are not comparable because of major differences in correlations. Under similar conditions, lowest and highest UL estimates differed by up to 500 per cent, but:

- If the same ρ was used with all eigenmodels,
- Then this difference was reduced to between 2 and 12 per cent.

According to expert opinions, the 500 per cent difference comes from the fact that some banks rely on CreditRisk+, others on KMV, still others on CreditMetrics. Each one of these models has its own way of assuming, and in cases computing, correlations. For instance, CreditRisk+ gives a relatively low ρ, whereas KMV produces a higher, and therefore more conservative ρ.

In conclusion, wrongly computed correlations contribute in a significant way to errors made in estimation of expected and unexpected risk, and associated financial losses. The best advice when studying correlations, and contemplating on their fitness, is to look at the figures and try to get the message that may be hiding:

- Behind 'this' irregularity
- Or 'that' periodicity in the distribution.

Then one should ask critical questions about the deliverables: are the time series really causally related? Is there an internal contradiction? What if wrong correlation coefficients misguide our hand in economic capital allocation, or in appreciating the level of exposure? It is most important always to keep in mind that sometimes correlations are an optical illusion.

One of the best teachers of statistics teased his students with two series that showed $\rho = 1$. One was the annual herring catch off Newfoundland; the other, the number of illegitimate children born in that same year in North Dakota. The opposite is also true: assumptions made in a hurry, and time series massaged to produce a wanted message or result, lead to the conclusion that risk drivers do not really correlate. Then, adversity hits.

14.5 The missing algorithm for unexpected losses

The choice of wrong correlation coefficients is not the only weakness in financial modelling. Chapter 7 referred to a fancy, unreliable and absolutely *wrong* model used by some banks for the computation of UL: this is a derivative of value at risk (VAR), known as $VAR_{99.97}$, or capital at risk.

Serious banks do not go for that sort of *model risk*, despite others considering it to be the 'in' thing. A Citigroup study found that the 99.97 per cent level of confidence implied by $VAR_{99.97}$ requires knowledge of the severity distribution at the 99.999999 per cent quantile, which is unattainable. In addition, direct calculation of VAR at even 99.9 per cent is impossible. What is possible is 99 per cent VAR estimates, then:

- Scaling up the outcome, or
- Conducting stress tests, which should be the first option anyway.

The irony is that $VAR_{99.97}$ implies a confidence level representing 11.7*s*, which is a stress test anyway. This stress result, however, is weakened by unverifiable assumptions and freedoms taken with mathematical rules. Citigroup also found that sample size plays a vital role in the accuracy of the $VAR_{99.97}$ output. In this test, it was necessary to increase the sample size from 50 to 1 000 000 data points, while the mean value ($\bar{x}$) remained stable from the small to the much larger sample.

- VAR_{99} increased by a factor of 2, of which banks should take note for their market risk estimates, and
- $VAR_{99.97}$ increased by a factor of 4.8, which is enough to cancel out any 'benefits' in the lower unexpected credit risk reserves, which some banks hope to gain by using this silly sort of measurement.

It is indeed difficult to believe how otherwise serious credit institutions assume a huge amount of model risk, while believing that they are in control of their exposure. Neither is this '99.97 level of confidence' uniformly used by all banks who go for that absurd formula. Some use 99.93 and others 99.95, at their pleasure. One of the better known big banks uses the algorithm:

$$\begin{aligned} RC &= VAR_{99.93} - EL \\ &= CF(\%) \cdot LGD(\%) \cdot EAD\ (€) \end{aligned} \tag{14.2}$$

where CF stands for *capital factors* derived from the output of portfolio models, and depends on obligor rating, industry sector, area of operations, size of firm, remaining maturity of transaction, portfolio granularity and portfolio correlation structure (see section 14.4 on this unreliability). The value for CF is computed using:

- Benchmarking,
- MKMV model, and
- Other credit portfolio models.

Several correlations, for the most part established arbitrarily by the board, are incorporated into the model. Benchmarking is done in collaboration with banks using a similar approach. It should be noted that benchmarking results typically show major differences between banks, often depending on the model that they use.

Another objection to arbitrary, ad hoc models is that the reliability of the resulting UL estimates is most difficult, if not impossible, to verify empirically. In addition, there is no backtesting, which is most necessary for all models. There are better alternatives for the computation of UL, one of which was presented in Chapter 12. As a reminder:

$$\mathrm{UL} = \mathrm{SPD} \cdot \mathrm{SLGD} \cdot \mathrm{SEAD} \tag{14.3}$$

Several banks however commented that this UL algorithm is a compromise with simplifications. For instance, obligor concentration effects are ignored (which is also true of $\mathrm{VAR}_{99.97}$), whereas they are considered in *their* eigenmodels. This argument should be studied with great care in the search for proof, because many eigenmodels are too simple to fulfil the stated functionality.

An alternative UL algorithm to be examined with care is the original economic capital equation advanced by the Basel Committee,[4] and promoted by the fact that it works in synergy with regulatory capital.

$$\mathrm{EC} > \mathrm{UL} + \max\left(0; (\mathrm{EL} - \mathrm{SP} - \mathrm{GP}_{\mathrm{nonRC}} - \mathrm{FMI})\right) \tag{14.4}$$

where EC = economic capital, UL = unexpected losses, EL = expected losses, SP = special provisions, or charge-off, $\mathrm{GP}_{\mathrm{nonRC}}$ = general loan-loss provisions other than regulatory capital, and FMI = future margin income (which is not well defined, but could be taken to be equal to business risk).

Subsequently, in January 2004, the Basel Committee advanced a UL capital requirements algorithm for *corporate* loans:

$$K_{\mathrm{C}} = LGD \cdot \left(N\left[\tfrac{1}{\sqrt{1-R}} \cdot G(PD) + \tfrac{R}{\sqrt{1-R}} \cdot G(0.999)\right] - PD\right) \cdot \left(1 - 1.5\tfrac{1}{b(PD)}\right) \cdot (1 + (M - 25) \cdot b(PD)) \tag{14.5}$$

where $\mathrm{N}[\cdot]$ = normal distribution of $[\cdot]$, $\mathrm{G}[\cdot]$ = inverse normal distribution of $[\cdot]$, practically a function of PD, M = remaining maturity, and R = correlation coefficient, a function of PD given by regulators. Note that $\mathrm{N}[\cdot]$ and $\mathrm{G}[\cdot]$ should not be confused with the meaning of symbols, N = effective number of exposures and G = nominal amount of credit protection. $\mathrm{G}[\cdot]$ can be computed using an Excel spreadsheet.

For greater accuracy in computation, Basel provides specific industry sector algorithms. For instance, high-volatility commercial real estate (HVCRE) is taken care of through risk weights. For residential exposure, revolving retail exposures, and other retail exposures, the algorithm is:

$$K_{\mathrm{RE}} = LGD \cdot \left[N \cdot \sqrt{1-R} \cdot G(PD) + \frac{R}{\sqrt{1-R} \cdot G(0.999)}\right] - PD \tag{14.6}$$

where K_{RE} = required capital for the aforementioned real-estate exposure.

In terms of a global UL calculation for a credit institution, this author prefers the UL algorithm that was developed some years ago by Deutsche Bundesbank. It is both simple and accurate:

$$UL_{\mathrm{BU}i} = a \cdot s\left(\textstyle\sum L_i w_i\right) \quad A < K \tag{14.7}$$

where a = a constant, function of risk appetite, s = standard deviation of aggregate risk, L_i = outlier of unexpected losses at business unit i, w_i = weight, representing the share of BU_i in the bank, A = assets of the entity, and K = economic capital of the bank.

If the risk factor R (not to be confused with R, which stands for correlation) is the enterprise-wide sum of extreme losses, then a worst case would assume no netting or compensation of risks. Hence:

$$\mathrm{R} = \sum_i \mathrm{R}_i \tag{14.8}$$

Economic capital allocation to BU_i is provided by the equation:

$$K_i = \beta_i \cdot w_i \cdot K \tag{14.9}$$

where β_i is the internal beta of BU_i, computed by:

$$\beta_i = \frac{A}{{s_{br}}^2} \sum w_i \mathrm{cov}_{ij} \tag{14.10}$$

and

$$\sum \beta_i \quad w_i = 1$$

where A = assets, ${s_{br}}^2$ = variance of aggregate bank risk, and cov_{ij} = covariance, returns of BU_i and the bank.

The original UL algorithm by Basel II (but not the ridiculous $VAR_{99.97}$) had two major dvantages: specialization by product line and a uniform base for UL estimates. However, the UL algorithm advanced by the Deutsche Bundesbank:

- Is very elegant,
- Provides a snapshot of UL exposure, and
- Can be used as a benchmark established by one of the best managed central banks.

One credit institution that tested Bundesbank's UL model against $VAR_{99.97}$ found that, by channel, the difference in computed capital requirements for UL varies between:

- –160 per cent, and
- +900 per cent.

This speaks volumes about model risk at large and, more specifically, the unreliability of $VAR_{99.97}$. It tells its user nothing about where the brakes are. With a difference of almost an order of magnitude between required economic capital and the one computed by the twisted VAR model, the bank would be driving full speed against the wall (see also in section 14.6 a much better approach to the measurement of UL than this $VAR_{99.97}$, which tells its usual business).

* * *

At this point, the reader should return to the *Warning* on page *xv*, which explains that the problems with establishing an appropriate computational procedure for UL have been made more complex, than they used to be, for no reason whatsoever. As if the UL computational challenge was not enough, in the aftermath of QIS 5 the Basel Committee has:

- Mixed up EL, UL, credit risk, market risk, and operational risk in one salad bowl.
- Tossed-up a procedure separating EL from UL, which was excellent – and it has been elaborated since Day 1 in June 1999, when the first document on Basel II was released, and
- Delegated stress testing - therefore, SDP, SLGD, SEAD - to the watch of national regulators, under Pillar II. But at the same time, it took away from them the UL watch which is the focal point in stress testing.

All this is very unfortunate and, as I underlined in the *Warning*, it weakens Basel II. Good governance should have seen to it that one does not drop by the wayside the all-important homogeneity in stress procedures and benchmarks. First-class professionals know that every great enterprise like Basel II, and the concept of unexpected losses, is fraught with uncertainty and bifurcations can lead to totally different ways of risk control:

- In a global economy, such uncertainty must be confronted in unison by all major central banks. That was the reason for the Basel Committee in the first place.
- Confusing by lumping together the anchor issues of UL and EL, of credit risk, market risk, and operational risk, threatens the whole Basel II – as documented by the American abstention from QIS 5. It can also severely damage the reputation of the Basel Committee.

In a globalized economy, the danger of having significant diversity in stress testing approaches and unexpected risk calculations – among national regulators and the banks they supervise – is undoubtedly recognized by clear-thinking people.

At the same time, however, this heterogeneity strengthens the attention national regulators and commercial banks should pay to the long leg of the risk distribution. Therefore, to stress tests, which this book has deliberately kept in the crisp definitions and algorithms they had till recently – away from the perilous amalgam.

14.6 Qualitative scenario for unexpected losses

No important subject should be ever studied through algorithmic approaches alone. Quantitative estimates are very important, but both preceding and following them there is need for qualitative scenarios that permit a sense of perspective to be gained. Typically, qualitative scenarios are designed:

- *Ex ante* to explore the field under study, and choose the more important risk drivers to be quantitatively expressed, and
- *Ex post* to make sense of quantitative results, interpret their impact and again focus on risk drivers, their domain of variation and fitness of choice.

As explained in Chapter 12 and the present chapter, macroeconomic factors, poorly chosen correlation coefficients, market risks that work in synergy with credit risks and an inordinate exposure by banks to highly leveraged institutions, are subjects that the *ex ante* qualitative scenario should address. For this purpose, the present section presents a comprehensive qualitative scenario focused on UL. A great many UL originally happen because:

- Loans officers, and senior management, misjudged the quality of borrowers,
- Economic circumstances, or mismanagement, caused once sound borrowers to fail,
- The bank's loans portfolio has been severely weakened, because of poor prognostication of macroeconomics,
- Senior management failed to diversify exposure, and the bank found itself on the wrong side of the balance sheet,
- Extreme events happened that were not accounted for in economic capital,
- The bank assumed a large number of derivatives and other trading risks that have turned sour, and
- As economic capital was eroded it should have been significantly augmented, but it was not.

It is not necessary that poor decisions made by highly paid executives lie at the origin of all seven bullets contributing to UL. It may also be that there have been conflicts of interest, or that the arteries of the organization were clogged. Therefore, one of the responsibilities of the board is to ask an independent consultancy for a factual and documented report on some well-focused queries:

- Are the feedback channels open?
- Is senior management receiving risk information in real time?
- Is the bank's information system able to collect and report the granularity of loss data in real time?
- Is senior management able to understand the implications of its decisions in regard to credit risk, market risk and operational risk?

Concentrations of risks, length of commitment and creditworthiness of the main counterparties should be on the agenda of such audits. The same is true of the quality of internal control and of the confidence that management places on organizational systems and procedures. A first class *independent* external audit would expose failings more harshly than an internal audit. It would also bring in evidence of the adverse consequences of top management's market perception.

Moreover, large institutions with global or multiple holdings need to pay attention both to details of counterparty, instrument and other variables, and to issues of consolidation in terms of total exposure by BU area of operations and the whole firm. They should determine whether there is another domain to be externally audited; and part of a risk scenario is the calculation of regulatory capital and economic capital requirements by jurisdiction.

The author has conducted audits for major institutions, as consultant to the board, which focused on the bank's information system, including the accuracy and timeliness of its deliverables. The board and members of top management should be provided with graphics rather than with long and confusing tables. A picture is worth 10 000 words, but it is vital that such presentation is interactive, with plenty of detail available to substantiate and document the message conveyed by the graphs:

- If historical financial information, on which graphics are based, represents years of transactions,
- Then it should not only be feasible but also easy to data mine on-line these years of information elements for verification, confirmation or any other reason the end-user has.

Moreover, graphical information (which typically has a quantitative background) should be enriched with a narrative scenario able to bring its user from 'here' to 'there' in terms of where, how, how many and how severe were, for instance, EL and UL suffered by the bank.

Just like quantitative methods, qualitative analyses require rich, accurate and fully updated databases on rating history, collateral history, custom relationships, investments and trades, portfolio positions, normal events, past extreme events, defaults by major counterparties, and other issues.

To strengthen their analytics, some banks are using complexity theory involving risk drivers, frequency of losses and impact of each type of loss. The deliverables of all methods being used must be tested and benchmarked. Argument is the lifeblood of analysis, particularly when investigating outliers.

14.7 The board needs tools to appreciate the value of assets

A fair conclusion from the discussion on EL and UL is that what distinguishes regulatory capital from total reserves, including economic capital demanded by the market, is whether provisions are made for EL only, or for both EL and UL. It may be recalled that:

- Economic capital, which accounts for the bank's farther out exposure, makes the difference in financial staying power.
- Short of a capital base beyond classical credit risk, UL can lead to bankruptcy, because after wiping out the bank's regulatory capital there are no assets left to face adversity.

Part 2 made the point that there is a difference between default and bankruptcy in connection with a credit institution. One bank's bankruptcy is not necessarily synonymous with systemic risk. Losses unsupportable by a single bank may well be supportable by the banking system as a whole. But the prospect of bank failures is not at all appealing, and many central banks choose salvage by taxpayer.

This, however, is a course that has a lot of strings attached to it, not least being change in management. Therefore, with the exception of criminal activities, no board and no chief executive officer (CEO) would wish the bank under their watch to fail. Management wants to be in charge. To do so, it must learn how to watch closely the *asset value*, which is a concept closely related to risk control.

A recent document by the Basel Committee brings management's attention to this dual issue. Whether applied to assets or to liabilities, in an uncertain business environment *value* generally means expected, or mean, value. The Basel Committee itself says that value is not an exact measure, but a best estimate. It also points out that there are numerous value concepts in existence:[5]

- *Market value* is understood to be the price obtained for an asset that is sold at arm's length by a willing seller to a willing buyer. This is also the definition of *fair value*.
- *Accounting value* is what is important for financial reporting at large, and regulatory reporting in particular.
- *Intrinsic value*, or *embedded value*, is a concept used by insurance actuaries and, by extension, in business or product valuations based on discounted cash flows.
- *Model derived value*, or *marking-to-model value*, is a technique used to derive a proxy for market value in situations where market values are not observable or there are no traditional markets.

In theory, but only in theory, these approaches should yield identical results when applied to a product, a portfolio or a company. In practice, this is never the case. Even so, to manage properly the company of which they are in charge, the board, CEO and senior management should be versatile with all four of them, and learn to appreciate the reasons for their differences in terms of the output produced.

Another basic business principle that must be observed by all responsible executives is that value must be preserved. After all, both regulatory capital and economic capital have that goal because, when adversity hits, a company does not generate value; it consumes what it has in store.

To test how well they positioned themselves in terms of their survival, some institutions use a method known as *time until first failure* (TUFF). In this, a sequence of days is plotted and the outlier is the occurrence of a loss exceeding a predetermined value. This method is interesting because either one or both of the following techniques, already popular in statistical quality control and reliability engineering, can be used:

- *Statistical quality control* (SQC) charts, by attributes, which allow a system for detecting limit abuses to be put in place,[6] and/or
- *Mean time between failures* (MTBF), leading to the use of the reliability algorithm (Weibull distribution).

Thoroughly tested for nearly seven decades in the manufacturing industry, quality control charts make it possible to bring to the immediate attention of both board members and senior management whether each desk (and each trader) is keeping within established limits. SQC charts can be very effective because they convey the seriousness of an exposure in value terms. They also enhance the spirit underpinning the right risk management culture:

- Setting guidelines, and
- Ensuring that these are enforced.

One of the best scenario analyses that the author has seen makes good use of SQC charts, mapping a pattern of sound risk-control policies. Figure 14.3 provides, as an example, a SQC chart developed to track currency exchanges. Such charts can be instrumental in mapping the behaviour of processes and products.

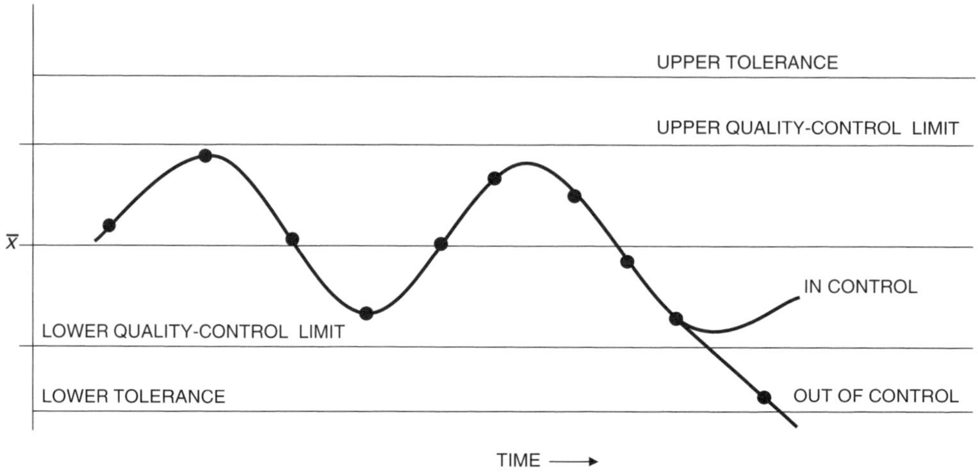

Figure 14.3 A statistical quality-control chart can be instrumental in tracking the behaviour of processes

This bank treats UL as a matter of *volatility* of expressed losses beyond a predetermined threshold. Then, it charges the institution's consolidated profit and loss statement with an amount that corresponds to the statistically derived EL beyond that threshold. Information is obtained from the institution's credit portfolio:

- The loss expectation is based on assumptions about developments over the medium term, covering a full economic cycle.
- This amount is posted in the balance sheet as credit risk reserve for UL, beyond EL provisions.

A scenario associated with the output of this model documents for members of the bank's executive committee, and the board, why such amounts are necessary to ensure that spikes in loss volatility can be taken care of (with the exception of catastrophic losses); also, why reserves and capital needs can balance each other out over the longer time horizon, on which the bank's economic plan is based.

The use of the more sophisticated algorithm of mean time between failures offers further advantages, among them the ability to prognosticate the reliability of the bank's internal control system. The reliability algorithm dates back to the missile studies of the 1950s:[7]

$$R = e^{-t/\overline{T}} \tag{14.11}$$

where R = computed reliability, $\overline{T}$ = mean time between failures (MTBF), t = time over which a system is projected to operate reliably under pre-established operating conditions, and e = Naperien logarithm.

In a financial trading environment, TUFF can be used as proxy of MTBF, while t is set equal to one day, one week or one month, depending on the time-frame under investigation. Experimentation along the foregoing frame of reference helps in documenting scenarios targeting gains and losses arising from changes in the value of the bank's assets and liabilities. This is an integral part of the economic capital challenge.

Notes

1. D.N. Chorafas, *Economic Capital Allocation with Basel II. Cost and Benefit Analysis*, Butterworth-Heinemann, London, 2004.
2. *USA Today*, 27 August 2003.
3. Deutsche Bundesbank, *Financial Stability Review*, Frankfurt, November 2005.
4. Basel Committee, *Working Paper on the IRB Treatment of Expected Losses*, BIS, July 2001.
5. Basel Committee, Joint Forum, *Regulatory and Market Differences: Issues and Observations*, BIS, Basel, May 2006.
6. D.N. Chorafas, *Reliable Financial Reporting and Internal Control: A Global Implementation Guide*, John Wiley, New York, 2000.
7. D.N. Chorafas, *How to Understand and Use Mathematics for Derivatives, Volume 2. Advanced Modelling Methods*, Euromoney Books, London, 1995.

15 Stress testing leveraged and volatile financial assets

15.1 Introduction

The first fourteen chapters of this book addressed the concepts of advanced testing, stress probability of default, stress loss given default, stress exposure at default, as well as expected losses and unexpected losses of regulated credit institutions, and the action of bank supervision authorities. The present chapter is different because it concerns non-regulated but *highly leveraged institutions* (HLIs), typically hedge funds. The reason for being interested in risks assumed by HLIs goes beyond the fact that they are geared. It is the practice of regulated banks to use HLIs as counterparties in lending and trading, which interests the financial community in terms of systemic risk, because it contributes greatly to the banks' unexpected losses.

15.2 Hedge funds: an industry born in the 1940s

A few years ago, in New York, the author was talking to one of the better known former central bankers. The theme of the discussion was: what could tear apart the world's economic and financial fabric? His answer was: four or five big banks or some of the HLIs defaulting at the same time, with central bankers being overwhelmed by these simultaneous big bankruptcies.

Highly leveraged financial institutions are better known as *hedge funds*. There are thousands of them around, but only a hundred or so are really big, and their failure can mean lots of pain in unexpected losses to the banking industry. The origin of the term hedge fund is related to the activities of the first institutions of this kind which, however, had a concept of hedging market uncertainty rather than one of speculating.

Since the late 1940s, when hedge funds first appeared, their activities have set them apart from other institutions. Hedging market uncertainty was not a big issue in the immediate post-World War II years. Over time, however, hedge fund activities evolved towards capitalizing on market risk and credit risk for profits. Over about six decades hedge funds have become increasingly sophisticated in using a wide variety of investment strategies that:

- Do not necessarily involve hedging,
- But take big bets on market fluctuations, on a more and more leveraged basis.

As a result of this change in goals and means, there is at present no generally accepted definition of what exactly a hedge fund is and is not. While alternative terms have also occasionally been used, such as leveraged investment funds, sophisticated alternative investment vehicles, private equity funds and vulture funds (the hedge fund of hedge funds), highly leveraged institutions is probably a more accurate term.

Part of the problem in providing a consistent, generally acceptable definition lies in the fact that hedge funds are not dealing only in financial instruments that are leveraged. Gearing characterizes everything that they do, including hedging, and they may also have other product lines on the side. An example of an almost pure financial hedge fund was Long-Term Capital Management (LTCM), which crashed in September 1998. By contrast:

- Enron, which crashed in December 2001, was a hedge fund with a gas pipeline, and it leveraged energy prices.
- Parmalat, which crashed in December 2003, was a hedge fund with a dairy products line, and it leveraged consumer staples.

Two key differences emerge between hedge funds and other investment pools such as mutual funds. The first is the gearing characterizing hedge funds. When it crashed, LTCM was 'managing' about US $1.4 trillion of leveraged assets, with a capital of $4 billion. This gives a leverage fact of 350, and speaks volumes about how leveraged the world's financial system can be, accounting for the fact that all sorts of hedge funds have currently available as 'capital' some $1.2 trillion.

The second big difference between hedge funds and other investment pools is that the latter have a focused objective. By contrast, the former give themselves broad investment mandates, with no (or very limited) regulatory restrictions on the type of instruments or strategies. Hedge funds also make extensive use of short-selling, repurchase agreements and derivatives.

The ability to pursue unconstrained and leveraged investment policies, with little control through prudential supervision, lies at the core of hedge fund activities. In addition, owing to political patronage, this almost unlimited freedom of action seems to be an enduring feature (see section 15.6), while other characteristics, such as the investor base, evolve.

- Banks, pension funds, insurance companies, university endowments and high net worth individuals who trust their money to hedge funds must appreciate that these can turn from assets to ashes overnight.
- Hedge fund investments are not only highly leveraged, they are also volatile. By being predominantly domiciled abroad, these entities also benefit from favourable tax treatment, but often profits are nothing more than wishful thinking.

For his or her part, a hedge fund manager receives performance-related fees while personally taking no risk. The fact that he or she can freely use various active investment strategies to maximize returns, involving any combination of leverage, derivatives, long and short positions in securities, or any other assets in a wide range of markets, poses a highly significant risk of *unexpected losses* to the banks financing the hedge fund and trading with it. As the LTCM meltdown has shown, even the best names in banking are exposed to hedge funds.

15.3 Stress testing highly leveraged institutions

Because of the reasons that have just been explained, and most particularly owing to the impact of high leverage on systemic risk, supervisory authorities have been looking with some concern into the business relationships of credit institutions with hedge funds. By the late 1990s, a preliminary document published by the Basel Committee contained an outline of possible direct and indirect approaches to HLI supervision.

- The Basel Committee seems to be in favour of the direct supervisory approach,
- But opinions vary on the degree of hedge fund supervision (see section 15.6), and some HLIs have the power to fire the regulator (see section 15.8).

As a way to circumvent such resistance to HLI supervision, the Basel Committee sought at first to encourage an improvement in banks' risk management practices, as counterparties to hedge funds. But the prevailing opinion remains that more direct regulation of hedge funds would be necessary should indirect measures, and an enhanced market transparency, prove to be insufficient.

According to some opinions, all hedge funds should be registered with the authorities of the countries where they operate. A depository of information on HLI, covering gross positions as well as net, would allow regulators to police them. Regulators who are in favour of hedge fund supervision say that this would lead to sound risk-control practices, for both hedge funds and banks. Areas where credit institutions must focus their attention in their HLI relationships include:

- Establishing clear policies and procedures that define a bank's risk appetite, and drive the credit standard setting process,
- Obtaining adequate information to make sound judgements of counterparty credit quality and associated default risk, and
- Performing due diligence in developing rigorous measures in prognosticating potential future exposure, including early warning of oncoming financial troubles.

As already mentioned, prognostication of exposure requires advanced technology, as well as sophisticated methods, tools and metrics. Of critical importance is the monitoring of meaningful overall limits for counterparties and their overrun. Adequate stress testing of counterparty credit risk and market risk, under a variety of scenarios, must take into account:

- Volatility, and
- Liquidity,

and the results of these stress tests must be stored in a corporate memory facility, which is accessible on-line to all authorized people. A rich, global database of HLIs' portfolios and transactions, as well as of the strategies that they follow, are necessary if regulators are to exercise any control on the impact of hedge funds on the economy, and most specifically on systemic risk. This database must also provide real-time information on the exposure assumed by credit institutions, which are simultaneously:

- Lending to hedge funds,
- Trading with hedge funds, and
- Using HLIs as means for bypassing the rules and regulations of their own supervisory authority.

Major bankruptcies in the HLI industry will significantly endanger financial stability. A capital of $1.2 trillion leveraged to probably $60 trillion (assuming a factor of 50) represents a couple of years of the world's gross domestic product (GDP).

Those in favour say that hedge funds are, in general, likely to enhance the efficiency of financial markets by contributing to price formation and liquidity, being ready to acquire risk, and pruning the market of weak and mismanaged companies. There is credit to this argument, but the 1989 LTCM crisis also showed that hedge funds can be a major source of risk to the global financial system. Neither is this the only example on a big hedge fund failure and its after effect.

HLIs have not found the elixir making them immune from bankruptcy. Hence, there is a need for stress tests specifically focused on which risks could potentially be transmitted to the banking industry, and more generally to the national and global financial system. The influence exercised by HLIs on market dynamics and market liquidity could be unfavourable to many market participants.

Emphasis also needs to be placed on closely linking leveraging to collateral arrangements, covenants and termination provisions in bilateral agreements between hedge funds and credit institutions. All of this is important to assessments of counterparty credit quality. Just as vital is timely monitoring of counterparty transactions and credit exposure, a prime reason why hedge funds have to be registered and supervised.

A similar statement is valid in connection with enhanced transparency. The Basel Committee sets out two guidelines: a general review of adequacy of public disclosures provided by global players, and the concept of a credit register for bank loans to be extended to the hedge funds, while providing adequate assurance of confidentiality of information.

- Even though, for many banks, credit risk exposure to hedge funds relative to their business volume may still be limited,
- There are plenty of indirect risks resulting from leveraged transactions with hedge funds, and their inability to honour contracts, if they go bust.

According to some estimates, hedge funds account for 40–50 per cent of all transactions in the New York Stock Exchange (NYSE) and London Stock Exchange; and their transactions represent almost the entire market for convertible bonds.

Both the high rate of equity trading due to hedge funds and the future of the convertible bonds market are prime domains for stress tests. The same is true of liquidity risks. Hedge funds that act as contrarians contribute to market liquidity, but the industry as a whole also harbours the potential to disrupt markets. In stress situations, hedge funds can amplify price movements in the financial environment, as was the case:

- In spring 2005 in the credit markets, and
- In May 2006, in the equity markets, particularly those of developing countries.

The need for stress testing the aftermath of hedge funds' trades and positions applies especially to tight markets, in which competition between hedge funds is particularly intense through convertible arbitrage and other methods. If unexpected events occur, let alone extreme events, loss-limitation strategies and margin calls often lead to the simultaneous unwinding of positions. Sharp price movements can endanger many of the HLIs' trading partners, leading to significant unexpected losses in the banking industry.

15.4 The proliferation of hedge funds and testing their risks

The proliferation of HLIs (hedge funds, vulture funds, private equity outfits and other entities), as well as their growing importance as participants in global financial markets, has raised questions about ways and means for risk control. As an increasing number of funds attempts to exploit profitable opportunities from similar strategies, concerns have been expressed that:

- The positioning of individual hedge funds is becoming more *crowded* in certain sectors, and
- An exit strategy by many of them will drain these sectors of financial resources, as happens now and then with emerging markets.

In addition, crowding by highly leveraged entities with fairly similar positions leads to diminishing returns and, as a result, can push HLIs into much greater risk-taking to satisfy the expectations of demanding investors. The result is not only adverse market dynamics, but also the likelihood of systemic risk. Under stress conditions hedge funds simply cannot afford to wait as leveraged positions begin to lose money. Therefore, they rush for the exit.

- The crowding of trades of similar positioning across hedge fund strategies magnifies the impact, and
- Entities with fledgling or exotic investments are the first to unravel, pulling other entities along.

Regulators are becoming preoccupied by the fact that since 2001, hedge fund returns have become less widely dispersed. This is an indication that hedge fund positioning is becoming increasingly homogeneous. Rising correlations in investment and trading strategies are a sign that managers of highly leveraged financial institutions are using models that:

- Are too similar, and
- Are no longer creating diversification in associated risks.

As markets start to become nervous and some types of trades are crowded, similar actions by hedge funds lead to more market uncertainty. Under stressed conditions, risks amplify, especially if trades are leveraged, and the ability of hedge funds to take offsetting contrarian positions is limited.

- High leverage and similar trading strategies contribute to the creation of worst case scenarios.
- The increase in pairwise correlations of yields is a sign of greater similarity of trading strategies, eventually leading to stress.

Pairwise correlations, for instance, picked up during the first half of 2005. Moreover, among hedge funds there has been an increase not only in the correlation of returns within specific strategies, but also in the co-movement of returns across all strategy groups, making stress tests of hedge fund exposures:

- More pressing, and
- More demanding.

Higher correlations imply that diversification possibilities have been reduced for HLIs specializing in any particular trading strategy. As a consequence of increased leverage and crowding of strategies, in the event of a serious market shock hedge funds are more likely to liquidate positions simultaneously, therefore:

- Amplifying price swings, or
- Causing liquidity to dry up.

A historical reminder helps in explaining the preoccupation of other market players (and supervisors) with HLI risk. In September 1998, when LTCM, considered to be the Rolls Royce of hedge funds, came to the edge of the abyss, the global financial industry only just escaped widespread bankruptcy.

- If a couple of major counterparties in the swarm of LTCM two-way financial bets had collapsed,
- Then almost every large bank that had traded in derivative instruments with LTCM would have been brought to the brink of catastrophe.

The system would have imploded, as Michael Camdessus, then head of the International Monetary Fund, subsequently admitted. The New York Federal Reserve saved the day by obliging LTCM's main shareholders to come up with funds to refloat the damaged institution. This was a swift and wise act that may not be repeatable because eight years later, in 2006, there are many more hedge funds moving, among themselves, ten times more capital around in financial distress than LTCM ever did.

Jochen Sanio, president of the Institute for Financial Services (BaFin), the German bank supervisory authority, has given a stark warning. At a conference organized by Goldman Sachs in New York City on 22 September 2005, Sanio shocked listeners by saying that a new derivatives catastrophe like LTCM was ahead: 'It will happen. And nobody at the moment is prepared for it. That is why I am scared as hell'.[1]

Nor is this the only warning. Answering a query posed in the course of an interview with CNBC at the end of October 2005, Felix Rohatyn, the former vice-chairman of Lazard Brothers and ambassador to Paris, said that nobody really knows when a big institution will go under until it happens, and then it is too late. On 19 May of the same year, however, Jochen Sanio had already pointed to hedge funds as the 'black holes of the international financial system'.

It is by no means a secret that a large part of the problem lies in the fact that hedge funds are not regulated, and any effort to bring them under supervisory watch is consistently thrown out by political intervention on the hedge funds' behalf. As we will see in section 15.8, William Donaldson, chairman of the Securities and Exchange Commission (SEC) and a former top investment banker, was fired in April 2005 after he suggested that hedge funds should come under supervisory oversight.

According to a study by the European Central Bank (ECB), banks that dominate in having close connection with hedge funds are: Morgan Stanley, working at the moment with about 400 hedge funds; Goldman Sachs, with 340; Bear Sterns, with 300; UBS, with about 100; ABN Amro, Citigroup and Deutsche Bank, each with seventy; Lehman Brothers, with sixty; Crédit Suisse First Boston, with fifty; Merrill Lynch, with forty; and Crédit Agricole, with thirty-five.[2]

As for capital put into these hedge funds, Morgan Stanley lead the pack with \$66 billion, followed by Bear Sterns with \$52 billion and Goldman Sachs with \$51 billion. Even a leveraging factor of 50, which is only one-seventh of LTCM's gearing, would put the valuation of derivative volumes of these funds at \$11 trillion, which is roughly the GDP of the USA. (These \$11 trillion would balloon to \$77 trillion if LTCM's level of leverage prevailed.)

Apart from the huge risk of tearing apart the world's financial fabric, another message that these numbers convey is that a very large chunk of the financial system has come under the control of hedge funds. According to some estimates, even the maintenance of the annual \$800 billion of capital inflows, essential for financing the US trade deficit, is increasingly a matter for hedge fund activity.

This is suggested by some estimates, which maintain that in July 2005 over \$50 billion flowed into the American economy through the purchase of debt and other instruments, not from the 'traditional' sources of Asian central banks but from financial centres where hedge funds are based. Half that money originated in the City of London. The rest came from offshore centres, such as the Bahamas and the Cayman Islands, none of which is known for its prudential supervision of financial entities.

15.5 The exposure of credit institutions to highly leveraged institutions

The previous two sections introduced the fact that over the recent years, the hedge fund industry has expanded rapidly, with an important role being played by HLIs, as participants in financial markets and as counterparties to financial institutions, especially banks. This has made it increasingly important to:

- Monitor their activities, and
- Assess the implications for stability of the banking sector.

A study conducted by the European System of Central Banks, at the end of 2004, revealed that for fourteen large European banks from six countries, the absolute amount of cash lending to hedge funds collateralized with securities, through reverse repurchase agreements, totalled almost €100 ($128) billion. Big banks from two countries clearly dominated in that sample.[3]

While, numerically speaking, these $128 billion are only a little more than half of the exposure to HLIs of the four US investment banks, discussed in section 15.4, that number is a first in Europe. At a leverage factor of 50, it rises to $6.4 trillion, and at an LTCM leverage factor of 350, it reaches for the stars at nearly $45 trillion.

Scary as they may be, these statistics have the advantage of dramatizing the fact that direct exposure of credit institutions to hedge funds stands at a very high level. In addition, direct credit exposures to HLIs are multifaced, including loans, credit lines and trading exposures in over-the-counter markets. The relatively mediocre investment performance of hedge funds in 2004 and 2005 has signalled that direct credit risks have become more relevant than ever before.[4]

To gain perspective, it is important to remember that the trend towards direct investments made by commercial banks in hedge funds was started as late as the end of the 1980s and in the early 1990s by Chemical Banking, the credit institution that also leveraged itself through mergers and acquisitions, by acquiring other big banks: MHTC, Chase Manhattan and J.P. Morgan, merging them into J.P. MorganChase, which acquired Bank One.

A decade on, by the late 1990s almost all global banks were investing plenty of their own capital in hedge funds. This accelerated after the bursting of the equity bubble in 2000. For instance, in early February 2004, Deutsche Bank said that it was investing $1 billion in a hedge fund by its former traders.

Given the strong inflow of bank assets to hedge funds, some experts are asking whether inflows into speculative-type investments are decoupling from a realistic expectation of profits. If yes, this is a sign of a bubble in progress. Other experts are worried by the fact that funds of funds that market their speculative instruments to consumers increasingly capitalize on the activities of the underlying hedge funds, which typically leverage their capital by:

- Buying securities on margin,
- Taking out major bank loans, and
- Extensively using derivatives products.

The best advice that can be given to the reader, and to investors at large, including institutional investors, as well as to banks thinking about taking the plunge, is to obtain information about the risks *before* taking them on board. Books and seminars are a good way to do this. As Mark Twain said, 'The man who does not read good books has no advantage over the man who cannot read them'.

As well as books, the best of the financial press offers valuable insight to its readers. According to an article in *The Economist*, the way in which credit institutions have invested many billions of dollars in large funds has, to a significant extent, been by exploiting a loophole in regulatory capital requirements.[5] The money poured into risky deals in this way is counted:

- As an investment, and
- Not as a trading position.

Therefore, huge amounts of capital at risk are not included in the banks' own trading books. The caveat is that such investments could be profitable only as long as markets behave along the framework of bets being made. However, markets have a nasty habit of following their own minds, which means that leveraged strategies put banks and hedge funds together in the same bucket of huge risk, particularly in the case of a severe shock.

In addition, while they invest into and trade with HLIs, banks are in no position to exercise counterparty discipline. Therefore, fate takes all. Essentially, banks are cornering themselves by increasing their exposure to hedge funds, because in a crisis they must either put up more capital at high risk or reduce their exposure by trying to exit through a highly congested door:

- Having overestimated their financial staying power by minimizing assumed risk, banks cannot add to their capital, and
- When they try to unload risky positions, they find that everyone else is heading for the exits at the same time, which quite evidently is moving prices sharply down.

Something else found to be wanting is risk management practices connected to highly leveraged deals, where unexpected losses are very likely. Most banks that extensively dealt with hedge funds have guidelines for this interaction, but as greed carries the day limits bend, and the strong emphasis on collateralization takes its leave.

- Hedge funds, particularly the larger ones, are successful in negotiating less rigorous credit terms, and
- Funds set up by former bank traders often obtain lower lending spreads, higher net asset value, decline triggers and trading on variation margin only.

There is something special about deals obtained by hedge funds set up by traders who used to work for the banks. These people often retain an inside track. As an article in *The Economist* pointed out, in 1999 Citigroup shut down its proprietary trading operations (temporarily, at least), but at the same time it invested a few hundred million dollars of its capital in a hedge fund set up by the dealers that had been running its proprietary trading.[6]

J.P. MorganChase is thought to be the most generous in doling out its cash, while Crédit Suisse, Goldman Sachs, Lehman Brothers and BNP Parisbas together invest hundreds of millions of their shareholders' money in hedge funds. The message that these examples convey is that there are hidden risk correlations, which filter through the value at risk report by banks to regulators, without leaving a trace. This turns on its head the whole argument of tracking, measuring and reporting market risk and credit risk assumed by regulated financial institutions. The supervisors only have a downsized view of the commercial banks' exposure.

15.6 Supervision of highly leveraged institutions

There are at least four good reasons why hedge funds, and all other HLIs, should be supervised and regularly inspected. In the USA the law should ensure that examiners from the Federal Reserve, the Office of the Controller of the Currency and Federal Deposit Insurance Corporation have the same rights to inspect HLIs as they have with banks. The same is true about regulators in all other countries, worldwide.

The first reason is the sheer complexity of the financial instruments with which hedge funds are dealing. This makes risk and return notions foggy, at best. The second reason is the rapid growth of the hedge fund industry. Not only have the sums under their management ballooned, but also the origin of these funds, particularly those from the regulated banking sector, raises many issues of concern.

The third major reason for HLI regulation is high-profile scandals. In one year alone, 2002, the SEC brought twelve cases of fraud against hedge funds, more than twice as many as in each of the previous four years, and the rate continued in the following years. *Moral hazard* is one of the domains where unregulated industries excel over those that are regulated. This should not be allowed to continue.

The fourth reason for regulating hedge funds is that whether directly or through bank-managed 'funds of funds', they are increasingly selling their leveraged and risky wares to a broader market, including consumers who know little or nothing of the risk that they are buying. This contrasts with the hedge funds' past policy of sticking to their traditional clientele of institutional investors and rich individuals.

In the USA, the SEC is worried that middle-market investors may not realize what they are buying. The retail market contrasts with *accredited investors*, who have more than $1 million to play with, or an annual income of at least $200 000, as well as *qualified purchasers*, which means individuals with at least $5 million in liquid assets (to lose), who may invest directly in hedge funds.[7]

As far as the riskiness of institutional investments and private investments is concerned, this is still under guidelines originally reflected in the Investment Advisors Act of 1940, which have not been updated. Therefore, the SEC has been right in its thinking that retail investors who do not understand the risks involved will probably bump up the accredited investor standard.

It is also advisable to take notice that under current regulations, at least in the USA, hedge fund managers are exempt from the requirement to register as investment advisors with the SEC. Registration means, among other things, regular audits. This lack of any sort of supervision is evidently a huge loophole. Arthur Levitt, former chairman of the SEC, wanted to change this when he called for mandatory registration in a speech on 7 May 2003.

A great lesson can be learned from past experience, albeit at a much lower level of gearing, on how the great bankers and industrialists reacted to the risk of extraordinary exposure. In 1907, the cash-starved governments of Germany and Great Britain, which had witnessed a depletion in their capital, particularly the British because of the Boer War, raised their interest rates to attract investors. This caused:

- Credit to tighten, and
- Money to drain from the USA.

In March 1907, in New York, public confidence had reached a low tide and, as a consequence, the stockmarket was floundering. Then president Theodore Roosevelt sought advice from Pierpont Morgan, the famous banker, and Andrew Carnegie, the equally famous steel magnate. According to Carnegie's biographer,

- He called for strict federal regulations to govern Wall Street, and
- He encouraged the US president by saying that 'we cannot trust this to the Gamblers, for such they are'.[8]

Then as now, however, the advice about the need for strict regulation came too late. In 1907, the US stockmarket crashed, and the Dow Jones index lost 25 per cent of its value. While men like Woodrow Wilson, then president of Princeton, blamed Roosevelt and his policies, Carnegie attempted to bolster the US president's confidence by supporting his position that the government must take a stronger hand in regulating private enterprises.

The wisdom of Andrew Carnegie's regulatory advice was proven a second time in the same year, when in October 1907 yet another banking panic hit American finance. It was precipitated by two Wall Street speculators, F. Augustus Heinze and Charles W. Morse, who attempted to corner the copper market and failed. (Compare this with the copper market crash of May 2006.)

- There was a run by depositors on the trust companies that had financed the speculators' ill-advised venture.
- This run on deposits caused those banks whose money had propelled speculative market action to fail.

Like gamblers in 1907 New York, a century later hedge fund managers worry about regulation because they understand that they will have to be more prudent, as well as more transparent, about their trading activities, complex instruments, creative accounting, hard sales, and profit and loss; as well as about their market practices, which are increasingly being criticized as propelling global systemic risk.

Short-sellers, who try to make money by selling shares that they do not own, in the hope of buying them back at a lower price, do not want to reveal their positions. They argue that investors do not really need detailed information about what is being done with their money. The managers of HLIs and their friends are afraid that:

- If the SEC were to demand that their outfits reveal all of their trading activities,
- Then hedge funds would be reduced to mutual funds, much less shiny but also less leveraged than they are today.

But can the economy as a whole afford this high-stakes attitude, and the swarm of uncontrollable risks taken by 6000 hedge funds, which among themselves manipulate over $1.2 trillion in derivatives and other risky instruments? In his book, *When Genius Failed*, Roger Lowenstein answers this through a practical example.[9]

He portrays, in the background, the final months of LTCM in mid-1998. Halfway through September 1998, sensing that the hedge fund was out of control, David Mullins, LTCM partner and former Federal Reserve vice-chairman, together with

Jon Corzine, chief executive officer of Goldman Sachs and LTCM controller, asked William McDonough, the then New York Federal Reserve chief, to survey the damage. The New York Federal Reserve had been monitoring the situation anyway, and its chairman sent Peter Fisher to take stock.

According to Lowenstein, after going through the books at LTCM, Fisher seems to have been shocked. The doomed hedge fund's massive trades and high leverage were linked to other equally huge exposures around the world assumed by banks and other institutions. Had these LTCM gambles failed,

- They would have threatened the integrity of the global banking system, and
- As an immediate effect, they would have destabilized LTCM's seventeen leading counterparties.

According to different reports on this abyss, Peter Fisher estimated the potential losses to between \$3 billion and \$5 billion, which proved to be an underestimate. The whole of Wall Street was on the hook. 'I'm not worried about markets trading down', Fisher confided according to Lowenstein. 'I'm worried that they won't trade at all'. The rest is history, but there is a lesson.

Prodded by the New York Federal Reserve to get LTCM off the hook by putting their own capital on the line, its trading partners had to commit large amounts of money and take the obligation not to unload their LTCM-related positions. In fact, to reach an agreement on LTCM's salvage two back-to-back meetings took place at the New York Federal Reserve over a twenty-four-hour period on 22–23 September 1998. Both meetings were convened by the Federal Reserve, and they were held in the boardroom.

Morgan's Sandy Warner broke the ice, declaring, 'Boys, we're going to a picnic, and the tickets cost \$250 million'. All of the banks that had so much to lose from the crash of LTCM paid the ticket. A deal was thrashed out and fresh cash was raised from fourteen banks. A contribution of \$3.6 billion was made on the spot. This was the minimum capital necessary to take over and salvage LTCM.

Could this last-minute salvage be repeated? Experts are not at all sure; they say that times have changed. In September 1998 derivatives exposure was minimal compared with today's huge numbers. The most recent available figures demonstrate that at the end of March 2005 one bank alone, J.P. MorganChase, had derivative investments of \$40 trillion in its portfolio, measured in notional principal amounts.

The trillions and trillions of dollars in notional amounts currently connected with derivatives trades; the much weaker banking industry, particularly in Japan; and the fast growth in unregulated hedge funds, many of which are small, secretive and elusive, make an LTCM-type return from the abyss a virtual impossibility. The only solution is to regulate the hedge funds *now*, as if they were banks.

15.7 Highly leveraged institutions at the peak of their might: No! to regulation

As the twentieth century turned into the twenty-first' and the go-go 1990s were nearly gone, the Commodity Futures Trading Commission introduced the text of a regulation that had become absolutely necessary to the health of the financial industry. It proposed Rule 4.27, which would have required operators of large commodities-trading pools, including hedge funds, to report periodically to regulators on their finances and risk. The aim was to prevent another widespread financial disaster.

As expected, hedge funds reacted rigorously through their lawyers and their lobbyists, with the hugely powerful Managed Funds Association (MFA) in the lead. MFA's 600 members represent a cross-section of big players in the HLI industry. Rule 4.27 was stopped dead in its tracks. Another proposed regulation, the Hedge Fund Disclosure Act, which was introduced to Congress in 1999, met a similar fate. Both cases prove that the industry of highly leveraged and risky institutions:

- Has significant clout,
- Benefits from very strong lobbying, and
- Prides itself on a history of stopping disclosure rules.

An array of high-powered law firms, political connections and strong pressure tactics help hedge funds and other HLIs to face down regulators. Money does not seem to be a problem, although the traditional lobbying techniques of letter writing, congressional testimony and frequent meetings with legislators also help.

In fact, MFA has a record of stopping regulation in spite of the evidence that this regulation constitutes prudential measures aimed at avoiding systemic risk. Between 2000 and 2002, the SEC brought no fewer than ten enforcement actions against hedge funds. Such allegations ranged:

- From Ponzi schemes disguised as hedge funds,
- To massive inflation of assets and misconduct.[10]

Subsequently, in May 2003, the SEC levied fines of $7.2 million against Ron Baron, manager of Baron Capital, a New York hedge fund, and two of his colleagues. The regulators alleged that he had manipulated share prices to influence the terms of a coming merger.

Equity manipulations and alleged fraud aside, one of the domains of regulatory focus is the increasingly ubiquitous *funds of funds* that invest in other funds, often for a high fee. There are also concerns that individual investors, and even institutional investors, may be underestimating the risks that they take by placing their capital in hedge funds:

- Pension funds are playing the hedge funds' highly leveraged game with retirees' money,[11] and
- By lending money to hedge funds, banks and insurance companies take risks with their own liquidity.

In August 2002, these concerns led the National Association of Securities Dealers (NASD) to issue an investor alert warning against hedge fund dangers, including their high fees and inordinate expenses. The MFA responded with a follow-up posted on its website, to weed out NASD's negative content and eliminate references to SEC's enforcement actions.

- To its credit, the NASD declined to bow to the pressure,
- But the urgently needed regulation of hedge funds remained a fantasy.

Finally, on 14 July 2004, the SEC decided on the need for hedge fund regulation through a three-to-two vote by its five commissioners. The initiative was taken by William Donaldson, a former senior investment banker and SEC chairman, and the two Democratic Party members on SEC's board.

A year or so before this action, during his Senate confirmation hearings at the beginning of 2003, Donaldson highlighted potential abuses in the hedge fund industry as a subject for the SEC to tackle. However, intensive lobbying by the HLI industry delayed any initiative through fake arguments that:

- The SEC has enough to do,
- It lacked proper funding, and
- It should not be concentrating on an area traditionally reserved for sophisticated investors who can look after themselves.

Surprisingly, even the Federal Reserve moved against the July 2004 SEC vote on hedge fund regulation. In an alleged letter to Congress, Dr Alan Greenspan stated that he saw no reason for regulating hedge funds. Coming from an intelligent, experienced and well-informed person, that was a surprise.

Even more amazing was the fact that when in a subsequent Senate hearing Senator Sarbanes asked Greenspan about 'that' letter, the Federal Reserve chairman answered he did not recall having signed one, leading Sarbanes to exclaim, 'Don't you recall?' (After consultation with his assistants, Greenspan confirmed that, indeed, he had signed such a letter.)

To understand this whole confusion, and the resistance to regulation mounted by HLIs, it should be stated that William Donaldson did not want to close the hedge funds down. What SEC's ruling said was that hedge fund managers must register with the SEC, which any honourable trader should be happy to do. Registration allows financial inspections similar to those to which the banks are subject.

Probably to ease the HLIs' anxiety, Donaldson said that registration would be used for targeted 'sweeps' of the hedge fund industry. This meant small probes of particular types of behaviour, which may represent risks for investors. As Harvey Goldschmid, one of the commissioners who backed Donaldson, aptly suggested, more work must be done by the SEC on how it would use the registration data to assess risk, because the hedge fund industry:

- Is vast and growing, and
- Definitely needs to be watched.

'What policy sense would it make for the SEC to turn a blind eye?' Goldschmid asked. But Paul Atkins, another commissioner who voted against the decision, said: 'I will not ask taxpayers to foot the bill for a fishing expedition'.[12] In other terms, it is better to have the taxpayer foot the bill for a megacatastrophe like that of Savings and Loans in the late 1980s, than to exercise prudential supervision.

15.8 The drama unfolds: highly leveraged institutions fire the boss of the Securities and Exchange Commission

Like so many other regulators who care about preserving the financial fabric, it is likely that Williamson and Goldschmid went down the road of registration and regulation of HLIs because they knew much more than the market at large, and maybe the HLIs themselves, about assumed megarisks. The following statistics document this point:

- An estimated $2 quadrillion ($2000 trillion) in derivatives is traded per year; even this may be an underestimate because nobody really knows the full dimensions of this huge gamble.
- The derivatives bets by the main players are so large, and so uncontrollable, that since May 2005 the financial press has been warning of an imminent blowout.

When in the third week of May 2006, stockmarkets in the USA, the UK and continental Europe moved south, while those of emerging countries dropped by more than 10 per cent and copper prices melted, on Wall Street rumour had it that the reason was two or three big hedge funds unwinding their positions, rather than profit taking. They had to do so because:

- They had overplayed their hand, and
- They had to sell their assets at any price, to avoid bankruptcy.

In fact, big HLIs were even behind the stellar rise of copper prices in early May 2006; they had misjudged the timing of copper price correction and had gone short on base metals, and as copper prices continued to rise they bought, again at any price, to cover their short positions.

These are examples on the gambles of HLIs, which Donaldson wanted to keep an eye on. In fact, on 6 June 2005, Dr Alan Greenspan admitted that 'the hedge fund industry could temporarily shrink, and many wealthy fund managers and investors could become less wealthy'. But as the SEC moved to put some controls on hedge funds, chaos broke out and this cost William Donaldson his job.

The head of the SEC was not the only chairman of a major regulatory body to ring the alarm bell about HLIs' exposure. On 19 May 2005, Jochen Sanio, president of BaFin, referred to hedge funds as 'black holes of the international financial system', and said that we need to 'systematically monitor the opaque sections' of the financial system, adding that, 'Regulation is a must'.

As the BaFin 2004 annual report warned, the HLIs' 'growth rate raises the question whether hedge funds could threaten the stability of the financial system'. The European Commission, too, stated on different occasions that it wanted a review of the hedge fund industry but, as had happened on the other side of the Atlantic, this effort is also dragging its feet.

William Donaldson was dumped by George W. Bush on 1 June 2005, while he was trying to place some minimum controls on hedge funds. As the founder of Donaldson Lufkin Jenrette (DLJ), the investment bank, the SEC chairman could appreciate the high risks of that unregulated financial industry; and as former president of the NYSE, Donaldson knew who does what in massaging equity prices.

In a 1 June 2005 press conference, announcing his early resignation, Donaldson made it clear that he was being forced to resign and that the primary issue of contention was his effort to regulate hedge funds. He noted that few of these funds were *actually hedged*, so that they would be more accurately known as 'pooled vehicles that you can do anything you want with'.[13]

'What is the job of a regulator?' Donaldson asked. He then answered his query with the statement that it would be almost impossible for him to conceive of an SEC that did not recognize a financial industry that:

- Was at a $3 trillion level, and
- Was not being regulated at all.

The former SEC chairman further stated that he had set about to regulate the industry of HLIs in a rather benign way, simply by obtaining the most fundamental knowledge about the hedge funds and how they work:

- Who is running the money?
- What is their investment record?
- How do they do their accounting?
- What is their track record in infractions of the law?

No matter which way one looks at this issue of hedge fund regulation, this was the simplest request for information to be provided by anybody who runs investors' money. As a bare minimum, this knowledge would have helped the SEC to understand better what impact the hedge funds are having:

- On investors, and
- On the market at large.

But HLIs and other investment funds were furious. The *Wall Street Journal* reported that Fidelity Investments (officially not a hedge fund) led the campaign by the Wall Street financial institutions to dump Donaldson. What seems to have particularly enraged hedge funds is that regulatory oversight would mean that they would also have to provide details of:

- Trading strategies, and
- How they value their portfolios.

This would have given the SEC a better sense of the goings-on in a highly leveraged business long shrouded in mystery. In opposition to any sort of regulation, the MFA argued that 'there has not been enough malfeasance' in the business to justify the rule change, but failed to define what is 'enough'. Aside from this, as far as malfeasance is concerned, even a small dose is poison to business, and to investors.

Notes

1. *EIR*, 14 October 2005.
2. European Central Bank, *Funds and Their Indications for Financial Stability*, Frankfurt, 2005.
3. European Central Bank, *Financial Stability Review*, ECB, Frankfurt, December 2005.
4. European Central Bank, *Financial Stability Review*, ECB, Frankfurt, December 2004.
5. *The Economist*, 21 February 2004.
6. *The Economist*, 21 February 2004.
7. D.N. Chorafas, *Wealth Management: Private Banking, Investment Decisions and Structured Financial Products*, Butterworth-Heinemann, London, 2005.
8. P. Krass, Carnegie, Wiley, New York, 2002.
9. R. Lowenstein, *When Genius Failed: The Rise and Fall of Long Term Capital Management*, Random House, New York, 2000.
10. *BusinessWeek*, 3 March 2002.
11. D.N. Chorafas, *Alternative Investments and the Mismanagement of Risk*, Euromoney, London, 2002.
12. *Financial Times*, 15 July 2004.
13. *EIR*, 17 June 2005.

16 Advanced testing provides a basis for better governance

16.1 Introduction

The process of globalization has led to a significantly increased integration of financial markets, a great deal of cross-border activity among credit institutions, innovative and risky new financial instruments, the use of collateralization for risk mitigation, and other significant developments that underline the need for more advanced testing methods and tools. These must not only contribute to daily risk management, but also allow the performance of the tools to be studied *ex ante* and *ex post*.

Advanced testing is a new approach to management control, aiming to improve the company's governance. Through Basel II, regulators have provided an impetus to stress testing. Better management is sustained not only by means of Pillar I, and its regulatory capital requirements, but also through Pillar 2 (see section 16.6), which strengthens regulatory supervision, and Pillar 3, targeting market discipline (see section 16.7). Financial institutions must contribute to these forward steps by implementing advanced testing methods.

16.2 A concept for better corporate governance

A company's corporate governance policies and procedures are defined over time, starting with the entity's status and subsequently through board decisions governing business strategy (see section 16.3), as well as corporate organization, staffing and daily management. The statutes define the firm's objectives and typically state that its management is committed to:

- Safeguarding the interests of all stakeholders, and
- Recognizing the importance of sound corporate governance in achieving this goal.

Some companies also make the point that transparent disclosure of important aspects of their corporate governance helps stakeholders to assess the quality of management and assists investors in their decisions. For their part, regulatory authorities believe that sound principles of prudential supervision can be instrumental in improving the survivability of companies under their jurisdiction, because they assist in focusing management's attention on crucial elements of:

- Risk control, and
- Successful business activities.

An example is the aftermath of Basel II in terms of better governance in the banking industry. Taken together, regulatory and economic capital (see Chapter 14) have added up to a significant increase in capital adequacy, while a structured risk-based approach provides greater accuracy in the calculation of a firm's financial staying power. Other benefits include:

- More meaningful differentiation of risks,
- Better appreciation of risk control requirements,
- An emphasis on unexpected losses, and
- Awareness of the need to address tail events in a risk distribution.

Among other advantages, a cultural change is effected through risk-based pricing, the observance of time horizons by means of maturity requirements; a global spread of Basel II rules and principles, including Pillar 1, Pillar 2, and Pillar 3 principles; and the inevitable upgrading of regulators' skills, which has proved to be necessary in many countries.

This evolution towards more advanced principles of governance is expected to be gradual, but areas also exist where Basel II is expected to have little or no impact. Examples are guidance towards more effective and documented diversification; a scientific definition and factual computation of correlations and weights; and massive change from the still prevailing palaeolithic information technology culture to high technology, including the appreciation of what models can and cannot do.

Typically, regulatory authorities do not interfere with the individual plans, objectives or goals of banking institutions, or their strategy and tactics on how to reach them. Neither do they play a direct role in the future economic performance or prospects of credit institutions, in any other way than assuring their capital adequacy, and eventually salvaging a bank that has defaulted.

It is the bank's own management that should administer the entity's fortunes, not only day to day but also with respect to potential effects on its future performance, control of risks, administration of contingencies, and assumptions underlying solutions to current and forthcoming problems. In this sense of better corporate governance, within the realm of Basel II,

- The Basel Committee advances the concept of and need for *advanced testing*, including stress-testing methods and tools,
- But each individual bank is responsible for effectively implementing these new approaches, to increase its competitiveness and keep its exposure in check.

This greater attention to risk management than ever before has been necessary because of globalization, deregulation, innovation and technology. Every business involves inherent risks and uncertainties, both general and specific, and it is always possible that projections and outcomes described or implied in management plans will not be achieved. A number of important factors could cause results to differ materially from the expectations outlined in an institution's strategic plans (see section 16.3), including:

- Unexpected changes in the strength of the global economy in general and in the economies of the countries in which the bank conducts its operations in particular,
- Political and social developments, including war, civil unrest or terrorist activity,
- The possibility of foreign exchange controls, expropriation, nationalization or confiscation of assets in countries in which the bank operates,
- The ability of counterparties to meet their obligations to the institution in a timely and correct manner,
- The effect of, and changes in, fiscal, monetary, trade and tax policies, and
- Interest rate and currency fluctuations, as well as the ability to maintain sufficient liquidity and to access capital markets.

As discussed in the preceding chapters, there are also operational factors, such as legal risks, which have been the potential to cause economic damage or even reputational prejudice to the firm. Other likely adversities are information systems failures; internal and external fraud; actions taken by regulators with respect to business and practices in one or more of the countries in which the bank is active; effects of changes in laws, regulations or accounting policies or practices; and human error, but also the inability to retain and recruit qualified personnel.

While overcoming the challenges outlined in the preceding paragraphs is, in itself, a demonstration of sound governance, it is no less true that management should be assisted through the most advanced tools and methods that are available. High technology is one of them; stress testing of risk being assumed is another. Such risks are the result of:

- Doing business with every counterparty,
- Developing and trading in new financial instruments, and
- Being active in markets anywhere in the world.

Advanced testing and the use of real-time technology not only are vital in terms of controlling exposure, but also contribute to the timely development and acceptance of the institution's new products and services by clients, including the perceived value of these products and services. They also promote the bank's ability to integrate successfully the produce of diverse business units, and of geographically remote global operations. Invariably, this proves to be a significant contribution to the timely and effective execution of strategic plans.

16.3 The contribution of strategic thinking

From sixty-two years of direct business experience, the author has learned that planning done on the basis of a limited, narrow perspective is ineffectual. Even if that plan does not fail, its results will be minimal and, therefore, unable to compensate for the amount of effort that has been put into succeeding.

This is true of both strategic and tactical plans. Tactical plans are very important only when they fit into, and serve, in an effective manner, a broader strategic perspective. *Strategic thinking* is at a premium, because this is fundamentally an investigative discipline that leads to:

- Questioning everything, particularly the 'obvious', and
- Challenging alternatives in positioning our firm against the market.

An excellent example on strategic thinking is that of Mervyn King, governor of the Bank of England, a professor of economics and former chief economist of the Bank of England. As *The Financial Times* reported on 17 January 2005, Professor King has no time for listening to amateur economic thinking. Since becoming governor of the Bank of England, there is one worry that has worked its way to the front of his mind: waking up one morning to a financial crisis that

- Threatens the international banking system, and
- Finds him and his associates without an emergency plan on hand.

The Bank of England has identified the rapid growth of hedge funds (see Chapter 15) and complex financial instruments such as derivatives as a potential threat to stability. This would be particularly true if investors were suddenly to switch in a massive way out of these relatively illiquid funds. Solutions to this megaproblem are not self-evident. An emergency plan worth its salt has two prerequisites:

- A steady stream of dependable intelligence, and
- Interconnections and links; essentially who should call whom on which salient issue, and where to have meetings.

Timely and dependable intelligence is crucial in all efforts, and that of spotting market threats is no exception. Therefore, the Bank of England has strengthened its intelligence on financial markets by training its own staff, encouraging whistle-blowers, picking up and distilling City gossip, and other means of intelligence gathering.

This move towards strategic goals of global financial stability is part of a root-and-branch review by Mervyn King, as he is turning the British reserve bank into a premier professional monetary authority. As an example, the Bank of England's markets team has been given a new role in uncovering emerging threats to the financial system. It is redeploying human resources to:

- Meet financial institutions, and
- Gather information about institutions and practices that could undermine the economic system.

In terms of practical details related to interconnection between units of supervisory authorities, the Bank of England and Financial Services Authority (FSA, the British supervisory authority) have set up a joint crisis committee, and drawn up areas of responsibility. Risk executives simulate crises in exercises involving senior participants, and focus attention on trying to defuse an emergency, when and where it develops.

- This proactive approach is one of the most basic roles characterizing good governance, and
- Simulation and advanced testing are the keys to effective analysis, synthesis and eventual execution of an emergency plan.

'It's quite possible that the FSA might find that there's no real risk to any individual financial institution, yet there still could be a risk to the system as a whole', King was quoted by *The Financial Times*. 'We still have to work out precisely what this means in practice and how we carry out the work'. This statement carries two messages:

- It documents a comprehensive change in the management and governance of the Bank, and
- It indicates how strategic thinking works in positioning an institution ahead of the curve.

Organization-wise, since he became governor, Mervyn King has reduced the Bank's former core purposes to the twin objectives of ensuring monetary stability and financial stability. The government does not see traditional payment activities as being part of the Bank of England's role in a modern, open and competitive marketplace. Therefore, areas outside these two core domains:

- Have been closed, as in the case of the registrar's division, which handled the registration of government securities, or
- Will be wound down to full exit, an example being retail banking operations.

The two core areas of monetary policy and financial stability, however, present an increased challenge to management. Even defining the job of financial stability is not easy. Neither is it obvious what sort of infrastructure is needed to monitor and assess threats to financial stability, and to manage a financial crisis. Effective solutions are necessary because this is the salient problem facing all central bankers today, and for which the contribution of strategic thinking will be felt the most.

Commercial banks and investment banks face a similar challenge. Like the top-of-the-line central banks in the globalized financial market, they will be the most affected by any major crisis, but without the ability to print money to improve from their liquidity. Therefore, as in the case of the Bank of England, excellence in governance means strategic thinking assisted by simulation and advanced testing to analyse the options, size up the risks and make choices in knowledge of what the likely, although uncertain, outcome might be.

16.4 Use of threat curves and S-curves: an example from the insurance industry

Every one of the strategies chosen by the board and chief executive officer (CEO) has its advantages, goals and perils. Projected gains and looming risks exist both in the short term and in the more distant future. The perils can be effectively studied through stress testing, in the knowledge that the worst of them will exist in the tail of the risk distribution.

Classically, for governance purposes, exposures and benefits associated with all types of decisions are studied by identifying the crucial factors affecting results, and by dividing risk and return into time buckets. The latter reflect a kind of time preference. In general, people and companies:

- Tend to discount positive outcomes, and
- Value them more, the nearer they occur in time.

The opposite is true with risks. As documented in the preceding chapters, the longer the life cycle of a transaction, the greater the likelihood that it will encounter adverse market conditions. This works in a way as if there were inverse discounting:

- The larger the exposure associated with a position or transaction,
- The more urgent the need for repositioning, closing and licking one's wounds before the damage increases.

Threat-curve graphics are an effective approach to the visualization of major exposures. Historically, they began to appear in the mid-1980s in NATO's intelligence offices. Their aim was to demonstrate the likelihood of certain dangers, through an ordering permitting intelligence officers to channel a good share of resources to *probable risks*, not only the *worst case*, which may be quite unlikely.

Credit institutions can effectively use threat curves for ordering the likelihood of their current and future problems associated with inventoried positions, and new risks that are being assumed daily. This exercise has merits, particularly within a globalized environment where:

- Classical internal control may be spread thinly,
- But strategic moves by independent business units must always be the subject of damage containment.

In addition, post-mortem walkthroughs based on threat curves help to demonstrate whether and where senior management action has been too little, too late in taking charge of unexpected loan losses, or in bending the curve of mounting derivatives exposures. They are also helpful in correcting internal control deficiencies and in restructuring ineffective audit programmes.

Another tool that can assist in top management's understanding of problem areas in ongoing business is the S-curve developed by Swiss Re in the mid-1990s. The results of research done by Swiss Re were based on regression analysis, with data from more than sixty countries over several decades. The S-curve pattern shown in Figure 16.1 reflects the global average relationship between:

- Economic development based on gross domestic product (GDP) per capita, and
- The behavioural insurance market expressed in premiums per GDP.

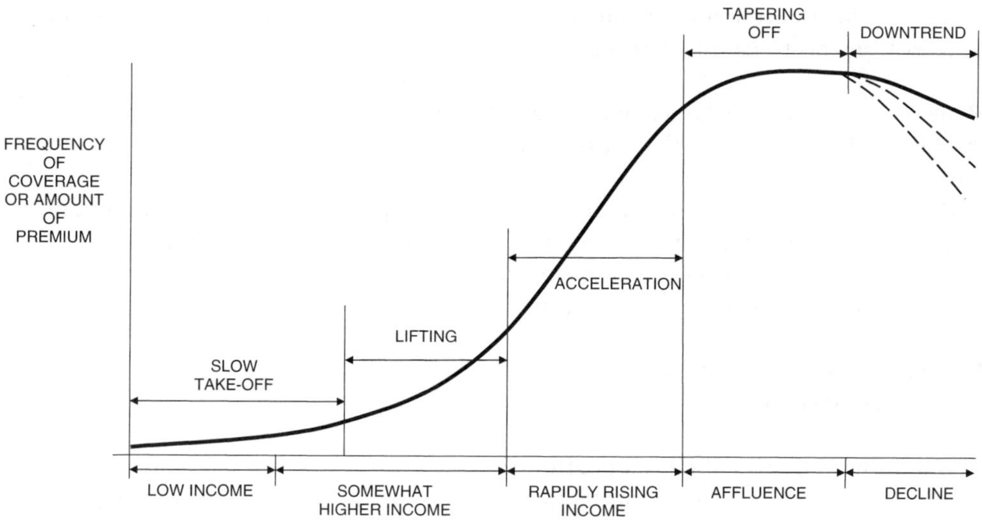

Figure 16.1 Swiss Re developed the S-curve to explain the global average relationship between economic development and behaviour of the insurance market

The Swiss Re research revealed that insurance spending rises particularly rapidly when GDP per capita levels are between \$1000 and \$10 000. In that income range, consumers seem to have a lot of ground to make up and insurance expenditures grow significantly more quickly than income. However, for lower and higher income levels, the income elasticity of insurance demand has been found to be closer to one.

- A point of saturation seems to have been reached in high-income countries, and
- In low-income countries, the level of insurance awareness is too elementary to cause the demand to grow more rapidly than income.

These two bullet points effectively identify the extremes of the S-curve shown in Figure 16.1: the slow take off and the tapering off. This is an income-based approach which can be made more sophisticated by factoring in other aspects such as cultural, institutional, social security orientated factors, as well as tax differences in different jurisdictions.

A test case in Swiss Re's study has been Asia. This S-curve implementation proved that, with some exceptions, Asia is underinsured with regard to non-life cover. A counterweight to this was found to be the popularity of savings-type policies in non-life insurance in several Asian markets; for example, above-average non-life insurance underwriting in Malaysia and South Korea.

Threat curves focusing on risk and S-curves targeting business opportunity can be effectively combined, the former supported by means of stress tests. Staying with the example from the insurance industry, a threat curve can be used to identify the risk structure confronting an insurance firm.

Let us start with the premise that well-managed companies follow stringent guidelines for assuming insurance risks. However, they still face several risk types stemming from their insurance underwriting activities. For instance, in non-life business, insurance risk relates to claims that may:

- Be more frequent or larger than forecast, and
- Have to be paid earlier than projected in the tactical plan.

Premium levels are developed considering the expected frequency and amounts of claims resulting from insured risks. Since better diversified insurance portfolios tend to imply smaller differences between expected and actual claims, insurance companies aim to hold a diversified insurance portfolio in terms of:

- Geographical structure, and
- Industry structure.

But, how well diversified is a portfolio? Only a stress test will tell, and the answers should be plotted on a threat curve. In addition, a well-diversified insurance portfolio with many business lines spread over many policyholders may be vulnerable to natural hazards, and therefore exposed to a large accumulation of risk.

- If adequate reinsurance protection were not in place, substantial losses could be triggered by a single natural catastrophe.
- Protection from insurance risk accumulations, and therefore exposure, is a core risk management activity performed within the insurance business.

On the business generation side (the S-curve), premiums earned by selling insurance policies are invested to cover claims occurring at a future date, sometimes many years later. For its part, the threat curve helps in managing insurance risk by focusing on key exposures, including managing the financial market risks associated with the assets and liabilities (reserves), as well as with reinsurance contracts.

16.5 An oil industry case study on risk factors and their background

There are prerequisites to the use of threat curves in connection with risk management goals. One of the most important is the clear identification of risk drivers, which should become the subject of a decision at the level of board and CEO, a decision to be reviewed 'regularly' becomes 'over time' as risk drivers change in importance and, sometimes, in their:

- Nature, and
- Structure.

It is not enough to decide on risks to be taken. It is just as important to define the most likely origins and behaviour of such risks. One of the most important principles is that it is impossible to control risks if their anatomy is unknown.

This is true for any company, no matter what its exact business may be. A corollary to this principle is that the primary objective of risk management is to protect not only the financial strength but also the reputation of the firm, across all product lines and risk types.

- Protection of financial strength targets the impact of potentially adverse events on the firm's capital and income.
- Protection of reputation is an overriding concern for the board, CEO, senior management and all employees; reputation takes decades to be built, but it can be destroyed in a few days.

Risk transparency and management accountability are a cornerstone to being in charge of both bullet points. The former ensures that all exposures are well understood by senior management, and can be evaluated against business goals; but without management accountability the various business units would not be under a strict obligation clearly and steadily to account for:

- The exposures that they assume, and
- Return for the risks being taken.

Both bullets benefit from inputs received from advanced testing. Enterprise risk management can only then be a structured process able to identify, measure, monitor and report risk when the definition, nature and magnitude of exposures being assumed in the regular course of business are well understood by everybody. Take as an example the oil industry: what risk factors is a company confronted with?

1. Competition in the oil and natural gas industry is intense, and some of the competitors may have greater financial, technological and other resources than our firm

The oil and natural gas industry is characterized by rapid and significant technological advances, as well as the introduction of new products and services using advanced technologies. The stronger companies are able to pay more for development prospects and productive oil and natural gas properties. They may also define, evaluate, bid for and purchase a greater number of properties and prospects than our firm's financial or human resources permit.

2. Reserve estimates depend on many assumptions that may turn out to be inaccurate, thereby causing quantities and the net present value of reserves to be overstated

Estimating quantities of proven oil and natural gas reserves is a complex process. Projection on future net cash flows from reserves requires the analysis of a list of variables, including geological, geophysical, production and engineering data, and their reliability, as well as historical production from the area compared with production rates from other producing areas, and so on. Equally important in an evaluation are economic assumptions relating to commodity prices, production costs, capital expenditures, severance and excise taxes, workover and remedial costs. Actual results will probably vary from such estimates, and it is likely that significant variance would reduce the estimated quantities and present value of reserves.

3. Drilling oil and natural gas wells is a high-risk activity, subject to a variety of factors that a firm may not be able to control

Drilling oil and natural gas wells, including development wells, involves many unknowns, including the risk that a firm may not encounter commercially productive oil and natural gas reservoirs, or recover all or any portion of an investment made in new wells. Exposures include title problems, unexpected drilling conditions; restricted access to land for drilling or laying pipeline; equipment failures or accidents; shortages or delays in the availability of drilling rigs, tubular materials and equipment; pressure or irregularities in formations; and adverse weather conditions.

4. Failure to replace the reserves can adversely affect a company's financial condition; hence, property acquisitions are a key component of growth strategy, while failure to do so successfully can reduce earnings and slow growth

It follows that continuing success depends on the ability to find, develop or acquire additional oil and natural gas reserves that are economically recoverable, a reason why oil companies' strategies emphasize growth through acquisitions. The risk is that in this highly competitive field, a firm may not be able to continue to identify properties for acquisition, or make acquisitions on terms that are economically acceptable. Moreover, acquisitions are subject to uncertainties of evaluating recoverable reserves and potential liabilities.

5. Oil and natural gas prices are volatile owing to a number of uncontrollable factors, and any decline will adversely affect the company's financial condition

Results of operations depend on prices received for oil and natural gas. Historically, the markets for oil and gas have been volatile and are likely to remain so in the future, with prices depending on political instability, armed conflict in oil-producing regions, weather conditions, supply of oil and natural gas, level of consumer demand, and the price and availability of alternative fuels. Other risk drivers relate to transportation facilities, domestic and foreign government regulations and taxes, the effect of worldwide energy conservation measures, and the ability of members of the Organization of Petroleum Exporting Countries (OPEC) to agree upon and maintain oil prices and production levels.

6. The use of hedging arrangements aimed at obtaining some price stability may result in financial losses or reduce a firm's income

To reduce exposure to volatility in oil and natural gas prices, oil firms enter into, and expect in the future to enter into, hedging arrangements for a portion of their production. These hedging arrangements, however, may limit the benefit they would otherwise receive from increases in oil and natural gas prices, and may also expose them to the risk of financial loss in some circumstances. Two important exposures are credit risk, including when the counterparty to the hedging contract defaults on its contract obligations; and when production is less than expected. There may also be a change in expected differential between the underlying price in the hedge and actual prices received.

7. Every oil and gas company is confronted by laws and regulations, including environmental protection, that could adversely affect its business

In the USA, for example, extensive federal, state and local regulation of the oil and gas industry significantly affects oil and natural gas exploration, development, production, storage and transportation of liquid hydrocarbons. Although necessary, environmental regulations have increased the costs of planning, designing, drilling, installing, operating and abandoning oil and natural gas wells, as well as other related facilities.

8. The marketability of a firm's oil and gas production is dependent on transportation and processing facilities, not only on the state of the economy and market demand

A crucial factor in marketability is the availability, proximity and capacity of pipelines, natural gas gathering systems and processing plants. Any significant change in market factors affecting these infrastructure facilities can harm an oil and gas company's turnout. Market linkages may be unavoidable, temporarily or in the longer term, owing to political upheaval, environmental conditions or mechanical reasons.

9. Oil and gas companies typically have substantial indebtedness and may incur considerably more debt than other companies. Failure to meet debt obligations would adversely affect a firm's business and financial condition

As a result of their indebtedness, oil and gas firms need to use a portion of their cash flow to pay principal and interest, which will reduce the amount available to finance their operations and pay dividends. This debt may also limit flexibility in planning for, or reacting to, changes in the oil and gas industry.

10. All oil and gas companies have substantial capital requirements and, depending on their financial condition as well as market liquidity, they may be unable to obtain needed financing on satisfactory terms

For reasons explained in the preceding risk factors, the firm must have, and continue to have, substantial capital expenditure for the acquisition, development, exploration and abandonment of oil and natural gas reserves. While management often plans to finance capital expenditures primarily through cash flow from operations, the options of borrowings and the offering of public and private equity and debt instruments are conditioned by the market. Moreover, lower oil and natural gas prices reduce cash flow and can also affect access to capital markets. If revenues decrease, or a firm is unable to obtain additional debt or equity financing, it may lack the capital necessary to replace reserves and maintain production at comfortable levels.

An orderly description of risk factors, as demonstrated by the above example from the oil industry, provides evidence of good governance. It also documents that senior management is in charge. Every one of the ten families of exposure, outlined in the preceding points, should be the subject of stress testing. Advanced testing should also address the greater detail of variables that influence the behaviour of a crucial risk factor, included in the above examples.

16.6 Pillar 2 and Pillar 3 require an enterprise-wide risk discipline

The emphasis on advanced testing methods and tools that has characterized the first fifteen chapters of this book has been primarily oriented to Pillar 1 of Basel II, which targets financial staying power by meeting the standards imposed by regulatory capital. By extension, the text has also discussed the role of economic capital as signalling to the market that our bank is here to stay.

The New Capital Framework by the Basel Committee also incorporates requirements for Pillar 2 and Pillar 3. For them, a clear definition of risk factors in the examples provided in section 16.4, through a case study on the insurance industry, and in section 16.5, through an oil industry case study, is necessary.

- *Pillar 2* is the steady review of capital adequacy, along with other criteria of *prudential supervision*, by national regulatory authorities.

The principle is that the more freedom credit institutions are given in computing their capital requirements, the more regulators need to inspect the bank's procedures, systems and models that are being used to establish capital adequacy. This responsibility comes over and above already existing supervisory duties.

- The object of *Pillar 3* is an active use of *market discipline* to encourage reliable financial disclosure and, by extension, bring the market into the regulatory picture.

The basis for market discipline is transparency in financial accounts, established according to standards and presented in an orderly fashion. Not only the regulators but also the market as a whole, including clients, shareholders, bondholders, corresponding banks and other counterparties, will be looking over the shoulders of financial institutions, scrutinizing their dependability. (More on Pillar 3 in section 16.7.)

To serve the requirements of Pillar 2 in an efficient manner, as well as the correct implementation of Basel II as whole, the Basel Committee on Banking Supervision has established the Accord Implementation Group (AIG). Its goal is to provide a channel for national supervisors:

- To exchange information on practical application challenges, and
- To discuss strategies and tactics aimed at addressing different regulatory issues, as they evolve.

The AIG will work together with the Committee's Capital Task Force, whose aim is to consider interpretations of, or modifications, to Basel II. The Basel Committee has asked a group of supervisors from several countries around the world, with participation from the International Monetary Fund (IMF) and the World Bank, to develop a framework for assisting regulatory authorities from non-G-10 countries, as well as credit institutions, in the transition from Basel I to Basel II.

Four basic principles characterize Pillar 2 and its implementation in the banking industry.[1] The first concerns the *capital adequacy assessment process* (CAAP), which poses a major challenge to many commercial banks, as well as to their supervisors. In a nutshell, CAAP requires:

- Conducting a steady analysis of capital levels,
- Evaluating internal processes for risk identification,
- Maintaining capital levels that incorporate future strategic moves, and
- Instituting a capital management policy committee.

The second principle is the *use test*. Supervisors should review and evaluate each bank's internal capital adequacy assessment, including the board's awareness of capital adequacy of the institution under its authority, the quality of risk evaluation and control, and the extent to which the concept and practice of capital adequacy are used routinely in day-to-day decisions.

Basel wants the bank's top executives not only to participate in use tests, but also to understand both the tests themselves and the issues involved. While practically everyone seems to agree that use tests are a prerequisite to good governance, there are differences of opinion in their implementation. Such differences mainly concern linking regulatory capital to reporting on:

- Exposure,
- Limits,
- Trading activity, and
- Management control.

The third principle of Pillar 2 states that supervisors should require all banks to adhere to a ratio above 8 per cent; elaborate bank-specific target ratios, based on risk profile; expect banks to operate above minimum capital ratios; and also establish industry-wide trigger ratios for corrective action. The fourth principle is that supervisors should seek to:

- Intervene at an early stage, to present capital from falling below risk profile, and
- Establish an appropriate legal basis for corrective action affecting credit institutions under their jurisdiction.

Taken together, these four principles of Pillar 2 provide regulatory authorities with a strong position in ensuring the integrity of capital adequacy and risk control processes characterizing banks under their jurisdiction.

The board, CEO and senior management at every commercial bank, or other financial institution, remain responsible for determining risk appetite; but it is the supervisors' job to implement all relevant risk policies, develop methods and tools to control exposure, and assess the overall risk profile of the firm. With Pillar 2, they have a mandate to exercise their duties in both a quantitative and a qualitative way.

16.7 The exercise of market discipline is a significant step in supervision

Disclosure requirements under Pillar 3 ensure that its contribution supplements Pillar 1 and Pillar 2 in the appropriate provision of risk information and exercise of prudential supervision. The aim of such information is to help market participants properly to assess a bank's financial staying power. The following disclosure requirements were added by Basel's consultative paper of April 2005:[2]

- Internal capital allocation for trading portfolio,
- Qualitative information on trading book valuation method(s),
- Standards used for modelling purposes, and
- Methodologies used to achieve internal capital adequacy assessment.

Because all disclosures must be consistent with established regulatory standards, Pillar 3 concentrates on an orderly expansion of elements traditionally included in disclosures. Market discipline is essentially applied through complementary use of market mechanisms, thereby enhancing prudential supervision. The central theme of Pillar 3 is that:

- The markets should be able to assess sufficiently the risk profiles of all credit institutions.

This becomes feasible when national supervisors require that banks disclose more frequently a greater range of their financial data, with emphasis placed on an objective presentation of own funds, capital requirements for individual risk categories, and a risk profile pursuant to Pillar 1 and Pillar 2. Part of the same drive for greater transparency at market level is:

- Provision of sufficient explanation for conspicuous changes in individual items, helping to avoid misinterpretations.

Providing information in a comprehensive way is one of the reasons why that Pillar 3 is expected to make a valuable contribution to improving communication between the banking industry, its clients and counterparties, and the financial market at large. The market can make up its own mind when credit institutions, and most specifically globally active banks, disclose a range of information about:

- The risks they take,
- The way they assess these risks,

- Their regulatory capital position, preferably including signalling capital, and
- Behavioural issues that reinforce market discipline because of transparency in the individual bank's level of risk and quality of risk control.

Current reporting requirements at the New York Stock Exchange are a proxy of what may be the new disclosure standards on a global basis, for market discipline reasons. For a publicly listed financial institution, market discipline is a multiple feedback loop providing evidence of a company's practices and their results, evaluations of the aftermath of performance on shareholder value, information on change in strategy by firms seeking to survive in a highly competitive environment, and resulting market reaction to the disclosure.

Several experts suggest that banks that are ahead of the curve will benefit from Pillar 3 disclosures, while the laggards are likely to suffer from Pillar 3. Invariably, the leaders in risk control and in open communications are those institutions who have a policy:

- Of advanced testing of their positions, and of the exposure these engender, and
- Of not being buried in the details of regulations, but move ahead of them through compliance and transparency.

Along this line of reasoning, a 2006 document by the Basel Committee brings into perspective the fact that advances in risk management techniques can significantly influence the development of risk management practices. Basel says that all respondents in a recent survey of large Dutch financial conglomerates have implemented economic capital models, and these models have a variety of objectives, including:

- Capital allocation,
- External reporting, and
- Performance measurement.

Moreover, according to the same Basel study, it is often the case that the manner in which a model is used for risk management purposes, within a given conglomerate, is broadly consistent across all firms making up the conglomerate, irrespective of the nature of the firms' business, be it:

- Banking,
- Securities, or
- Insurance.[3]

Tier-one banks look at advanced testing of risk modelling as a means of improving internal exposure control practices. The principle is that, if a company is in charge of its exposures, management has no difficulty in communicating such information, by adopting a policy of transparency.

The development and implementation of new regulatory capital frameworks, such as Basel II in banking, and Solvency II in insurance, reflect a growth in supervisors' acceptance of elements of firms' internal risk models and stress-testing techniques.

In turn, this influences the continuing evolution of advanced technological solutions in the banking industry.

In conclusion, positioning a credit institution against the evolving regulatory environment, and forces released by the market, requires an enterprise-wide strategy of being ahead of the competition in risk management. This often calls for adapting an existing organization to a new structure, giving the board of directors and CEO with oversight responsibilities in risk governance, the implementation of advanced testing techniques and ultimate risk control action.

16.8 Use of stress testing by central banks and regulators, for better governance reasons

The effective use of stress-testing methodologies, and its tools, has expanded not only in the landscape of commercial banks and investment banks, but also in the domain of regulatory authorities and central banks; with the goal of better governance in monetary policy, central banks are combining stress tests with their existing macroeconomic models (see Chapter 13).

For instance, macro stress testing is implemented at a country level, to help in quantitative assessments of resilience of the financial system to adverse economic conditions. This approach capitalizes on the results obtained by commercial banks in conjunction with the *Financial System Assessment Programme* (FSAP; not to be confused with the European Union's Financial Services Action Plan, also known as FSAP), conducted by the IMF. According to the European Central Bank (ECB), the following Euroland countries have IMF FSAPs: in 2000, Ireland; 2001, Finland; 2002, Luxembourg; 2003, Germany; 2004, Austria and the Netherlands; 2005, France; and 2006, Belgium, Greece, Italy, Portugal, Spain and, for the second time, Ireland.

According to the ECB, the direction of further work on stress testing, by regulatory authorities specific to Euroland, could develop into a system for addressing risks in an extended geographical area. This is important because of the increasing degree of cross-border economic and financial integration, which might:

- Imply a higher level of dependency between national banking systems, and
- Involve, in times of adversity, potentially negative externalities across countries that cannot be fully captured by stress tests applied at single-country level.

Macro stress tests by central banks and regulators are also seen as a means to evaluate the after effects of regulatory changes, such as Basel II, expected to impact all credit institutions in the European Union (starting in 2007). This is particularly true of banks adopting the internal ratings-based method (advanced IRB and foundation IRB).

Experimentation along this line of reference can provide a framework for a more rigorous analysis of vulnerabilities, enabling central bankers to quantify the likely impact of assumed exposures and facilitating the ranking of risks by their impact. Stress tests have already been applied to a certain level of complexity, which depends on the sophistication of a country's practice and the type of risk under study. The input is the *initial shock* connected to a major risk event affecting the banking sector.

- A simpler approach is when single shocks are examined one at a time.
- A more complex one involves the combination of two or more shocks simultaneously.

This initial shock may be credit risk, market risk, liquidity risk, operational risk or a combination thereof, leading to fairly complex stress testing. Each of these shocks can be further subdivided into component parts, to provide greater accuracy of obtained results. For instance, the measure of focusing on credit risk is a well-established indicator of default, in conjunction with recovery rates. The banks' lending portfolios may be composed of:

- Loans to the corporate sector, analysed at individual industry sector level and in conjunction with one another,
- Lending to households, divided into consumer and mortgage loans, as well as other classes,
- Or a finer grid involving sectors such as lending to hedge funds, higher risk counterparties and concentrations of credit risks.

Central banks have also developed methods for adapting the stress examination of market risk to the analytical framework under discussion. An example is global value at risk. A more complex approach involves the joint treatment of market and credit risk, where regulators suggest that considerable further work is needed to develop appropriate stress models.

A similar example is *liquidity risk*, which has not yet been extensively worked out in macro stress tests at a country level. At present, the ratio between liquid assets and short-term liabilities is commonly used as an indicator against which an initial shock is evaluated.

In this and other cases, the initial shock, or shocks, is embedded in a stress-testing scenario, the type of which varies with the method used. As discussed in Chapters 3 and 4, stress scenarios can be historical, replicating extreme events that took place in the past, or hypothetical, made to evaluate the aftermath of unlikely or plausible major risk events.

- Scenarios used for macrotests may be *probabilistic*, constructed to reflect the empirical distribution of relevant risks corresponding to extreme events,
- Or they may be *reverse engineered* to match a predefined, but significant, amount of loss to be suffered by the banking sector and, through this, test this sector's resilience.

To obtain a more holistic approach to stress testing, several central banks have also used their macroeconometric models, originally designed as forecasting tools for monetary policy. As noted by the ECB in the *Financial Stability Review* of June 2006, this approach benefits from providing a comprehensive picture of the macroeconomy. At the same time, it allows a consistent representation of the economy under stress.

The results of macro stress tests by central bankers and regulators lead to better governance of the economy as a whole. Experimentation that permits assessment of the risks embedded into the banking system is essential in monitoring financial stability. One of the tools in use is *extreme value theory* (EVT), which is suitable for the analysis of financial instabilities connected to *tail risk*. EVT has been used to examine:

- The severity of stockmarket crashes,
- The pricing of catastrophic loss risk in reinsurance, and
- The extent of operational risk in the banking industry.

In connection with very small probability events at the long leg of the risk distribution, EVT helps in estimating the likelihood of financial market crashes, as well as in measuring the risk of financial market contagion. Extreme value theory addresses the families of distributions for which the minimum and maximum outcomes behave asymptotically.

Regarding the banking industry's holistic risk, the fact that the tails of leptokyrtotic distributions are thicker than for the normal distribution means that very large and very small returns are more frequent. An example is the out-of-proportion occurrence of crashes in case of financial crises. In tests by central bankers based on EVT,

- Tail dependence parameters are estimated from daily bank stock returns, and
- For reasons of robustness, different very low percentiles of the return distribution are tried to describe critical situations.

The advantage of EVT is that, in contrast to most other approaches, it can capture rare events that are of great interest to the study of financial instabilities. Moreover, it is multivariate, and hence appropriate to the system-level dimension, particularly when the events under study concern crisis situations in a cross-country setting.

The downside of EVT is that assumptions about the underlying semi-parametric distributions are weak, particularly when hypotheses being made concern crisis situations in a cross-country setting. Therefore, EVT should be used with care, with its results being subjected to cross-checking through other modelling solutions.

Finally, in terms of current implementations of stress testing by central banks and regulators, two approaches are followed. So far, both have focused mainly on conducting stress tests at the country level.

- *Top–down*, where the central bank designs the tests to be conducted by credit institutions in-house.
- *Bottom–up*, in which commercial banks are requested to run an identical stress scenario, but do so by using their own in-house model.

Subsequent to the bottom–up approach, the central bank aggregates the results at systemic level. A similar procedure is followed with top–down. Each approach has advantages and disadvantages, leading regulators to look at them as complementary methods.

The disadvantage of top–down is that it does not benefit from institution-specific information; therefore, it is less precise than bottom–up. By contrast, the challenge with bottom–up stress tests is their cost in terms of aggregation, as well as a relatively limited flexibility. It should, however, be added that, in this domain, the state of the art is still in full evolution, and some of the downsides may be taken care of through more advanced methods.

Stress tests used by central bankers and regulators are, to a significant extent, *cognitive models*. Their aim is to evaluate events propelled by market forces whose aftermath remains unknown to classical tests. If there were no unknown risks, the whole financial world would have been an earthly paradise which, as Descartes said, can be proposed only in the land of novels.

Notes

1. Basel Committee, *Implementation of Basel II: Practical Considerations*, BIS, Basel, July 2004.
2. Basel Committee, *The Application of Basel II to Trading Activities and the Treatment of Double Default Effects, A Consultative Document*, BIS, Basel, April 2005.
3. Basel Committee, The Joint Forum, *Regulatory and Market Differences: Issues and Observations*, BIS, Basel, May 2006.

Index